Get Mahoney
A Hollywood Insider's Memoir

Get Mahoney
A Hollywood Insider's Memoir

Jim Mahoney

Table of Contents

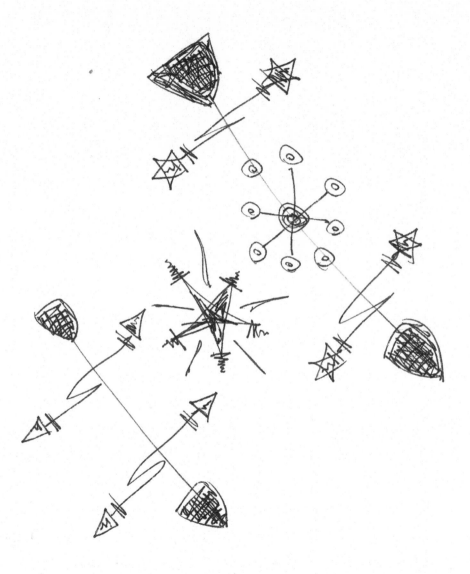

When asked to provide some doodles for a book of celebrity doodles,
Sinatra said, "Here Jim, you doodle, I don't doodle!"

Preface

THE BEST PIECE of advice I ever received was from my first boss at MGM, who used to preach to us on a daily basis: "Avoid being the story, at all costs!"

That man was Howard Strickling. He was Louis B. Mayer's right-hand man, my mentor, and the head of publicity for MGM during its heyday. MGM's motto at the time was it had "More Stars Than There Are In The Heavens," and a big reason for that was the genius of Howard Strickling.

Strickling's career was based on two opposing principles: knowing how to get press and knowing how to suppress it. My entire career and success were built around perfecting that delicate balance, so I find it a bit awkward sitting here writing my own story. I wonder how Howard would have felt about this endeavor.

Fortunately or unfortunately, I've outlived and outlasted most of my contemporaries, which has given me a unique perspective on how the PR business has changed and evolved over the years. From courting influential newspaper columnists like Louella Parsons, Hedda Hopper, Earl Wilson, and Walter Winchell to the advent of the internet and the marketing power of social media; from the Hollywood independent public relations firms such as Rogers & Cowan, PMK, Baker/Winokur/Ryder, Foster & Ingersoll, McFadden & Eddy, Guttman & Pam, and my own business, Jim Mahoney and Associates, and later on Mahoney/Wasserman and Associates; to the giant corporate marketing machines of Edelman, Finn Partners and French/West/Vaughan, to name a few.

Regardless of modern technology, or the new and different distribution streams, some things never change. It's always about the story. If you've got a good story, someone will always be interested in hearing it, no matter what the delivery platform.

Telling one's own story is never an easy prospect, especially when one spends seventy years trying to stay out of the spotlight. When I took on this challenge, choices had to be made. Do I write a "tell-all" book to please publishers and risk subjecting former clients and their loved ones to unnecessary public scrutiny and embarrassment, or do I write a "lessons learned" primer on my walk down memory lane with some of Hollywood's most charismatic characters? With a little luck and a lot of sage advice, hopefully I've included enough titillating stories of fascinating Hollywood notables without defaming their images or breaking Howard Strickling's key dictum.

You may wonder why I titled my book "Get Mahoney?" Well, it was suggested by my daughter Monica that I call it "Tell 'Em I'm Not Here" because every time the phone would ring at home I'd yell that out because if it was for me, it was never good news. Ever! I decided on the current title because over the years my particular area of expertise evolved into crisis management and communications. That's not to say that there's anything wrong or less important with planting a story or creating creative marketing campaigns, but when the shit hits the fan, when careers and corporations' livelihoods are on the line, they need someone with "crisis" experience that can come in and calm the rough waters, create a message for the media that's truthful but in the client's favor, and ultimately condition the atmosphere. After handling mercurial characters like Clark Gable, Johnny Carson, Jack Lemmon, George C. Scott, Lee Marvin, Steve McQueen, Alan Ladd, Judy Garland and others, I got a PhD in crisis management and publicity. In Chapter 34 ("Crisis Management") I get into a few of these delicate PR situations where one wrong quote or story could devastate a company or career.

From the late 1940s into the internet age of the 2000s, I hope my story provides a unique perspective on the history of Hollywood and some of its most notorious characters and events. These pages hold my personal insider's point of view on Hollywood, most of which has never been told before.

In all honesty, I consider myself one of the luckiest people in the world. I'm just a kid from Culver City, a kid who grew up behind the back lots of a magical land called Hollywood, and I never forgot that.

I was lucky to have started my career at MGM and have my first assignment be Clark Gable.

I was lucky to be there from the beginning with the Rat Pack when they were riding high, and getting into all kinds of mischief.

I was lucky enough to travel the world with the likes of Frank Sinatra,

Bob Hope, Peggy Lee, Lee Marvin, Steve McQueen, Jack Lemmon, Glen Campbell, George C. Scott, Johnny Carson, and many others.

And yet, I never lost sight that I was just that kid from Culver City. If you asked me what the key to my success was, I'd say in the beginning it was learning how to listen, a trait that did not come naturally to me. Next was inherently knowing a good story, and learning how to write and package that story. And finally, I surrounded myself with a very talented staff of publicists, writers, and marketers.

Of course, balancing business and family life in Hollywood can make for a never-ending high-wire act. I would never have reached the levels of success that I did if it were not for my wife of sixty-three years, Patricia "Marston" Mahoney, whose love and support gave me the confidence and ability to perfect my craft and solidify my career.

As a matter of fact, I think most of my clients preferred my wife to me on most occasions, since she was always a breath of fresh air, while I was always the bearer of bad news. I also want to give a shout out to my kids Jim Jr., Marilee, Sean, Mike and Monica, for not only their love and support but for keeping me grounded in this make-believe world of Hollywood. You can't raise five kids and escape the little league games, parent-teacher conferences and bloody noses. All of these were, as I learned, much more important than the egos I encountered on a daily basis.

I would also like to thank my friend and colleague Bob Chew for not only motivating me to complete my book, but for his expert collaboration, editing, and marketing of it. Without his nurturing, suggestions, and attention to detail, this probably would not have happened.

This book is the story of a kid who made good with nothing more than a little moxie and a gleam in his eye, who through hustle and street smarts made his way to the brightest stage in the world, Hollywood. Sit back and enjoy. It was quite a ride.

Chapter One

Taken

IT WAS DECEMBER 8, 1963, and by the time I arrived in Reno it was twelve hours after I got the call. This was not going to be an average day at the office. Nothing was average in those days. It was just a few weeks since JFK was gunned down in Dallas and the world was already turned upside down.

It was near midnight when Frank Sinatra's lawyer, Mickey Rudin, called me in Beverly Hills.

"Jim," he said. "You gotta get up to Reno." "What's wrong," I asked.

"It's Junior," he said, speaking about Sinatra's son, Frank Jr. "Get a flight up there as fast as you can."

"What about Junior?"

"He's been kidnapped from his hotel room at the Harrah's Club in South Lake Tahoe."

As Frank Sinatra's publicist, I had to swing into action. Fast.

It turned out nineteen-year old Frank Jr. was sitting in his underwear, eating a chicken dinner before a show, when men masquerading as room service waiters broke into his hotel room and took him.

"There's a terrible blizzard in Tahoe right now, all planes are being diverted to Reno. Frank's just left from Palm Springs," Rudin said. "He wants you to join him there as quickly as you can."

I wouldn't say the news kicked me in the gut in terms of the crisis factor. I had a celebrity crisis or two, but this was different. First, there was a human's life at stake here, and second, he was the son of Frank Sinatra!

I was part of Frank's "inner circle," and I had been in plenty of outrageous situations.

My job was always to advise and guide a client so they'd be put in the best possible light.

I listened to Rudin and understood why he called and why I was needed. This was going to be a major news story and it needed to be handled correctly, on multiple levels. This wasn't some scripted film. I had to brace myself for a father's frustrated torment and the explosion of worldwide media coverage. The relationship between Frank and Frank Jr. had never been an easy one.

Living in the shadow of a supernova star could not have been easy for Frank Jr., who at every turn was compared to his father. Similarly, Frank Sr. had high expectations for his son, which only pressurized the two. Much has been written about this father-son combo, and about their distance after his split with their mother, Nancy Sr. But above all else they were father and son, and the kidnapping hit Frank hard.

This highly personal criminal act was a vulnerability no one considered. It created a serious chink in Frank's iconoclastic armor, which had been hardened and reinforced by Hollywood. Sinatra always had a sense of being, and if not invincible, certainly untouchable. So, this kind of crime against his family hit him at his core. He was an Italian street fighter, but he was now helpless.

"Where's Frank going to be?" I asked Rudin.

"I have no idea."

I hung up and immediately called the airline and booked the first flight to Reno in the morning. Early the next day I got a call from Sinatra's secretary saying that I was to meet Frank in Reno at the Mapes Hotel. By the time I arrived in Reno twelve hours after that call, Frank was ensconced in the Presidential suite at the art deco Mapes Hotel in downtown Reno. The Mapes was as luxurious as Reno had to offer. It boasted the dubious distinction of being the first post- WWII skyscraper built in the United States. It was a high-rise built to accommodate both a hotel and casino, what everyone was calling the prototype casino of the future.

Frank knew the Mapes well, having performed there in the legendary Sky Room.

But this was hardly the place he wanted to be. He tried in vain to get up to Lake Tahoe the night before, but the same blizzard that nearly downed my flight had made the highway to the lake impassable, even for Frank Sinatra. And as sumptuous as a Presidential suite can be, the Mapes was nothing more than a bunker at this point, a waiting room. The good news was, if we couldn't get up to Tahoe, Frank Jr. and his captures surely could not get out either. In addition, the police and FBI had instituted roadblocks around Tahoe to ensure there'd be no escape.

The hours passed in the suite, and Frank, restless, growing impatient and chain smoking, seemed oddly composed and cool. His composure set the standard for the room, as usual.

"God help the bastards if we find them first," he said, and kept smoking. "God help them."

Eventually, word got out and the media began to circle. They found out where we were staying.

"How did they find out?" Frank asked, looking at me.

"Listening to any police band radio, anyone can put two and two together," I said. Frank agreed and went back to smoking.

"We're going to need the media at some point," I said.

Frank: "Can't we keep this quiet?"

"Not something like this, Frank," I said. "This is worldwide news."

I explained we should provide initial statements, explaining how Frank was understandably nervous and concerned for his son. The media would also act as a delivery vehicle for our messages to the kidnappers. "Who knows," I said, "they might talk with the media before they talk to us."

As word spread, the phone lines lit up. Everyone from the media to well-wishers to sympathizers started calling. People never seem to realize that in times of crisis their well- intentioned wishes and concerns are a pain in the ass, of little comfort, and at worst they are potentially huge obstacles in the process of solving the problem.

I took over handling the phones and as I fielded calls, being careful not to tie up the lines in case the kidnappers called. One of the first calls was from the FBI. It was J. Edgar Hoover himself. A voice on the other end simply said, "The Director would like to speak to Mr. Sinatra."

I asked if he could hold the line. Frank was in the other room. As I put the phone on hold, the second line rang. I asked who was calling.

"Just tell him it's Momo... he'll know who it is."

It was the mob boss Sam Giancana, from Chicago. Giancana was probably the only other person in the country with the kind of resources to rival Hoover and track down the kidnappers.

"Sam," I said. "It's Jim Mahoney, I was at the party with Dean Martin and Frank in Chicago. I need to put you on hold."

I went into the bedroom and told Frank about the calls.

"One is J. Edgar Hoover and the other is Giancana," I said. "Who do you want first?" "I'll talk to Momo," he said. "Tell Hoover I'll call him back."

I paused briefly to take in the moment. Between the personal support of J. Edgar Hoover, who assured Frank of the full resources of the FBI, and Momo, whose resources could be downright lethal, these poor bastard kidnappers were now being chased by both the good guys and the bad, and Frank chose Momo first. Afterward, Frank took it all in stride, for the most part, and chuckled at my observation.

It was at this point the FBI arrived and set up shop in the suite. The FBI Special Agent in charge of Nevada, Dean Elson, took charge of things and helped calm Frank down. I was ready for Frank to explode, but he didn't. Hours ticked by and Sinatra lit up cigarette after cigarette, enough so that by the time contact was made, some sixteen hours later, Frank's voice from the smokes was raspy and an octave lower than normal. It was about then that the kidnappers called.

Frank started talking, but the smoking made his voice unrecognizable. "It's fucking me," Sinatra said. "Where's my kid?"

The last thing anyone wanted to believe was that unfiltered cigarettes could be the very thing that might make kidnappers snap.

"You want me to sing?" he screamed. "You want me to sing a fucking song, you assholes?"

In fact, he calmed down enough to have the common sense to string the kidnappers along. He got them to talk and kept them talking with the hope of being able to trace the call.

During that first conversation there were no negotiations, no demands. The most that came out of this initial contact was to convince Frank that these goons did in fact have Frank Jr. and that, more importantly, Junior was still okay. The call ended with an odd gentleman-like question from the captors asking Frank if he would be available the next morning at nine, for the second phone call. Of course he was going to be available.

By now word had gotten out to the world's media and it spread like gasoline on embers. This wasn't just news, it was a global crime event happening to an icon.

Whatever logistical problems I had faced getting to Reno clearly had dissipated because these guys faced none and descended like locusts on the Mapes lobby, all wanting an update and a "word with Frank." The nation had lost John F. Kennedy to an assassin's bullet. It was as if the country wasn't ready for another tragedy, or injury, to someone as legendary as Frank Sinatra.

In the suite, we watched it all unfold on television. Sinatra, still chain-smoking, switched from one TV channel to another looking for and hoping for any word, any tidbit of information on Frank Jr.'s well-being. One local newscaster didn't help matters when he proclaimed to his co-anchor to "look at the statistics."

"Kidnapping," he said to the viewers, "is the same as dead eighty percent of the time."

"Bullshit!" Sinatra shouted back.

This was the kind of situation where people like me earned my keep, and then some. No reporter was going to get that career-making "word" with Frank for no other reason than he was a nervous wreck, and that is a side of a client no PR pro wants shown to the world. Second, Frank was just liable to make a threat or worse to these captors via the press. My job was the delicate balancing act of keeping the media informed without actually giving any significant information. This was my specialty.

While the melee continued downstairs, things weren't much better upstairs where we stayed. Well-wishers, including Robert Kennedy, Dean Martin, and Judy Garland, kept calling in their support nonstop, but that was the last thing we needed as it clogged the only phone lines.

Although the FBI set up specific lines for outgoing calls, we only had the hotel lines available for incoming calls. And while someone called in their support, the obvious fear was: what if the captors called?

Throughout, Frank was getting nervous and was damn near at the end of his rope. Frank's only escape was the few minute respite he would take occasionally up on the roof. But the extreme cold assured us he was never going to be too long or too far from the phone.

Before long, Mickey Rudin showed up, as well as Jack Entratter, the president of the Sands Hotel. Out of earshot of the FBI agents, Entratter let Frank know he had more than a hundred thousand dollars on him, stashed within a series of well-tailored and hidden pockets with plenty more where that came from if it were needed to "get the kid back." Sinatra told him he appreciated it more than he'd ever know, but he's already got it covered through his long time banker Al Hart at City National Bank in Beverly Hills.

I was fast getting the feeling that more money would be circulating within that suite, maybe more than the gaming tables downstairs. My instincts were to keep mum, but I couldn't help thinking about the reporters and newscasters downstairs and how any number of these news bits were front-page headlines.

As luck and The Big Clock worked, I answered the phone when the kidnappers called. It was just after nine.

"Where's Frank?"

I shouted out. "It's them!"

Now, everyone was looking at me. I pointed to the phone receiver. There was nothing distinctive about the voice at the other end, and as much as my gut said to try and get some information out of this guy, I wanted off the line as much as he wanted me off.

"I represent Mister Sinatra," I said.

"Where is he?" the voice asked.

"I'm trying to find him," I said. "I'm handling the phones."

"Who are you?"

"My name's Mahoney," I said.

"I know you," he said. "You're his press agent, right?"

"Yeah, that's right."

"Good," he said. "Keep up the good work about saying nothing."

Ironically, when Frank took the phone, he once again had trouble convincing them that he was THE Frank Sinatra. The kidnapper then put Frank Jr. on the extension and let them speak briefly for the first time, long enough to convince Senior that Junior had not been harmed and was well, considering the circumstances.

Pursuant to the FBI's instructions, Frank labored to stretch the conversation long enough for a trace to be put on the line, but anticipating this, they said they'd call back at two that afternoon and quickly hung up. Fortunately, the FBI was able to partially trace the call. They narrowed it down to Southern California.

It was unclear if they were handling the negotiations from Southern California, or if Frank Jr. had been taken there too. But there were roadblocks and a blizzard stopping everyone, so the belief was that Frank Jr. was still nearby.

Frank, for the first time, breathed a sigh of relief. Junior was alive.

True to their word, the phone rang at precisely two o'clock. This time Frank answered.

No sooner had he started to talk than he motioned for me to get something to write on. They were giving instructions for the ransom. It was precise. They wanted 700 one hundred-dollar bills, 700 fifty-dollar bills, 4,000 twenty-dollar bills, 4,000 ten-dollar bills, and 3,000 five-dollar bills.

All told, it amounted to $240,000. All the money was to be used currency and no more than eight bills could be in a sequential serial series. The package to hold the money should be no more than twenty-two inches and the courier delivering the package should have his driver's license and a pen and paper. Additionally, he should bring along one dollar in dimes, eleven dollars in quarters, and 200 dollars in used five- and ten-dollar bills.

All had to be ready to go by early that evening. There was no real explanation given as to why the variety of cash, but we all presumed it was so it couldn't be traced. As for Frank, they told him he should proceed to the home of his ex-wife Nancy on Nimes Road in Bel Air to wait for further instructions.

Al Hart, Frank's good friend and banker, would eventually assure Frank there would be no problem putting the ransom money together. One problem solved. Ironically, years later I would be partnered up with Al Hart at Tamarisk Country Club in Palm Springs, and it was one of my most memorable golf outings. (Please see Chapter 31: "Putting My Putter Where My Mouth Was.")

As the FBI settled in, things were not going along so smoothly. They wanted every bill photographed and treated with some traceable substance. Frank's face went white.

"There's no time for that," he said.

"Yes," the lead FBI agent said. "We have time, we've got to do it, or else we may never get them. It's non-negotiable, Mr. Sinatra."

Time was ticking, as Hart's people and the FBI went to work immediately in the vaults of Hart's branch in Beverly Hills. Impressively, they were well on their way to having the job done by the time Frank, Rudin, and I, along with a smattering of FBI agents, boarded Frank's plane for the trip back to L.A.

By the time we got to Nancy Sr's house, the FBI had already set up a communications system in one of the guest bedrooms. It was a war room.

When I saw Nancy, she looked like a woman who was going through hell. Not only was her son kidnapped, but now the FBI had taken over her home, too. As reassuring a presence as the FBI can be, the sight of all that was going on was both overwhelming and daunting. A gloom set in over Nimes Road. She retreated to her bedroom and rarely came out.

Fortunately, the first call came from FBI Director Hoover, who reassured both Frank and Nancy that everything was being done to apprehend the kidnappers and that he was personally involved with the investigation. It was hard to tell if this came as some comfort to Frank and Nancy. They were no different than any parents in a similar situation. They were scared.

In the meantime, word had gotten to the media that a command post had been set up at the house. They descended en masse, hundreds of reporters from print, radio, and television making the winding road in Bel Air almost impassable. If it wasn't already, this was fast on its way to being a "crime of the century" story. As one of the only people allowed in the house outside of the FBI and who was not an immediate member of the family, I had a unique perspective.

My first instinct was to protect the privacy of the family, but one news nugget after another ran through my head, each more headline-grabbing than the last. The media knew me and expected me to throw them a bone. No details, nothing that could tip the kidnappers, but something that could appease them. And if I was going to keep my credibility with the media, that was what I needed to do. But the FBI stopped me. I was not to give them so much as the time of day.

That was easier said than done. I certainly didn't want them making up stories, so despite what the FBI said, I threw them the occasional bone, such as how Frank and Nancy were feeling, the mood, and so forth. Then I came up with an idea to keep them at bay, without having to say a word. In a quiet moment, I took Frank aside and told him the press had been very patient and downright respectful of the family so far and that it might be a good idea to show some appreciation in return.

"Like what?" he asked.

"It's past dinnertime," I said. "Yeah, they're hungry for a story, but I think it's more likely they're just hungry, too."

"So, what you do suggest, have Nancy start cooking?"

"No," I told him, "but we could call Chasen's and have them cater the whole thing in no time."

"Do it."

Now, if you know the media, take-out Chinese food or even pizza would have sufficed, but a chance to dine on the delights of one of the town's more famous night spots—a place I could imagine most of them had only been on the outside looking in—would be more than appeasement.

With a quick call to Ronnie Clint, Chasen's major domo, the restaurant catered its first, and presumably only, kidnapping. Chasen's chili was world famous—Elizabeth Taylor even had it flown to Rome while she was filming "Cleopatra."

At around eight o'clock, Al Hart's number one man, Bill Olsen, arrived at the house with two suitcases filled with the doctored ransom money, all $240,000. As we sat down in the middle of the living room staring at the cases, wondering what the next move was, Olsen announced that we had yet one more problem.

"Like what?" Frank asked.

"We got the money all put together like you asked, but we didn't have the correct cases to put it in."

"So where did these suitcases come from?" Frank asked.

"That's just it," Bill stuttered, "None of us doing the counting had enough money to buy these cases. So, I took a couple of hundred dollars from the ransom money, ran across the street to Saks Fifth Avenue and bought these."

"Now," he said, "Saks has a couple of hundred dollars in marked bills and the kidnappers have been shorted?"

"We can live with that," laughed one of the FBI agents.

Even Frank broke a smile, which was nice to see after all the hours of stress. But then Mickey Rudin asked me if I'd like to step out on the patio for a smoke.

"Frank talked to Hoover a little while ago," he said.

"I know," I said, "Nancy told me. I don't know what the hell he can do in Washington D.C., but I am sure it was reassuring, at least to Nancy."

"He asked Frank if he had anyone in mind to make the ransom exchange with the kidnappers."

I assumed, up to this point, that the FBI would handle the ransom drop off, being trained in these matters, and that they had weapons. It was a strange question, I thought, but not as strange as who Frank and Rudin had in mind: Me!

"You've got to be kidding," I shouted.

"No, we're serious," Rudin said. "Someone's gotta do it, and you certainly have every right to tell them to take a hike, but you're the only one the kidnappers would know wasn't a set up since they've talked to you."

"Me? You mean there's no one else?"

"Look, it's up to you," he said. "If you don't want to do it, just say so, everyone would understand."

He walked inside, leaving me alone to smoke and ruminate. The words echoed in my brain. "Everyone would understand."

"Everyone" was Frank and Nancy and, well, my clients, and the world. How do I look them in the eye and tell them I'm too chickenshit to carry a couple of suitcases of money off to some drop point to free their son? I had carried Sinatra's bags plenty of times in the past, everything from briefcases to bags of money out of Vegas, and it certainly wasn't the first time I'd been asked to clean up a mess or do the dirty work on behalf of my benefactor.

But this was different, really different. Any number of things could go wrong, but Frank and I went back too many years. He had been too important in my life, my career, for me not to help at this critical moment.

He wasn't just a client. He was a friend, a real friend who was in need. Still, I could not help but think then, alone and smoking on that cold patio, how did a kid from Culver City end up being asked to be the bag man in the Sinatra kidnapping?

The $240,000 ransom was procured, photographed and readied. The next call from the kidnappers came around 9:30 p.m. with instructions for Frank to leave the house alone and drive to a gas station on Little Santa Monica in Beverly Hills. He was to wait by the public phone. Once there, he was to receive another call advising him to have his courier, me, wait for further instructions.

"Tell your courier to use the name Patrick Henry," the caller said. "My name will be John Adams."

These were patriotic bastards.

It was then that a fateful decision was made. I was off the hook. It was decided an FBI agent would be better suited as the courier. They were, after all, trained in kidnapping techniques. If anything went wrong, they said, I'd be in trouble.

Before Frank left the house, he made one more call to Hoover. He told him in no uncertain terms that he "didn't give a shit about the money," and only wanted his son back alive and unharmed.

Frank left the house, made his way to the phone booth at a gas station on Little Santa Monica Boulevard, and waited. The call came. The instructions were that the courier was go to another public phone, this time in the Western Airlines terminal of Los Angeles International Airport. He was to wait for a call at 11 p.m. with new instructions.

When the agent arrived at the airport, he was instructed to go to another location, a gas station not far from the airport, where he would be sized up and approved from a distance. He was then ordered to go to yet another location to wait for further instructions. We were getting the updates by phone from each location.

He was finally told to drop the money between two yellow school buses at a closed Mobil gas station near the corner of Sepulveda Boulevard and Montana Avenue. He was additionally told that after dropping off the money, he was to go check into a hotel and await further instructions as to where and when Junior would be released.

While all this was going on, Frank, Nancy, and their daughters Nancy and Tina, as well as Rudin, myself, and a few FBI men were squeezed into the makeshift control room in one of the bedrooms, listening to every exchange between the kidnappers and our agent courier.

When Hoover promised to put his entire force on the job, he wasn't kidding. He must have had over a hundred agents fanned out all across West Los Angeles, in the most unsuspecting places and attire. They were driving cabs, mail trucks, ice cream trucks, and emergency vehicles. All of them were in continuous communication with the temporary Bel Air headquarters. Every time the courier made a stop for further instructions, there must have been twenty agents in and around the surrounding area.

The courier dropped off the money as instructed. He found the spot between the two buses shortly after midnight. Within minutes, Frank received a call from one of the kidnappers. Junior was free. He had been dropped off along the San Diego Freeway near Mulholland Drive, and somehow, we learned, the kidnappers got the money too! They got away with everything without the FBI nabbing them, but Frank didn't care. He just wanted Frankie back.

Frank and I got in one of the FBI cars, with the FBI's Dean Elson driving, and crouched down in the back seat. The media was waiting outside the gates. The agent drove fast, we ducked low, and we headed to the drop point, but we saw nothing, no one.

We drove back and forth between Sunset Boulevard and Mulholland Drive six or seven times during the next hour, creeping along the shoulder and privately praying that we would find him healthy and unharmed. We feared all we'd see was a body. We finally determined that if he had been dropped off there, he certainly wasn't there now. With very heavy hearts, we decided it might be better if we just returned to the house.

Later, when we were about to go out and take another look, there was a knock at the door. People had been coming and going all afternoon and evening without a single knock. When I opened the door, it was a Bel Air patrolman, the neighborhood private security department.

"What can I do for you?" I asked.

"I've got Frank Sinatra Jr.," he said.

"Where?"

"In the trunk of the car," he smiled.

With all the cops, agents, and press waiting, Frank Jr. was squired right past them without anyone knowing.

True to their word, the kidnappers had dumped him off near the Mulholland offramp. But Junior had walked all the way to Roscomare Road, a couple of miles away, to where the Bel Air Patrol is stationed, all the while hiding behind bushes whenever headlights appeared for fear the kidnappers would come back and get him.

As he approached Roscomare, he spotted a patrolman making the rounds, and flagged him down. The patrolman recognized Frank Jr. and agreed to take him back to Nimes Road. Rather than face the barrage of press, the patrolman had the good sense to hide Frankie in the trunk. He was safe, and not a scratch was on him.

Was this a cause for celebration? You bet! And celebrate we did, but it was a not-so-happy ending for the kidnappers. The three of them—John Irwin, Joe Amsler, and ringleader Barry Keenan—were apprehended by the FBI and taken into custody within days.

They were real amateurs. The man who called was Irwin, the kidnappers' designated spokesman, who was following a script dictated by the mastermind, Keenan. It turned out Keenan was a business whiz kid and former schoolmate of Junior's sister, Nancy. He dreamed up the whole scheme to get some seed money for investments. In his trial, he said the first idea was to nab Tony Hope, Bob Hope's adopted son, but he felt Hope had done so much for the troops over the years, that taking his son would be un-American.

Somehow, he figured it was a better idea to kidnap Frank Sinatra's son.

When their trial ended on March 7, 1964, Keenan and Amsler were both given life sentences, which were subsequently reduced to twenty-five years imprisonment. Irwin got sixteen years and eight months as a co-conspirator.

The Los Angeles Times and several other major papers throughout the world headlined stories alleging the kidnapping was engineered for publicity purposes to give young Frank's career a much-needed shot in the arm. This infuriated Sinatra, and he never forgot the treatment. After that, Frank Sinatra's view of the media was never the same, and I couldn't blame him.

As for me, I couldn't help but wonder: how the hell did I get here?

photogragh by Don Cravens
Behind the scenes on Nimes Road at Sinatra Junior's homecoming.

photogragh by Don Cravens
Tina & mother Nancy embrace Frank Jr. after his release from kidnappers.

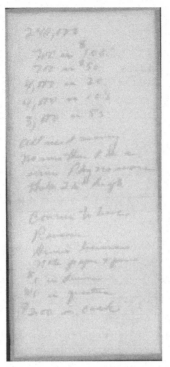

Kidnapper's demands, in Frank's handwriting.

The press transcended Nancy Sr's home, as Chasen's chili was served.

Chapter Two

The 40 Acres

I GREW UP in Culver City in the 1930s, within blocks of the most famous movie studio back lots. We lived at 8939 Carson Street. At the end of the block was the Hal Roach Studios, home to the "Laurel & Hardy" and "Our Gang" comedies. I remember my mother gloating over the location fees she used to get for allowing them to shoot in and around our house. Across the street and down a few blocks was the David O. Selznick Studios, and further west was MGM. To a kid growing up during the Great Depression, these back lots were dream worlds, with the only barrier to entry being fences, and not good ones at that.

Everyone called the Selznick studio's back lot "The Forty Acres," and when nothing was going on behind the fence we made it our ultimate playground. There was every kind of outdoor movie set you could possibly imagine, from New York streets to western towns, from desert forts to Indian encampments, and from sailing ships to a mock prison.

After school, on weekends, and during vacations we'd work our way under the barbed wire, being careful to avoid the watchman, a pudgy guy in blue cop uniform, and his tall-eared, sharp-toothed Doberman Pinscher. He didn't have a gun, but we knew his routine, patrolling the property in an old flatbed truck. We never knew his name, but we knew when he wasn't in his truck, he mostly hung out by the studio buildings where the stars walked by.

One day we'd play cops and robbers, and the next it was cowboys and Indians. Kids everywhere in America played these games, but the difference here was we had our own make-believe western towns and Main Streets to shoot off our B.B. guns.

We had it all to ourselves, until the watchman chased us back under the barbed wire. As I think back, he probably knew we were there and pretended to act shocked and upset every time he ran us off.

It was the end of the 1930s, and a section of The Forty Acres was transformed to look like a southern town during the Civil War. We snuck in and watched as workers reconstructed a big house façade and new town from the remains of the old King Kong sets. They were planning a rail station, loading docks, and homes of Southern gentry. My mother said it was a new Clark Gable film, something called "Gone with the Wind."

My friend Rex and I knew this was different, a bigger deal than most films. We were both ten years old when one Saturday night we worked our way under the fence to watch what was going on. There was a crowd standing back from the old sets and about ten fire trucks with firemen standing by. There were five or six cameras in different places and spotlights everywhere. The whole place was lit up like daytime, and in the middle were some actors in a horse-drawn carriage. Everybody seemed to be following the carriage, shouting at the driver to turn around and go through the old dirt streets once more. I remember the horse was jumpy and reared a few times. Then, in the glare of light, we saw men on the rooftops. They each started to pour kerosene over the buildings.

"What're they doing?" Rex asked.

"I don't know," I said. "I think they're gonna burn the 'Kong' set down."

We watched the commotion and the studio people pointed to the carriage, to pull it back, as the fuel was poured over the old sets, stables, a Main Street saloon, a bank, and an old African village. A man with a sweep of dark hair and glasses, shouted through a bullhorn, "Action!" Then three men with fiery torches dropped their flames to the fuel-soaked wood.

Rex's face went red and yellow from the fire. The flames and smoke rose into the night against the backlot hill. It didn't take but about ten minutes for the carriage and horse to make it through the fake towns burning up, and for the man with the bullhorn to shout, "Cut!"

My father, an independent painter with his own business crew, often worked for studio executives on their homes, and he said the set was supposed to look like old Atlanta.

"They burned it down, just like they did in real life," he explained at dinner the next day.

I didn't fully understand what he meant, but he said it was a clever way of destroying old sets to make way for the new ones needed for the film. From that night on, our little town of Culver City was abuzz with stories from the set of "Gone with the Wind." Everybody talked about Gable and Olivia de Havilland, and this new British actress Vivien Leigh. What was going on in our playground, under the barbed-wire fence, day and night, seemed to be the biggest deal in Hollywood. Even my mother would bring up the movie around the dinner table.

"I wonder how she's playing Scarlett with that British accent?" she'd ask.

My older brother, Jay, and I didn't care a lick. We shrugged and ate quickly, then left the table as fast as we could to get back to what was going on over at The Forty Acres. We saw it all. We saw Gable dressed as a southern gentleman and we saw the actresses in their hoop skirts flitting about, and then smoking cigarettes and leaning against wood stands the crew built so their costumes wouldn't get wrinkles.

It was about then that Rex came to me with an idea.

"My dad's getting a couple of cases of Coca-Cola," he said. "How about we sell them to the crew and extras?" (This was obviously the era before craft services on sets.)

"You mean take 'em under the fence?" I said.

"You want in?" he asked. "I'll give you half a case and we'll sell them for ten cents apiece, you can keep two cents for every bottle you sell."

Was he kidding?

"What's the catch?" I asked.

"No catch," Rex said.

It was no investment on my part and all profit. How could I lose? "I'm in," I said.

We sold out within an hour, but what Rex didn't know was that I was selling my bottles for a quarter, paying him eight cents, and keeping the rest. By mid-afternoon, I was in business for myself, and in the days and weeks ahead while filming on the movie progressed, I'd put away at least a shoebox full of coins and dollar bills. Our little business became so popular that Rex and I became regulars on the set and the guards let us through untouched with our boxes of supplies.

Before too long, we were selling the extras—everything from gum and candy to cookies and whatever they wanted to buy. And the extras numbered in the hundreds. Business was great, and during one scene, at the train depot, where hundreds of wounded Confederate soldiers were stretched out on their backs in an area the size of two football fields, we made a real killing selling our gum and sodas.

Off to the side, Rex and I watched the whole scene being shot. We stood by as Vivien Leigh, playing the Scarlett O'Hara my mother talked about, walked through the dead and dying men, looking to help, overwhelmed with grief. We watched as a camera on a crane (it turns out the first crane ever used in movies) rose over the scene of made-up devastation. Rex and I laughed as Leigh walked among the dead, half of whom were stuffed dummies dressed in Confederate uniforms.

I didn't know it then, but the idea of making a living off Hollywood started right there, during those "Gone with the Wind" days. From this inauspicious beginning, I thought I clearly had a future in the movie business.

But it was a few years later in the summer of 1943, when I was fifteen, that I got my first real Hollywood job. It was at the Meralta Theatre on Culver Boulevard in Culver City. The Meralta was not as grand as The Orpheum on South Broadway in Downtown Los Angeles or Grauman's Chinese Theatre in Hollywood, but for Culver City, it was our movie palace.

I found myself in management from the get-go. I was put in charge of popcorn. This lofty position didn't last long. One night, shortly after I started, I made my way to the theater for my evening shift. When I arrived, all I found there was the skeletal frame of the old stoic movie house, and that was ashen and wet with water from fire hoses. One fire truck remained, and there were still a few firemen shoveling up the mess on the sidewalk.

"What happened?" I asked.

"Someone forgot to turn off the popcorn machine," a fireman said.

I ran home faster than I ever imagined and locked myself in my room. I was sure they were coming for me.

"Jimmy," my mother called from the other side of the door. "What's wrong?"

"Nothing, Ma," I said. "Nothing."

Maybe my Hollywood career wasn't going to be so bright after all.

Chapter Three

Welcome Aboard

IF THERE'S A theme to my life, it is usually centered around luck and timing. Looking back at all the good fortune I've had, starting with our little house on Carson Street outside the studio gates, I get the feeling the Big Clock that runs it all had a special place in its mechanism for me.

Sure, there was The Depression and Pearl Harbor, a war raging in Europe, but it didn't seem to touch the Mahoneys. There was no dust bowl in Culver City, California, no "Grapes of Wrath." If I wanted for anything, I certainly didn't know it. To say I was a lucky kid is a monumental understatement. That isn't to say I came from a family of privilege. The Mahoneys, Irish on both sides, were solidly middle class. We were of the O'Mahony clan from County Cork, Ireland, though some distant cousin got the clever idea of dropping the "O" and adding an "e" and we've held that name ever since.

My father was the second eldest of fourteen children of John D. and Molly O'Houlihan Mahoney. Dad never took time to enjoy anything… except work. He worked from seven o'clock in the morning until seven at night, six days a week. My brother and I barely saw him. He was tough but gave us a long leash. On Sundays after church, he and my mother met with clients to talk over painting and decorating jobs. He never worked for anybody but himself. One time he figured it out on the kitchen table that he probably painted every house in Cheviot Hills, a big development of new homes by developers Neff & Hurst. Some were even owned by big shot studio executives. My father was their guy and his little painting business, J.D. Mahoney Painting and Decorating, never lacked for work. The company's motto was, "Painted to Stay Painted."

Sometimes my father brought things home from his jobs. One time, a Cheviot Hills client gave him an old bag of golf clubs.

"You want them?" he asked me. "I don't have time for the game."

He handed me the round canvas bag filled with wood and metal-shafted clubs. "Sure," I said. I took one club out, a mashie, and took a big clumsy swing.

"Maybe they'll let you play the little course up at the California Club," he said. "I see kids sneaking on that all the time."

It was true. The California Golf Club was tucked into the rolling hills of wheat and bean fields along Motor Avenue on the way to Pico Boulevard, toward Rancho Park. If you pushed through the chain link fence on one side of it, you could get onto a few short par- three holes that were used for practice. And so, with the hand-me-down gift of golf clubs, I'd sling the bag over my shoulder and ride my bike up Motor, or through one of the cement storm drains that headed north toward the course. The drainage canals, usually dry but with a single channel of water down the center, were our secret underground highways running north, east, south, and west. They were interconnected and we rode our bikes in the partial darkness up to Pico to shoot B.B.s at rabbits in the bean fields above. But sometimes I strapped the golf bag over my shoulder and rode up the drains toward the golf course, sneaking my way through yet another fence, to another gated fantasyland, but this one of green rolling fairways and wealthy men playing the game of golf.

My father was a striking man, with sandy red hair, strong build, and movie star looks. He epitomized rugged independence and California optimism. Town leaders from Culver City even asked him to run for mayor, but my mother said he didn't have time for that nonsense. She told him more than once that he had a family and a crew of painters to feed, and they needed to work. He was a soft touch, never yelled at us, was mildly religious and though the larger Mahoney clan was known as semi-professional troublemakers and drinkers, my father was not. He drank occasionally and played some poker. My mother hated that, and when he did stray, her stern mood tempered the Mahoney curse, though not always.

One Sunday, visiting my father's parents in Inglewood, CA, the Mahoney clan was in fine form. A normally rowdy crowd even when not drinking, on this Sunday they were well into the booze and squaring off into boxing matches. Mike Mahoney, my uncle, was a bruiser and big kidder. He started boxing with me, showing me moves, counters, and then wham! He hit me square in the mouth, open-fisted, and chipped a tooth. My father never heard the end of that one. I was never allowed back to my grandparents' house again.

The real sheriff and disciplinarian in our house was my mother, Marie Ellen, who was the eldest of two by James and Anna McGreevy of Grand River, Iowa—hearty Midwesterners to the core.

Some summers, we packed up the car and made the long trip back to the family farm in Iowa. My brother and I loved the expanse of the farm, the nothingness but the corn and empty roads. But it was dull as dirt after about a week in, and we longed to get back to our little neighborhood of fame and fortune.

As childhoods go, we were lucky, and we knew it. But more than the luck, it was all due to timing and geography. Our quaint, well-appointed, solidly middle-class home was square in the land of make believe, not corn fields and big skies. We were living in the center of Hollywood during its brightest days of the Golden Age of picture making. And I had a front row seat to see it all.

My mother was the perfect homemaker, as perfect as anyone can be— handling all the domestic tasks, including having a tight fist over the household funds. She was the one that kept our financial accounts and built our security. Their first house was on the back part of the lot and was so small they called it The Cabin. Later, my parents saved enough money to build a new house on the front part of the lot, where my brother and I grew up. Then, my mother rented out The Cabin. She liked the income so much she bought the two empty lots on either side and built two apartments on each. Those five rental units kept the Mahoneys in good shape and allowed my mother to get a new car every other year.

Marie Ellen had meticulous taste when it came to the home and she kept it clean and well appointed. She infused her husband with some of this talent and it helped his growing clientele. Suffice it to say she did her best to keep us clean, well dressed, well groomed, shopping at only the finest stores, like Desmond's and Silverwoods on Wilshire Boulevard in the Miracle Mile. These classy stores were beyond her pocketbook, but she knew taste and style made a difference. It gave a person confidence, made them feel stronger, and it opened doors. She instilled that sense of style in my brother Jay and I from the start.

My mother was the driving force in the family and a firm believer in education. It was the rock that everything else was built upon and she'd be damned if her children weren't well educated. To that end, they did well with Jay, who went on to graduate from Loyola High School and then the

University of Southern California, and then on to the Navy. I, on the other hand, was a major disappointment, a bum in comparison. I could barely handle the eight years of Sisters of Mary and Joseph at St. Augustine's Grammar School, which was directly across from the walls of MGM. School was the last thing I was interested in, and the idea of real work, like what my old man did, was even less appealing.

My father never depended directly on the studios for employment, but instead got most of his work from executives at Selznick's, Hal Roach's Studio, which during the war was called "Ft. Roach," and the sprawling Metro Goldwyn Mayer lot, which was just a little farther west down Washington Boulevard.

He kept his family afloat with his consistent studio executive home painting assignments, and sometimes he was brought in to paint the homes of the biggest stars on the lots. He was a true artist in his field. He could take a piece of plywood and make it look like wormy chestnut. He could do anything with paint and colors and carpentry, and, with my mother's help, interior design. He slowly crept up the ladder of the Hollywood Contractors' Who's Who List and was becoming the go-to guy for painting and interior design, not only in Culver City but neighboring Cheviot Hills, Beverly Hills, Brentwood, Pacific Palisades and even Encino, always with his loyal crew of five-six guys at all times. I, on the other hand, didn't pay much attention, instead focusing on the newly discovered fairer sex.

As busy a Dad as he was, The Depression and the war had its impact on the moviemaking business. Some hit rough times, even with 100 million people a week buying tickets. This wasn't bad considering the entire country's population was 130 million in the late 1930s and early 1940s. Despite those huge weekly box office tallies, the studios all over Hollywood seemed to be taking a financial bath, at least according to my father.

"RKO's getting hit," he'd say, reading the *Los Angeles Times*. "Paramount's done and now Fox and Twentieth Century have merged."

It seemed like each morning's news brought another bankruptcy, another reason for the old man to shake his head with worry about his next project with the executives and the stars. He'd look at me like it was time to start thinking about a paycheck. "United Artists has suspended production altogether," he once said, folding the paper over and looking straight at me.

But the Culver City studios somehow managed to keep going after the attack on Pearl Harbor. MGM, in fact, was bustling, and Carson Street was taken over by Hal Roach's "Laurel and Hardy" (1926–1940), "Our Gang Comedies" (1922–1944), and earlier, Harold Lloyd (1918–1924) movies.

Our little dead-end street was a hive of moviemaking. Carson Street, it seemed to everyone, was the very picture of America. In fact, the studio production manager at Roach made a deal with everyone on our block to vacate the street. If we would vacate the street and our front yards as well, they paid us $15 a day, which was serious money in our little world outside the gates.

I remember my dad cashing plenty of those checks; he called them our "studio bonus." Before I was even aware of it, our family was now part of Hollywood, and making a living off it. I didn't know it then, but for next seventy years Hollywood and its stars would continue not as an imaginary world on the Big Screen, but as my bread and butter.

In those early teen years, with the war effort building up, I'd help my father paint and scrape, but I hated it. I got a better job delivering mail with the Post Office, but that didn't last. Then, during the war, my father got me a job at Paramount Pictures up on Melrose in the real town of Hollywood, where I pulled nails and took down sets for re-use. My mother drove me, and I hitchhiked back or took the streetcar. There were soldiers everywhere. We had air raid drills some nights, and periodic wild explosions from anti-aircraft firing. It was always a false alarm, but the town was jumpy with the thought of Japanese submarines and planes blowing things up.

Rumor had it that the Japanese actually fired a missile at Santa Barbara, but other than that, life was good. The pictures and the stars were still being made, and famous directors like John Ford, Frank Capra, and William Wyler shifted their attention to making war films in the Culver City Studios. During this time, my father was an air raid warden, and maybe because of that we didn't worry much about war rationing. We had all the ration stickers for gasoline ("C") and meat ("D") we could use.

As I mentioned before, my mother was a big believer in a good education, so when it was time for my brother and I to enter high school she enrolled us both into Loyola High, an all-boys Jesuit school on Venice Boulevard near Vermont. My brother was a good student, studied hard, and had a knack for never getting caught, but I, on the other hand, had finally met my match with these warden-esque priests.

Loyola was as good as it got for an education as far as my mother was concerned, and it still is! It's a solid and respected institution, and a natural stepping-stone to college. Higher learning aside, graduating from the right high school held almost as much prestige as the right college in those days. But I blew the whole thing and my mother never forgave me.

I had a pretty good idea I was in big trouble when Father Caroline, the vice principal and the toughest of badass taskmasters, told me I was flunking both my religion and R.O.T.C. classes. I was also far from a shining star in Latin, history, and algebra. Combine that with my steady stream of schoolroom pranks, and you can assume my name was regularly coming out of Father Caroline's mouth.

There were warnings, but I didn't pay attention. Why should I? I was a comfortable junior in High School. There was no need to work any harder. The future? Who cared? Things were good. Why screw with success?

The final straw came at a noon assembly. The entire student body was squeezed into a quonset hut as a makeshift auditorium unfit for a group half its size. My good pal Al Pollard and I were shoulder to shoulder against the wall with a fire hose at our side. Al was a fellow wiseass but was also an athlete everyone knew was destined for greatness. I was just a joker.

"You got any balls," Pollard said, "you'd take this hose and spray the whole fucking crowd."

"Bullshit," I said, but it didn't take much back then to get me going. "Here," Pollard said. "Take this end, and pull"

So, I looked around and no one was paying any attention. The place was too jammed.

"Pull," he said.

So, I pulled the hose a little and it started unraveling from its ring. I got it about six feet out and Pollard turned the handle and water fired out like a wet snake over the crowd.

Oh. It worked.

The crowd started running and everyone screamed and we ran like hell out the side door. The assembly was cut short, but that wasn't all. In the excitement of it all, I failed to calculate the fact that there were 500 witnesses who saw me holding the hose, with Pollard twisting the valve. Somehow, I thought I could talk my way out of it. Somehow, I thought I would find enough creative flair to come up with some kind of excuse so my mother wouldn't find out. Can't anybody take a joke?

Father Caroline's final and only words to me were, "Mr. Mahoney, get your books and get out." He repeated those words over and over, between my interjecting of "But… but… but…"

My mother was devastated. I don't think she ever recovered from that incident, not even years later when she attended the graduation of two of her grandsons from Loyola.

Word quickly spread throughout L.A.'s religious academic administrative network that this Mahoney kid was a real troublemaker. I tried to make it at other schools, but the word was out about the "bad seed" named Mahoney. I lasted a total of two weeks each in three other Catholic high schools, Cathedral, Mt. Carmel, and Saint Monica's. This school thing, as it was turning out, just wasn't my forte.

My mother could not have been more brokenhearted. For some reason, she believed that a Catholic education was the only education. It didn't help that my brother was a perfect student and excelled at everything he put his mind to.

I finally ended up at Hamilton High, the local public school. When I arrived for registration, I was immediately told by the registrar to report to vice principal Homer Eaton's office. After three pretty rough years being battered around verbally and physically by the Jesuits, the Christian Brothers, the Carmelite priests, and finally the Sisters of the Holy Name of Jesus and Mary, I was more than ready for something more gentile.

"Mahoney," Vice Principal Eaton said, "one fuck up... just one fuck up, and you're off to Jacob Riis. No bullshit about it, kid. Do you read me?"

"Yes, sir," I said. Everyone knew about Jacob Riis. It was all the way in East Los Angeles and was the next thing to a penal institution. I got the message.

Hamilton High turned out to be the best thing that ever happened to me. Aside from never having serious scholastic problems again and maintaining a B average or better, I also behaved (for the most part). Maybe Vice Principal Eaton's "kind" welcome had done its job, but I also hated the thought of going to Jacob Riis, or disappointing my mother any more that I already had. Even after my mother's grand talks of the benefits of a fine Catholic education, the public schools were probably where I belonged.

One of my final classes during my senior year was journalism. My assignment for the school paper, *The Federalist*, was to cover any and all sports going on at the school. I often hung out in the gym, watching practice and shooting the breeze with players and the coaches. On one of these days, the gym was being prepped for a Saturday night dance.

As I interviewed one of the coaches, I turned around and there in front of me was the cutest little gal I had ever seen. I did my best to talk to her, but all I could do was stare at her. She was a goddess, with a perfect figure, and as my eyes ran up and down her frame my mouth was uncharacteristically frozen.

"It's Sadie Hawkins this Saturday," she said.

"Yeah," I said, dumbfounded she was talking to me. "I'm looking for a date, you interested?"

As is the tradition with Sadie Hawkins dances, all the girls were going around asking the guys. This was uncharted territory for the both of us, and this little freshman beauty was asking me.

How could I not say yes? Her name was Pat Marston. Pat Marston was the best-looking girl in school, and everyone knew it. It was love at first sight, right then and there. Pat was asking me to the dance and that's all that mattered.

High school ended shortly thereafter for me, but I kept seeing Pat, stopping by Hamilton to pick her up after school. We were more than steady. We were inseparable. Her family lived at 1623 Pointview, near Pico and La Cienega. If my Ford was running, I'd take that. If it was busted, I'd hitchhike over to see her. She lived with her mother, but her father came around every now and then. He didn't care much for me, thought I was too old for his daughter, but understood what I was after. He was a peanut butter salesman, and knew all the lines. Maybe from my time with Tina, I learned to keep my distance from wary fathers.

One night we would go to the drive-in to catch a movie, another night to a party or a dance. There were clubs we all joined. The boys club was called The Bachelors and the girls club was the Demoiselles.

The clubs had loose rules and we swore allegiance to them for some reason, but the best part was getting the leather jackets with "The Bachelors" written across the back. It was all about chasing girls and having parties, and Pat was a good dancer. There were trips to Lake Arrowhead and Big Bear, and overnighters to Balboa Island and Catalina, and it was nothing but one great party after another.

I had no interest in furthering my scholastic education. During the day, my only interest was finding Pat, heading to Sorrento beach, and getting as close to her as possible in my coupe. I figured a bum like me had to take advantage of this while I could, before my old man took me by the neck and made me come work for him.

The notion of college was constantly pushed, but in those days it seemed unnecessary. To make up for my earlier bad behavior with the Jesuits, I reluctantly enrolled, for my mother's sake, at nearby Santa Monica City College.

It was just a two-year junior college stint. I could deal with that, and to me the campus was like a country club. You could arrange classes to get out by noon, which made it easier to get down to the beach. I went one step further. I arranged my classes for three days a week. The rest of my time, I worked as a lifeguard at the Del Mar Beach Club. There were five of us watching the pool and beach, taking turns at each location. Why would anyone do anything else? But my mother prevailed, and so in my last year at SMC I transferred to the University of Southern California. Because of the immediate threat of war on the horizon, I signed up for the National Guard, to avoid any possible draft situation. My mother was finally smiling.

It was then, one Sunday morning, when my father asked me to go for a ride. "I can't Pop," I said. "A bunch of us guys are heading to the beach."

"No," he said. "I have a better idea."

"What's that?"

"There's this house," he said. "I just finished the painting and decorating it. It's one great place and I'd like to show it to you."

"Where?" I asked.

"Encino."

"Encino?"

Once he told me the house was all the way over in Encino, at least an hour's drive from Culver City, I knew this was going to be an all day trip. I could kiss the beach and Pat goodbye.

"The man who owns it is very private," my father said.

I had never shown an interest in my father's work. In turn, he didn't have the kind of ego which required showing off, not even to his family. But on this day, he clearly had it in his mind for me to see this house and no discussion or salesmanship on my part was going to get me to the beach. My dad had never asked me to accompany him anywhere before, so knowing that, and the fact that it must be important to him, I had no choice but to say "Yes."

We started the long hot journey up through the Sepulveda Pass in my mother's new 1948 Chevy two-door. My father's truck would not be appropriate for Sunday client visits. We eventually made our way to the top of the pass and then down the winding roads on the backside that led to the San Fernando Valley.

My father didn't talk much on this trip, which made me uneasy. I sensed something was up but didn't know what. Finally, we pulled up to a giant gated driveway.

"This the place?" I asked.

"This job was referred to me by Howard Strickling, a very important man at MGM. I did a job in Cheviot Hills for his number two, Mr. Eddie Lawrence. He recommended me for this job."

"Incredible place, who owns it?"

"You'll see."

The address was 5525 Petit Avenue, and this was the first time I'd ever been to a home where, instead of ringing a doorbell, you phoned the main house from the gate.

"Who is it?" a voice asked through a speaker.

"It's Jack Mahoney."

The gates immediately opened, and we drove for a least a quarter of a mile up the winding driveway to a huge parking area. On either side were manicured lawns, flowers, rose bushes, and orange trees. There was a stable with several horses and groomsmen working them. My father parked the Chevrolet and we walked toward the main house, passing the garage with five spaces on either side of the house, each housing one gorgeous automobile after another. There was a Jaguar, a Mercedes roadster, a Rolls Royce convertible, a Cadillac convertible, three motorcycles, and even a few old Fords, rebuilt and looking new.

Like a lot of teenagers, I knew what make a car was just by the sound of it. After the war, new cars were something of a novelty, but this was like a top-of-the-line car showroom and museum combined. My father was right. I was duly impressed.

"Whose place is this?" I whispered.

He smiled. "You'll see soon enough," he said.

As we neared the house, my eyes widened with the blue of a swimming pool. Off to the side of the pool sat two men. One wore a suit and the other was in a flannel shirt, dungarees, riding leathers, and boots. The man in the riding clothes called my father over.

I stopped walking.

My father took my arm and dragged me forward. It was the same man I saw years ago when I went under the fence on Selznick's Forty Acres. The man with the ladies in the hoop skirts, the man everyone in the world knew. It was Clark Gable. He was right there in front of me, and I stopped cold.

"Who's this?" Gable said, looking dead at me.

"It's my son," my father said. "Jimmy."

Gable was as big as you could get. My mouth was agape, and as I stood there in awe I began to understand who owned all the cars, the horses, the English Tudor style mansion, the gates.

Gable got up to shake my father's hand and then he came toward me. It was all so easy and unassuming in a completely assuming place. Perhaps it was the way he conversed with my father, as equals doing business together, which in turn lessened my anxiety about the whole business of meeting a movie star. I shook his hand in silence. There were no airs or attitude, a true gentleman.

"Pleased to meet you, young Mahoney," he said, the way Clark Gable would say it.

The little smile off to the side. "Come meet my good friend Howard Strickling."

It was The Big Clock at work again. Timing working in my favor, timed to perfection just for me, just as the universe ordered. Clark Gable, the biggest star in the world, and Howard Strickling, who I would learn was the most powerful behind-the-scenes player in Hollywood, and my father, were all lined up there for me, or so it seemed the universe was ordering special delivery. I couldn't have known it then, but whatever success I ever hoped to achieve would be because of these three men.

After introductions, Gable and my father went into the house to discuss business. I sat there alone with Mr. Strickling. It turned out this man was not only Gable's closest friend, but he ran the Publicity Department at MGM. More importantly, he was also Louis B. Mayer's closest advisor. He knew how to get things done and undone in Hollywood, whether it was bringing up a young starlet to be America's sweetheart or keeping her off the booze and out of cheap motel rooms along Washington Boulevard.

"You in school?" Strickling asked. "Enrolled at USC," I said. "What're you majoring in?" "Girls," I said flippantly.

He smiled a little at that, but you could see it didn't come easy for him. Strickling was all business, and he had a slight stammer.

"College doesn't come che...cheap," he said. "I work a little too. What kind of work you interested in?"

"Oh, I don't know. I have a few odd jobs here and there. I'm taking journalism classes. I don't really have any great ambition to be a reporter, but it just seems to come easy to me."

"We can use young talent over at the studio, people that understand journalism, but want to do something bigger," Strickling said. "You ever want a job, come on by the studio and ask for me." And he gave me his card.

It suddenly dawned on me that this little tete a tete with Mr. Gable and Mr. Strickling was all set up and orchestrated by my father. He arranged this whole afternoon just for me, so I'd get the opportunity to meet with Clark Gable and this studio big shot. Little did I know then what a position I was in, sitting down with Howard Strickling of MGM. Hundreds of graduating journalism students throughout the country would have given their eye teeth to land in this spot, sitting around this pool at Clark Gable's mansion talking to this man.

When Gable and my dad came back, Strickling reiterated what he had just said about having me come around for a job at the studio. I didn't say a word, but I watched my father. He had a smile on his face as wide as the Pacific.

"Howard," Gable said. "If he goes to work for you, I want him to handle me."

I had no idea what "handle" meant, but even in my naïveté I could see that lady luck had just landed in my lap again.

I looked at my father, and his grin was still as wide as ever. On the ride back home, again, not much was said, not much was needed to be said, but we never communicated so well.

Chapter Four

What A Ride

THE NEXT DAY, I called Strickling's office.

"Mr. Strickling," I said. "I was considering your offer yesterday about coming to work for you and was wondering if it was still good?"

"Good?" Strickling said. "Come in tomorrow and ask for my office."

The next day, a Tuesday, I decided I was out of USC and now hopefully employed at MGM, in the Publicity Department. I put on my best jacket and tie that morning and, as directed, I went to the front gate, where the guard, a Mr. Keating, greeted me with, "Yes, Mr. Mahoney, Mr. Strickling gave us your name, go on in, it's the building on the right."

I had to smile. How surreal life had become. My former playground was now possibly my employer—my past was in fact my future. I walked through the gates, invited to be there, not crawling under the barbed wire, trying not to get caught by whatever back lot dick was patrolling the studio. But as impressed as I was walking those pristine paved streets, it all paled when I was ushered into *that* office.

I had never seen an executive's office before, except in the movies. When I first walked in, I thought I was in Strickling's office, but it was his secretary's office, or rather the secretary of the secretary's office. I was finally ushered past them and into *the office*.

The ceilings inside Strickling's office were twenty-five feet tall and the walls were upholstered in leather. This seemed a bit ostentatious for a man like Mr. Strickling, who I thought looked more comfortable poolside than in this grand space, a commander's office.

"This used to be Mr...Mr. Mayer's office," he said, reaching out to shake my hand.

Strickling cut an impressive swath in that office, though he seemed somewhat embarrassed by the grandeur. He was impeccably tailored in a severely conservative dark gray suit with a white shirt and a maroon tie. He wore black wingtip shoes, handmade at MacAfee's in London, I found out later. His one quirk was that slight stammer, which only came out during times of stress or when he needed to make a very important point.

He took me around the offices and introduced me to the nearby publicity staff, giving me a brief rundown as to what my primary duties were to be— the usual gofer tasks within the department.

After the introductions, Strickling asked one of his two secretaries, both of whom were named June, to send in Ted Harbert, a member of his staff, who was to give me a personal tour of the studio, take me to lunch and show me where I was to be spending the better part of my ten-hour days. Ironically, as my life played out years later in nothing short of a Shakespearian comedy, my son Sean met and married Ted's daughter Sarah, and I have two beautiful grandkids from that union in Amy and Timmy,

It turned out Harbert was one the Publicity Department's best "planters." Right off, you could tell he was a good storyteller.

"You got Gable?" he asked as we walked.

"Yeah," I said. "Not sure how, but Mr. Strickling set it up."

Harbert was charming, witty, and likeable—three characteristics which made him one of the best at taking stories or photos from other department publicists and "planting" them with hungry reporters and columnists.

"Our biggest job here is the care and feeding of the press," he said. "They're always looking for material, it's the beast you have to keep at bay and happy at the same time."

I nodded like I knew what he was talking about. The Beast? Feed them material? I was told later about Harbert's leg up. His uncle was Richard Berlin, William Randolph Hearst's top aide, and one of the most important people in the field of communications. Harbert, it seemed, was plugged in to "the beast" as directly as anyone could be in Hollywood. I followed Harbert along the tour with wide-eyed awe.

Even though I'd grown up in the shadow of MGM, selling Cokes and gum on the set of "Gone with the Wind" and dozens of other films, and had attended St. Augustine's parochial school directly across the street for eight years, I had no idea what really went on inside the gates. I actually knew nothing about the place or the making of movies.

Harbert pointed out the various departments, explained their functions, peppering his conversation, as he was so good at doing, with interesting anecdotes about each. As one of Strickling's best "planters," Harbert took press releases "by hand" to the big shot syndicated columnists like Walter Winchell, Earl Wilson, Hedda Hopper, and Louella Parsons. Every paper had at least one.

"It's easy being friends with them," he said. "Especially, when you represent the stars at MGM."

In a relatively short time, and with Harbert's help, I could weave stories like nobody's business, too. With the kind of access I had to the top brass, and Gable, I thought I might move up the ranks of the Publicity Department fast. But I was soon told otherwise. There was a lot of grunt work in this business, and as the newest member of the team, Harbert explained as we walked the studio that first day, there was going to be a lot newspaper and magazine clipping of important articles, taking new studio contractees to events, giving studio tours to important guests, and helping put together press kits.

"Here it is," Harbert said.

"What?" I asked.

"The Commissary," he said. "The most important place on the lot, and the best food in town. We want to keep the stars happy, L.B. wants only the best for his assets."

I knew "L.B." meant the big guy himself, Louis B. Mayer. "Assets?" I asked.

"It's a crazy business you're in now, Mahoney," he said. "L.B. says this is the only business where the assets drive home every night. We gotta keep them smiling for the cameras. We don't want them driving off the lot for a three-martini lunch. Better to keep them right here where they can't get in trouble, where we can keep an eye on them."

"You'll be spending a lot of time in here," he explained as we walked in. "It's when we can talk to the stars, between breaks in shooting."

The Commissary was one big food hall with photos of the biggest stars blown up huge on the walls. At first it looked to me like a more glamorous version of Hamilton High's cafeteria. Harbert, under his breath, told me each studio department ate together and had its own table, some larger than others.

"You have to eat with the publicists unless one of your clients invites you over," he said. He pointed to the back and side of the room. That was where the publicists ate.

It was true. More often than not, the Make-Up Department ate with the make-up people, the Art Department people ate with the art people, and the Property Department, Sound, Publicity, and so on, ate with their respective peers. There was no question about where you belonged in The Commissary.

The best tables in the place were set up for the stars.

"They are all here, Mahoney," Harbert said. "Every star in the world is right here in front of you."

It was true. I looked around and there were Elizabeth Taylor and Peter Lawford and Van Johnson at one table. At another were Janet Leigh, Howard Keel, and Ricardo Montalban. Marilyn Monroe, Jane Powell, and Ann Miller sat behind them, and Cyd Charisse, Donald O'Connor, (future First Lady) Nancy Davis, and Roger Moore sat at the table next to them. It was hard to take it all in. Everywhere I looked, there was another famous face, or someone I thought I knew, and they looked just like they looked in the movie magazines my mother kept in the kitchen.

"Yeah, kid," Harbert said. "This is the center of the universe. You've officially arrived."

In the very middle of the room there was a large table. No one sat at this table unless they were invited, or were one of the "untouchables" who sat there regularly.

"Don't even think about sitting at that table," Harbert said. "L.B. or Mannix are the only ones, or the biggest stars, that sit there."

Eddie Mannix was the studio's vice president of operations, and even though there was private dining room adjacent to The Commissary and an executive dining room across the lot in the Thalberg Building, he came in sometimes to mix with the stars he watched over.

Harbert gave me the quick inside story on Mannix.

"Don't cross him," he said. "He'll cut your balls off."

Mannix, it turned out, was as rough as an Irishman comes. He was known as The Fixer. A former bricklayer, he came from Long Island and was sent by the New York financial office to look over Mayer's shoulder, to keep a tab on his spending habits. The arrival of Mannix was a sign that New York was claiming a dominant position over operations.

"L.B. likes the guy," Harbert said. "Go figure."

I learned later there was something in the gruff henchman that Mayer found useful. He became a "Mayer Man" nearly instantly, even though most "Mayer Men" were smooth as silk and smart as hell in legal and money matters, Mannix was different. He was the kind of guy who could eliminate a problem with a pissed-off Spencer Tracy or moody Clark Gable with a bottle of Jack Daniels and a little bullshit. He was good at greasing palms and burying bones, too. Actors and actresses, as it turned out, loved Mannix for what he did for them behind the scenes, how he saved their asses time and again.

"Get to know Mannix," Harbert said. "He'll like you."

I didn't press him on that, but I figured it was an Irish thing. He nodded like that was true, but I didn't believe it or care at that point. I was just looking at all the stars eating their ham sandwiches and French Dips.

"These kids are generally stupid, so you gotta take care of them," Harbert said as we looked for a place to sit down. "They have more money than common sense."

So, this special table in the center of the big room was reserved for the biggest of the studio's big stars, like Gable, Tracy, Hepburn, the Barrymores, Ava Gardner, Lana Turner, Fred Astaire, Gene Kelly and Greer Garson, as well as visitors like Bill Holden and John Wayne.

As I stood scanning the room of famous faces, a very distinctive voice yelled out my name. There standing in the middle of the room, which had suddenly become eerily quiet, was Clark Gable calling out to me.

"Mahoney... Mahoney... over here," he shouted.

He motioned me over to the special center table, to sit down with him. In something of a daze, I stumbled around a few chairs and made it to his side. He was bigger than life, the real Clark Gable, not the one sitting poolside in riding dungarees and cowboy boots. He wore a snappy gray chalk suit, shook my hand, and said, "Jeem, Howard just told me you were here so let's have lunch."

It was Clark Gable talking to me. Seeing that I was totally petrified, he smiled and said, "Sit down kid, let's eat."

My first day on the job and I was sitting at the "A" table, with MGM's most important "asset."

Holy Christ, what a ride this was going to be!

Chapter Five

Keeping My Mouth Shut

TIMING. IT ALWAYS came back to timing.

I'd be a bag boy at Safeway or in the insurance business like my uncles Pat, Mike, and Tommy, if I hadn't skipped the beach that fateful Sunday morning and taken that drive to Encino with my old man.

My father was thrilled with my new position. It may have been the happiest day of his life. He was officially off the hook for my college tuition, although he would have gladly paid it. My mother, however, was not happy in the least. She wanted me to follow in my brother's footsteps and get a good college education. Somehow, I would have to make it up to her.

Gable was true to his word. I started working for him as a gofer and soon helped give studio tours. I was the envy of every junior publicist at the studio, but I was still very much a grunt. I had little to do with "handling" Gable. Strickling was his man. But there was some backbiting about the "new kid" getting the plum spot, but I wasn't the first Gable flexed his considerable muscle for at the studio. He wanted guys around him that he could relate to and for some reason I fit that bill, albeit at a minor level. Or at least he saw something in me, something raw, that maybe I was something like he was when he was nineteen. He did this for actors, too. There was a young up-and-comer named Bob Wagner that he took under his wing. It turned out Wagner, the son of a steel executive, was also his regular caddie at Bel Air Country Club.

Looking back, it was clear I didn't know squat about what was going on in the Publicity Department. I had no real clue as to what I was supposed to do for Gable, either, but I guess I was smart enough to keep my mouth

shut and stand at the ready when either he or Strickling called. I knew I
was learning from the best, so being a grunt at MGM was just fine with me.

And then there was Otto Winkler.

When I got Strickling alone, I asked him what kind of personal stuff
Gable asks for. "Not much," he said. "You got the easiest racket in this place.
Mostly, just keep the press away." You didn't have to sell Gable as a product
or worry about him mouthing off, Strickling said. "The press wants to talk
to him, but just tell them he's not available, got it? Leave the tougher stuff
to me."

I got it. I didn't know what the "tougher stuff" meant, but I nodded and
followed him around like a sidekick. There were senior, junior, and a few
apprentice publicists all handling the important stuff each star demanded. It
seemed like my main role was to help out the staff wherever and whenever
they needed help, from fetching coffee to running laundry.

"But remember," Strickling said. "Gable is the king around here, you're
here because of him."

It didn't take me long to understand just how important Strickling was to
the place, or Gable. One day, I was called to his office and when I arrived Ava
Gardner came out of his door in tears. She was sobbing. I thought to myself,
Strickling had to be "somebody" to make Ava Gardner cry.

It wasn't my place to ask questions. It was always better keeping my trap
shut. I assumed it was about her not toeing the company line. It went for
everyone. My days of being a disrespectful, smart-assed prankster were well
behind me now. I needed this job. There was no going back to college. In
fact, where else could a nineteen-year-old collect a paycheck for watching
Ava Gardner cry, or sit at the "A" Table with Clark Gable? Even then, as the
lowest of low in the PR department, I knew it didn't get any better than this.

Strickling had run Publicity for a long time, in the end more than twenty
years, and he had put together the best in the business. Everyone said it,
the media, the other studio guys, even the wiseguys. Strickling's department
handled publicity better than any of them. Strickling always said, "Publicity
is not only your first line of defense, but also your first line of offense."

When Mayer gave the go-ahead for a film, Strickling was one of the very
first to know about it. With a scrap of a script idea or a new star they were
eyeing for the part, he set his troops in motion.

First, a "unit publicist" was assigned to the project. He or she stayed with
that unit from start to finish, from pre-production right on through to the
film's release. It was the job of the publicist, with the help and support of the
permanent staff of P.R. specialists, to see to it that millions of moviegoers

throughout the world heard about the movie and wanted to see it months, sometimes even a year, before it came to their theaters. It was an effective and cost-efficient way of getting "asses in seats," as Strickling liked to say.

Some publicity specialists dealt with news magazines, while others handled everything from sports to fashion outlets. There was even a separate department for foreign press. Still another department of Strickling's dealt only with still photographs, not just the glamour shots, but also the still pictures that came in daily from every unit filming either at the studio or from around the world. In those days, every motion picture in production not only had a publicist on the set every day, but also a still photographer.

Clarence Bull headed up portrait photography in the studio's Still Department. He took the glamour shots, too. Most were on the walls all over the place. Greta Garbo. Lana Turner. Ava Gardner. Elizabeth Taylor. He took the portraits of the guys, too, like Robert Taylor and Clark Gable, and everyone else famous. But glamour shots were just part of the business. There was poster art, too. A movie wasn't complete until the poster was carefully crafted, posed and photographed with the stars of the film.

Posters proved as provocative a selling tool for advertising and in theater lobbies as Bull's eight-by-ten glossies were at gaining fans. There was something called "holiday art"— dummied up pictures of the stars in their Christmas or Easter finery—all ready for a seasonal story. And never, ever, was a still picture released to the press without careful scrutiny and retouching if necessary. All the still photographers on the MGM staff were world class. So were the cinematographers. The Gables, Turners, Gardners and Taylors (Elizabeth and Robert)—all had favorites who were assigned to their films.

From the start, I was schooled in the concept that image was everything.

I watched Strickling's careful handling of our assets. These were primarily the actors, but also included directors, producers, and executives under contract. Never were we to confirm the fact that anyone, contract players or stars, were sick or had any kind of personal problems. And when it came to potential scandals of the day—affairs, divorces, homosexuality, spousal abuse, abortions, and a whole myriad of crimes and misdemeanors—those were quashed long before the press caught wind.

If anyone under contract ever got into any kind of scrape with the law, thanks to the power of the studio and the influence of certain people such as Strickling or Whitey Hendry, the studio police chief, most incidents were buried, and buried deep.

At MGM, Hendry had a police force the size of most municipalities.

People were "taken care of," and the unfortunate incident just went away. These weren't domestic problems or drunk driving citations. This was a minefield of potential career-ending stuff kept under wraps from the public and police.

There was Loretta Young's affair and subsequent child with Gable. Another was a film distributor's rape of a young showgirl on the back lot. Then there was the questionable suicide of Paul Bern, the MGM executive and husband of actress Jean Harlow. Strickling "handled" them all, and the bigger the "investment," the faster and more efficiently the studio circled the wagons.

There were always rumors, and Gable himself was no exception.

The one I never had the guts to bring up was about him driving his Cadillac convertible on Sepulveda Boulevard near Santa Monica Boulevard and killing a jaywalking pedestrian crossing the street. It was in 1945, and the word was that the family was taken care of. And it was all courtesy of Whitey Hendry and Howard Strickling (and his deep pockets).

When it came to public relations and crisis management, this was the place. It was as if the sun shone and the skies rained every day. I learned fast to roll with it and keep my mouth shut, or I knew I was out. There was never a dull moment, and the media beast kept the edge on us all.

Chapter Six

Feeding the Beast

THE PAPERS WANTED dirt. The legitimate news outlets had a relationship with us, and vice versa. If something unseemly popped up by one of the contract actors, we just told the reporters not to print it. But it wasn't free. There was a quid pro quo. For each magnanimous gesture from the press, we rewarded them later with a scoop, or something better. There was no sense of impropriety in these relationships. It was standard stuff, though Strickling's magnanimity was better. Besides the usual gifts of booze or clothes or tickets, there were trips to exotic and foreign film locations, too. All of it was fully paid, gratis. It was a win/win, but with the studio getting the bigger percentage of the win.

Still, the whiff of scandal occasionally surfaced in the papers. There were often veiled threats and innuendo and blind items—mostly regarding trysts between stars.

Strickling more than once hastily arranged marriages for stars like Robert Taylor and Barbara Stanwyck. It helped tamp down the real story, that they were both "allegedly" gay. Then there was the Gable and Carole Lombard affair. Strickling was able to quell the backlash of that scandalous 1930s adultery, when Gable carried on not so secretly with Lombard while still married to his second wife, socialite Rhea Langham. Gable and Lombard eventually married and, like always, the press bought Strickling's story hook, line and sinker—on the surface anyway. More often than not, the papers ran with the subsequent "happily ever after" photos we planted.

From the start, Strickling had me taking important stories or studio announcements and "hand planting" them—literally placing them in the actual hands of key columnists or editors. "It ain't as easy as it looks," he said. "You have to track them down, find them in restaurants or gin mills all over town."

He was right. Just when you thought the reporter was inside Musso & Franks, or some dive bar on Western, they were gone. They said it took years to establish a rapport with the big press names. They were a suspicious lot and anyone new to the game, especially new "planters," had to earn their trust, as columnists were extremely guarded. It was gold to know these writers, to have a personal rapport, to be on a first name basis, to drink, and shoot the shit together. It wasn't uncommon for a studio planter to keep his job just because he could get powerhouse gossip columnists like Louella Parsons or Hedda Hopper on the phone. These two could make one's career as a publicist in Hollywood or make it pure hell.

Hand planting was all about accuracy. Just talking a story over the phone invariably led to an error that showed up in the paper. More often than not, that little error ruined the story, or maybe cost you your job. A misspelled name or wrong title or incorrect opening date was enough to erase whatever confidence and credibility you had with Strickling. Hand planting and explaining the story directly to the reporter was the best way to go.

One of my first hand-plant assignments came when Strickling asked me to take an envelope over to Louella Parsons at her home at 619 North Maple Drive in Beverly Hills.

"I need you to give this to her personally," he said. "You understand? This has to be a hand plant."

For all I knew, there was money in the envelope.

"You know what hand plant means?" he said.

I nodded. "Yes, sir."

"It means this envelope goes from your hand to her hand, and nothing else, you don't give it to anyone else, get it?"

"I got it."

When I arrived at the house on North Maple I was greeted by a man, her butler.

"Yes?"

"I'm from Mr. Strickling's office at MGM. I have an envelope for Miss Parsons."

"I'm Collins, her personal assistant, I can take it."

"I have strict orders from Mr. Strickling to hand it only to her."

"I'll give it to her."

"I'm sorry, but I have my orders."

Collins, painfully thin with a blade-like face, turned to go back inside the house, but then turned around. "What's your name?" he asked.

"Mahoney," I said. "Jim Mahoney."

"Come inside Mr. Mahoney, and make yourself comfortable while I get her."

When he left, I took to sizing up the place. There were autographed photos of just about everyone you'd see at the studio, and a few presidents and kings, too. They were in frames on the tables and on a large grand piano. As I waited, my eyes went from one framed photo to another. And then to my amazement, right there among the stars, kings and presidents, was Father John O'Donnell, the pastor of our church, St. Augustine's, in Culver City.

Parsons entered the room. She appeared anxious and upset.

"Why didn't you leave the envelope with Collins?" she demanded.

She was a formidable woman. I was told she had a job for life with the Hearst papers, something about a payoff for not blabbing the real story about the death of director Thomas Ince aboard Hearst's yacht parked off Santa Monica. She milked this leverage to get to her pampered position. She sized me up in an instant.

"You're from Howard's office?" she asked, rather curtly and with an intonation that sounded for all the world like, "The kids Howard's hiring these days!"

"Yes," I said. "I'm Jim Mahoney and I have this for you, it's from Mr. Strickling." I handed it to her, she took it, said nothing, and started to walk away.

"By the way," I said. "I see you know Father O'Donnell?"

She stopped and turned. "Why yes," she said, somewhat surprised. "Why do you ask?"

"He baptized me and he's one my parents' best friends. My father painted the church!"

That did it. I was "in."

Miss Parsons asked me to stay for tea and meet the rest of her staff. From that day forward, Howard Strickling had a new planter for Louella Parsons. I could get her on the phone whenever I needed and that was career gold. I knew I was safe, for a while. I knew I could probably get a job in any publicity department at any studio anywhere in Hollywood after making this connection.

Hollywood celebs feared her. Between 1915 & 1960 Louella Parsons was America's premier movie gossip columnist and in her heyday commanded a following of more than forty million readers.

It turned out the note I planted was an early tip about the big Africa movie being planned for Gable called "Mogambo." They were working on getting Gene Tierney to star and thought the actress needed a little push to get her interested. It was to be directed by John Ford, and Parsons got the exclusive. It was my first "plant." I'll never top this, I thought.

Maybe in some way Catholic school paid off.

Little did I know what was coming. It wasn't too long after that that I planted another letter with her from Strickling. Turned out Tierney didn't get the part. Ava Gardner did.

It all seemed rather innocuous, but I learned quickly all the jobs in publicity, no matter how menial, had some sort of critical importance to the studio's greater cause. The grunt work never bothered me. I occasionally drove Strickling to various appointments around town and to and from the airport, and I'd also meet and see off other bigwig executives from New York. It was on one of these occasions that Strickling asked me to take him and Howard Dietz to the airport. It was a mid-afternoon drop-off.

"Don't allow him to miss the plane," Strickling warned me.

I had no idea what he meant, but I got a studio sedan and we headed out to the Bel-Air Hotel, where Dietz was staying. Dietz happened to head up MGM's East Coast Publicity machinery. In fact, he was Strickling's boss.

As we drove north toward the hills, Strickling told me about Dietz.

"A real talent, but he's always late, always."

Strickling was just the opposite. He was always early to a meeting and hated anyone who came late. Dietz drove Strickling crazy with his tardiness and apparently Dietz couldn't have cared less. Dietz was flamboyant in the way he dressed and in the way he spoke, while Strickling was dour and dull in comparison.

It seemed Dietz's real talent was being a Broadway producer and lyricist. He wrote *Dancing in the Dark* and *You and the Night and the Music*, both big hits. His Broadway shows included *Three's a Crowd* and *Bandwagon*. He also created the MGM trademark, Leo the Lion, and its Latin motto, Ars Gratia Artis, or Art for Art's Sake.

At the hotel, Dietz ambled toward us about twenty minutes late, early for Dietz, according to Strickling, who was about ready to fume.

"You never change, Howard," Strickling said, introducing me quickly. "Let's get going."

"Change?" Dietz said. "And why would I change at this stage of my life?"

"Doesn't it bother you that you're always late?"

"I can't deny it," Dietz admitted, smiling, "but I always leave early."

Nothing seemed to bother Dietz. Life was a big carousal ride for him. On the way to the airport, he complained about how exhausted he was from the trip.

"Too many glamorous parties?" Strickling said.

"I need my little helpers," he said, looking at me. "Maybe young Mahoney can help here."

I kept my mouth shut. I didn't know what he was talking about. "I can't do this overnight trip without some help," he said.

Strickling saw I was lost. "Sleeping pills," he said. "See what you can find."

"Of course," I said, as if I could pick them up as easily as a pack of cigarettes.

At the airport, while Dietz checked his baggage and talked with Strickling, I made a beeline for the airport Red Cross emergency unit. If nothing else, I knew how to improvise.

The Red Cross was a block away, and I asked one of the residents if he had a couple of sleeping pills. "It's for my boss, he has an overnighter to New York and can't sleep for shit."

"Are you kidding? You need a prescription for sleeping pills."

"What am I going to do?" I pleaded. "Can you put something in a box for me, otherwise it's my ass."

The resident intern went back to a storeroom and came out with a small pillbox. I gave him ten bucks, thanked him, and ran back to the terminal. I didn't care what the pills were, it did the job for the moment.

"Thanks, Mahoney," Dietz said. "I'll remember this."

Dietz took the pillbox and we walked him to the plane. On the way back to the studio, Strickling turned to me and said, "Where'd you get sleeping pills so fast at the airport?"

"Red Cross," I said. "I don't know what they are, probably aspirin."

Strickling burst out laughing. "I hope for your sake he never finds out."

The next morning, Strickling buzzed me on the intercom. "Dietz has just called from New York," he said. I cringed. I knew I was done for. "He slept like a baby all the way back."

We both had a big laugh over that one. Some things you can't be taught, I thought. Some things were just instinctual.

Chapter Seven

Leo's Lair

STRICKLING'S RULES WERE our commandments. We learned to live by his every word and action, and the trips to the airport seemed to be the place he'd lay out the rules. It was on one of these occasions when he first mentioned his most important rule: Don't be the story.

"P.R. people should keep their names and faces out of the papers," he said. "It's bad for business, takes the light away from our assets, our product. Never get your face in the papers, it never turns out well."

He was adamant. He continually reminded the staff of this, but with the press doing their job, it didn't always work out that way. The example that steamed him most was Ralph Wheelwright, one of his right-hand men, and another one of my father's clients. Every time he mentioned Wheelwright, he steamed just a little more.

It was about Judy Garland, who was, at that time, one of the studio's biggest stars.

Her then husband, Sid Luft, and she were going at it again, part of their continuing marital battles, which had become well known around the studio and town. Garland was a mess. Fighting on the set, fighting in L.B.'s office, fighting with Luft at home in Brentwood, fighting booze and pills and just about everything in life. There wasn't a thing anyone could do about it but watch and turn away. Then, one day, we got the call. She was in the hospital. Suicide.

It turned out it was attempted suicide. She slashed her throat with a knife, but not very well. She was still alive, and now the news was getting out. There was no covering up a big star like Judy Garland trying to kill herself and ending up in the hospital. We could keep the wraps on for a while, but not for long.

Word got out that she was okay, recovering nicely even, but the knife business leaked and the press inundated the Garland-Luft estate. Here's where Strickling's Wheelwright Lesson came into play.

Strickling sent Wheelwright out to Brentwood to calm everyone down. He was to advise the press that everything was blown out of proportion.

"Judy's just swell," Wheelwright told the assembled media outside the house gates. "Just a small accident, a scratch really, she and her husband are as happy as lovebirds that she's back home."

One of the crafty wire service photographers asked about the cut to the throat doctors mentioned in the official report.

"Nothing to it," Wheelwright responded and then added, "just a scratch."

"Where?" asked the shrewd photographer.

This is when Wheelwright made his mistake, injecting himself into the story.

He pointed to his neck. Right then flashbulbs exploded all around him. It was this photo that the newspapers printed. The headline and caption read: MGM PUBLICITY MAN SHOWS WHERE JUDY SLIT HER THROAT.

Wheelwright was now the national story. "It never turns out well, kid. Never."

After a few months, I was getting used to the place. I'd enter The Commissary by myself and find the right table. Sometimes I'd shake hands with Gable and others at the "A" Table and then I'd go find Harbert or some other publicists and sit down with them. I was developing my routines. On this particular day, I had just ordered my favorite, a Green Goddess Salad, when Strickling walked up and said, "Mahoney, you're coming with me."

"I just got my salad."

"Leave the salad."

He was stammering, and everyone around knew something was up.

He led me across the dining room, and we proceeded to open the door to a room adjacent to The Commissary. He waved me inside. There, surrounded by dark paneling and leather chairs, sitting alone at a table for ten was the number one man, Louis B. Mayer—all of five foot nothing and as round as Humpty-Dumpty sitting on a throne. But somehow, in this regal setting he pulled off the mogul role. There were bone china set-ups, expensive silverware, and two waiters standing by.

I fixated my glance at a platter of tomatoes. They were red and perfectly round, so round I thought they were movie props. Somehow, Mayer simply had the power to make the most innocuous of objects around him seem important and ideal.

"Mr. Mayer," Strickling said, the stammer nearly under control, and always using great formality in his boss' presence, "this is a new addition to our department, Jim Mahoney. I thought it was important that you two should meet."

"Mahoney," bellowed a smiling Mayer. "That's a good Jewish name, you should go far in this business."

"Well, I'm learning from the best," I said, improvising whatever bullshit I could come up with in front of L.B. and my boss.

"This is the best team in Hollywood," he said. "And Howard is the best publicity director ever! Do what he says and you'll do well."

Howard stopped stammering after that, and then the head of MGM proceeded for the next hour to tell me what a great opportunity I had working at the studio.

"My door is always open," he assured me.

I learned later that the small, regal dining room was known as Leo's Lair. Mayer used it often to entertain visiting dignitaries, but I will always remember it as a throne room, the place where I was knighted by the king.

At this point, in 1947, it was not uncommon at MGM to have a dozen movies filming concurrently. With thirty sound stages and four huge lots with every conceivable outdoor set, movies shot side-by-side would not interfere with one another. There was even a small zoo for jungle movies, and there was Stage 15, the biggest sound stage in the world.

Stage 15 was an engineering marvel and spanned more than an acre in size without one supporting beam. For "Battleground," the decorators created a snow-covered forest for the Battle of the Bulge. An entire western village was built on the stage for "How the West Was Won."

There was Stage 5, too, and its purpose was for the many musicals being produced for Gene Kelly, Fred Astaire, Mario Lanza, Judy Garland, Marge and Gower Champion, Howard Keel, Vera Ellen, and Jane Powell. Sets could be brought in to make the stage look like anything from the Paris Opera House to Ford's Theater.

Then there was the famous Stage 30, where beneath the floor was the largest indoor swimming pool in the world. This was where Esther Williams did her thing with the likes of Fernando Lamas, Ricardo Montalban, Van Johnson, and Peter Lawford.

Contract actors and actresses were each assigned a publicist. Everyone in the department, short of Strickling and the secretaries, was assigned at least three or four contractees whom the publicists had to take care of, and they needed a lot of handholding. That meant contacting them at least two or three times a week, writing column inches about their activities, setting up interviews and photo layouts for them with various periodicals, and generally letting them know that someone at the studio cared.

Even on my lowly perch, in addition to my duties with Gable, Strickling and later Mayer himself, I was assigned to young contract players, too. I remember they sent me over to meet a new one on my birthday, February 22, 1947.

Strickling informed me one morning that I was to be at the Talent Department at noon. I was to meet Al Trescony, one of the talent executives. He was bringing up a new actress they found locally, in Burbank. This young starlet had won a contract at Warner Brothers by having been crowned Miss Burbank. The word was Jack Warner didn't want to give her a raise to $65 a week, so he dumped her on us. I went over to see Trescony and he introduced me to his new find.

"Jim," Trescony said. "I'd like you to meet one of our newest stars—or soon to be stars, with your help."

She was a cute little blonde and as All-American as apple pie. Her name was Mary Frances Reynolds. It seemed that Solly Baiano, the talent scout at Warner Bros., won her in a coin toss with Trescony after the Miss Burbank Pageant. Now she was here.

"Pleased to meet you, Miss Reynolds," I said.

"Call me Debbie," she said, and reached out and shook my hand with the firmest grip I ever received from a gal.

My first impression was unimpressive. She was too apple pie, too midwestern, too cute. The studio was all about glamour and stars. I couldn't picture her in sequins.

"Make her a star," Trescony said, with a wry smile.

"It's what we do," I said. "It's what we do."

Still, I wasn't too sure about her, but I figured all starlets start out like this. Some make it and some disappear down Culver Boulevard. But from the first moment Debbie and I started working together, I could tell she had something special, a sparkle in her eyes, a great smile, and a great figure, too. She was ready and eager for all that was ahead.

"All I wanted was the blouse and scarf," she said.

"What blouse and scarf?" I asked.

"This whole thing is a mistake; I entered the Miss Burbank contest just to get the free blouse and scarf. I had no interest in it, my father forced me, and now here I am at MGM. I can't believe it."

I shook my head and proceeded to wonder what I was going to do with her.

"Well," I said, "now you can get a hell of a lot more than a blouse and a scarf."

When Debbie Reynolds walked through that gate that first day, she couldn't dance or sing any better than Mr. Keating, the security guard. Louis B. Mayer wanted his stars to always look the best, but he also wanted them to sing the best, walk the best, speak the best, dress and be the best. No one took more or better advantage of the University of MGM than this young beauty queen.

The studio had a full time dentist, a doctor, comportment and style teachers, and the very top people in their respective fields were available to teach anyone under contract to do and be better than anyone else. When North Carolina-bred Ava Gardner was discovered by MGM talent topper Billy Grady and was brought to the studio, she had a honey-coated Southern twang. After a year of daily appointments with "voiceologist" Gertrude Fogler, she sounded as if she were raised in New England.

By the time they were ready to put her before the cameras, Miss Burbank would be able to handle whatever was offered. It was amazing to watch this young lady absorb everything thrown her way, and then some.

Her first outing was portraying Helen Kane, the "boop-boop-a-doop" girl in "Three Little Words." It wasn't much of a role, but it had enough flash and pizzazz for me to work with, and the press ate her up. Debbie was off and running.

Wherever she went, I went with her, and now I was beginning to understand why Strickling's rules were so critical to the studio's success. There were events and stage shows jammed with fans, thousands of them, and managing all that was a handful. Staying out of the way of all this mayhem wasn't easy either, but I never forgot Mr. Strickling's creed: "Don't be part of the story."

I could see how a star could get in trouble fast, with everyone pawing at them and offering things. The media following us was like a pack of jackals, popping off flash bulbs by the hundreds and shouting questions.

It wasn't too long before one of my jobs was to fix Debbie up with dates with the rising male stars from the studio. The publicity helped both actors, and the media and fan magazines fed off the made-up romances, sightings at movie premieres, and new nightclub openings. Debbie understood the game, and to get some pizzazz next to her name she let me fix her up with any number of young actors, like Carleton Carpenter, Rock Hudson, or producer and MGM shareholder Arthur Loew, Jr., but there was never a real spark. I wasn't having much luck finding a date she really liked. Sometimes, I even escorted her to premieres.

"I don't know, Jim," she said. "I'm just waiting for the right guy."

Everything was just a laugh for the cameras, but she was looking for someone she could be serious about. I fixed her up with Tab Hunter and then coffee mogul Bob Neill, but both were duds. I asked her if there was anyone in particular she wanted to go out with.

"There is one, Jim," she said.

"Who?" I asked.

"Bob," she said.

"Bob?" I asked. There were a lot of Bobs in Hollywood.

"Bob Wagner," she said. "I think I'm stuck on him, I think he's the one."

"Wagner?"

Of course, through Gable I knew Bob (R.J.) Wagner and I knew he was making his way through Hollywood's leading actresses. But I also knew he was signed to Twentieth Century Fox Studios, which wasn't ideal for us.

"Let me work on that," I said.

It wasn't too many days later when Debbie was called up to L.B.'s office for an important meeting on a new production they were working on, a musical. Strickling invited me along too, to see if I could do something with her and this new picture they were working on called "Singing in the Rain." It was starring Gene Kelly and Donald O'Connor, and now maybe Debbie as the female lead.

Debbie and I went into the L.B.'s office and Gene Kelly was right behind us.

"Gene," Mayer said to Kelly, "here's the leading lady you'll be working with."

Kelly looked at this young girl from Burbank. He looked over at Strickling. He even looked at me.

"You gotta be kidding?" he said.

"No," L.B. said. "This is Debbie Reynolds, she's going to be a star."

Kelly walked over to the blonde teenager and asked, "Can you sing?"

"A little," she said.

"Can you dance?"

"A little."

"Let's see," he said.

Kelly asked her to do a few pirouettes and then a few other moves. She was hopeless, and Kelly walked out.

"I thi..thi..think it'll work out," Strickling said.

For the next three months, Kelly had Debbie running through dance drills, singing lessons, and voice coaching until he worked her into the form he needed to make this new "musical within a musical" work. He worked her ass off and she had no time for dating anyone until after the picture.

Of course, when the pictured opened, everything changed. She was now Debbie Reynolds, MGM leading lady and movie star.

Afterward, there was a whirlwind of press and publicity tours to manage and the media pounded down my door for scoops about the young sensation from "Singing." In what seemed like an instant, Trescony's find and Jack Warner's lament became the toast of the town. She was invited to every promotional event and we booked her in most of them, from the Pasadena Rose Bowl Parade to the Los Angeles Coliseum Fourth of July Celebration.

There I was, in the middle of this media storm, arm-in-arm with our newest star, Debbie Reynolds. And sometimes, in the crowd, like at the Coliseum, there were some of my old school chums watching me walking with America's newest sweetheart. It was surreal. And to think, I was getting paid for this! I felt like I was submerged in fields of beautiful women. Debbie was really cute, and there were others, but I had no interest. I was still dazzled by Pat. To my way of thinking, Pat was better looking than all of them, except maybe Elizabeth Taylor. But Pat had a better set of wheels.

I felt I was the luckiest guy in the world. And there was no shortage of dates for Debbie after that, but she still pined for Bob Wagner. They finally met on their own terms and they were both serious about each other for a time, getting to know each other's families, and writing letters when they were both away shooting films. But love is fickle, and in time they drifted apart from one another and went their separate ways, an all too familiar direction in the make-believe land of Hollywood.

Chapter Eight

A Dark and Profitable Art

PUBLIC RELATIONS WAS never something I thought about going into as a profession. I'm not sure anyone did in those days. It usually starts out with a desire to get into journalism, or writing the Great American Novel, and then somehow you end up in the dark art of publicity, PR, public relations, flacking. Thinking on your feet is part of the business, and sales is part of it, as well as pitching stories to the press, and taking the heat when things go sideways. It's all part of the business. Sometimes I felt like a junior lion tamer, holding a whip against the beast of the press on the one side while on the other side holding a chair against my clients. Improvisation and lion taming should be part of the job description for any PR person.

My primary responsibility at the studio always came back to handling Gable. When he had a need, everything stopped until it was fulfilled. And because he carried such weight, it gave me the opportunity to work with the biggest of the big stars right out of the gate. As a result, a big star never intimidated me, because no one came bigger than Gable.

Strickling had me carry out a lot of "secret assignments" for Gable. One was to quietly work with him on getting Gable married to Lady Sylvia Ashley. This was 1949 and the number one star in the world wanted to marry this elegant, titled-by-marriage divorcee and didn't want anyone to know.

Marriage was never good to Gable. His marriage to Carole Lombard was hastily prepared by the studio, too. Under their breaths, the publicity staff said this one looked no better. But we all kept our mouths shut.

It was typical Strickling work. He had clandestine connections seemingly everywhere, even in Solvang, where the wedding was to take place. He knew a judge outside of town and arranged for all the paperwork and blood samples to be taken care of without the press hearing a word of it. My job was to pick up the simple narrow gold wedding band Strickling purchased at a local Culver City jeweler, and meet bride and groom at Alisal Ranch, a fashionable dude ranch near the quaint Danish town just north of the seaside city.

I was to arrive at the ranch an hour prior to the wedding and check the resort for any newsmen and photographers. Having scanned the place, I was to then call Strickling, who was with the happy couple. I called and assured him, "It's all clear."

Trying to keep Gable under wraps in those days was the toughest job in Hollywood. The owners of Alisal, Lynn and Patsy Gillham, happened to be friends of Strickling's and they were in on the scheme. But they didn't know me, so when I arrived, the Gillhams immediately assumed I was with the press.

"Who are you?" Lynn Gillham asked.

"Just visiting," I said.

I didn't want to even hint that something was up, so there was a standoff with both of us not saying a word about what we both knew. Finally, I called Strickling and he confirmed that the Gillhams were indeed in on the deal and to work with them. So, the Gillhams and I laughed for about thirty seconds and then it was back to work.

Strickling was sending Eddie Hubbell, one of the studio's top photographers, to shoot the proceedings.

"I thought you said no photographers?" I asked

"They changed their mind," Strickling said. "You gotta roll with things."

Strickling advised me that the bridal party was on their way from San Luis Obispo, where they picked up the marriage license.

"They'll be there in an hour," he said.

Gable and Lady Sylvia arrived and both were dressed in navy. The Gillhams had decorated the ranch living room with chrysanthemums, palms, and evergreen boughs in front of a crackling fire. There was a three-tiered wedding cake and champagne for the small, private reception. The wedding was at three o'clock and took place without a hitch. There was a lot of picture taking, which, needless to say, Strickling stayed out of.

I rushed the negatives back through the MGM photo lab and hand-planted the best ones to the downtown newspapers and wire services that night. Strickling arranged for the couple to meet the press the next morning at Gable's ranch before the honeymooners motored to San Francisco, where I was to join them to assist in their travels. They then were to board the SS Lurline Luxury Liner bound for Hawaii.

The wedding publicity dominated the papers that whole next week. Everything went perfectly, Strickling said. "Everything except for one thing," he said.

"What's that?" I asked.

"The ring," he said.

"What about the ring?"

"It didn't fit, too small."

When Gable returned, I went to his office and apologized.

"Maybe it's an omen. Jeem," he smiled. "A lot of things didn't fit quite right between she and I, if you know what I mean."

The marriage lasted two years.

Chapter Nine

The Letters

IN THE SPRING of 1949, something happened that changed everything. I was headed back to the studio after one of my now routine "planting" missions, this time with Hedda Hopper's office. It was about Gable and Lady Sylvia's Hawaiian honeymoon, how swell it was, and there were photos of them on the beach. I decided to stop at one of the corner newsstands at Santa Monica Blvd. and Sawtelle before I went back through the MGM gates.

I saw the headline and it shouted out at me: "CALIFORNIA NATIONAL GUARD TO BE ACTIVATED."

I had joined the National Guard Reserves when I turned eighteen, which allowed me to be exempt through a student deferment from any national draft. I was assigned to the 40th Infantry Division if anything happened, but I pushed war far from my mind. I was attending my monthly meetings and "summer camps," and was ready if called, but here I was on the top of the world, just back from traveling to San Francisco with Gable and Lady Sylvia, and now I was being called up for General MacArthur's Korean Conflict.

I worked my eyes down to the small print. My Guard division, the 40th, was listed. All I could think about was, "I can't go to war now, not now, things are too good."

The order came in September, and my father drove me to the Culver City National Guard Armory and I boarded a bus for Fort Hunter Liggett military base near San Luis Obispo, California. I had said my goodbyes to my workmates at MGM, to Gable, to Debbie, to Strickling and finally to my family and especially my mother, but the hardest person to leave was definitely Pat. As the bus pulled away, I looked out the window to see my

father, his hands in his pocket, looking at me. He was expressionless. I had
a sick feeling this was not going to end well and somehow the blank look on
his face confirmed that feeling. At a minimum, I knew the curtain had fallen
on my Hollywood dream. To me and everyone else on the bus, this was the
start of one long, miserable ride.

My unit was the 143rd Artillery Battalion attached to the 160th Infantry
Regiment of the 40th Division. I knew a little bit about what was coming. The
summer training camps prepared us all, but these were anything but camps.
The most critical skills I learned were how to drive a jeep and navigate using
maps. The skills came in handy one day when I directed our commanding
officer, who was hopelessly lost on maneuvers, and got him safely back to
camp. We were that kind of a unit—a bunch of Beetle Baileys.

Most of the guys in the unit angled to get out of duty using any excuse
they could come up with, like mysteriously broken kneecaps, flat feet, or
just plain crazy. Even our division psychiatrist was finally sent home and
released after three months of continuously wearing both his pistol belt and
helmet backwards. Somehow, I made it through those training days, and at
the end of it they awarded me with the rank of Sergeant in the U.S. Army.
All I could think of was, "God help the war effort."

After Hunter Liggett we were shipped off to Camp Cooke northwest of
Lompoc, California, now Vandenberg Air Force Base. Cooke was even more
like the Keystone Comedies than the actual pictures they filmed on my street
back home. No one wanted to be there except the officers. These guys loved
the uniforms and the discipline and the medals. They loved playing soldier.
And, like a flashback to my high school days, the brass certainly didn't know
what to do with me. I was the odd sergeant in more ways than one.

It wasn't more than a month after I'd been activated that I was ordered
to division headquarters to meet with Col. Worth Larkin of the Public
Information Office. Larkin, it turned out, was one of those reserve officers
who just couldn't or wouldn't let go of the army. He loved the military
and everything about it. As a civilian, he was in charge of publicity for the
Los Angeles Junior Chamber of Commerce, so we had that in common,
but I could tell the uniform gave him an inner power that was beyond his
capabilities. Larkin knew something I didn't.

"You've got some friends in high places," he said.

"I do?"

" Don't kid me, Mahoney, I know you worked at MGM." And he held up
two letters.

I looked at them close. One was from Clark Gable and the other was from

L.B. himself. They were written to the National Guard's Commanding General of the 40th Division, Major General Daniel H. Hudelson.

I sat back in my chair and smiled.

"Yeah, I guess I do have some friends in high places," I said.

I was sure these were written by one of Strickling's top writers. They both suggested Sgt. Mahoney could better serve our country promoting the Army rather than digging foxholes and chasing Communist Chinese out of Korea. This was normal in the world of Howard Strickling, but I knew this kind of "juice" was new to Larkin. It made him nervous right off the bat in figuring out how to handle me.

"You won't get dirty here," he told me. "And if we ever get into it, you will be at Division Headquarters with me in Public Information and never on the front lines."

"Sounds good to me, Colonel, how do we go about it?" I asked.

"Well Mahoney," he said, "we don't have room in my section for a sergeant, so you'll have to be reduced in rank to corporal."

Forgetting where I was, I blurted out, "Are you fucking serious?"

I wasn't expecting a demotion after all this.

"Another outburst like that you'll be back to private!" he shouted.

Larkin stood up, I saluted, and that was it with Larkin. I was back to being the "odd" sergeant in artillery.

Someone finally decided I should be the battalion intelligence sergeant. I didn't know what that meant, but it sounded a hell of a lot better than Seoul.

Soon, I was shipped off for a winter at Fort Riley, Kansas, to learn what an intelligence sergeant did. There was no cloak and dagger work. The most secretive aspect of my training was finding whiskey in a dry state. I threw myself into the job.

With departure pending, I was looking for any kind of way to stay stateside, at least for a while longer. I went to my commanding officer and asked him if there were any other special assignments he might have for me in California.

"I'll make you a deal," he said. "I'll make you a sergeant first class immediately if you go with us next week to Japan."

"Where's the deal part?" I asked.

"Don't be a wiseass."

"Okay, but seriously, it doesn't sound like much of a deal."

"A master sergeant after two months there."

"What's my alternative?"

"You're on your own, a month's leave, and then you'll be reassigned to god knows where."

"Can I think about it?"

"Sure," he said. "Take as long as you like so long as it's in the next thirty seconds."

This time I kept my ego in check. A raise in rank was the bait. I thought about it for ten seconds.

"A month at home is better than Japan any day."

I took full advantage of that month. Pat and I looked at each day like it was our last. We went to the beach nearly every day and there was a party or drive-in movie at night. Talk of the war was everywhere, but it didn't seep into our private world. We had each other, for now, and we were making the most of it.

When the month was up, I reported back to duty and was immediately sent to Camp Stoneman, across the bay north of San Francisco. It seemed like just weeks before I had been there with Gable and Lady Sylvia, flouncing and flaunting through the city traveling first class. What a time. Back then, I didn't know much about the city, nor did Lady Sylvia, but Gable was like a native son. He was anxious to show us the town. We went to a place called Finocchio's. I had never seen female impersonators, and they absolutely wiped Lady Sylvia and I out. Gable took us to his best haunts, from Ernie's to Fisherman's Wharf, the Tadich Grill and Amelio's, his favorite Italian eatery. Moving about with Gable was something one would have to experience to truly believe. He stopped action wherever he went. Men admired him and women adored him.

I was told the camp was short of N.C.O.'s—non-commissioned officers— and that I, being a sergeant, would probably be held for two or three weeks, to process several "specialist" groups, before I'd be on my way to whatever hellhole country they had planned for me. Korea. Japan. Philippines.

"It won't be too bad here," the C.O. told me. "You can take off most every afternoon, and there is plenty to do in the city."

My job as barracks master was to see that each group woke up for reveille and made their morning formations. It was all routine stuff until I was introduced to one motley crew after another. These specialists were delivered right out of the worst disciplinary barracks. True jailbirds. L.B. could have cast them perfectly in a jailbreak movie. Once you got to Stoneman, there was no way out, not even for these guys. Everyone knew it the moment they passed the guard and passed through the gates. The only departures were on troop ships headed straight for war.

In the days after my arrival, I saw they were moving dozens of graves registration experts into my barracks. Morticians. Things were going so bad in Korea they were rushing embalmers and funeral directors to the front.

The best part was San Francisco. On my first night off, I went back to Amelio's, Gable's favorite. The owner remembered me, and I told him my sad state of affairs. He took care of me like it was The Last Supper. Afterward, Amelio himself said two ladies across the room, good customers, would like to buy me a drink. As it turned out, they were two little old ladies, both widowed, and in the course of the conversation one asked me what I had in mind for the rest of the evening.

"Well," I said, "I'll probably take in a movie and get back to camp."

"What if we fixed you up with a date?" they asked.

"And what did you have in mind?" I asked eagerly.

"Well," she went on, "I own an apartment house two blocks from here and I rent to more than thirty airline stewardesses, and I'm sure there has to be one or two of them there that would just love to show you the town. It'll be on me."

Within half an hour, I had a beauty on each arm, and we were off and running. From then on, every night, it was heaven. At that point, I would have stayed at Stoneman forever, no matter who they put in the barracks. And I knew Pat—ever in the back of my mind—was safely ensconced back home with the coeds, studying teaching at the University of California in Santa Barbara.

Surely, she would understand that war was hell.

Chapter Ten

The Crabs of Yamanaka

WHEN IT WAS finally my time to ship out, I bade goodbye to my heaven-sent stewardesses and boarded the U.S.S. Nelson M. Walker. Little did I know that I'd be in for the most uncomfortable journey of my life. The route was through the Great Northern passage, the Aleutian Islands. I never saw such big waves or so many people standing in their own puke. It was just a preview of coming attractions.

When we arrived in Yokohama, we all expected a brief stopover en route to the battlefronts of Korea, but as we docked a voice over the loudspeaker told us that any personnel formerly attached to units now stationed in Japan would be rejoining those units in Japan. So, twenty of us found our way to the 40th Division, ensconced in a tent city known as Camp McNair, on the slopes of Mt. Fuji.

The nearest village was a farm and rice paddy town called Yamanaka, population 100. But with the camp so near, the population tripled with prostitutes. Within a few months, the camp had more cases of the clap, and various other social diseases, than the rest of the Army, Navy or Marines combined in all of the Far East. As a result, the entire 40th Division was quarantined, with only those of us uninfected allowed passes off base. It didn't matter since there wasn't much to do anyway. Mt. Fuji was no Nob Hill.

The quarantine didn't work. At one point, the commanding general held meetings with his top medical aides and all the chaplains. Then, a massive outbreak of crabs hit the camp. Experts discovered the crabs were multiplying and thriving on the powder the army had been issuing each soldier to apply twice a day.

As things in war are prone to go from bad to worse, and I was the sergeant without assignment, they put me in charge of all the dirty work details nobody else wanted, until we shipped out. And like all my assignments, it was temporary until they found an even shittier one to take its place. But the best part of my new temporary assignment was getting off from noon Friday until Monday morning at daybreak. That was just enough time to get out of that God-forsaken volcano.

Word was that one of my old public relations friends from Los Angeles, who had the unfortunate luck of being called out of the reserves, was stationed in Tokyo. His name was John Dickson and in Hollywood he was a military advisor. The studio used him often for its war pictures, for clearances and usage of military equipment. He was now a Captain stationed at the Dai Ichi Building and was one of General MacArthur's army of public information officers. Dickson lived with about a dozen other officers in a Prince's palace in Meiji Park, a fashionable suburb of Tokyo the army had commandeered during the occupation. The palace had tennis courts, an Olympic-sized pool, a pitch-and-putt golf course, and two bars open twenty-four hours. It sure beat our crab-infested rice paddy.

I called Dickson and he insisted I come to visit. After a few visits to Tokyo and the usual sightseeing, I found that just hanging out at the palace was more interesting and comfortable than the local N.C.O. clubs or the bars on the Ginza. One Saturday night, Dickson suggested I come with him and some of his other pals to a party at the exclusive Washington Heights Club.

"I can't do that, John," I said. "That's an officer's party and they won't let me in. And I can't show up in civilian clothes. It's a court-martial offense."

"Bullshit," he shot back. "No one there knows you from Adam, just put on one of my blouses and you'll blend into the woodwork. None of your officers are within miles of this palace and they wouldn't be invited if they were. We'll come up with some kind of story and believe me, no one will pay any attention to one extra person."

The story Dickson and his buddies came up with was foolproof. I was a captain. I was assigned to a "very secretive operation" out of MacArthur's headquarters. The story was wild. I was parachuted into enemy territory every Monday morning and brought out every Friday to advise MacArthur's staff as to what was going on behind enemy lines. If anyone asked questions, we were told to say it was top secret, the worst assignment anyone could have, and certainly not something that should be discussed outside of G.H.Q.

Dickson's blouse fit me like it was tailored. Having served heroically in the last war, he wore three rows of military ribbons stitched on in silk. It was nearly impossible at twenty years old that I could have served in the last war and sport this kind of garbage, but nobody bothered to ask. Like movie stars, I was never overly impressed with rank, or what passed for stardom in the military, as I had been surrounded by it before I arrived here. So when it came to crashing HQ parties, surrounded by MacArthur's top brass, I could not have been more cool, calm, and collected. After a few vodkas, I really was Captain Mahoney. I was playing a role that fit me well.

After that first party, we closed the place down and as we were leaving, well-oiled and loud, we came across a 2nd lieutenant in the parking lot grappling with this very attractive Japanese hostess. I called him to attention.

"What the hell are you doing?" I asked.

"Nothing sir," he snapped, drunk as a dog.

"Like hell," I said. "Don't you realize we are the guests of the people of this country and you are acting like an asshole?"

"Yes, sir!"

"What's the name of your commanding officer?"

He started to tell me, but I cut him off.

"Oh hell, just get the hell out of here and don't do it again."

"Yes, sir."

The guy took off running.

Dickson and I both had a good laugh at that one. After he left, the only proper thing to do was take the hostess back to the palace for a nightcap. It was easy to be chivalrous in a uniform of such note.

Every weekend for three months, I masqueraded as Captain Mahoney at some of Tokyo's finest parties. I played the role well, it fit me, all the way up to Christmas of 1951. It was then that I found out we were headed to Korea, for the "real" war.

Chapter Eleven

Who Goes There?

ON CHRISTMAS EVE of 1951, we were finally told we were going to Korea. Some holiday. This time lady lucky seemed to have failed me. I was among the first to board the ship. Along with this "good fortune," I was told I would be attached to the advance party in my bastardized assignment as liaison sergeant with the 160th Infantry.

"Liaison sergeant?" I asked my C.O. "What's that?"

"Fuck if I know Mahoney, just get on board and figure it out."

There was no such position in the Army.

We arrived at the harbor of Inchon on New Year's Day. I'd be lying if I didn't admit to some feelings of fear and concern as to what was in store. Maybe I shouldn't have mouthed off after all and taken that job at the public information office.

My first impression of Korea was not good. As we stepped ashore from the landing craft, I saw what appeared to be several hundred prisoners in a temporary stockade. They were Chinese, and they looked to be wasting away. Their eyes were hollow and they stared as we passed. Some had their hands out for food or water. I was told they were being hauled out on the same ships that brought us to this hellhole. They were headed for some islands. Holy shit, what had I gotten myself into?

We were put aboard trucks for our trip to the front. We made our way to Seoul, or what was left of it. It was a mess. Not one building stood without a scar. After all, U.S. and Korean forces had gone back and forth from the Chosin Reservoir and the Yalu River all the way back down to Pusan on the southernmost tip of the country three or four times, blowing up everything in sight. We drove over the Han River. There was another bridge a quarter of a mile to the south, and somebody had strung up three bodies underneath it.

I knew nobody. I was with an advanced group.

"Traitors," a captain said. "Communist sympathizers, it's who we're fighting."

It was snowing hard when we arrived at camp. We were twenty miles northeast of Seoul. Our temporary headquarters was on the partially frozen Imjin River, about thirty yards wide. The river dissected a small valley, which might have been nice if it wasn't frozen and bullets weren't flying. The valley was no more than half a mile wide with steep snow-covered mountains tucked in on each side. An officer pointed to a hole in the ground. There was a canvas cover over it.

"That's your home, Mahoney," he said.

"Ah, shit," I said.

"Yeah, that's right. Don't complain, it could be worse. It's where you're living for a few days until things get organized, and one other thing: don't move around too much after dark, the guards are a bit nervous around here."

"Got it," I said, and jumped into the frozen hole.

"One other thing," he said. "We've been having gooks," he said, using the derogatory term of the day, "infiltrating at night right up the river on the frozen ice. They're hard as hell to see. They wear reversible quilted uniforms, khaki on one side and white on the other. White's in fashion this week in this fucking snow."

The first night was the worst. When Mother Nature called we were told never to go anywhere without your "piece," your carbine rifle. Getting fully clothed to ward off the icy, windblown rain and go out looking for a place to do your number under these circumstances leaves much to be desired. We were told there were makeshift toilets down by the river. They were made of mortar boxes, with holes cut out to sit over.

I eased myself down to the riverside and found a box, but by the time I got my pants down, wiped the snow off, and balanced my 'piece' against my body, the urge left. I waited and waited. Every time the wind rustled, I knew it was the enemy ready to pounce with a bayonet. Just as I was about to give up, I felt a presence and in a microsecond I heard the most God forsaken noise I'd ever heard of in my life. I looked skyward. There, not more than 150 to 200 feet above me, a plane screamed, a Corsair from one of our aircraft carriers, and it was lit up with every cannon blasting away. I shit. Boy, did I shit.

After that, I wiped myself off and ran as fast as I could back to my hole, and waited the night out. The next day, my immediate commanding officer was a Lt. K. Carlyle, who happened to be from Santa Monica. He told me I was nothing more than added baggage. The next day, I heard that the attack blew up our medical unit and the division post office at the other end of the valley.

"I gotta find a place to plant your ass," he said. "Just look busy, Mahoney."

"Yes, sir," I said. "But I have to do more than sit in that hole."

I was part of the artillery's "liaison force," and as a result the infantry group I was assigned to hardly noticed me. Carlyle was a good guy and was only interested in getting the hell out of Korea and back to the sunshine of Santa Monica.

"I'll find something for you, but just keep out of my way for now, okay? I'll figure something out."

"Got it."

Before long, the first troops moved on and new troops were on the block, and we all moved up a notch in terms of accommodations and assignments. I found myself the best hole in the ground and took it over, along with a kerosene stove and makeshift tent above. I made a deal with the departing corpsman and shot the handle off one of their stretchers, rendering it useless but invaluable to me. I placed the disabled litter on two mortar boxes for a bed. A departing supply sergeant sold me an air mattress for ten bucks and threw in half a case of beer. I'd secretly brought along a fifth of Ballantine Scotch from Japan. I was living high, and before long we had card parties in my makeshift suite.

I started to become invaluable to the top brass on the line. Booze. Hollywood stories. Cards. As a result, I got to know the regimental commander better than most. He was Colonel Warren Benoit, and we hit it off right from the very beginning. Wherever Colonel Benoit went, he wanted Sergeant Mahoney, his artillery support, along with him. So, like Gable, he was the king of the place, and I was happy to make his life as comfortable as possible.

During this time, the Panmunjom Peace Talks had just started, so fighting was spotty. The Chinese sent their patrols out every night, and we would counter. It got to the point where we weren't allowed to fire artillery shells unless there were at least a dozen of the enemy sighted at any one position. Nevertheless, smaller numbers were lurking, and we were in our holes, waiting and watching for all hell to break loose.

The Chinese were crafty with their psychological warfare, nothing elaborate but effective in its own way. I never saw a plane, but almost every night, without fail, a single engine aircraft flew over our lines and dropped hand grenades. It played hell with sleep. They were ingenious with their mortar shells, too. On one occasion, they dropped one on the hood of the chaplain's jeep which was moving along at a pretty good clip on an open road. The good Padre never made it to church.

Speaking of Church, I was in Korea a month when the colonel told me he had a new operations sergeant and he wanted him to move in with me.

"Sir," I said. "I don't think this hole is big enough."

"Dig it wider," he said.

I tried a few more angles, but he wouldn't listen.

The new sergeant was Daniel Patrick O'Shea, with whom I'd gone to Loyola High School for three years and spent a good amount of time in Chapel with. He was a dear old buddy, and O'Shea's old man was one of Howard Hughes' top executives running RKO Studios. It was like old home week in our little foxhole. Dan and I drank and played cards day and night. He wrote letters to his old man telling him what a shitty place Korea was, how wet, cold, and brutal it was. We were all freezing our asses off and waiting to get shot in the head as we pissed.

After a few letters home, it wasn't long before the packages from O'Shea's father arrived. Soon, O'Shea and Mahoney were sporting the finest duck hunting gear from Abercrombie and Fitch. Never again did we wear those godawful ponchos with the cold rain slipping down between our necks and collars. Under the guise of jams and jellies, Mr. O'Shea also saw to it we had a continual supply of miniature bottles of Remy Martin Cognac, to keep us even more comfortable in this winter wonderland.

O'Shea and I hired a Korean houseboy, too, and every morning the kid would wake us up with a canteen cup full of steaming hot coffee topped off with a generous shot of Remy. If nothing else, we knew how to survive the elements.

As operations sergeant for the regiment, O'Shea made frequent visits to division headquarters.

"Guess what?" he asked, returning one afternoon.

"What?"

"Guess who's our new brigadier general?"

"Fuck if I know."

"Homer fucking Eaton."

"Eaton?"

The Principal of Hamilton High School, Homer Eaton, was now a brigadier general commanding the 40th Division.

"Holy shit," I said. "You think he knows I'm here?"

"For your sake, I hope not. And guess what else?"

"What now?"

"We got a new chaplain, Father Caroline."

"Are you shitting me?"

"No," O'Shea said.

Father Caroline was the same chaplain who had kicked me out of Loyola High School just a few short years earlier I had a sick feeling this wasn't going to turn out well.

Late one night the colonel and I were playing gin when one of his company commanders sent him an urgent message.

"Get with it, Mahoney," Colonel Benoit said. "They need artillery support on the line, like right now. Get it done."

As luck would have it Captain Carlyle was back at artillery headquarters, and the colonel ordered that I get my ass up on "the line" and solve the problem.

I didn't have a clue as to what the problem was and didn't know how to get there. I located a driver, and we were on our way. There was a light snow falling. We couldn't see anything in the cold, dark night. I knew enough to take the road right up the center of the valley and turn right at the second intersection. So, we headed down that road.

We all knew that if we made one wrong turn, we'd head into no man's land, and another two or three hundred yards would put us face to face with some nasty people.

With no lights and with it being so dark, we must have missed the first intersection. We were well past the second intersection when the driver, a Notre Dame graduate no less, stopped the jeep.

"This doesn't feel right," he said. "I have a terrible feeling we missed a turn back there. We could be in deep shit."

I told him to turn off the engine. We sat in the quiet pitch black cold for a few minutes contemplating our next move, listening to the night. We knew there were land mines everywhere.

"We can't go forward," I said.

"Do we go back?" the driver asked.

"Let's take this right," I said. I noticed a dark path right where we stopped.

As we drove, it got even darker under the trees, so I told the driver to stop again. I got out and walked ahead with a white towel over my shoulder, to guide the driver. We didn't seem to be getting anywhere, so we stopped again.

"Shit," the driver said. "We're lost… in no man's land!"

"Hold on," I said. "We'll figure this out."

We sat there for ten minutes, listening for movements. "Stay put," I said.

I went a little bit farther on foot. About thirty feet down the road, a voice yelled out.

"Halt! Who goes there?"

I froze. Oh, shit. "Sergeant Mahoney," I yelled, hands over my head.

"What's the fucking password?" the voice screamed.

In a panic I yelled back, "I don't know the fucking password! I'm Sergeant Mahoney from artillery and somebody up here called for help."

"What's the fucking password?"

"Hell if I know."

"Who is your battalion commander, Sergeant?"

"Colonel Benoit."

"Okay, Sergeant Mahoney, move forward very, very, slowly, you don't want to make any more stupid mistakes, do you?"

I was frozen in fear because I knew there were rifles—a lot of them— zeroed in on yours truly.

"No, sir!" I shouted.

After that scare, I called in the coordinates. It didn't take long before the artillery shells started dropping. The threat was eliminated.

I got a reaming from the company commander after that little incident out in the dark, but in the end he thanked us for solving the problem. The screw-up never went further than that, for which I was thankful, and I kept my mouth shut about it. Back at headquarters, Colonel Benoit even complimented us on a job "well done."

The rest of my stay in the Land of Morning Calm was spent with the colonel, playing cards, drinking beer, all while the Panmunjom Peace Talks carried on, along with the battles, patrols and firefights. At one point, Colonel Benoit, now my best friend, wondered if I wanted a promotion.

"Sure," I said.

"Great," the Colonel said. "When you reenlist, I'll get you transferred to my unit and promote you to second lieutenant."

"Thanks," I said, "but no thanks."

Six months later, miraculously, I was out of my foxhole. I was shipped back home and returned to work at MGM. Just as I was settling back into the soft life at the studio, I was notified to report to Ft. MacArthur in San Diego.

To my surprise, I was invited to a ceremony where I was to be presented with the Bronze Star for my so-called heroic actions. Word got around the studio, and you'd think I was a Medal of Honor winner or something. There was a write up and photo in the local papers of me receiving the commendation, and afterward Strickling and the others I worked with, even Gable, looked at me differently, like I was some kind of war hero. How wrong they were.

The Panmunjom Peace Talks eventually fell apart, and the heavy fighting resumed. No more than two weeks passed when I opened the newspaper one morning to read that my unit had been caught up in a firefight and suffered heavy losses.

My dad and his loyal painting crew. That's me on the left.

My gang, "The Bachelor's," in High School. That's me in the center.

Married Pat on 11/29/52. Best decision I ever made.

Bronze Star ceremony. "Mom was never so proud!"

Pat & I kicking up our heels for one of
Debbie Reynolds' costume parties!

Out with Debbie in costume
on one of our quieter nights!
Credit: Bert Parry

It all started with Gable!
I'm the kid on the left

photograph by Don Cravens
Here with studio head Jack Warner

Years later with my first boss,
mentor, and L.B. Mayer's
"Fixer," Howard Strickling.

Ava Gardner and I, hard at work.

On the town with Peggy Lee and her short time husband,
Dewey Martin, and haberdasher Sy Devore.

Chapter Twelve

Back to Work

I WAS OFFICIALLY discharged from service on May 6, 1952, from Fort MacArthur. Returning to MGM after Korea was a bit surreal. The juxtaposition was mind-bending: foxholes to movie stars. To my surprise, people at the studio kept making quite a big deal of my war "contributions." Why should the truth get in the way of a good Hollywood ending? In fact, listening to them, one may have thought that I singlehandedly won the war, even though nobody won and the war officially continued.

I was welcomed back with a party and made a full-fledged junior publicist, which allowed me to join the Publicist's Guild. My new duties were not a helluva lot different than my former grunt duties, but I was allowed to work with the news media and seek out story ideas on the stars I was assigned. I was allowed to be a "planter," rather than just planting stories when there was no one else to handle the task. I was now one of five planters in Strickling's department. The other twenty or so publicists worked in the art department or specialized in magazine feature story placement, worked the foreign press, or were "unit publicists," the ones assigned to pictures from pre-production all the way through to the red carpet premiere. They fed the "planters stories and updates every day on the stars, the progress of the movie, and any acceptable gossip that would grab a headline. I was given an office—a sort of cramped cubicle—that I shared with two others.

It beat a cold foxhole any day.

Feeding the press with scoops kept us all busy. The Los Angeles market had six major daily newspapers alone, and each had their own daily entertainment section and columnist. New York had a dozen newspapers, not to mention the radio outlets, and all of them had Los Angeles entertainment columnists, too. We had our hands full managing the demands of Louella Parsons, Hedda Hopper, Sheila Graham, Army Archerd, Mike Connolly, Harrison Carroll, Jimmy Starr, and Jimmy Fiddler. We worked with New York columnists like Dorothy Kilgallen, Ed Sullivan, Earl Wilson, Walter Winchell, Lee Mortimer, and many more. Then, there were other big market columnists, like Chicago's Irv Kupcinet, San Francisco's Herb Caen, and Detroit's Shirley Eder.

We were each assigned a half dozen of them, and they were hungry for something nobody else had. They wanted news exclusives, and scoops. These beasts of Hollywood needed to be fed every day. Just as Harbert had said, it was no easy trick keeping them sated, but we worked them as best we could, and in the end our little army of MGM publicists gave them what they needed to keep their readers, and our moviegoers, happy.

I picked up where I left off with Debbie Reynolds, but was soon assigned to others, like Ann Blyth, Howard Keel, Roger Moore, and Vic Damone. Like riding a bike, you don't forget how to do this job, but now I was a lot more appreciative of what I was handed.

On Thanksgiving Day, 1952, I was assigned to pick up Ava Gardner at her home in Nichols Canyon. She shared it with her sister Bea. Gardner had to be on board the noon flight to New York. It was the first leg of her journey to Africa, where she was to start "Mogambo" with Clark Gable and Grace Kelly.

MGM had arranged for a stretch limousine, so when I arrived, I rang the bell and that gorgeous creature appeared at an upstairs window and suggested in the sexiest southern drawl, "Honey, come on in, fix a drink and make yourself comfortable. I'll be right down." As I previously mentioned, MGM insisted that she lose her rural accent when she came to Hollywood, but away from the studio it snuck back out.

The foyer opened into a living room that had a great view looking down at the entire Los Angeles basin. I noticed a bar off to the right and set out to mix myself a little holiday cheer when a voice from behind asked, "Who the hell are you?"

I turned and there on the couch in the far corner sat Frank Sinatra.

"Jim Mahoney," I said. "I'm with the studio, here to escort Ms. Gardner to the airport."

"Yeah, okay," he said. Nothing more, not much of a conversation.

He seemed to be on edge and distraught. Everyone heard these were troubled times for Sinatra, not only because of the turbulent on again, off again, marriage to Ava, but his career was in shambles. Nothing was working. His recording contracts had been canceled, his movie career was in the toilet, and the club business, for him at least, was almost nonexistent. I'll never forget the sad and forlorn look on his face as I made myself that drink.

Ava came down, and I put her bags in the limousine. She and Frank had a moment inside the doorway, and then she came down the steps, got in in the limousine, and as we backed down the driveway, he stood with the rain falling over his shoulders and watched us drive away. I didn't know the man at the time, but I really felt for him. As for Ava, she was sobbing.

We hadn't gone two blocks when she broke the silence. "I've got to have a drink," she said. "No problem," I said, and asked the driver to stop at the first available watering hole. It took a while, but we found one, a nondescript joint along La Cienega. "I don't want to go in honey, just get me a large Bloody Mary."

So, I went inside the dark bar and asked for two Bloody Marys "to go." One was for her, the other for me.

"You've got to be kidding me," the bartender said. "There's a law against 'drinks to go,' and I am not about to spend the holidays on the bread line."

"You don't understand," I pleaded. "I have Ava Gardner in the limo outside and if I don't get her a Bloody Mary, I am more fucked than your Thanksgiving turkey."

"Pal, if you've got Ava Gardner out there, then she's not only going to get the biggest and best Bloody Mary in the world, but I am going to serve it to her personally."

With two Bloody Marys in hand, I brought the bartender toward the waiting limousine. I knocked on the window. She rolled it down. Sunglasses covered her tear-filled eyes. I introduced the two of them.

"Miss Gardner, it's a pleasure to serve you," the bartender said, and he handed her one of the glasses through the window. He gave the other to me.

"Thanks, friend," she said. "You have no idea how needed this is."

On November 29, 1952, a scant couple of days after the trip to the airport with Ava, I married Pat Marston, that pretty girl who'd asked me out on a date seven years earlier and who I could not live without. She'd finished college in Santa Barbara and waited while I toiled in Japan and Korea. We honeymooned in Palm Springs and Las Vegas and set up housekeeping three blocks from the MGM studios on Motor Avenue.

After the war, a lot of things changed and moved fast. Of course, Pat and I got busy making a family, but by the early 1950s the film industry started to change dramatically. Not least of it were Louis B. Mayer's problems at the studio, the coming age of television, and the ascendancy of Dore Schary to the throne as head of production. He was no L.B. The kingdom was in serious disarray.

People weren't buying tickets like they were before and during the war. America's attention had shifted to watching the little box in the living room. Nobody I knew had a television set in the 1940s, but by 1950 five million sets were sitting in American households. By 1953, there were already a million-and-a-half sets in Los Angeles alone. Studios saw it coming, and it wasn't too long before they started getting on the small screen bandwagon. United Paramount Theaters board approved the $25 million acquisition of the ABC Network.

To this end, I sat down one weekend and wrote a memo to Howard Strickling, which I thought was pure genius:

To: Howard Strickling

Subject: WHY SHOULDN'T MGM BE THE FIRST STUDIO TO HAVE ITS OWN TV NETWORK!

From: Jim Mahoney
Date: 3-3-53

It seems ridiculous for the motion picture industry, with all its facilities, to either consider or accept TV as a handicap.

Actually, through TV, the industry has a rare opportunity to not only develop new talent and stars for tomorrow but also to bring added profits into studio coffers by releasing great motion pictures of the past over TV before 3D makes them obsolete.

The film industry is at an all-time low with no change in sight. It is getting to a point where the ole adage, "Good pictures make good box office" doesn't make sense. One of the reasons for this is the fact that TV is good and getting better... so much so that people are staying home on good box office nights to munch popcorn in their own living rooms. Monday night is spent watching "I Love Lucy." Saturday night is spent watching "The All-Star Revue," "The Jackie Gleason Show," etc. Sunday night "The Colgate Comedy Hour," "The Ed Sullivan Show," and others. All a person has to do is glance at a TV Guide to be awakened. These are just a few of the many top shows now available to a million-and-a-half TV owners in Los Angeles alone.

Why should the average family with, say, two children spend $10.00 to see

a movie when they can stay home and enjoy themselves just as much? $10.00
sounds like an absurd price to see a movie. However, that's the price people
have to pay.

To prove it, I'll break it down: $4.00 for a babysitter ($1.00 an hour) and
a $1.00 tip, making $5.00 before they leave the house. $2.40 for admission
to the theatre. Oh, yes, 50 cents for parking, 35 cents for refreshments once
they're inside the theatre. A bite to eat after the show runs a person at least
$1.75. A 25-cent tip brings the evening to a total of $10.25.

The only solution to all this is to get into TV up to the hilt—not 'half
way,' such as the method being used to plug "Jeopardy" and "Battle Circus,"
but full scale...BUY A NETWORK EQUIVALENT IN SIZE TO NBC
OR CBS. This wouldn't be a gamble such as the jump into sound pictures,
but an intellectual move that has already been proven by both the above
mentioned. Cost to an organization of this size would be secondary if it
can afford to produce pictures costing SEVEN MILLION PLUS, as well as
buy and operate radio stations that ring a familiar goose egg on the cash
registers.

Now, the question is asked: What would MGM do once they owned and
operated a TV network?

They'd continue making films of the caliber of "Mogambo," "All the
Brothers Were Valiant," and "Young Bess"; however, not for TV. A completely
separate unit, similar to the Schnee project, would be set up to make
films expressly for TV. They wouldn't use the Gables or the Taylors or the
Barrymores on these TV films, but instead, they'd use the young, relatively
unknown people that sometimes sit around the studio for two years without
working a week because of the gamble it would be to give them a responsible
part in a big picture. This way, the studio could find out very quickly if these
young people have "IT." If they do make a hit on TV, they could then be
given a good supporting role in a big picture and then you are going to bring
these TV bugs out of their homes to see their favorite co-star with a Gable
or Turner. This whole theory will be proven at our own studio with Desi and
Lucy in "The Long, Long Trailer."

Let the public decide who are to be our great actors and actresses of the
future. That's what they've always wanted to do. However, up until now,
they've never had the opportunity. The public is the one who makes stars, as
well as the dollars for the film industry.

There's more to be gained by a move such as this than throwing thousands
of dollars into second-rate films annually. The studio could sell time just
as CBS and NBC for one thing. They could also plug pictures as often as

they pleased. The pictures they would plug would be similar to the two mentioned a few paragraphs back. This is just one of the ways of getting people out of their living rooms and into the theatres.

The initial cost of a move such as this would be practically zero since we have facilities here far in advance of anything TV City ever thought of having. The big cost would be the network and Lord knows, it'd be worth it.

In addition to these, one or two-hour films on say Monday nights, the studio could release the old films stacked in their vaults and show them on say Thursday nights.

These films aren't doing the studio any good as they are, whereas, they could be thrown on TV and pay for the high cost of the studio overhead. It's a gamble, but so is it a gamble allowing them to sit in the vaults when 3D threatens to make them <u>completely obsolete</u>.

In the last paragraph, I mentioned, "pay for the high cost of the studio overhead." This, of course, would be the answer to all our troubles and it can be done.

There have been many suggestions on how to get TV films to pay off; however, there is only one answer. That answer is Phonovision. It too would take money, as well as time. However, it will be accomplished sooner or later and there is no reason why MGM can't be the first to make it pay off.

I'm positive that if the studio took the time, money and patience being spent on 3D, which is also a gamble, and spent it on an idea such as this, the dividends would be insurmountable.

In closing, I would like to make one example. By charging 50 cents per TV set in the greater Los Angeles area alone to see an MGM hit of a few years back, the studio would net <u>$750,000 in one night</u> from the 1,500,000 known TV owners.

Several days passed, and there was no response. Nothing. Strickling never said a word. The silence was odd. He usually responded to any memos within hours, even if he was out of town. Finally, one day I was chauffeuring him somewhere and asked what he thought of my TV idea.

"Jim, don't ever talk about television," he said. He was emphatic. "Don't even bring it up, don't even mention the word. Mr. Mayer views television as the enemy."

By 1954, ABC had made deals with Walt Disney to produce "The Wonderful World of Disney" and Jack Warner to create three series launched under the "Warner Bros. Presents" banner.

By 1955 more than half the homes in America had television sets, but I never mentioned television to Strickling again.

_ It was about this time that word came down from MGM headquarters in New York that there was going to be some severe cost cutting. There was a palpable cloud of tension and unrest over the studio. Everyone potentially would be affected, and you could feel it in the Commissary, in the halls, on the sets, and in the executive suites. Executives earning more than $1,000 a week would have to take a pay cut from twenty-five to fifty percent for at least a year. There was to be an immediate reduction in the number of producers, directors, and writers under contract.

While I was away in the army, many of the big stars and contract players had been dropped from the studio, and it looked to be getting worse. Judy Garland was gone. Mickey Rooney was gone. Contracts for Greer Garson and Clark Gable were allowed to lapse. Gable had made some fifty-four pictures over twenty-three years at MGM, but his $300,000 a year was too much for the Lion to swallow. He was gone without so much as a handshake from the studio toppers. Spencer Tracy, after twenty-one years, was gone the next year. So too were Van Johnson, Esther Williams, and Jane Powell. Some, such as Grace Kelly and Lana Turner, were put under a contract that called for one picture a year. This allowed the studio to have the option on the services but relieved it of the expense of a forty-week deal.

Things were decidedly different now. Strickling, in an unheard-of move, had to let several people go from his department. It wasn't much of a consolation, but having been honorably discharged from the army, I was assured at least one year's employment by an act of Congress. With what I was being paid, I was the least of Strickling's worries. But still, the cuts got my attention. It just wasn't one big happy family anymore, and the cost cutting became more apparent each day. The studio that once bragged of having "More Stars Than There Are In The Heavens," was letting them fall away.

One extravagance that got eliminated was the chauffeured limousines that were assigned to the producer, director, and stars of every film in production. These limos, with their drivers, used to be available at the studio's beck and call from morning until night. There were a few limo drivers at the studio who had put away enough money in overtime that they were independently wealthy. I knew of one who owned three twelve-unit apartment complexes adjacent to the studio in Culver City.

My first indication that there was trouble in my own little paradise was when I was called into a meeting with Strickling's two top lieutenants, Ralph Wheelwright and Eddie Lawrence. They wanted to know if I was happy in publicity and if I'd ever given any thought to possibly working in production or one of the other departments on the lot.

"Well, no," I said. "I love it here. Why would I want to do something I didn't like?"

Little did I realize at the time that Strickling didn't really think I was suitable for a long-term career in the publicity business with my lack of writing experience, and had to put his two henchmen up to trying to persuade me into changing careers. They were both really great guys, both clients of my Dad, attempting to do me a favor, and many years later Wheelwright told me he didn't really have the heart to tell me what Strickling really felt. And the truth was, I could have taken advantage of the University of MGM and trained in any department on the lot. It was just that I had no inclination to make movies.

I figured I'd just wait and see what was next, and I would look around myself, too. Timing and luck, I was learning, were proving to be my strong suits. I'd wait to see what the Big Clock had in store for me.

Chapter Thirteen

Leg Man

WORKING AT MGM, it was only natural that I forged relationships with a number of newspaper columnists. One was Harrison Carroll, whose column appeared locally in the *Los Angeles Herald-Express*. Carroll's columns were syndicated through the Hearst Syndicate. Carroll was a legend in the business, but he wasn't as well known as the major national columnists like Hedda Hopper or Louella Parsons. Their circulation was vast, but Carroll was just as respected, and even more so in some circles.

Harrison made legions of fans among the celebrities not only for his honesty and fairness over the years but also for his reputation for checking every story for accuracy before printing. He'd stop by the studio weekly, cover sets, talk to the stars, and have lunch. One day, he asked me a simple question.

"Jim," he began, "you want to be my leg man?"

The offer took me by surprise. Practically every columnist in the business had at least one assistant, or "leg man" as they were called. Leg men did everything for their columnist, including writing the column on occasion. There were just too many openings, previews, premieres, parties, screenings, and even just phone calls to answer for one person to handle it all.

"I've been at the studio quite a while," I said. "Strickling's been good to me."

One of Harrison's earlier leg men was Army Archerd, who worked for him up until he was offered his own "Just for Variety" column, for *Variety*. Then, Bill Latham followed Army as Harrison's assistant. I'd be replacing Latham, who went over to Warner Brothers as assistant publicity director.

Carroll saw how I worked the personalities on the lot and thought I was the right person at the right time to schmooze from the other side. I knew I wanted to stay in some sort of publicity job, and I thought this might add to my education. The writing was on the wall at the studio and so I considered his proposal.

Harrison didn't cut a sophisticated swath. He was strictly second-tier, even if he was a legend. He was all of five foot eight inches tall, overweight, jowly, and stooped over. He suffered from an arthritic condition that made him look almost hunchbacked. He was a workaholic, putting in thirteen-hour days, and he lived for Hollywood and his column. Fancying himself some kind of Raymond Chandler, he was a sucker for any story that involved "broken bones" or "broken homes."

"I'm flattered as hell," I told him. Then reality flashed before me. "But I can't write well enough to work for you." The mere thought of writing every day sent me into a panic.

At that moment, I was thinking back to my conversation with Strickling, Wheelwright, and Lawrence, and their continual chorus about my lack of writing skills. They bitched constantly that if I didn't attempt to write, I'd never learn to write. "Learn to write," they'd plead with me. "You have to write, if you want to be good in this business, you have to know how to write."

"Of course you can write," Harrison said. "I've used many of your stories." There was a pause and then, "The most difficult part of this business is getting good stories in the paper first, not writing them. And I'm doing the writing anyway."

"But what about when you are on vacation?" I asked, groping for an out.

"That's not for another six months and by that time you'll be doing just fine." Panic aside, he made a convincing argument.

That night, Pat and I discussed the move and agreed maybe it was the right thing to do. It was made obvious to me that there was no great future for me in studio publicity. And I was in doubt as to whether I had a future in publicity at all. At least this would give me an opportunity to get out into the open marketplace and see just what I should be or would like to be doing. Pat was about two months away from delivering our first child, and we agreed that the timing could not have been better.

The next morning I told Harrison that I would love to give it a try. There was no epiphany or Aha! moment. I just felt the end of this phase of my life all around me. I had a good run. So, that afternoon I went in and told Strickling about my decision. He knew it was time, too. There was no sense in fighting against the tide. Opportunity was knocking and he knew I had to grab it. Nevertheless, he didn't talk to me again for six months.

Working at the *Herald-Express* was an unbelievable stroke of good fortune. It was the perfect move at the perfect time. A typical day went like this: get up in the morning, check around the studio publicity departments to see where the most production was being done, then decide which one to visit. I'd get to the action around ten or ten thirty, visit a few sets before lunch in the studio's commissary, more often than not with an actor or actress whom the studio was pushing for one reason or another, and with a studio publicist. After lunch, I'd drive to the paper—arguably the worst part of the job, as the paper was located in downtown L.A. Once I got there, I'd write up the morning's notes.

The atmosphere was right out of "The Front Page," a city room that was equal parts loud, chaotic, frenetic, and intense, with City Editor Agness "Aggie" Underwood at the helm. She was legendary, and had one of the sharpest minds in the business, a trait most found intimidating. Her voice was rough as a horse, and she was tougher than most of the guys in the editorial department. She always had a baseball bat nearby, too. When she wanted to make a point, she'd pick it up and slam it down hard on her desk. The joke around the newsroom was that she had a voice that "would seduce a foghorn."

Aggie was the first female city editor of any major metropolitan daily paper. Known as much for her infamous home-cooked spaghetti dinners she served as often to mobsters and movie stars as to her own two children. She was an expert four-fingered typist, and her near encyclopedic knowledge of phone numbers, inside scoops, and even the middle names of those she reported on was unmatched. She could be as tough as a Marine drill sergeant, but boy did she have her hand on that City Room. Thankfully, the entertainment department had a separate office upstairs.

Most afternoons, around two-thirty, the phones would start to ring. Calls from the studio press agents to guys like me would fill the air. I was immediately surprised by the amount of "other calls" that would come in—from the stars themselves, would-be actors, hangers-on, and those just hoping to curry favor with Harrison. Anything for a mention in the column.

Most days, I left the paper around five, unless there was an opening or party Harrison wanted me to cover. I never knew a life could be so sweet on this side of the publicity equation. And I was making a better than respectable $160 a week, too.

Besides the paycheck, there were an enormous number of perks by way of invitations. I never knew I could be this popular! Stars, producers, directors, up-and-comers would do anything to get their name in the paper. Fortunately, having worked on the other side of the fence, I was well aware that if I ever severed my ties with Harrison or the paper, the party would be over… and fast.

I never fell for the belief, as many others did, that it was charm, wit, or personality that garnered you an invite to a swell party. Harrison was a great guy to work for, and if he didn't particularly want to cover an event, he'd always ask if I was interested in attending. Knowing that we were expecting our first child, he never pressed me to work nights. But four months in, Harrison fell seriously ill and was hospitalized.

My worst fear was coming true. Now, I was to write the columns and weekly movie reviews, and cover the studios, and the nightclubs and parties, all by myself. Harrison's only advice from the hospital bed, after telling me the column was temporarily mine, was, "Oh, by the way, don't ever write anything about the Hearst family or Howard Hughes."

Fortunately, the press agents of the time could smell blood in the water and knew I would be hungry for anything they could throw at me. Thankfully, I was never short for subject matter, no matter how trivial.

The Carroll column now read: "BY JIM MAHONEY" and underneath in small print, "Harrison Carroll is ill." In what seemed like one day, I went from planting stories for Strickling with guys like Harrison, to being Harrison. I was in over my head, at least I thought I was.

But I did find support with two other members of the entertainment news section, Dave Bongard and George Jackson. They kept me sane and were always there when I needed help either with grammar or punctuation. The biggest problem I had was deciding each evening, as I sat down to write the column, which story to put in the lead. I'd sit and stew, smoke and drink coffee for more than an hour trying to decide. So much of it was by gut instinct, but I had no writing instinct to fall back on. Usually at that point, either Dave or George came over, knowing the deadline was fast approaching, and made the decision for me.

"Don't sweat it, Mahoney," George said. "Pick anything and slug it up at the top. It's all good stuff, nobody's gonna care what you start with." They were right. By merely putting it in the lead, I simply gave it more importance than the other tidbits I had.

When I finished writing a column, I'd mail one copy out to the syndicate and take another down to the composing room—an ink-splattering dungeon of a place.

After a few visits to the composing room and ruining a couple of suits and plenty of shirts with ink, I took to changing into a sweatshirt and jeans as soon as I got to the paper. I found out many years later that many of my colleagues there thought that was my usual working attire and assumed I was just some kind of far-out, goofball bohemian columnist.

During Harrison's illness, which lasted more than three months, I found myself working almost every night, except weekends. But Pat didn't mind. We now had James Jr., and she was four months pregnant with our daughter Marilee.

Life evolved quickly for the new Mahoney family. Gable, Strickling, and L.B. were fading further and further in my rearview mirror, and up ahead was a new road, untraveled and I hoped full of surprises. Now, like my father before me, my goal was to work and keep working. I had mouths to feed.

Chapter Fourteen

Byline

IT WAS NOW 1955, and we all saw it coming, the final curtain on the Hollywood as everyone had known it. There were still big openings each week and the regular haunts, like Ciro's with its art deco paneled walls, The Mocambo along the Sunset Strip, and the intimate clubs like The Interlude and The Crescendo, which were still the crown jewels of Hollywood nightlife. The Coconut Grove in the Ambassador Hotel, with its life-size palm trees flanking the stage and dance floor, had the feel of tropical Miami, Havana, or Rio. It was still the place to be seen. There were always big names appearing in town, so there was always a good reason to go out, but the heyday of the L.A. club scene as I knew it was fading quickly.

I never had a favorite club. Restaurants were more my thing. In this new job, I became a regular at Villa Capri, Romanoff's, and Chasen's. Sinatra and Peter Lawford even opened their own Italian place, called Puccini's. It was a natural hit. Still, the clubs had their own panache and elegance, and on any given night you could see Gary Cooper at Ciro's or Gable at Mocambo. There was always a big-name star—or two or three—at any opening; everyone from Marilyn Monroe to George Raft, all looking their best for the fans and photographers. Being seen was still good for studio business, often covering up some underlying controversy. After all, if Monroe was on the town, all was good.

I was in the thick of it, a player, whether I liked it or not, but there was a subtle yet distinctive line between me and them. For the most part I was treated like a king, but on the odd occasion I was reminded I was just a pretender to Harrison's throne.

Most top restaurants had their own press representatives. They called me almost every day with what went on at their *boites*. There's no doubt that a columnist, syndicated or not, could eat out every meal for what seemed the rest of his or her life without ever reaching for a wallet. It was a way of life, and at times I was as bad as any newsman taking advantage of free food and drink.

At one Coconut Grove opening, I remember ordering an expensive bottle of wine at the suggestion of another columnist, Jimmy Starr. The reason I remember this incident so vividly was twofold: one was the embarrassment of being told by the manager that I could only order domestic wine as I was merely "filling in for Harrison." Starr got the good stuff, the imported hooch; and two, the manager who nixed the fancy wine was none other than Fred Hayman, who was in charge of the Grove at the time, and soon left to open a clothing store on Rodeo Drive called Giorgio's. In its heyday, Giorgio's became a top destination in Beverly Hills, selling its signature fragrance internationally and welcoming all sorts of glitterati in for designer clothes and cocktails at the bar. Hayman hosted all of Hollywood for fashion and fun during the late 70s and 80s.

It was different being on the other side of publicity, part of the internal workings of the media machine, filtering stories from the studio publicity men and making interesting reading out of it all, day after day. The slights were minor, but then some things stopped you cold, like the night out with Robert Mitchum.

It was one of those evenings when I had three fast appointments to cover and then a fourth event. The evening could have started with a new act opening at the Coconut Grove, and then I could hustle over to Mocambo, and then after that another show at the Interlude. But fourth on my list was something special.

I wanted to get home to Pat and Jim, Jr., as fast as I could, but there was that one special event I had circled, a private party at Romanoff's. I was avoiding this one. It was a black-tie soiree hosted by Mitchum, a man not known to hang on formalities, let alone pick up the tab for the experience.

Knowing the other events were routine, I decided to hit the Mitchum party first, pick up a few column items, and then wander on down to the Grove for dinner and the show, and then see how it went.

I was running a little late when I got to Romanoff's but I couldn't have gotten there any later than seven o'clock. Still, with several stops ahead, I decided to get to Mitchum as quickly as possible to see if I could pull some kind of story out of him and then bail.

The party was well underway when I got there. Prince Michael Romanoff—

the colorful faux-titled owner and maitre d' and all around social icon—
greeted me at the door and directed me to Mitchum at the bar at the far side
of the room.

Romanoff's was a large, elegant place on Rodeo just south of Wilshire,
with a bar to the left and booths both surrounding the walls and in the
center a step-down dining room. It took some negotiating to get through
the crowd and find Mitchum. I had only worked with Harrison for a short
period of time, so the crowd didn't know me. It was an "A" party, with all
the top personalities, and I ordered a drink and waited until it appeared
Mitchum was momentarily alone.

"Hello, Mr. Mitchum," I said. "I'm Jim Mahoney with the *Herald* and I was
wondering why you decided to have this party?"

From that moment, everything seemed to suspend in space.

"Who the fuck are you to come in here and ask me anything?" Mitchum
bellowed loudly enough for the valet to hear.

Everyone turned and stared. Conversation halted. He kept going.

I don't know how long his tirade went on, but to me it seemed as if it were
an eternity. There I stood in the middle of this glamorous black-tie event,
dressed in a blue suit, being screamed at by the host. I should add that at
this point in our brief conversation, it became apparent he'd begun partying
much earlier than the rest of the guests. He was not only pissed off, but very
well oiled.

If it weren't for my old friend and *Variety* columnist, Army Archerd, I
think there could have been serious bodily harm inflicted here. I was about
5'10" and some 190 lbs. at the time, and in pretty good shape, but against
a gassed up 6'3", 200 lb. wild man, I didn't like my chances. Both Army
and Prince Mike Romanoff were between us before it got any worse, and
thankfully they calmed him down. I left as carefully as I could.

Considerably shaken, I went off to the Grove without a story, and with
my reputation somewhat tattered. That night, I had learned an important
lesson: not everyone thinks they need the press, but even if you think they
do, be tactful in your approach, take it slow, feel things out first.

Since it was part of the gig, I'd stopped for a bite at any number of the
great restaurants in town before going on to nightclub openings. One of
my favorite places at the time was Martoni's in Hollywood, near Cahuenga
Boulevard. Martoni's served some of the best Italian food in L.A. at the time,
along with Villa Capri. It was a place for local media types and celebs to
hang out. Hollywood press agent Sam Wall was there on the phone almost
every hour with his latest item.

On one occasion, I was at Martoni's for a cocktail and an early dinner. The place was empty except for what sounded like a couple in a back booth whooping it up and having a hell of a good time. Much giggling and laughter trickled my way. I didn't pay much attention to it, other than to note it seemed like an early hour to be on such a roll. I was waiting at the bar for Wall when the barman noticed my interest in the goings-on in the back booth.

Prying eyes of the press aside, curiosity was killing me.

"Just a fun-loving couple," he winked.

Just about then, who should emerge from the darkened booth but Anita Ekberg, the best-looking thing on the face of the planet. She was breathtaking. By the time this gorgeous creature waltzed by me and out the door, I realized the guy she was grappling and hugging with was the happily married Gary Cooper.

I sat there dumbfounded. When Wall, the press agent, showed up, I told him to keep a lid on the juicy story. I needed time to decide what to do with it. If I saw it in any other column, due to Wall's big mouth, Carroll and I would never run his stuff again. Trust me, people like Wall needed people like me more than I needed him.

It was a real conflict for me. My old studio days protecting Gable and the other stars at MGM tugged me in one direction, to keep them safe, while my column job tugged in the other direction to get readers to consume my scoops. Seeing Cooper with Ekberg got me thinking about what I was doing. Did I really want to be part of the scandal business? Did I want to be the source of pain for these celebs?

Right then and there in Martoni's I started to think about my future in this newspaper business. I was not a particularly gifted writer, but I did network well. If forced, I could turn a phrase and find a scoop. Everyone in the newsroom would have a laugh and pat me on the back. I was not really interested in gossip and finding success in other people's misfortunes. I hated the twenty-hour days, too. And with another kid on the way, I started seriously thinking about the future. Never in my life did I want to be the next Walter Winchell, but that was the road I was on, the road all of us "legmen" were on.

I sat on the Gary Cooper/Anita Ekberg bombshell and just sort of let it fade away. It wasn't uncommon for columnists like me to sit on horror stories about certain red-blooded, all-American celebrities. We let the celebrities know, and it earned us credits down the road. Besides, if the story about a major actor or actress was too hot, their studios could get a story killed with one phone call from the Stricklings of the world.

I went back to Martoni's the next week, and Cooper and Ekberg were there again— same booth, well oiled, and oblivious to the world. But I still sat on the story.

I happened to be at Paramount the following week on my usual rounds, and press agent Bob Fender was giving me the rundown on who was working on the lot that day. When he ran the name Gary Cooper by me, he was aghast that this was the first set I wanted to visit.

"You've got to be kidding, you'll never get a story out of him, all he ever says is 'Yep' or 'Nope.'"

"Never mind," I told my old pal, "just do me a favor and ask if he'll see me alone."

Cooper was an imposing figure, and the look he gave me when I was ushered into his trailer was like ice. Like Gable, he was one of my heroes. I stammered and stuttered and told him how much I'd always admired him and would hate to see something in the paper that could cause him untold embarrassment. I assured him I would never write a story like that.

"What the hell are you talking about?" he asked.

I kept talking and assuring him I was there to write great things about him and then I dropped the name Anita Ekberg.

"Holy shit," he said, and leaned back in his chair.

"She's a real beauty," I said. "I sure as hell don't blame you."

Over the next five minutes, I proceeded to tell him that sooner or later someone would print the story and it would cause him undue discomfort at home. I reassured him I would not print it and that hopefully the press agent at the restaurant would keep his mouth shut, too.

"If I were you," I said, "I'd stay away from Martoni's for a while."

"Are you serious?" he pleaded. "Where the hell can I go and NOT be recognized?"

Now, like an old pal, I began to advise the great Gary Cooper on where he could take his broads.

"There's La Venta Inn in Palos Verdes, which is fantastic. They don't serve hard liquor, but you can get all the wine you want. The rooms are super, and you can see up and down the coastline for a hundred miles."

I went on to tell him about a place in Malibu, the Holiday House, and another in Brentwood. He listened as I gave him my secrets.

And this little bargaining chip provided me with one more little career lesson that I would carry with me: sometimes you can bargain a good story away for a long-term relationship... and it is well worth it. I never wanted for a story from Cooper after that—I got one every time.

Cooper and I became fast friends, I mean really good pals and a regular stop on all my future visits to the studios when he was before the cameras. I had a feeling Gary Cooper and I were going to see a lot of each other in the future.

At this time, I didn't have a clue as to what writing a column could lead to in the entertainment business. But the job was giving me the greatest opportunity in the world to meet every top entertainment personality, studio mogul, singer, comedian, songwriter, director, producer, and writer you could possibly ask for, and all of them on a special, one-on-one basis. Between my work at MGM and now at *The Herald*, there wasn't anyone of importance in the entertainment industry who I didn't know on a first-name basis.

This really hit home one weekend when I was invited to producer Bill Dozier's home in Beverly Hills for an afternoon "garden party." The Doziers' idea of a garden party was a full-on affair, with guests dressed in their party best. It was every bit as elegant as any black-tie evening gala.

As the party progressed, none other than Louis B. Mayer himself cornered me for what seemed like half the afternoon. At this point, Mayer was now over a year removed from running MGM.

L.B. was livid. He was in the twilight of his career and needed a familiar ear to bend. I was more than happy to listen to his bitching. After all, it was L.B., MGM or no MGM.

"That son of a bitch Dore Schary plotted all along to get me out, Jim. You know it!" he wailed. "It was a set up all along and now they want me back and I'm not going. Fuck 'em. Poor Howard, I don't know how he can put up with the shit that's going on over there. You did the right thing by getting out when you did, but I am not going back. Fuck 'em." Mayer was so riled up tears formed in his eyes.

"I'll get it back," he said, "but not at MGM."

That was the last time I spoke to Louis B. Mayer. The legend died a few months later.

Chapter Fifteen

Enter Sinatra

AT THIS POINT, The Big Clock ticking away was ever present in my mind. I knew when it was time to make a change and leverage the moment. Luck and timing had always been my greatest assets. That being said, you don't get anywhere in this business without help, and I had a list of friends I could call. One was the beauty queen of Burbank, Debbie Reynolds, who one afternoon inadvertently introduced me to the man who would shape my future.

On this particular morning, I was looking for a studio to visit and have lunch, my usual routine, before going to the paper. I hit upon MGM, which was always a pleasure to revisit since it was like going home. Despite the changes, the cutbacks, and layoffs, the studio was still abuzz with activity. It was infectious just being around it again. I called Bill Lyon, who was the head planter now. It was great catching up, and he gave me the rundown on what was going on that day.

"Let's hit some sets," he said.

"Great, who's shooting?"

"Debbie's making a great film, 'The Tender Trap.'"

"The Tender Trap" was based on a 1954 Broadway play by Max Shulman and Robert Paul Smith, and it marked Sinatra's return to MGM some six years after "On the Town." The second film under his new MGM contract was "Guys and Dolls," which was actually released one day ahead of "The Tender Trap."

It was an exceptionally good day to visit sets, since four or five films were in production on the main lot and two or three were either on lot 2 or 3. If I couldn't get half a dozen good stories from the stars of that many pictures, I should just hang up my quill.

When I got to "The Tender Trap" set Bill pointed to the sign, "Closed Set. No Visitors."

"I'm not a visitor," I reminded him. "I'm Debbie's former press agent and a pretty good friend."

"You don't understand," he said. "Sinatra's working today, and for one reason or another Chuck Walters has shut down the set."

Walters was the director, but more importantly to me, he happened to be an old friend as well. Still, you have to respect the process, and I wasn't there to ruffle feathers.

None of what Bill was saying was a surprise. Many actors, actresses, and directors don't allow visitors of any kind, especially press, on the sets, as it tends to disrupt filming. It especially didn't surprise me after I heard Sinatra's name. Right or wrong, he was having problems with many members of the press and I, for one, didn't want to become one of those problems. My encounter with Robert Mitchum still stung.

Bill took me through several other soundstages before we set out for The Commissary and a late lunch. As we entered, who should be leaving but Miss Burbank herself, Debbie Reynolds. She asked if I was coming down to the set after lunch.

After we explained the shutdown by Sinatra, she laughed and said Sinatra wasn't even expected until later that day and maybe not at all. "Besides," she said, "that's crazy. You're welcomed and expected on any set I'm on, so get your Irish ass down to the set."

She was and always had been a no-bullshit kind of gal. That was one of the qualities that made her so endearing even though it flew in the face of her "America's Sweetheart" public persona.

"Besides," she said, "if he does show up, you should get to know each other. Hey, why not come on down to the set with me now." With that, Bill excused himself to get out of harm's way, and I accompanied Debbie down to Stage 30. We entered to the usual unique commotion of a movie set that always seems to prevail until the assistant director yells, "Quiet!" and the director says "Action!"

Grips, soundmen, and cameramen were all talking at once, giving orders back and forth, nothing unusual. But when we entered it fell silent as a tomb. I got a sinking feeling, and rightly so. Standing no more than ten feet in front of me in what appeared to be a heated discussion with Chuck Walters was Frank Sinatra.

Walters looked at me as if I were a Mack truck bearing down on him at

90 mph. A member of the press on his closed set! I can't expect that Sinatra would remember me from our brief encounter nearly two years before at Ava Gardner's place, while whisking her off to the airport for "Mogambo." And being back walking the streets at my old MGM home, I didn't consider myself a member of the press, but Walters did, and his face certainly gave away his concern. Most everyone on the set knew that I was now indeed a member of the press and were all waiting for an explosion.

Sinatra clocked my entrance. I heard him ask, "Who's that?"

At that point, loudly enough for everyone to hear, Debbie stepped between Walters and Sinatra and said, "Listen, Francis, this here is my good friend Jimmy Mahoney, he works for Harrison Carroll and I want you to be nice to him. Don't give him any shit!"

She explained me in seconds, including how I had done her publicity when I was at the studio and how I was a Korean war hero. Debbie got away with doing and saying things most people would be arrested for, and more often than not her inimitable style worked. It certainly did this time. Sinatra and I, the war hero, got on just fine after that. I didn't get a story out of him, but from that day forward I was welcomed on any Sinatra set, thanks to Debbie.

Several months passed, and I continued working with Harrison. He was fully recovered by now, and my duties were less pressing. I was more adept at picking up news stories and continued the nightclub beat whenever Harrison asked, which was usually about twice a week.

It was quite the life. Pat and I would go to Ciro's, Mocambo, the Coconut Grove, or one of the other hot spots. I was literally getting paid to take my wife out on the town, and these were glamorous, cocktail attired evenings. Who wouldn't want to be a part of this on someone else's dime? If we were to pay for any of those nights, my salary wouldn't have covered one evening. Equally important were the people I was befriending, from stars, to managers, to agents, to studio heads, to club owners. On any given night, we could be sitting and watching Sammy Davis, Judy Garland, Vic Damone, Peggy Lee, Harry Belafonte, or whoever else was playing in town, and then Pat and I would go back to our little rental house and growing family on Hughes Avenue in Culver City.

As luck would have it, Pat and I would run into Sinatra at these outings and we became fast friends. It was hard to explain to outsiders, but we had a communication with each other that was unique. We understood each other, but I did most of the listening.

Whenever he was working, whether it was on a film set or TV studio, I was always invited and treated like I was part of his team. This was somewhat unusual for a member of the press, since there were very few to whom he warmed up, for good reason.

We were also making frequent trips to Las Vegas together for various openings.

New hotels were opening fast along The Strip, as were acts. These always provided a good excuse for us to get out of town for a few days. Most of the hotel openings were star-studded events and I was getting to know more and more of the movers and shakers on a first name basis. And, in those days, a major entertainer was opening at one hotel or another on a weekly basis, and Pat and I were always invited.

Harrison never wanted to go anywhere, so I was "stuck" with the assignments. I looked at this as if I were getting paid to do what most only dreamed of doing, and Pat loved it too. On these trips to Las Vegas, my portfolio of contacts and new friends widened considerably. I got to know the new singers like Eddie Fisher, Peggy Lee, and Tony Bennett, and the up-and-coming comedians like Bob Newhart.

Back in L.A., on one of our many freeloading trips on the town, Pat felt like Italian food, so I called up my old friend, press agent Sam Wall, who represented not only the Villa Capri but also took on other clients as well. Sam said he'd fix us up for dinner, but I had to promise I'd drop in at the nightclub Zardi's after dinner to see a new comedian he was representing. I told him it was a deal.

The Villa Capri was a hot spot, known for its authentic Italian food. It was a small place, not far from the Chinese Theatre on McCadden Place. It had a bar lining the left wall and banquette booths lining the right, with just a couple of private booths in the back. Aside from the fact the food was good, most of its celebrity status came from the fact that it was Sinatra's favorite hangout.

Anytime Frank said, "we're going to Patsy's!" he meant Patsy D'Amore's restaurant, The Villa Capri. Or more casually, The Villa.

The Villa has spawned more great restaurateurs than can be counted. First there was Jean Leon, who was a waiter at the Villa and who went on to much success with his La Scala restaurants. Then there was Matty Jordan, a bus boy at the Villa, who opened the successful Matteo's restaurants in Westwood, Newport Beach, and Honolulu. Martoni's, La Famiglia, and La Dolce Vita could all trace their roots back to the Villa.

When we arrived at the Villa on this particular evening, we were greeted at the bar by Sinatra himself, who asked us if we would like to join his dinner group, which was gathering at the rear of the restaurant. Naturally, we said yes and sidled in along with guests legendary baseball player and manager Leo Durocher (nicknamed "Leo the Lip"), Don Drysdale, Peter Lawford, and their respective wives. We had a great time, and I picked up enough information to fill two columns. In the course of the evening, Sinatra asked me when I was going to visit the set of "Kings Go Forth," a movie he was shooting with Natalie Wood and Tony Curtis. I told him I would be thrilled to come by and would check with the studio and arrange for a visit.

After dinner, Pat and I headed down Hollywood Boulevard to Zardi's to see Sam Wall's new comedian. Zardi's was a sleazy hole-in-the-wall joint. It couldn't have seated more than fifty people, and when I arrived there was a grand total of six people, three of which I was sure worked there.

Sam ushered us down to a table directly in front of the stage and told us the show would begin shortly. Awkward, I'd say, since there was no one else within thirty feet of us. In an attempt to make myself comfortable in a most uncomfortable chair, I leaned back and put my foot on the corner of the stage to balance. The lights went dim, and the spotlight hit a rotund little man who entered stage left and screamed at me.

"You in show business?"

"No," I replied sheepishly.

"Then get your goddamn feet off the stage!"

The comedian's name was Don Rickles. Right off the bat, I knew I would love this guy. From that evening onward, I mentioned Don Rickles in the column every chance I got. No one was funnier than Rickles.

With Rickles' voice still ringing in my head, the next morning I was trying to decide what studio to cover. At around 9:30, I got a call from the MGM press agent covering the Sinatra film, "Kings Go Forth."

"Mr. Sinatra just asked if you were coming out to the set today?"

I hadn't planned on it, but it sounded like a pretty good idea.

"Yeah, tell him I'm on my way."

The set was at the fabled estate of silent film comedian Harold Lloyd, a few blocks behind the Beverly Hills Hotel. It was known as Green Acres, one of the finest homes in all of Beverly Hills. Until now, the closest I had come to this legendary estate was a glimpse through the gates. Aside from the manicured lawns and gorgeous landscaping, what I remember most was that Lloyd kept a thirty-foot, beautifully decorated Christmas tree in the foyer year-round.

When I arrived on the set, the studio publicist, my old friend Emily Torchia, told me Sinatra wanted to see me alone. He was waiting in his dressing room, a mobile home the size of a Greyhound bus.

I was ushered aboard, and Sinatra was talking with someone on the phone. Everything in the dressing room was unbelievable: a king-sized bed in the back, full service bathroom, complete kitchen, and most important, a stocked bar. It was state of the art, the best Hollywood had to offer.

Sinatra got off the phone and his valet, George Jacobs, appeared from the far reaches of the vehicle. He whispered something to Sinatra and was out the door.

"Jim, I'm glad you could come over," he began. "How long are you going to stay in that hokey business you're in?"

Stunned and barely able to answer, I blurted out something like, "Until something better comes along."

"It just has," he said. "I want you to work with me."

He went on to explain that he had just made a big deal with ABC television network for his new production company and he was going to need some help.

"What exactly would I be doing?" I asked.

"I don't know yet," he said, matter of fact. "But there are plenty of areas in which I know you could help."

He went on to tell me that he had another few weeks on the film in Europe and was scheduled to fly to Paris next week. He wanted me to talk to Pat and think it over while he was away, but I was to consider this a firm offer and he'd call me as soon as he returned. We talked a little while longer, said our goodbyes, and then he was called out to the set. I floated down the canyon and went directly home to tell Pat. I had a hard time filling the column that day.

After some ruminating, I decided this was a step in the right direction; the potential would be endless, and it meant more money. We needed that more than anything at that point. Pat was pregnant with our third child. We thought it best not to mention the Sinatra proposal to anyone until it was official. I had to wait. And it was tough.

It took three weeks for Sinatra to come back from Europe. I waited another three weeks after that. I began to doubt the whole thing.

Finally, I got a call from Frank's secretary, Gloria Lovell, who asked me if I could meet Mr. Sinatra at Romanoff's for cocktails the next afternoon at five. Romanoff's was a regular spot for Sinatra. For me, all I could think about was that damned Mitchum confrontation.

I arrived early, but so had he. He was seated at the bar with Mike Romanoff, and, but for the bartender, they had kept the room for themselves. I knew

Romanoff, professionally, but not very well socially. Even at that stage in his career he had legendary status. He always addressed me or prefaced any statement to me with "Dear boy."

Romanoff, as if on cue, excused himself and Sinatra suggested we take a booth.

"How's the little mother," he asked as we settled in.

When I told him that we were expecting again, he ordered a bottle of Dom Perignon.

"That's for her," he said and partook of his usual Jack Daniels. Frank adored Pat, and always treated her like royalty whenever we were all together.

When he finally got around to the real purpose of our get together, he told me there had been some changes to the ABC deal, but those changes wouldn't alter our arrangement.

"I still want to work with you and I have been giving it some serious thought," he said. "How would you like to handle my publicity?"

Before I could answer, he told me that he had some kind of "fakakta deal" with Rogers & Cowan, one of the largest independent entertainment public relations firms, but that he'd like me to handle him through their office.

"That sounds fine to me," I said. "But what will they say?"

"Don't worry, I'll take care of it. You can expect to hear from them shortly." Sure enough, the next morning I got a call from Warren Cowan asking when he and Henry Rogers could get together with me. I suggested lunch. They were desperate to keep Frank as a client, and as Frank was their ace client, my negotiations were more like a *fait accompli*. By two-thirty that same day, I had a new job that more than doubled my salary from the *Herald Express*.

It didn't surprise me that Harrison was very happy for me and my new assignment. He was a good guy and had only originally asked me to help him out for a year or so, but the months stretched out to almost three years. He just asked me to give him enough time to find a replacement, something that luckily only took two weeks. The transition could not have been smoother.

I remember visiting Universal Studios a few days after word got around about my job change. Les Mason, who was one of the founders of the Screen Publicists Guild and a longtime friend, greeted me.

"You want some good advice, kid?" he asked.

"Sure," I replied.

"Don't do it, Sinatra's a has been."

When word got around the paper that I was leaving, Aggie Underwood asked me to drop by. In spite of all the noise of the busy newsroom, Aggie's voice carried far, and she had that baseball bat. "Mahoney!" she yelled. She picked up the bat and slammed it on the desk. "Word has it you're going to work for Sinatra."

All eyes turned and work in the newsroom stopped.

"I'm going to make it easy for you and I'll put him on page one. Just call me when that son of a bitch gets hit by a truck!"

I think it was one of her photographers that Frank tried to run over one day at the airport, so understandably she had no love for Frank Sinatra. The old broad was tough, but like everyone in the newsroom, you had to love her.

Chapter Sixteen

Rogers & Cowan: Creating Activity

MY TRAINING IN the publicity department at MGM taught me to be totally truthful with the press, allowing for evasiveness on only the odd occasions. Truthful meant the stories had to have their basis in fact. You could say "X" star was up for "X" role because every star under contract would theoretically be up for every role. But at Rogers & Cowan, I learned the rules were about to change. "Truth" at R & C was more of a guideline, if not a downright fabrication. But it was our truth and we stood by it. At public relations agencies, ink was what it was about, always. Ink was the original black gold.

More often than not, an unusual amount of creative work went into the stories we placed with the press. Despite that, or maybe because of that, Rogers & Cowan had a solid reputation in the business. And if I was going to learn this side of the business, the PR agency business, I was going to learn from the best.

Warren Cowan was one of the more creative publicists in the business. His motto was, "Activity Breeds Activity." His theory was that if an actor or actress appeared in the columns and papers on a regular basis, they were busy, and therefore hot, even if they really had nothing going on. Publicity got them work, and they paid Rogers & Cowan to make them look busy.

Our days at the agency were spent in strategy meetings followed by more strategy meetings. We talked about everything from crisis aversion to creative marketing. Everyone was expected to contribute, from juniors on up to Henry and Warren. Rogers & Cowan had more than a few success stories.

One such star that Cowan literally resurrected was Tony Curtis. There was a time, before Curtis made "The Defiant Ones," when he couldn't get arrested, but if you read the daily columns across the country you would have thought he was the hottest actor in town. Curtis was so appreciative of the efforts to keep his career alive that he wrote a gushing thank you note to Cowan. Cowan kept the note in his wallet for years, pulling it out at a key moment when talking to a prospective new client.

At PR agencies, we all had to live or die by how much ink we generated in the entertainment columns, and every newspaper had one, even the *Daily Racing Form*. Some papers had two or three Hollywood columnists and they were all hungry, ravenous for new material, even if it was for the smallest deal or set-side story. If names were good and the story legitimate, it ran. The media beast was thirsty for it all.

In New York, there were eight daily newspapers and in Los Angeles there were five, and in the rest of the country there were hundreds. Our job was to fill those columns with as much about our clients as possible, in a positive way.

A typical example of Rogers & Cowan's "creative publicity" would be nothing more than an announcement that Tony Curtis was being sought to be in "X" movie by "X" producer to be filmed next year on locations in France and Germany.

Or another item might be "X" producer just bought the story from "X" writer and is talking to "X" about doing the screenplay. Or such items as "talks are also underway" with a big European star, like Sophia Loren, to co-star with Curtis. It was all just talk, but there was the possibility, continuing the theory that activity, or at least the hint of activity, begat more activity.

More often than not, Cowan also represented producers. They were just as eager to get ink. In fact, an unemployed producer was more eager for the press than an unemployed star. For them, it meant paying their mortgage on their Bel-Air estate or tuition for private schools. This was the type of story Louella Parsons and Hedda Hopper loved. If either one of these ladies wanted to talk to either Tony Curtis or "X" producer, the star and producer would be available on a moment's notice.

What really made this entire scenario crazy, and successful, was how many times the whole "story" was so well scripted by the PR agency that real deals actually happened as a result. We put together "X" producer and mentioned a few scripts "in the works," and lo and behold, a major studio called the producer we represented and asked for an exclusive distribution deal for the film. Voila! Activity begat activity. Rogers and Cowan mastered this kind of PR packaging.

Another surefire publicity trick I learned was to associate our star clients with a charity, and then to make them their national spokesperson. The purpose was to gain national press for both the charity and the client. It was foolproof, and an easy win/win.

Each year, charities from Easter Seals to The National Multiple Sclerosis Society went on a search for hot celebrities to bring them national attention. Charities called, and we'd have strategy meetings on the best fit. It took some work to fit the right personality with the right charity. Sometimes, we came up empty. In one infamous meeting, after running down the list of charities and associations we wanted to connect our stars to, we came up with the sum total of zero. At this point, someone in the meeting said, "All the good diseases are taken!"

Another surefire method for getting ink was to create a list. So, I came up with lists like the "Mr. Blackwell's Best Dressed List." It was always perfect copy. He was a TV personality and client so we gave him this honor. There were any number of ways to go with this technique, but we made sure the lists were genuine, or as genuine-sounding as we could make them. We did this by creating the actual organizations that created the lists, such as The United Secretaries of America Guild.

We'd have stationery printed up for the group, supposedly headquartered in Washington, D.C. There were always three or four Rogers & Cowan clients on whatever list we created, as well as a few real names one would expect to appear on such a list, if it were legitimate.

These lists were always planted in unsuspecting newspapers and wire services. We released them on "slow news days" for maximum play, like over long holiday weekends when the newspaper staff was thinnest. On those days, they were looking for anything to fill space. The celebrity stories fit the bill perfectly. If they called to fact check the source, well, the offices were closed for the holiday weekend.

But not every trick was surefire.

Those first few months at Rogers & Cowen were somewhat of a breeze, since my only real responsibility was Sinatra. Since most of my work with him was done over the phone, my time was relatively free. It got to be somewhat boring. So, like a fool, I told Henry and Warren that I had time on my hands. I could handle more clients if they needed help.

I should have kept my mouth shut.

In no time at all I was given a dozen personalities to handle. I was given a part time secretary to help. My old friend Gary Cooper was one of my first assignments, but he was a lot like Sinatra, preferring to stay away from the press. Then came other clients, including Tony Bennett, Alan Ladd, Dean Martin, and Zsa Zsa Gabor.

Zsa Zsa loved publicity, and she had fun with it as well.

One night, she and I were in Chicago for her appearance on Irv Kupcinet's TV talk show. Afterward, she insisted on having dinner at the famous Pump Room in the Ambassador East Hotel.

The maitre d' escorted us to booth No. 1, and Zsa Zsa promptly told me we were at the best table, in the best restaurant in town. The place was packed, and all eyes were on Zsa Zsa. Without missing a beat, she turned to me and whispered, "Dawlink, these people think you're SOMEBODY!"

Back at the office, Henry Rogers appeared at my door with a worried look on his face.

"We're going to lose Tony Martin if we don't do something fast," he moaned.

Good," I said. "He's a major asshole with an ego the size of Manhattan, good riddance!" Tony Martin's ego and hunger for publicity was the bane of existence for anyone who had the misfortune to work on his account.

"No Jim," he went on. "You'll learn that clients are hard to get and you can't always be picky and choosy. Tony pays us a lot of money, and we've got to figure out a way to save him. He's up in Las Vegas and opens Friday at the Flamingo. Go up there, spend a few days with him, and maybe come up with a few ideas that'll save him as a client."

Henry didn't realize he just hit the magic button: Las Vegas.

The idea of going to Vegas for a few days, even if it was for Tony Martin, suddenly was a great idea.

"Okay," I said. "I'll make it work. Give me a few days."

I checked into the Flamingo Hotel the next afternoon and put in a call to Martin. The operator said he wasn't available to take that call, or several of my subsequent calls. Two days later, I called Henry Rogers.

"Henry," I said. "You're right, we do have a problem."

"What's going on?" he asked.

"He won't even take my calls."

Rogers finally got through to Martin and set up a meeting poolside the next afternoon, at two. It was ninety-five in the shade, and when two-thirty struck, the singer finally arrived, oiled up and all ready to stretch out on a lounge chair. He could've been a well-paid thug.

"You guys stink!" he started.

"Wait a minute," I said. "I just got on the case, don't blame me for past problems. I'm here to help."

"Well, maybe it's not your fault," Martin said. "But those so-called geniuses in your office know I'm the top paid act in Vegas and they can't get a word in the paper about my opening. They deserve to be fired."

Before setting my mind in gear, naively associating success with money, I said, "I thought Liberace was the highest paid performer on The Strip?"

"That's pure bullshit!" he roared.

Now, he was off the chaise lounge, standing, and pacing.

"Let me tell you something, that crap you read about that fag," he said, using the slur of the day, "making more money than anyone else on The Strip is pure bullshit. I make more than anyone else. It's part of my deal. Anybody who knows Vegas deals knows that. Liberace making a hundred thousand a week is a joke."

Before he could continue his rant, I told him I had an idea. "What's that?"

"It's a hell of a story."

"What's a hell of story?"

"The hook is that most people are under the impression that Liberace is number one, but it's not true, you're number one."

I told him I could write a story in an hour and with his approval, get it properly placed, and we would blow the lid off the Liberace myth. It was a PR dream come true. Everyone wants to know about money, breaking the bank, or rags to riches stories.

"Print it," he shouted. "It's about time you guys did something to earn all that money I'm paying you."

I made a quick exit and called my good friend Vernon Scott at United Press International in Los Angeles. I told him I had a hell of a story for him and then fed him the details.

"Are you serious?" he screamed over the phone. "Did he really say those things, and can I quote him?"

I put Martin on the phone. He spoke with Vernon for ten minutes, and the story was out, and sizzling

I caught Tony's opening act. When he saw me in the crowd, he was all smiles. I was taking the late plane out of Vegas back to L.A., and so before I left, I went backstage to say my goodbyes. "Jimmy, it's good to have you on the case," Martin said, slapping me on the back. "Maybe with you, things'll improve now."

Back in the office the next morning, I rushed to get the early edition of the *Herald-Express*. Right there on the front page of the second section, it blasted out like a war headline: "TONY MARTIN BURSTS VEGAS SALARY BALLOON."

The story went out just like we discussed with Vernon. I had done my job. I was able to come to the rescue. I thought maybe I'd even get a bonus.

Generally, when a client gets that kind of headline, the office staff gives you a little praise, maybe even asks you to lunch. But nobody said a word. I didn't think much about it after the first day. I went about my business with Sinatra and Cooper and the others, but I was expecting at least a word of thanks, or something, from Henry Rogers. Practically every paper serviced by UPI picked it up. Vernon called and thanked me for the great tip. It was a huge scoop for him.

God, I was feeling good.

I was reminded that Martin was winding up his Vegas stint and he'd be back in town the next day. I thought, being the proactive PR guy that I was, and learning the airport trade at Howard Strickling's knee, maybe I should go to the airport and welcome him home. I knew clients appreciated that kind of service.

I waited at the bottom of the arrival stairs fully anticipating a big hug from my happy client. He spotted me the second he appeared at the doorway.

"You son of a bitch!" he screamed. "You ruined me! That story ended my fucking career. I'll never work in Vegas again! I've been blackballed. Do you know what that means, you asshole?"

I hadn't counted on the mob. They ran Vegas, and I learned then and there they never wanted anyone to talk about money, publicly. Tony's salary was now the benchmark for all headliners. The mob paid those salaries. They were not happy. It appeared that, thanks to my PR work, every entertainer in Las Vegas got a big fat raise, except my client. Tony Martin was now officially out of work.

By the time he got to the bottom of the stairs, I melted into the crowd and prayed people thought he was addressing some other poor asshole.

Back at the office, Henry told me Martin didn't appreciate our work.

"We're better off without him," he said.

Lesson learned: sometimes you follow your gut and not your wallet.

After the Tony Martin fiasco, I went back to focusing on Sinatra. He was the first call I made every day, to check in, to see how I could be of help. Whenever he traveled to Las Vegas, Chicago, Miami, New York, or New Jersey, for either a singing engagement or a film role, I went along.

When you were with Sinatra, you were all in, all the time. Whether it was a dinner or a party in his suite, there was action every night. And that action lasted until dawn. And he didn't like people to give up on him. If you faded first, you weren't invited back. I don't remember ever sleeping before dawn in Las Vegas when traveling with Frank. It was exhausting, but a hell of a great time.

We also spent a great deal of time socially, which was nothing but fun. On the spur of the moment, while having dinner at a place like the Villa Capri, Sinatra would decide we should all go to his place in Palm Springs for a few days.

An hour later, we'd be on his plane. He was single during this time, and being a night person, something was scheduled for every evening. If he wasn't having a group together at the Villa or Romanoff's, or catching an opening at one of the many nightclubs, he had a group up to his house for dinner and a screening of a new movie.

To keep up with Sinatra, you had to be in shape. He was an iron man. His workout was booze, women, and smoking. He never wanted for anything, anytime, anywhere. It was fun, and intoxicating to be around the man. On one occasion while performing at the Fontainebleau Hotel in Miami, he fell under the weather and asked me to call "Deafey" to get a doctor up to the suite post haste, or he wouldn't perform that night.

"Deafey" was Frank's nickname for Ben Novak, the hard-of-hearing owner of the hotel. Within minutes, an aging, well-tanned, and very uptight doctor was taking his newest patient's blood pressure and asking the usual questions.

"What seems to be the problem?" the doctor asked.

"If I knew, I wouldn't have called you for Christ's sake," Sinatra snapped.

"Do you have any specific pain anywhere," the doctor continued.

"No, I just feel lousy. Everything hurts."

"It could possibly be something you ate," the doctor probed. "Your blood pressure is normal. Are you allergic to anything like shellfish?"

"No," Frank insisted. "It is not anything I ate. I haven't eaten anything but a little pasta early this morning."

"What do you mean early?"

"Like three. Isn't that early to you?"

"Do you smoke, Mr. Sinatra?"

"Yeah, I smoke."

"May I ask how many cigarettes you smoke in a twenty-four-hour period?"

"A couple of packs, maybe more."

"WOW!" was the doctor's reply. "Do you drink?"

"Yeah, I drink," Frank responded.

"Do you have more than a couple of cocktails when you drink?"

"Hell yes!" Frank was testy now.

"Three or four?"

"More," Frank snapped.

"Well just how much do you estimate?"

"I estimate about a bottle, doc, and I'm thinking that's what I need right now. Thanks for your help. Send the bill to Deafey."

The doctor's face turned ashen as I escorted him out the door and shut it. It was then there was another knock on the door.

"Who is it?" I asked.

"The sheriff," a voice said.

I looked at Frank. He shrugged. "Let him in."

I opened the door and there was the top cop from Miami, along with two deputies behind him. They were all smiling.

"We just wanted to thank Mr. Sinatra for visiting our city," the sheriff said.

Frank came over immediately and shook his hand, saying the pleasure was all his.

"We want to give you a little token of our appreciation," the sheriff said. With that, he handed Frank a police badge and a gun.

"Thank you very much," Frank said, shaking all of their hands and holding the gifts in one hand. "I'll do my best here in your lovely city. I love Miami."

With the door shut, Frank and I looked at the badge and the gun and started laughing. It was just another typical day with Sinatra. He insisted I take the gun and badge. I begged off on the gun but still have the badge to this day.

Frank's recovery was miraculous. Within an hour, he suggested we get some "action," the suite was driving him "stir crazy."

"Frank," I said. "It's a Sunday afternoon at four, where are we gonna find action?"

"Not to worry," he smiled, while leafing through the Miami yellow pages. He got his prey on the phone. "Is Harry there?" he asked. "Just tell him Frank is calling."

He looked over with that look that said he didn't want me to miss a moment of this conversation.

"Yeah Harry, I'm fine but we got a serious problem up here and unless you send half a dozen of your best girls within an hour, your joint will be a parking lot by midnight."

Harry filled the order and within less than an hour the party was on. All the girls waltzed into his suite.

Frank, ever the super host, suggested I take my pick. "Sorry," I said. "I got something I have to get to downstairs."

"Yeah, sure," he said. "Don't worry about it."

Chapter Seventeen

Debbie, Eddie, Liz, and Mike

I WAS SETTLING in at the agency and they were giving me more clients to handle. Then, there was one more: Eddie Fisher.

I first met Eddie though Debbie Reynolds. She introduced me to him on the set of "Hit the Deck" in 1955. Overnight, Debbie and Eddie became the darlings of Hollywood. Louella Parsons named them the *"it"* couple of the year. It was hard for me to figure the connection, the nice Jewish boy and America's sweetheart. This was especially so since I knew deep down how much Debbie still pined away for Bob Wagner. But I kept my mouth shut.

It wasn't long into their courtship when Debbie pushed for me to represent her new boyfriend. Photogenic, popular, charismatic, headline-grabbing and beloved, both of them should have been a PR man's dream. I wished she'd never met him. Eddie went after Debbie like a barracuda. He proposed to her on their third date, and despite his radio and TV success, plus the fact that he was the top-selling recording artist in the world, Eddie felt he was still just a high school dropout from South Philly. Debbie Reynolds dazzled him. She was the adorable, wholesome girl-next-door that he had no possible chance winning over under any circumstance, except that he was now a huge star.

The more I got to know him, the more it struck me that he looked at her as more of a trophy than as a lover. Their courtship was a perfect storm, a massive torrent of publicity and chaos. Before long, neither could stop the momentum. They were married under a deluge of photographer flashbulbs and gossip stories. They realized their mistake almost instantly, but it was too late. They were young, immature, and rich, and they had gone too far down the road to pull it all back. But Debbie had her own agenda, too—

marriage, at any price.

Debbie wanted to get married in the worst way. Yes, her first true love was Bob Wagner—she thought the sun rose and set with him—but her strict puritanical upbringing was more than most guys could handle. R.J., as Wagner was known, was not ready to settle down, and so their relationship could only go so far. Debbie was brought up to believe good girls waited. And what you saw on the screen was what you were going to get on a date. But worse, she feared with this philosophy she might end up an old maid, too. Debbie used to ask me, "How old was Patty when you got married?"

She asked me this more than once, and I knew the age issue gnawed at her confidence. Years later, after divorce number three, I said her taste in men sucked and that she should have married me.

"You never asked," she said.

So, because both Debbie and Eddie walked... or ran... into their relationship for selfish reasons, she worked her damnedest to make the marriage a shining example. We who were close to it knew it was doomed from the start. Eddie had his complaints. In private, to me, he said, "Debbie lives to maintain that character she plays on the screen, Miss Goody Two Shoes."

Then he said under his breath, "She's a cold fish."

Romance, or the lack thereof, was an issue but hardly the only one. From the very beginning, the two seemed to agree on very little: where to live, whose career was more important, even the size of the engagement ring. She said it was eleven carats. He said it was seven.

According to Debbie, as hot as he was to spend every waking minute with her before the wedding, Eddie turned as cold as the proverbial well digger's ass soon thereafter. He claimed the opposite was true.

Maybe he enjoyed the chase too much, and she was going to settle before old age kicked in. I loved Debbie, but my job at Rogers & Cowan was to handle Eddie, to make him look good. He was the client. So, I just listened, got him ink, and watched the disaster unfold.

Fisher took to burying himself in work and then hanging out with the boys, including his idol, Mike Todd, the Hollywood and Broadway producer extraordinaire. Todd's biggest hit was the film "Around the World in 80 Days," an Oscar winner.

Mike and Eddie were friends before Debbie was even on the scene. Todd was both a confidant and a father figure. It was hard not to be impressed with Todd, who was about as charismatic a showman as they came. He could have been a great politician; he could talk you into anything, a real

Pied Piper.

Aside from an unhappy marriage, Eddie had another problem—drugs. He told me he knew the exact date he got hooked: April 17, 1953.

I'm not sure why this date stood out for him. It was as if he always wanted to remind himself of that big mistake, emblazoned like a birthday in his memory. There was Eddie before April 17, 1953, and then there was the other Eddie, the one born April 17, 1953. The old Eddie was dead and buried.

I first became aware of the problem on one of the many trips we took together to New York. This time it was to promote one of his hugely popular television appearances. He was the Coca-Cola Kid when he met Debbie, doing twice-weekly television shows for the sponsor at $1 million a year. This was big money. Then, when Coke pulled its sponsorship, Chesterfield cigarettes entered the picture. Eddie was now the Chesterfield Man.

We flew most of the day and arrived in New York just in time to shower and change before going to a reception and dinner, where he would entertain later in the evening.

We were ushered into our suite—a three-room apartment he kept at the Essex House on Central Park South—when a strange-looking man knocked at the door asking for Eddie.

"Who may I say is calling?" I asked.

"Just tell him it's Max," he grumbled.

Max, as I was soon to discover, was a New York doctor who administered "vitamin shots" to Eddie to sustain what he called his "energy level."

Max was actually none other than the infamous "Dr. Feelgood," Max Jacobson. Dr. Feelgood was known around town for administering these same "vitamins" to some big names, including John F. Kennedy, Cecil B. DeMille, Alan Lerner, and Zero Mostel.

Dr. Max ironically could have passed for Yul Brynner in a dark alley. He was bald, with high Slavic cheeks and powerfully built. I don't think Eddie had any idea or cared what the doctor shot in his arm and ass. He claimed the shots did everything from keeping his energy up to soothing his tired throat during grueling performance schedules.

It was his manager, Milt Blackstone, who had first introduced Eddie to Max. Blackstone was on the same "vitamin" regimen. At the time, I never gave the doctor's visit a second thought, and sure enough Eddie was full of energy and ready to go when he needed to be. That was all I worried about. It wasn't until much later, on another trip to New York, that I realized Dr. Max was administering more than vitamins. As it turns out, Eddie was getting a dose of multivitamins. But Jacobson's concoction, as we were to discover much too late, also included 30-50 milligrams of amphetamines, or in simple terms "speed." It was enough to get anyone hooked. The result was an instantaneous euphoria, but also paranoia, extreme depression, and even symptoms of schizophrenia.

On another occasion, we were at the Essex House and Dr. Max arrived at the suite shortly after we did. He told Eddie that Milt Blackstone had asked him to come over and administer a shot. Eddie motioned him into the bedroom, and Max followed. From where I was sitting in the living room, I could see Dr. Feelgood proceed with his bag of tricks. He then produced a syringe and began filling it with his magic potion. It was a little from this bottle and a little from that bottle. He made his cocktail from five or six different vials. Then, he motioned to Eddie to drop his drawers and bend over. He took the needle and shot Eddie in the ass.

Not more than thirty seconds later, I heard a crash. The sound came from the bedroom. Eddie had passed out cold, and Dr. Feelgood was working with a vengeance to revive him. Eddie wasn't particularly big, maybe 150 pounds, no more. Dr. Max was in a panic.

"Holy shit!" I shouted. "What's going on?"

"Stand back, it's nothing."

Dr. Feelgood picked up Eddie by his feet and held him upside down. Nothing.

He then spun Eddie around and around by his feet and swung him on to the bed, as if he were a rag doll. Dr. Feelgood was a cool as a cucumber as he worked on bringing Eddie back to life.

"You want me to call someone?"

"It's nothing, a slight reaction."

Then and there, I knew Dr. Max was a problem. Still, he was a doctor, and I could not have been more naïve about drugs. Debbie was equally naïve, but thank God she never succumbed to the need for, as she called him, "Dr. Needles."

The next time I ran into the doctor was on a return trip to Los Angeles from Las Vegas, where both of us had been visiting clients, or patients in his case. We happened to be seated together for the hour-long flight, and along the way, he asked me if I ever tired of my hectic schedule.

"I'm always tired," I told him, "but it's all part of the business. If I'm not there to service the client, someone else will be." I heard the echo of my father's voice.

"But do you ever find yourself tired in the morning," he asked, "and have to be extra sharp for a meeting or presentation?'

"More often than not," I admitted.

"Well here," he said, handing me a small bottle of pills. "Take one of these thirty minutes before one of those meetings and you'll be better than ever. You'll never be sharper."

The doctor was, if nothing else, a persuasive salesman. I could see how easy it was for others to fall into his trap.

"What the hell is it?" I asked.

"I call it a psychic energizer. Let's just leave it at that. When you run out, just give me a call. Eddie or Milt Blackstone will tell you how to reach me."

I never ran out because I never took the pills. They scared the shit out of me. And that bizarre performance at the Essex House did nothing to sway my misgivings.

Fortunately, things caught up to Dr. Feelgood. His license to practice was revoked by the state of New York, but not before he'd taught Eddie to administer his own "vitamin" shots.

As seemingly bad as things were going for Eddie personally and from a marriage standpoint, everything was coming up roses for his pal Mike Todd. His movie, "Around the World in 80 Days," was fast becoming a worldwide success, and just as importantly, or maybe even more so, he'd been romancing Elizabeth Taylor, who happened to be married.

But soon, Eddie and Debbie were best man and matron of honor, respectively, at the Acapulco nuptials of the newly divorced Elizabeth to Todd. The attractive foursome was inseparable, and the press couldn't get enough.

Eddie's and my next visit to New York was scheduled so that it would coincide with a dinner at the Waldorf Astoria. The event was to honor Todd at the Friars Club "Showman of the Year" dinner. Eddie was scheduled to make an appearance for Chesterfield in Winston-Salem, N.C., and then another in Washington, D.C. for NBC before arriving in New York.

Todd and I had been talking about doing business together, and he assured me that as soon as we were all back from New York our arrangement would begin. I was truly looking forward to this trip, and what followed. Todd suggested that since we had so many stops on our agenda, we should fly on his plane. I'll never know why, but Eddie opted for commercial flights and I, traveling with Eddie, was therefore relegated to commercial as well.

I remember that the flight to New York was horrendous, the violent weather pitching the plane from side to side. On our approach, we were told we would circle for an unspecified time before it was safe to land. The comedian George Gobel was on the flight, too, and was clearly nervous. I turned to him after the announcement and said, "This is the most dangerous part of the whole flight, when you're circling in a storm, because other planes are circling about 100 feet apart."

Of course, that was an exaggeration, but he bought it and quickly ordered a large gin on the rocks. George never needed an excuse for a cocktail, but this was a good time to have one. By the time we touched down, Gobel had drunk himself into a calm serenity, but left the plane by wheelchair.

We arrived at the Essex House, and Eddie received a call. I was there as I watched Eddie's face drain of blood.

"What is it?" I asked.

"Mike's plane, it went down, somewhere in New Mexico," he said. "They all died."

Eddie was a wreck after that. We caught the first flight available back to the coast. I'll never forget how bad the weather was when we were leaving the city. Our limousine veered from one side of the highway to the other, slipping on the ice and the heavy snowfall.

It turned out our flight was the last to leave New York for the next three days. We were lucky to arrive back in L.A. and Eddie went directly over to comfort the widow, who had been sick with the flu and opted, at the last minute, not to travel with Todd.

It's difficult to criticize Eddie for what happened afterward. He idolized Todd and would have given anything to be just like him. He dressed like him, drove big Mercedes convertibles like him, walked like him, talked like him, and even smoked large Cuban cigars like him. He was even making plans to produce movies like him. It was at this point and time that Fisher was working on an acquisition of Lerner and Lowes's hit musical "Paint Your Wagon," as his first film production. The fact that Eddie was spending so much time with Elizabeth was understandable, given his relationship with Todd. After all, he was his best friend, and the widow needed help.

Eddie asked me to accompany him back to Chicago for Todd's funeral. Howard Hughes, a longtime friend of Elizabeth's, furnished a Constellation, a commercial airliner fitted out for private luxury, to make the trip somewhat bearable. It was on this trip, however, that I could see Eddie was losing it, to Elizabeth. It was nothing in particular that he did. It was everything he did—the glances, the mooning, you name it. It all added up.

In defense of Eddie, I'd like to meet the man who wouldn't fall under the spell of a helpless, suffering, and lonely Elizabeth Taylor. Even Debbie conceded that point, much later of course.

When we got back from the funeral, Eddie continued his daily visits with Elizabeth. It became bizarre, what with Debbie taking care of their two young children, but also babysitting Elizabeth's as well, while Eddie vigilantly helped the widow recover from her tragic ordeal.

After a short period of time, Elizabeth returned to work and finished "Cat on a Hot Tin Roof," the movie she was making at the time of Todd's death. Eddie also returned to work, but they managed to see each other. The exact point in time when they became a "relationship" was unclear. They were discreet, at least at first, and even I hadn't heard anything. There was no buzz, no gossip at all. But it wasn't long before the next storm hit.

I started to hear from various friends who knew my involvement that they saw Liz and Eddie at the better watering holes around town. Most of these tipsters didn't think the Polo Lounge or La Scala were where the average bereaved widow should be hanging out. I brought this to Eddie's attention, and he assured me it was just gossip.

"If you don't believe me," he said, "just ask Debbie, she was with us."

Jean Leon, the owner of La Scala, confirmed that the three of them were in just a few nights earlier. Further checking with one of the headwaiters, however, confirmed something different. Liz and Eddie were frequent visitors to one of the La Scala back booths for late afternoon cocktails.

Part of my job as a publicist was being a part-time psychiatrist and morality cop. I called Eddie and told him there were certain rules in life to which one must adhere. "First of all, you never lie to your doctor, and secondly, you never bullshit your press agent."

I went on to tell him that fortunately the press hadn't picked up on the story yet, but if he continued to be as flagrant as he had become, they'd be on him like a dirty shirt.

He continued to bullshit me, and himself, and explained it all away as misconceptions and evil minds. I told him that I wouldn't be doing my job if I didn't advise him on what was being said. He thanked me and told me everything would be okay. The poor bastard couldn't get out of his own way.

Not too much later, perhaps a few weeks, Eddie called to tell me that he had to go to New York on business but that there was no need for me to come along. I didn't make anything of it until the next morning, when I read in Hedda Hopper's column that Elizabeth was also en route to New York on the first leg of a holiday in Southern France.

The two of them hadn't been in New York for twenty-four hours when the first rock was thrown. The New York tabloids were getting information via a vast web of tipsters from every powder room, restaurant, bar, and dive in Manhattan.

"What's with Elizabeth Taylor and Eddie Fisher?" was the first question I got from columnist Earl Wilson at 11:30 p.m. my time, which made it 2:30 a.m. his time.

I went through my song and dance, assuring him they were just best friends and that they just happened to be in New York at the same time, what with her going off on vacation and he with some music business, and how he and Mike had been such good pals and on and on and on.

Earl wasn't buying. He told me the whole thing looked kind of weird, and I was silently agreeing with him, but he wouldn't write anything for the time being.

The next morning, the stone throwing turned into a shitstorm. Every paper, wire service, and columnist wanted an answer to one simple little question, "What gives?"

I put a call into Eddie at the Essex House and didn't hear from him all day. That afternoon, an old friend of mine from the MGM publicity department, Rick Ingersoll, called from New York. He was there doing some publicity for Eva Marie Saint and happened to run into Eddie and Elizabeth at the Blue Angel night club. Rick didn't even have to ask the question, he knew the answer.

"You might have a problem," he said.

Rick always had a way of underplaying the most serious of crises. He went on to tell me that he and Eva Marie Saint were invited by Elizabeth to join her and Eddie for the floorshow featuring Elaine May and Mike Nichols. He also told me that Eddie was doing a lot more than consoling the widow Todd.

"No shit," I told him, "and what other good news do you have to report?"

"Well," he went on, "if you think it's a secret, it isn't anymore."

"It's all bullshit!" I wailed. "They're just good friends."

I wasn't too convincing. "Sure," he laughed, before he hung up.

Eddie called that night after ten my time. Now, he wanted some advice.

"Look," he began, "you know what's happening, all hell is breaking loose and we can't even leave the hotel."

"I know, I've been getting reports all day."

"Elizabeth and I are in love and we leave tomorrow for Europe," he declared. "Jesus Christ, Eddie," I screamed. "Are you crazy? You're asking me for advice and in the next breath you're telling me you're going to Europe with Elizabeth Taylor. You've got to have some kind of death wish. Did you forget that you have a wife and two kids back in Los Angeles? My advice to you is to get your ass back home tomorrow before the press really gets their act together and figures out what's going on. At least be sensible and go home for a little while. At least be smart enough to go through the normal routine of a separation before you announce your undying love. People might understand that, but what you're doing is absolute suicide."

He said he'd talk it over with Elizabeth, as if she was the last bastion of levelheadedness at this stage.

Eddie opted to come home the next day. At least he listened to me a little, or so I thought. It turned out that he got a call from Debbie, too. She couldn't reach Eddie all day at the Essex House, and she put two and two together. Finally, she found him in Elizabeth's suite at the Plaza Hotel. She told the operator it was Dean Martin calling. It was two in the morning.

Whatever the case, Eddie listened and returned to their Holmby Hills house the next day. He told America's Sweetheart he wanted a divorce. It was definitive, it was over, he was marrying Elizabeth.

After that, Eddie's career went into a tailspin and Debbie was heartbroken and left with two kids, a girl named Carrie and a boy named Todd, after Eddie's old friend. Elizabeth went on to win three Academy Awards and have four more marriages with three husbands, with Richard Burton getting the nod twice.

Debbie had no interest in the six-piece matching bedroom set she and Eddie had just ordered so naturally she offered it to Pat and I for our new home. It's the bedroom set we continue to use to this day.

Yes, you do learn from each and every experience with a client. From this, I could only glean that no matter how much you try, you can't always stop someone from getting in their own way. And there's not a damn thing you can do about it.

Chapter Eighteen

The Next Big Move

BY THE SUMMER of 1959, I had been working at Rogers & Cowan for three years without an increase in salary, a bonus, or anything resembling either.

"The Fisher-Taylor Debacle" got me thinking about my next move. It was a perfect example of how a client can screw up not only his own life, but other lives as well.

The press went at Liz and Eddie non-stop for months. While I was fending off that beast, I still had Sinatra to worry about, and a dozen or so other agency clients who were lobbed my way. What I had learned at the agency, even more than what I learned at MGM, was how many clients needed to be babysat.

At MGM, it was in the studio's best interests to keep their stars in line, and they listened. They were under contract. A publicity agency didn't carry the weight of a studio. The client was the boss. It never ceased to amaze me how many genuine movie stars just wouldn't listen to common sense.

So, adding things up with the work, the time put in, the Eddie-Liz craziness, I felt it was time for a raise. Pat and I now had a growing family and more mouths to feed. What with the cost of living and everything else going up, including the need for a bigger place to live, I asked Warren Cowan first. He said he'd talk to Henry.

Nothing happened. The silence began to get under my skin. I started to add things up. And it wasn't like they threw a real assistant my way, or anything resembling support staff. I didn't like playing the role of a complainer, but things were at the breaking point. Every time I brought it up, Warren said Henry hadn't gotten back to him. And Henry was always out of town.

I talked it over with Pat and told her I thought it might be time to look for something else. She was wonderful about it all. At a time when most women with a growing family would fear the future, would buckle under the weight of family and finance, she got stronger. She was a rock throughout it all.

"You do what you feel you have to do," she said. "Don't worry, we'll always get by."

Perhaps it was the challenge of something new, maybe it was the natural evolution of one's career, but whatever the rationale, I made the decision. Nothing was going to change my mind. The next day I walked into Warren's office and told him I was leaving.

It was Labor Day weekend, and so he assumed I was leaving for the holiday.

"No," I said. "I'm out of here, gone, not to return. Thank you for a pleasant three years, but, like I said, I'm gone."

"Henry will be back next week, and we'll get this thing straightened out first thing," he said.

"No Warren, it's too late, I've given it a lot of thought and made up my mind."

"What are you going to do?" he asked.

Generally, this kind of exit was well thought out with a plan. I had no plan, nor an idea what I was going to do. All I said was. "I am going to go into business for myself."

"Who are you taking?"

The kind of Rolodex pilfering he was referring to was normal practice in the publicity business, but below my intent. In a town where romancing and stealing clients was a way of life, I could see the relief in his eyes when I answered: "Nobody, I came here with no clients and I'll leave the same way." It was an unwritten "Honor Among Thieves" code that there would no poaching of clients.

Warren asked for one concession. He wanted to be the one to tell my clients I was leaving, that is, if I hadn't already advised them of my decision.

"Be my guest," I told him. "The only person to know about this, besides you, is Pat. I'll have to tell Sinatra since he brought me in here, but it isn't my intention to start a new business at your expense."

With that quick meeting, I was out of work but still had all the usual expenses of a small family and no more than a thousand dollars in the bank.

When I left Rogers & Cowan, I no longer represented Eddie Fisher. That was my bonus. But that didn't stop Eddie from calling and asking for advice. One call I'll never forget was from Rome, where he was hanging with his new bride on the set of "Cleopatra."

"Richard Burton is fucking Elizabeth," he said. "Everyone knows it, and I look like an asshole. What should I do?"

"Shoot the son of a bitch."

I told him Italian courts would consider it an honorable deed and never prosecute. How's that for constructive advice? I didn't care. The damage was done, I was out of his life, and sadly Eddie never recovered from the broken heart or the busted career.

* * *

On my own now, my first call was to Maury Samuels, an old friend and golfing buddy, who was also Dean Martin's partner in the very successful Dino's Lodge restaurant on the Sunset Strip. Dean was also a Rogers & Cowan client and one of my assignees. Samuels had been nagging me for months to go into business for myself. I thought he'd like to hear the news.

The restaurant itself had never been a client of Rogers & Cowan, but because of Dean's involvement, we'd always gone out of our way to promote it, sort of pro bono.

Probably the most meaningful bit of PR with the restaurant was getting Aaron Spelling to use it prominently in his hit series, "77 Sunset Strip."

Samuels invited me over for dinner that evening to celebrate my decision and give me my first account, Dino's Lodge. My fee: $150 per week and all I could eat.

The next morning, I called Sinatra's office at MGM and told his secretary Gloria that I needed to meet with "himself" as early as possible.

Since it was his idea that I join the agency, I felt it only right he should hear from me directly about me leaving. She told me he was due in early and it would be a good idea to be there when he arrived. He was, and when I arrived he invited me in before anyone else that morning.

"When are you doing this?" he asked.

"It's done," I told him. "Warren didn't think it was such a good idea that I start building a client list on his and Henry's time, so I am out of there as of now."

"What are you going to do for clients?"

"I want to be fair," I said. "I don't want any of their clients, I don't expect you to defect, but I thought it was only right to let you know first."

"Who do you have in mind?" he asked.

"I don't know, I gotta get off my ass and hustle up some clients. I've got

Dino's Lodge as my first account."

"That's a good start."

"And this meeting is not about trying to get you to leave and come with me," I said.

"Where are you going to office?"

"I have no idea," I said. "All I really need is a typewriter and a phone."

"Wrong," he shouted. "I've got an office at the William Morris Agency that I never use, you can have it for as long as you want. Henry works out of there, but you will probably never see him, and the secretaries can help you get set up."

The Henry he referred to was Henry "Hank" Sanicola, Sinatra's longtime manager, confidant and sometimes co-songwriter. Hank was a jack-of-all-trades, if you will. He not only looked tough, but was tough. He had a large belly and was nearly bald, save for a few wild hairs on top. He always had an anxious, worried look, like he was expecting trouble at any moment. Many times while accompanying Sinatra, Sanicola was mistaken for Frank's bodyguard. He could have been. He was built like Rocky Marciano.

Sinatra then picked up the phone and started dialing. The conversation was short.

"Hi, this is Frank," he said. "Starting immediately, I want Jim Mahoney to do the publicity on Puccini's. You'll be hearing from him this afternoon. Okay? Fine, I'll be in later."

I now officially had two clients: Dean Martin and Frank Sinatra's restaurants. Not bad for a start.

"You're off and running, why don't you and Pat join me for dinner tonight and we'll celebrate. Puccini's at eight, okay?"

At that point, Puccini's was the hottest restaurant on Beverly Drive. It didn't hurt that any night Sinatra and Lawford were in town, patrons could find them there.

"You gotta be kidding, Frank," I said. "How can I thank you?"

"Forget it," he said. "And one other thing, take out ads in *Variety* and *The Hollywood Reporter* announcing your new business and location and send me the bill."

As I left his office, I was floating on cloud nine. I went straight home to tell Pat the great news and then not more than a minute after I walked in the front door the phone rang. It was Peter Lawford.

"Congratulations," Lawford said. "It's about time you went out on your own, I've been telling you that forever. Since I'm without representation, let's have lunch and talk about it."

"Where and when?"

"I'll see you at Romanoff's at one."

I couldn't believe what was happening. Over the last twenty-four hours, everything had turned completely. Later, my wife reminded me that if I had concerns about my future, they were for naught.

"See," she said. "Every new baby brings more good luck."

She was right. And still again, I had the graciousness of Frank Sinatra to thank.

Though Sinatra gave me full use of his office and staff in the William Morris building, he remained with Rogers & Cowan. What Warren failed to do, however, at least in a few cases, was tell my clients I was departing the company. One of these clients was Alan Ladd.

One day Ladd called the agency looking for me. The operator advised him I was no longer there.

"Then can I speak to Henry Rogers?" he asked.

"He's in New York this week."

"Then how about Warren Cowan?"

"I'm sorry, Mr. Ladd, he is not here today."

"Very interesting," a frustrated Ladd sniped. "When you hear from Mr. Rogers or Mr. Cowan would you tell them that I am no longer there, either?"

Ladd tracked me down in my new digs and took great joy in retelling that conversation.

Alan Ladd became one of my earliest clients and was a joy to work with. He was one of the few stars who literally had two major careers. He was nobody in 1942 when Paramount cast him in "This Gun for Hire" and was, overnight, the hottest property in town.

After several big-time box office years, his career started to wane and he could barely get arrested. In 1953, he was cast as the title character in "Shane" and he was once again bigger than ever. The media interest in Ladd, especially the fan magazines, was insatiable. Only Elizabeth Taylor's fame compared. With Ladd on board, business continued to get better and better in Sinatra's suite.

My client roster grew daily, as if all the seeds I ever planted in my life started sprouting at once. New clients included Steve McQueen, Peggy Lee, Vic Damone, and now even Debbie Reynolds, and producer/manager Pierre Cossette.

On the subject of Pierre Cossette, I'd feel remiss if I didn't pause here and give a little background and perspective on this crazy immigrant from Montreal. He was truly one of Hollywood's biggest characters, and one of its most successful managers and producers. Pierre started at the talent agency Music Corporation of America (MCA), currently NBC/UNIVERSAL, booking clients into Las Vegas hotels and elsewhere, as well as serving as personal manager to Andy Williams, Vic Damone, and discovering Ann Margaret. He helped start Dunhill Records with Lou Adler, helped discover The Mamas and the Papas for the label, and won the Tony Award for the best musical "Will Roger's Follies."

But his crowning achievement has to be bringing the Grammy Awards to CBS in 1973, and ironically I was there to witness Pierre at his P.T. Barnum best when he "closed" that deal. It was around mid-1972 and ABC had just informed Pierre that they were not picking up the Grammys for the following year. Pierre and I were having breakfast as we regularly did and I told him that I was going back to New York for business in a few days and I'd been invited to stay at Bob Wood's house in Connecticut. At that time Bob Wood was the president of CBS network and a good friend, and he was also an old friend of Pierre's from college days at USC. Pierre jumped all over me, begging to join me, and so of course Wood said yes and we were roommates for the extended weekend. Whenever Wood, Cossette and I got together after hours it was usually an overindulgence of see-through drinks, an excess of wild tales and fond memories, and always a ton of laughs, and this first evening in Connecticut was no different. It was late when we all packed it in for the night, Pierre and I sharing one of the kids' rooms, and within minutes we were both out cold. In the middle of the night I heard Pierre rustling around, then open the door and walk down the hall, clothed only in his 50+ inch boxer shorts, presumably in search of the toilet. Then, as Bob's wife Laurie tells it, their bedroom door opened and you could sense a presence in their room. Pierre then leaped on to their bed, putting one leg across Laurie and yelling: "Wood! If you don't buy my show, I'll do to your wife what you've been doing to me for years!" With that Wood sat up and yelled back: "Cossette, get the F... off my wife! I'll buy your G.. Damn show, just get the hell off my wife!" That, my friends, is how the Grammy Awards was sold to CBS, and it's been a mainstay on the network for nearly fifty years.

I could write a book on my escapades with Pierre alone and it would be 300 pages. We spent a lot of time together, our families spent a lot of time together. I miss him.

At the time Cossette was doing television specials for big corporations like General Motors. Soon, I started representing his television interests. GM led to Ford and then to General Electric. Business begat business. To that end, I became fearless in my pursuit of clients— approaching Jack Lemmon on the street in Beverly Hills at the corner of Wilshire and Rodeo offering my services right there and then. And it worked. I signed Lemmon. Beverly Hills is such a small town.

One of the toughest parts about going out on your own is determining what your time is worth. I had always been a salaried employee, but now it was me who had to justify my own worth. So, I went with what I thought was reasonable. The industry standard rate for my services was $1,000 a month for a personality. The truth of the matter is that salary quotes are arbitrary. You simply have to determine just how much of your time you think a particular client is going to require and charge them accordingly. Some paid more, while others haggled their way south.

McQueen, a cagey young television actor, wanted to work out some sort of percentage of his earnings instead of a flat fee. I wanted no part of that deal. At the time, he was starring in the TV series, "Wanted Dead or Alive." He wanted out of it desperately. He thought he could make it big in movies and he and his manager, Hilly Elkins, were making life miserable for everyone connected with the show, especially the production company, Four Star Television, which, also happened to be a new client.

I saw the writing on the wall. If he did succeed in getting out of the show, I'd have a percentage of nothing. I stuck to my guns and got a fee of $1,500 a month. I can assure you that as frugal as McQueen was, my percentage would have been long gone from his camp by the time he was earning his expected mega-millions.

Another tough negotiator was dear old Debbie. She thought that if I had done it for free for so long while working at MGM that, well, why not just continue at that rate? When I asked for a lowly $750 a month, she was flabbergasted.

"You've got to be kidding!" she gasped. "My father worked twenty years for the railroad and never came close to making $750 a month."

But I was off and running, I set my own rates and schedule, and I was my own man for the first time in my life.

Chapter Nineteen

Hanging with The Pack

SINATRA WAS WITH Rogers & Cowan for two more years, and then he joined me. By that time, business was booming. I had a mix of Hollywood, movie and television, and corporate clients. I even set up an office in New York to handle both centers of the media universe. Corporate clients were the best. They were happy for my help in navigating Hollywood's back alleys and egos, and they were clear and decisive in their mission. But most importantly, they always paid on time.

In signing Sinatra, there was nothing underhanded, no raiding, just a simple transition when it was contractually appropriate. Contrary to popular belief, Sinatra was far from my highest paying client, but the cachet of having Sinatra on my roster was worth its weight in gold. Keeping up with Sinatra was a fulltime job, and doing strange and crazy things on the spur of the moment was becoming the norm.

One night, for instance, while dining at Puccini's, he decided that we should have dessert at his place in Palm Springs. Within the hour, the entire dinner party including Pat and Peter Lawford, songwriter Jimmy Van Heusen, Prince Michael Romanoff, and the Mahoneys were winging to his desert compound on his Lear jet.

One might ask about the essentials needed for a short stay. Need toiletries or a change of clothes? Not to worry. Sinatra took care of everything. He was the perfect host.

At that time, Sinatra's desert compound consisted of several separate cottages adjacent to the main house located on the 17th hole at Tamarisk Country Club.

Architecturally, it wasn't much to look at. It's what it had to offer that held the real value.

Along with the multiple bedrooms, there was a screening room, a train caboose converted to a massage room, a cottage specifically designated for his collection of vintage toy trains, garages, rooms for staff, two separate pools, a tennis court, and even, for a short period of time, a helipad. But the living cottages were what got my attention. Each of these was equipped with all the amenities known to man or woman.

Pat marveled at how her favorite perfume Shalimar was always there. The small kitchens were stocked with enough to satisfy a family of six for two weeks. The medicine cabinets were the size of small closets and looked like miniature drug stores. Everything you might possibly need or want was there. If a change of clothes was needed it was always there—always casual, but right for the occasion. In an article written by syndicated columnist Joyce Haber around this same time, she wrote:

"Several years ago, Mrs. James Mahoney, wife of Sinatra's press agent, was one of Frank's houseguests in Palm Springs. There were two cars, only one of them air-conditioned, and Pat Mahoney, then pregnant, climbed into the first. Sinatra noticed, insisted she switch to the air-cooled car. "You're a mother," he explained, and Ruth Koch, wife of Sinatra's talented producer, Howard, says, "He treats every woman like a lady, and yet he's supposed to treat all women like tramps." (Pat Mahoney seconds this, says she's seen Sinatra treat Tramps like ladies.) Sinatra's patience can be extraordinary."

On this particular visit, we didn't arrive until the wee small hours. It was a beautiful and warm summer morning, and we sat by the pool until daybreak when Frank decided to "put it to bed."

In this same regard, if you were privileged to be Sinatra's guest, you didn't decide to call it a night or "put it to bed," as he aptly describes it, until he faded first. As previously mentioned, failure to adhere to this simple rule could quite possibly banish you from future invitations to the kingdom.

More often than not, one imbibed throughout the evening. Then there came a time with most imbibers, when another drink was the last thing one wanted. That's just about the time Sinatra hit his stride and moved everyone over to the bar. I found these to be the best times, as Sinatra would tell stories about his early days when he was on the road as a band singer. One time, he revealed that it was just a quirk of fate that he ended up with the Tommy Dorsey Orchestra, a gig that really kicked his career into high gear.

"The night before I signed with Dorsey," he said. "I had a meeting with

Glenn Miller, who offered me a much better deal. Miller, of all people, convinced me that I'd be better off with Dorsey."

Glenn Miller knew the singer wasn't a good fit.

"He said he was an instrumentalist music-making machine," Sinatra said, about Miller. "Dorsey would feature me much more and he'd accelerate my singing career, if there was one there to be had."

Frank spoke on any number of subjects, politics, music, women, and golf. I don't remember how we got on the subject of Howard Hughes, but he said one night he set out to kill him. Drunk as I was that night, this admission got my attention.

"I was upset," he said. "Ava and I weren't married yet, but he knew damned well we were together. She told him to take a hike, but he wouldn't give up, wouldn't take no for an answer. It got a little out of hand. He used to hang out at Mocambo and Ciro's and a few other fancy places, so one night I got a gun and went looking for him."

I couldn't help but wonder what would have happened if Frank had found him. Frank had no problem stepping up to the plate if he or someone he cared about was being done wrong.

In 1958, just such an occasion arose another night when he called to ask if I'd like to join him and his pal Jack Entratter, who ran the Sands Hotel in Las Vegas, at the Coconut Grove for Judy Garland's opening night.

Who wouldn't?

Frank was always a big fan of Judy's. He was there for her at every opening he got a chance to attend. I told him I needed to be home for an early dinner with Pat and the kids, but I'd meet up with him at The Grove on Wilshire Blvd. before Judy went on stage.

When I got there, the place was jammed to the rafters, loaded with celebrities. The Grove, with its old Havana ambiance, was one of those places where there was not a bad seat in the house. Banquettes and tables all faced the stage, and life-sized palm trees lined the dance floor and bandstand. Still, this being Hollywood, there was a pecking order at The Grove.

The coveted seats were ringside, and Frank was well placed in the thick of it by the time I got there. The atmosphere was electric that night, and Judy was at her very best. Perhaps it was because she knew the treat that was in store for the audience.

Quite unexpectedly, in the middle of her act, she stopped the show and asked the crowd if they would mind if she indulged herself. Judy wanted to introduce someone, "Someone very, very special to me."

With that, she asked her twelve-year-old daughter Liza to come up on stage. Judy told the audience that Liza one day hoped to follow in her mother's footsteps and asked if they would like to hear her sing. That little girl knocked the audience on their collective asses, both as a solo act and as a duet with her mother. She was just great—a little bit gangly and awkward as one would expect of a twelve-year-old, but she was a smash hit.

After the show, Judy invited what appeared to be half the audience to a party set up in another part of the hotel. It was a large meeting room, which ordinarily handled a group of sixty. When we arrived, there were at least a hundred and sixty.

Sinatra, Entratter, and I worked our way through the crowd in an effort to congratulate Judy, then get the hell out of there. Sinatra wanted to get over to Patsy D'Amore's Villa Capri for a nightcap, and all of us were going along.

As we worked our way through the party shoulder to shoulder, Sinatra came across the young Liza, who was being bumped from side to side by the adults. She, too, was looking for her mother. In the middle of this chaos, Sinatra told little Liza just how much he appreciated what she had done, and how he and everyone marveled at how well she sang and how professional she was on stage.

Then, out of nowhere, a massive, overly intoxicated guy dressed like a carnival barker interrupted Frank and Liza.

"You were an embarrassment to yourself and your mother tonight!" he said. "You need to work harder, and practice a lot more, before you ever set foot on a stage again."

It was one of those moments when everything goes into surreal slow motion and then stops. Frank's steely blue eyes were glazing. Entratter, a bouncer at New York's Copa in an earlier life, was frozen. Liza immediately burst into tears. Frank picked her up. The loudmouth disappeared into the hustle of bodies.

Over the roar of the party, Frank shouted to me, "Keep an eye on that guy and don't lose him."

I told Entratter to stay with Frank and I'd see where the jerk was headed.

I caught up with the guy mid-lobby. I watched as he took a left down a long hallway, toward the main ballroom and restrooms. He turned at the restrooms. A minute later, Frank and Entratter were at my side.

"He's in the john," I said.

"Stay here," Sinatra said. "I'll be right back."

Fortunately, the long hallway was empty. Frank made his way about halfway down and stopped, waiting for this guy to come out. As he exited the bathroom and met up with Frank, they had a few words. I don't know what was said, but the loudmouth raised his hands as if to push Frank away. It wasn't a wise move. A well-executed left-right combination by Frank dropped the man right there.

As Frank passed by me, he said: "Let's go to Patsy's for some pasta." I told him I'd catch up with him later, I just wanted to make sure that this guy didn't say anything that would or could implicate Sinatra.

Moments later, a crowd started to form around the loudmouth still on the floor. He was on the floor being aided by a security officer. I worked my way close enough to ask the officer what had happened.

"He thinks he was mugged," he said. "He can't remember what happened."

"Probably too much to drink," I suggested. "You know how people get with the free booze."

This was just one example of Frank's tough side. He came to Judy and her family's aid many, many times. One night coming out of Ciro's, while waiting for his car, someone shouted, "Who's the broad?"

"She's not a broad, Pal." Sinatra fired back. "She's a lady."

One word led to another, and the poor schmuck found himself face down in the parking lot. I learned later that the victim was Ciro's press agent, and the lady in Frank's company was Judy Garland. As expected, charges were filed, and later dropped.

More often than not, if Sinatra got upset it was because someone was being picked on or taken advantage of. Despite the reams of publicity about Sinatra's supposed tough guy image, Sinatra rarely got physical—there were others to handle that—but he never seemed very far from landing a solid right. And once, and only once, it was my turn to step up.

It was 4:30 a.m. and we were sitting at a booth in the bar at the Sands Hotel in Las Vegas. Sinatra had finished his second show more than three hours earlier, and he was well into the Jack Daniels. It was the usual gathering of what they called their "Rat Pack," members including Dean Martin, Sammy Davis, Jr., Peter Lawford and Joey Bishop as well as others who might have been working The Strip that week. There were other honorary members too, like Marlene Dietrich, Peggy Lee, Shirley MacLaine, Tony Bennett, Eddie Fisher, Judy—and me!

All of a sudden, we heard this loudmouth making trouble at a nearby craps table, and he wasn't letting up. Sinatra looked across at me and said, "Get rid of that guy!" Sinatra's request was loud enough to hear over the combo playing across the bar. Suddenly, all eyes were on me.

The table where we were gathered was separated from the casino by a thin latticework wall. The gaming area was sometimes so loud it was hard to carry on a conversation without yelling.

The guy Sinatra asked me to get rid of could be heard above the music. For the past thirty minutes or so, he had been yelling obscenities at the croupiers and pit bosses over his mounting losses at the crap table. Ordinarily, a casino boss would have been aware and had the jerk removed. But for some reason, none of the security people or casino execs were around. He just kept calling the dealers around him every name in the book.

Sinatra usually made such a request of his long-time pal Jilly Rizzo or another of his muscle men, whom I referred to as "the crowd dispensers." Unfortunately for me on this night, ever since Debbie Reynolds told him I was a war hero, he thought of me as a tough guy. Nothing could have been further from the truth. My specialty was typewriters and bullshit. That particular morning, there were no "crowd dispensers" present. All I had to fight with was my smoke-and-mirrors tough guy reputation.

As I got up from the table, both Dean Martin and Peter Lawford gave me side-eye looks.

"Are you crazy?" Lawford asked under his breath. Yes, it seemed I was.

But what was I supposed to do? Sinatra had spoken. When Frank asked you to do something, you did it. But this was a first.

I ambled around the table, continued out of the bar area and into the casino. At first, I thought I'd find one of the security guards and tell them Sinatra wanted the guy quieted down or, better yet, thrown out.

I scanned from one end of the casino to the other looking for security, but there was no one. I had to bite the bullet.

The loudmouth was now in the middle of the casino floor. He was drunk and still shouting obscenities at the top of his lungs. He was wearing coveralls. I figured he had blown his paycheck on his way home from work. Whatever the cause, he was roaring and pissed, but appeared to be in total control of his faculties. In my experience, going back to my uncles in Culver City, there was nothing more combustible than a drunk who was still in control. As I got closer, I saw he was bigger than I was, by a lot. And, he was in much better shape, too. Bracing myself for the worst, I sidled up to him and leaned forward.

I put both hands on the craps table. I felt beads of sweat running down my sideburns. I was no more than a foot away, knowing full well Sinatra and everyone else were watching, awaiting the outcome. This was my moment. I owned it and I had no idea what was about to happen.

It was then, terrified my brain would do something stupid, that the loudmouth slammed his fist down on the table. Bam! He screamed another obscenity, turned on his heels, and bolted out the front door.

With trouble vanquished, I returned to our table.

There were hushed murmurs floating around the table. Sinatra was stunned. Martin and Lawford were laughing. All of them had a clear sense of disbelief over how I handled the drunk.

I sat down and lit up a smoke. Sinatra leaned over and asked, loudly enough for everyone to hear, "What happened?"

"It was easy," I said. "I just told him to get the fuck out of here, or there'd be a problem."

My reputation and, more importantly, my teeth were left intact.

Millions of words have been written about Frank Sinatra, both praising and criticizing. As popular and famous as he was, he was also a very, very private individual. But Sinatra was always where the action was, and if it wasn't there before he got there, it was soon there after he arrived. He made the party. Other than gaming, he was probably more responsible for the success of Las Vegas as a worldwide destination than anyone or anything else. When Frank Sinatra appeared on The Strip, the town came alive.

In the late 1950s and into the early 1960s, Frank Sinatra was news.

There was always a buzz around him, be it in the recording studio with just a handful of lucky invited guests or at a concert with thousands in attendance.

It was always interesting and amusing to walk into a restaurant or meeting with Frank Sinatra and watch the silence begin. The only other person who had that unique ability was Gable. I've walked down the streets of New York with Gregory Peck, Kirk Douglas, and Leo Durocher, but Frank was who the people clamored for. They literally just wanted to touch Frank Sinatra. He was golden.

And he had a nose for news, too.

Unlike any star I've worked with, he knew exactly what he was doing when it came to the media.

A case in point was the time he filed a multimillion-dollar lawsuit against CBS to block them from airing a documentary on his life. Front-page stories appeared the next day wherever papers were sold. Ink was not an issue for Frank. Not a day went by when I didn't thank my lucky stars for Frank Sinatra.

He made everything look easy. He made everyone look good. He even made politicians look good. During election years, some senator or congressman always wanted the "real story" behind Sinatra's involvement with organized crime, and they used it against candidates Frank endorsed.

There were always a few hardcore syndicated columnists who took great joy in printing stories about the mob, either fabricated by themselves or by some tipsters. People like Dorothy Kilgallen, Jack O'Brien, and Louis Sobol.

All made Sinatra paranoid, so much so that one morning some years into our relationship he called to ask if I had read the latest Earl Wilson column. Wilson was the patriarch of entertainment news on the East Coast. I told him I hadn't heard from my office.

"Is there a problem?" I asked.

"Yeah, there's a problem," he said. "Call that son of a bitch and tell him to never use my name in that fucking column again, okay?"

Before I could answer, he hung up. I didn't understand. Wilson was a big Sinatra supporter. He loved Frank.

I called Larry Eisenberg, who was running my new New York office, and asked him to read me the column.

Wilson wrote that Sinatra had just finished a sold-out engagement at the Fontainebleau Hotel in Miami Beach. As an aside, he wrote that he made the hotel employees extremely happy when he left.

Sinatra read the item to mean that the employees were happy to see him go.

I found out later from Wilson that the item had been messed up by the copy editor. He meant to say the employees were happy with the generous gifts and tips Sinatra had given out when departing, but there was no changing Frank's mind. Wilson, in Frank's eyes, was a creep and he never wanted his name mentioned in the column again.

I made the call to Wilson, one of the tougher calls I ever made.

Now, *my* reputation was on the line. Maybe time would heal the wound, I thought. Maybe not. Wilson was one of the biggest and most important columnists in the business, and Sinatra had literally told him to fuck off.

I made the call and Wilson listened, but he didn't understand.

"I love Frank," he said. "Jim, tell him I apologize, it was a big mistake. I'll make it up to him."

"No," I said. "Don't write anything, let some time pass."

Months passed and I accompanied Frank back to Miami, where he was filming the picture, "The Lady in Cement," and working one show a night at the Fontainebleau. I happened to be backstage in Frank's dressing room opening night, minutes before he was to go on before another packed house. If one has any sense at all, you leave a performer alone before a performance. It's their time to collect their thoughts, to compose themselves before the curtain goes up. But there was a knock at the door. It was the hotel's press agent. He had news. It was "great news," he said, and he wanted to share it personally with both Frank and me.

"Earl Wilson just arrived with his wife and I set them up with a ringside table." I wanted to die.

"Get that motherfucker out of here or I don't go on!" Sinatra screamed. "Get him out of this fucking building or I am out of here. Who the fuck invited him?"

Thank God it wasn't my assignment. That poor press agent had to trudge down to ringside in that jam-packed room and ask Earl Wilson, the mightiest columnist in the East, to leave the building.

To make the moment even more awkward, Wilson's wife opted to stay for the show, even as her husband was escorted out. Five minutes later, Sinatra was on stage singing romantic ballads, as if nothing had happened at all.

Of course, Wilson blamed me.

Taking the hit for a client was part of the job, too.

Chapter Twenty

Brother Jack

THE 1960S WERE shaping up to be the best decade of my life. My family was expanding, my business was booming, and my firm's reputation in the business was stronger than ever.

I was never really into politics, but the 1960 Democratic National Convention was to be held in San Diego, and the presidential candidates were making their moves. My first foray into politics started in early 1960, when Senators Stuart Symington and Hubert Humphrey were working the California trail, raising funds and votes, as was two-time presidential nominee Adlai Stevenson, while California Governor Pat Brown sat comfortably in Sacramento.

The presidential race included Richard Nixon, and to me it seemed like a foregone conclusion that Nixon would be a shoe-in in November. He had the support of President Dwight D. Eisenhower, whose popularity rivaled that of Elvis.

More often than not, what was left of the Rat Pack and other assorted friends of the Lawford's would gather at his beachfront home on Sunday afternoons for cocktails, barbecued hamburgers, poker, and a lot of talk. I particularly liked the poker games and won more than enough to furnish our first house. Not that I was a shark at poker, but inevitably everyone else was drunker than I. The house, formerly Louis B. Mayer's place on the beach not far from the Santa Monica incline, was casual but refined. It was a comfortable place where the atmosphere was always open and free flowing.

The well-lubricated conversation usually got around to politics, and most of it centered on Pat Lawford's brother, the young senator from "Bawston," John F. Kennedy. I did a lot of listening, but concentrated on my seven-card stud or hold 'em hands. Frequent guests at these gatherings included Judy Garland, Milton Berle, Angie Dickinson, Dean Martin, Elizabeth Taylor, Eddie Fisher, TV director Dwight Hemion, and producer Joe Naar. It was always one big party at the beach.

After one of these sessions, early the next morning, everyone was saying that it was almost a foregone conclusion that Jack Kennedy not only had the nomination but, unbelievably, was going to win in November. Either I had too many bad hands at poker or too many cocktails and decided to tell the gathering why I believed in no uncertain terms why "brother Jack" didn't have a chance in hell of getting the nomination and wouldn't even be in the race.

I went on to explain that the young senator, whom I met at the Lawford's several times, had no presence in the state. The only image of Kennedy on the West Coast was a highly publicized appearance with the Rat Pack in Las Vegas—not necessarily a positive or well thought out move. In fact, the McClatchy papers in Northern California were ripping "brother Jack" a new one on almost a weekly basis. They were not impressed with the young, tanned upstart. If he had any presidential aspirations at all, he'd best get his ass out here and get to work, because he wasn't nearly as well-known as they may have thought.

These observations were not well received.

Before we called it a night, there were many grumblings and asides that I was full of shit. But to me, I was just talking common sense, not picking sides. From what I could see at this point in the race, the honorable senator was not so much campaigning to the masses as he was preaching to the choir.

Early the next morning, I got a call from Pat Lawford, who I honestly thought was going to tell me that my services were no longer needed. Instead, she thanked me for my observations and said she'd just gotten off the phone with Jack, who would be most appreciative if I would please write him a letter immediately and fill him in on these constructive ideas. I told her that I should have kept my mouth shut and obviously had too many cocktails.

"No, no, no," she insisted. "You were right on. He needs to hear this. His people aren't giving him the right information. Please do this for me."

I told her that I felt it was presumptuous of me to advise the rising star senator of political maneuvering, but I would jot some things down and give them to Peter. I was having lunch with him in a few hours, anyway.

Here's what I wrote down and gave to Peter Lawford during the lunch.

Kennedy-For-President clubs should originate in the rural reaches of California, not San Francisco or Los Angeles. As almost all Democratic clubs are youthful in age, vigor, and aims, as well as in name, it will not be difficult to get a groundswell going, particularly as no one else is sowing seeds in this territory. Symington is now here and proving pretty sagacious in his choice of subjects when he makes addresses.

Kennedy-For-President clubs could appear locally inspired—and well they could be. Although Pat Brown, at this point, controls the delegates—or will control them by the convention in the summer of '60—he by no means is so personally popular that he could inspire any Brown-For-President clubs.

In fact, at this point, a few would argue that Brown's personal popularity is diminishing. His recent tax proposals in the state legislature have hurt him with the Democratic electorate, particularly with the rank-and-file labor—which so solidly supported him when he won the governorship.

By waiting, there is presently a void that Humphrey is sure to leap into. He does have some slight support from so-called Demo-fringe groups—groups which are very vocal (as they are elsewhere). Many are pretty prominent in Demo politics and many are erstwhile Stevenson supporters.

The many polls harping on Catholicism have hurt you in California, stirring doubts, when actually the whole matter is greatly magnified. The recent Gallup Poll stressing Catholicism of a candidate particularly hurt in California, where Republican press played it considerably.

The upstate McClatchy papers, the only ones who are nominally Democratic from year to year, should be discretely courted, for they wield considerable influence in their areas, particularly with rural voters.

Another good wedge in California would be provided by veteran's groups. With your war record, a very strong hand for a little political poker playing. An invitation could be arranged for an appearance and an address at a state convention of vets.

With as many new Congressmen from California who sit on the Democratic side of the House, a few seem in anyone's camp. By cultivating several of these freshmen Congressmen, much ground could be gained, and a great deal learned. There is one, for instance, from the northeast sector of L.A. County, George Kasem, now occupying the seat Nixon once held. He won in an upset last November and isn't at all well known on Capitol Hill. Yet he is very well known now in his district and can exert quite an influence there. Before the most important decision must be made, on entering the California primary next summer, it would be well to sound out, rather subtly, the feelings of some of these Congressmen. Brown would be, at this writing, no shoe-in.

On your next visit to California, the address should zero in on subjects which have a local bearing—agriculture, defense plant employment, public water. Oddly, these seem to grip the imagination of California voters more than do the much more vital matters dealing with the Cold War, global policies of the country or even labor legislation. However, one bold stroke on the higher level, one headline-grabbing stand, is needed in any speech in California, if it is really hoped to gain wide attention from such an address.

These, Peter, are the few pearls of wisdom I would like to pass on to the senator.

Several days passed, and I had all but forgotten the entire incident, letter and all, when I got a call from Peter late one afternoon.

"What are your plans for this evening?" he asked.

"I haven't got any plans, I was just getting ready to go home."

"Good," he said. "Jack's coming in from San Francisco and I'm meeting him at Puccini's at six. He wondered if you could have dinner with us."

Jesus, I thought, what have I gotten myself into? I told him I'd be there. Brother Jack arrived on time and was accompanied by two gentlemen he introduced as Pierre Salinger and Hyman Raskin. I recognized Salinger's name from the many times I heard Peter and Pat speak reverently of Jack's press aide.

Raskin, I was to later learn was a Democratic bigwig from Chicago, had served in various executive capacities within the party. Among other duties, he served as deputy manager, executive chairman and co-chairman of the failed nationwide Presidential campaigns of Adlai Stevenson in 1952 and 1956. He was subsequently hired by Joe Kennedy to work as western chairman of Kennedy's 1960 campaign. Salinger and Raskin took a table in another section of the restaurant, and Kennedy, Lawford, and I took a booth in the bar.

It was truly a memorable evening. Conversation flowed easily and covered a broad number of topics. I have never been so impressed with anyone in my life. He was charming, captivating, witty, intelligent, and most attractive. In another place at another time, he could have been a movie star. In the course of the evening, he asked if I would consider giving up my business and joining him on his quest for the number one job in the world. I was very rarely thrown, but this offer stopped me.

I told him I was flattered by the offer and would give it a lot of thought, discuss it with my wife, and give Peter an answer within the week.

We closed Puccini's and I got home at 2 a.m. It was more than a delightful evening, it was inspiring. If he could translate that inspiration to the masses, I thought he might just take this thing. I was still on such a high that I called my mother at three in the morning to tell her, "I've just had dinner with the next President of the United States."

I gave the offer a lot of thought and discussed it in detail with Pat. We went back and forth. It would require a move to Washington D.C. and a disruption in our lives beyond what we could imagine. I felt things were just now taking off for me, for our family, for our kids. Besides, in my heart of hearts, I felt Nixon was a shoe-in, and it could all very easily be for naught. I felt like I was in the heady swirl of the Lawford and Kennedy clans, and admittedly it was intoxicating. But then Nixon had Eisenhower's support, too, and that was formidable. Pat and I took a deep breath, and we decided to pass.

Looking back, it was the right decision for numerous reasons, but every now and then I find myself thinking, what if...?

Chapter Twenty-One

Boy From the Block

A GOOD DEAL of Sinatra's fame rested on the fact that he was always admired by his fellow stars. He was the Chairman of the Board of Celebrity. Billy Wilder, one never at a loss for words, once told me that he believed Sinatra's allure went beyond talent. "It is some sort of magnetism that goes in higher revolutions than anyone else, anyone in the world of show business," he said to me one night before an opening at The Flamingo. "Wherever Frank is, electricity permeates the air, it's like Mack the Knife is in town and the action is just starting."

The fascination, in no small part, seemed to stem from his natural style, grace, and confidence, how he conducted himself without worry about looking good or bad.

I had the great fortune of playing a lot of golf with Frank, Dean, and a lot of the big names that liked the game. Bing Crosby, Frank's longtime friend and singing idol, was another I often played with at Bel-Air and Lakeside country clubs. We often talked about what it meant to have that rare talent, a charismatic connection with millions of fans. Bing had a special philosophy about Sinatra.

"Frank is quite a fellow, a paradoxical cuss," he said. "He does it without taking any bows or making a big fuss about it. He goes about doing many wonderful things for people who are in a bind, who need help. He can be incredibly generous, kind and completely selfless, but then he'll turn around and do something so inexplicably thoughtless, so unnecessary, that you wonder if it's the same fellow."

Bing and I both believed Sinatra nurtured a childish desire to be a tough guy, a hood. But deep down he had too much class, too much sense to go that route. He made up for it by barking at people instead, including reporters, photographers, and directors, and sometimes PR guys.

It wasn't surprising that he was such a good actor. The best singers were actors of song. They had to be in order to get into the song's "character," and Frank Sinatra was the greatest of them all when it came to inhabiting a song.

Surely, no other superstar aroused so many mixed feelings about his private and public lives. He was the champ who made the big comeback, the man who conquered everything, lost it all, and then got it back, letting nothing stand in his way.

Sinatra's public persona was, of course, the better known. He was the singing star who almost singlehandedly raised popular music to new critical respectability, coupled with the flamboyant personality and charisma that was off the charts.

The private Sinatra was a whole different animal. Even to his closest showbiz friends, Sinatra remained close to the vest. Even fellow members of the notorious Rat Pack felt constrained when dealing with him.

"I don't discuss women with Frank, or who he is going to marry," Dean Martin once told me. "All I discuss are movies, TV, golf, maybe politics and drinking. I'm certainly aware, from my own relationships with the fairer sex, that you never talk women with Frank."

"When talking to Frank, we substitute wit for logic," Joey Bishop said.

Sammy Davis Jr., acknowledging the aura about him, saw it as a professional virtue.

"Only two guys are left who are not the boy-next-door—Cary Grant and Frank
Sinatra."

There was every good reason to think Sinatra was never the boy-next-door, not even to the other boys next-door in Hoboken, New Jersey, where he grew up. He was set apart first by his family's ability to provide well for him in a fairly uncomfortable minority neighborhood, and then by his own relentless determination to make it to the top.

Things were written about Sinatra at all levels, from the gossip pages to the literary magazines to academia. I'll never forget one book by sociologists Moynihan and Glazer, who wrote in their research study, "Beyond the Melting Pot," that the "set of qualities that seem to distinguish Italian-Americans includes individuality, temperament, and ambition. Perhaps the ideal is the entertainer—to give him a name, Frank Sinatra—who is an international celebrity, but still the bighearted, unchanged, boy from the block."

This was a dead-on accurate description of Frank Sinatra, the skinny kid from Hoboken turned mega star. Sinatra tried to keep his generous side under wraps. In many cases, that was my job, but this part of my work as a publicist can be marked down to "lost opportunity."

Much of Sinatra's charity work will never be known, and that's the way he wanted it. There are many examples and to list them would be endless, but to publicize them would go against his philosophy of humbly wanting the extent of his charity work to remain low-key. Bing, Dean, Sammy, and most of his close friends knew about this generosity, but we left it quiet. These things were both big and small, from how he paid Lee J. Cobb's living expenses to giving George Raft a blank check when he ended up down and out. Then, there was the time he handed over a blank check to young Liza Minnelli to cover the costs of her mother's funeral.

Modesty and shyness are not words one usually associates with Frank Sinatra, but they fit him well in these circumstances, especially to those who knew him best.

Later in our relationship, I was leaving the office at Warner Brothers and getting into my car when Sinatra rushed out to catch me.

"There is something I want to talk to you about and it slipped my mind," he said.

"What's that?"

"Well," he said sort of sheepishly, "you know those hand and foot things at the Grauman's Chinese Theatre?"

"Sure. What about them?"

Now almost whispering, "I was just wondering if they'd want me to do it."

I didn't know if he was putting me on, or what, so I played it straight.

"Frank, I am sure if you wanted to mess up your hands and shoes, all they would want from us was a date and time you wanted to do it."

"That's great," he smiled. "Let's see if we can get it done."

Before I could say another word, he was gone.

As I drove away, I had to laugh. Here was one of the most celebrated entertainers of all time questioning whether or not he was important enough to leave his imprints in the forecourt of an aging movie palace along with John Wayne, Marilyn Monroe, and Donald Duck. Within two months, we had the ceremony in front of Grauman's.

Sinatra had one motivating force when it came to charity: he had to believe in the cause. Once he did, he devoted the same drive, energy, and personal involvement to it that he did to his professional career. The sheer amount of his giving over the years that I worked with him was always astonishing to me, and to anyone else who knew this side of the man.

About the time I started to work for him, he went on a world tour for children's charities that is still a hallmark to the social agencies involved. He personally paid for all the expenses and insisted that all the monies raised stay in the country in which it was raised and be donated to specific children's charities.

In Japan, for example, his appearances resulted in the construction of a new building and supplies for five orphanages, including six million yen for the construction of the two-story Sinatra Educational Hall at Shoja Yojien orphanage.

In Hong Kong, funds were used to continue the work of the children's orthopedic hospital, aid the children of fishing villages, and to benefit a blind children's foundation.

In Israel, under the sponsorship of the Israeli Labor Organization—Histadrut—a Frank Sinatra Youth Center in Nazareth was created, and he endowed scholarships annually for the children of the youth center.

In Athens, the money provided operating funds for a nursery at the St. Sophia Children's Hospital. In Paris, the money went toward a home for crippled children.

Many organizations benefited from his concert appearances in Great Britain, including Invalid Children's Aid Society, Variety Group Fund, the Sunshine Home for Blind Children, SOS (an organization for epileptic children) and a fund for mentally challenged children. In Italy, it was Boy's Towns of Italy that reaped the major benefits from the appearances there. In one three-year period, through appearances for which he personally absorbed all the expenses, Sinatra raised more than a million dollars for half a dozen charities in St. Louis.

Later, he began to focus on one of his more personal goals, the Martin Anthony Sinatra Medical Education Center in Palm Springs, named in honor of his late father. He also endowed the Christina Sinatra Teen Center for high school youth, named for his youngest daughter, in Cathedral City, near his home in the desert.

One day, he woke up and read about the plight of U.S. Diplomat Dan Mitrione, brutally kidnapped and slain while on a State Department assignment as a police advisor in Uruguay.

"Jim," he said over the phone. "Stop whatever you're doing and get to Richmond, Indiana, and find a place suitable for a benefit concert."

I got right on it and forty-eight hours later he flew in a planeload of musicians and his pal Jerry Lewis to Indiana. He raised more than a hundred thousand dollars for the widow and the education of her children.

Another time, he called and asked me to check out a story in *The New York Times* about a seventy-one year old woman from London who had arrived in New York to visit her relatives. A slick cabby charged her $237 to take her from JFK to Woodbridge, N.J.

"Can you have your New York guys find the lady?" he asked.

"Yeah, sure," I said. I had no idea.

"I have a letter I want you to give to her. And I want to give her her money back."

I had my New York office find the lady. They handed the $237 check to her from Frank Sinatra's account, along with the letter. In the letter, he wrote, "Everyone treated me so well when I visited England, and I feel this was the least I could do."

Sinatra took the plight of others personally. Immigrants held a special place in his heart, as well as those who were damaged in some way by circumstances beyond their control. He was particularly moved by the story of a University of Maryland student, Steve Gold. Gold and Sinatra had more in common than I realized.

At birth, Gold was injured by a doctor's instrument. The result was a life-altering scar from ear to chin. The scar left him psychologically and socially debilitated. Sinatra too had been scarred by a birth instrument, and after reading his story felt compelled to write a letter to the young man:

Dear Steve,

Through a mutual friend in Baltimore…I received a letter about the problems you felt you had to face because of the birth-instrument scar you received, much like mine.

Well, Steve, in a small way I think I know how you feel because I felt the same way—at one time. Now, no one can really know the depths, emotion and nuances another person feels. One can only try to place himself in another guy's shoes through his own experience. And I don't think my experiences have been that atypical—or that my sensitivity is that dulled— that my words would be meaningless.

Now I'm not exactly a religious person. I guess fatalist would be a much better word to describe myself. And I think everything that happens… happens for a reason. We may not know the reason all the time…but we have to assume there is a reason…and then go from there.

You can let your scar…scar your whole life…or you can conquer it right now…and rise above it. That's it in a nutshell. Know it's easy for me to say this—but then I am speaking from similar experience.

I magnified my scar all out of proportion—until I got hold of myself as a result of some ministering from a family friend (the same friend who got me my first singing job in a New Jersey roadhouse).

I don't even think about it anymore. Fact is, when I first came to Hollywood there was some talk about a plastic surgery operation to greatly 'tone down' the effects of my scar. MGM had the money…and the doctor…to do the job. But I would have none of it.

Without sounding pontifical, and blowing my own horn, I decided against the operation for one reason and one reason only. The scar was part of me. It helped shape me— for better or worse. It was part of me. I didn't ask for it. But I wasn't going to cop a plea. It was there—and that was the only explanation needed. People have to learn to accept me—as me. Finish.

I hope that these words will have some meaning for you. If not today… perhaps tomorrow, or later on. In the meantime, if you want…please write to me and let's strike up a correspondence.

Best wishes, Frank Sinatra

Sinatra's generosity was demonstrated once again when he and I were at NBC for an appearance on "The Tonight Show Starring Johnny Carson." Outside Carson's studio was a shoeshine stand, run by a legend of a man, Floyd Jackson.

Floyd was a Black man who, despite having shined the shoes of all the greats in show business, was unimpressed with celebrity. It was why everyone loved Floyd.

I suggested to Frank that we get a shine rather than simply killing time until he went on. At the end of the shine, Sinatra turned to Floyd and said, "What's the biggest tip you ever received?"

"$100," Floyd answered quickly.

Sinatra then peeled off two $100 bills and handed them to Floyd.

"Who was the asshole who gave you $100?"

"You did, Mr. Sinatra."

I never saw Frank tip less than $100, no matter the situation. He never carried anything but Ben Franklins.

His generosity came my way on several occasions. I am not talking about tossing me work or providing me with office space when I first started out, but things friends do for one another.

There was the time when we were in Las Vegas a couple of days prior to his opening at the Sands. It was during the halcyon days of the Rat Pack. The two of us were on our way to dinner at a little Italian restaurant off The Strip when he turned to me and said, "I think you will get a kick out of our dinner companions."

Naturally, I asked, "Who?" With him, you never knew what was up. It could have been Marilyn Monroe or John F. Kennedy or Martin Luther King, Jr.

As it happened, the two were Joe Louis and Billy Conn, two boxing legends. I sat enraptured by their conversation, talking about their one fight in which Conn damned near beat Louis only to have Louis pull it out in the final round. For a kid from Culver City, this was one hell of a night for me.

Then, Sinatra found out my father was born in Brooklyn. He knew a little bit about my background, but my job was to stay out of the story, to focus on him. But this one time, I mentioned that my father had never been to a Major League Baseball game. Without so much as a second's beat, Sinatra turned to me and said, "He's going to a game with us next week."

"What are you talking about?"

He informed me that he was taking us to the 1959 World Series as his guests to watch the newly transplanted L.A. Dodgers play the Chicago White Sox.

When we entered the reconverted Los Angeles Memorial Coliseum, my father was dumbfounded. Before he knew what was happening, he was seated next to Frank Sinatra and Dean Martin at the World Series. My father looked at me with that same little grin that was on his face that day at Clark Gable's estate, the day I got my first break. His son set this up. He couldn't believe it. He just looked at me with that smile frozen on his face the entire game.

Following the game, we all went to the Dodger locker room for a visit with their manager Walter Alston, as well as Sandy Koufax, Don Drysdale, and Duke Snider. The Dodgers won the Series, beating the White Sox four games to two. It was one of the happiest days of my life, and maybe one of my father's, too. I still have a photo of that memorable day hanging in my dressing room with the autographed ticket stub wedged in the frame.

photograph by © Bernie Abramson

My Dad and I enjoying the 1959 World Series game with Frank Sinatra and
Dean Martin. It was my Dad's first ever major league baseball game.

Joe DiMaggio's autograph, a ticket worth keeping!

Chapter Twenty-Two

Momo and Friends

THE GREATEST CROSS Sinatra had to bear was his association with the underworld. He never denied the fact he met members of the Mafia. He admitted as much to a multitude of investigative bodies, both federal and state, coast to coast. How could Frank Sinatra not know these characters? They were part of his trade: nightclubs, casinos, bars, and shows. All types gravitated to Sinatra, from heads of state, to reigning monarchs, to senators and congressmen, to cab drivers and bus boys. Who wouldn't want to shake his hand?

In New Jersey, he was backstage with a group of local politicians following a sold-out performance. He shook their hands had photographs taken. A few months later, he was called to appear before the New Jersey State Investigation Commission. He was being accused of financial involvement in an illegal racetrack scam.

The first question they asked was how well he knew a few of the big-time New Jersey crime family members. He said he'd never heard of them. The commissioner then displayed a poster-sized photo of Frank posing backstage with them at the New Jersey Arena. There stands Sinatra arm-in-arm with the two characters in question.

The entertainment journalist James Bacon came to his rescue with these writings in one of his columns:

"Frank knows Mafia figures. So does every top entertainer in the business. The Mafia either owns or used to own all the top clubs.

"But I have never known any entertainer, Sinatra included, who ever wanted to be too friendly with any of the boys…

…Lots of people over the years have told me they were great friends of

Sinatra and I knew Frank hadn't the slightest idea who they were."

The photo and other negative press coverage forever plagued Sinatra, including a highly publicized investment in a Massachusetts racetrack, Berkshire Downs. One of its investors was one Raymond L.S. Patriarca, the head of the New England crime family. These perceived associations lead to a subpoena by a Congressional Select Committee on Crime.

Sinatra struck back in two ways: first, a well-worded op-ed in *The New York Times* defending everything from his position and celebrity to his Italian heritage; and second, he sent the Honorable Claude Pepper an invoice for $18,750 for fifteen hours of the lease of a private jet and five days of living expenses for his time while testifying.

But the cost of these supposed or real associations was not just his expenses but also his reputation. It cost him the Cal Neva Lodge in Lake Tahoe. The Cal Neva, eponymously named for straddling the California-Nevada border, was Lake Tahoe's premier gambling location, and Sinatra owned a good piece of the action. That was until Sam Giancana checked in.

Giancana and Sinatra had been "pals" for some years. It was not the kind of relationship you'd think of though. When Sinatra was starting out, Giancana was in a position to hire him. And he did. Ever since, the Sinatra-Giancana connection wouldn't die. The simple fact was, if you wanted to work the club circuit or in Las Vegas, you had to deal with guys like Sam Giancana, even peripherally. Of course, to his friends, Giancana was known as Momo.

But Giancana was black booked by the Nevada Gaming Commission. His name literally was printed in a book of people banned to enter any casino or gambling establishment—including the Cal Neva.

Phyllis McGuire, a Vegas headliner with her sister singers The McGuire Sisters, was far from banned from the casinos. The problem was that she was also the girlfriend of Sam Giancana. And on one particular occasion, Phyllis was booked to perform at the Cal Neva. What she didn't mention was that her boyfriend would be there, too.

As a result of Giancana's brief stay, the Nevada Gaming Commission revoked Sinatra's gaming license. Ironically, Frank wasn't even in Nevada at the time and had no clue as to who was registered at the hotel.

Sinatra not only lost his hotel and casino operation; his ability to hold gaming interests anywhere in the state was jeopardized. It was a sad irony for someone who did more for the state's economy and tourism than anyone else in history. Needless to say, this was a highly publicized infraction and did nothing to quell the rumors of Frank's involvement with the mob. It wasn't until years later that Sinatra redeemed his role in gaming, when he petitioned for a stake in the management of Caesar's Palace. In a two-hour testimony by Sinatra himself, he said to the committee, "I have never in my life, sir, ever received any illegal money. I have had to work hard, very hard for my money, thank you."

He was grilled about everything from the Cal-Neva incident to the photo backstage in New Jersey. In the end, it was determined by Richard Bunker, the board chairman, that, "I'm not suggesting he's a saint by any means, but in the areas we investigated we have not found any substantive reason why he shouldn't have a gaming license."

A *New York Times* article covering his reinstatement to the gaming world stated in return that:

"Virtually every book about organized crime published in the last two decades had reported alleged social and sometimes business links between Mr. Sinatra and members of the underworld. The most recent, 'The Last Mafioso,' is based on recollections of Aladena (Jimmy) Fratianno, an admitted Mafia assassin."

The sad thing about Sinatra's so-called "association with the Mafia" is something that the media sensationalized, even to this day. He never sought their help or went out of his way to socialize with them. Quite the contrary, they wanted to be around him. And there were a lot of them.

Jilly Rizzo, Frank's closest friend, was a New Yorker who moved to Palm Springs on Sinatra's insistence. Frank wanted to open a club in the desert, and he needed someone to watch over it. Pat and I were invited to the opening night party, where I had the honor of introducing Pat to Charlie "Tomatoes," Joe "Bananas," Jimmy "The Hook," and Jerry "The Crusher" Amaniera —all friends of Jilly's, and therefore de facto "associates" of Sinatra. Pat loved to tell that story.

I remember the first time I was acutely aware of these men hanging around Sinatra. It was when he asked me to accompany himself and Dean Martin to Madison, Indiana, for the location filming of one of their better movies, "Some Came Running."

Frank and Dean had agreed to stop in Chicago and join a luncheon honoring an old pal of theirs, a onetime nightclub impresario who was not in the best of health, physically or financially. I didn't bother to ask who it was. It was just another in a long list of generous appearances a guy like Frank Sinatra made. I was along for the ride, and to make sure the media behaved. I got the distinct impression it was an appearance neither of them was looking forward to but felt obligated to attend. No matter the reason,

Frank loved going to Chicago.

We were met at the airport by two characters definitely not from the Mayor's PR office. Neither appeared thrilled with this assignment. Little was said on the way to the hotel. The weather was lousy, things were running late, and the man to be honored was more than a little upset that the luncheon had to be postponed twenty-four hours to accommodate Frank and Dean's schedule.

I knew better than to ask who "the man" was. They dropped us off at the Palmer House and told us they would be back to take us to the luncheon the following morning at eleven. I had a slight problem with the luncheon's timing. In this case, we were flying commercial, and I knew we had a 3:00 p.m. flight out of Chicago en route to Madison for the start of filming Monday morning.

We checked into the hotel, where the three of us shared the Presidential Suite. Neither Frank nor Dean offered any explanation of this surprising and unusual welcoming committee. So, I decided it best to keep my mouth shut and get a good night's sleep.

The next morning, I was up bright and early and ordered a large pot of coffee before jumping into the shower. I hadn't made it to the bathroom when the doorbell rang. I threw on a robe and rushed to the door hoping they had not awakened Frank or Dean and praying they wouldn't ring it again before I got there. I needn't have worried. As I entered the living room, one of the guys from our original welcoming committee was already opening the door and the other was on the phone at the bar. How they got in or how long they had been there were questions I didn't feel comfortable asking. I asked the first one if there was anything I could order or do for them. He just stared at me.

"Naw," said the second guy. "We're going for a big lunch whenever your two friends get their act together."

Saying this, he then took off his coat and tossed it on a chair, revealing a holstered pistol. I grabbed a cup of coffee and headed for Dean's room. I knocked and he yelled to come in.

"Jesus Christ," I whispered, "those two characters who met us at the airport are out there. I don't know how long they've been there. And what's worse, one of them, maybe both, are packing pistols."

Dean's first response was to lift his finger to his lips, suggesting I should keep my voice down. "Today's going to be very interesting," he whispered.

He was right. We left the hotel around 11:30 for the noon luncheon. Frank, Dean, and I were in one limousine and the other two were leading us in another. Where we were headed, we didn't know. It was Sunday, which was quiet by normal conditions in Chicago, but for some reason this ride to wherever seemed unusually eerie. I asked the driver where we were headed but he said he didn't know.

"All I know is I've been told to follow that car," he offered. "We're in a section of Cicero now, if that helps." He also told me, as we finally arrived at our destination, that he only did this chauffeuring to pick up some extra money on weekends.

"What do you do when you're not driving?"

"I'm a sergeant with the Chicago Police Department," he said, smiling.

We arrived at an Italian restaurant, Villa Venice, near Northbrook, which from the outside appeared as if it might have been closed, but when we walked inside it was pure pandemonium. The place was jammed to the rafters. It was like New Year's Eve, but there was one difference: there were no women.

Suddenly, someone started singing, "For He's a Jolly Good Fellow" and everyone else chimed in as Frank and Dean were escorted to what appeared to be the head table. I assumed it was Frank they were honoring. I was wrong. Let the feast begin. I retreated to the bar. I'd no more than ordered a drink when one of the guys who brought us approached and said Frank wanted to have a word with me.

There was still too much noise to carry on a normal conversation, so when I got to Frank I leaned down close so that he could talk directly into my ear. I didn't hear a thing he said. I glanced up as he started to speak, suddenly aware of who was seated next to him. My brain went blank. I was staring into the face of Sam Giancana, six inches from nose to nose. An honest to God crime boss. I suddenly remembered the reference to "the man" the previous evening. I also suddenly realized who was being honored at this unique gathering. He was balding, well-tanned, and his eyes were bluer than Frank's. He was very soft-spoken.

"Frank' not going anywhere," he said to me. "Understand?"

He didn't appear to be very big, but hard to gauge since he was seated. He had none of the charm and charisma of other Chicago crime bosses I remembered from movie matinees, nothing like Cagney or Bogart.

"Did you hear me?" Frank asked, finally getting my attention.

"No Frank, I didn't. It's too loud."

He cut me off and repeated himself. "Get us out of here in time to catch the plane. We have to make that flight otherwise we're here for the night."

"We'll make it," I assured.

"He's not leaving," Giancana repeated, rather sure of his dictum. Suddenly, the soft-spoken voice was the only thing I could hear.

Frank gave me a look that said it all. We would be leaving, we would make that flight, and it was my responsibility to make it happen. Taking on the mob was not part of my job description, but there I was between Frank and Momo.

As I left to find our driver, the "police escort," Giancana was making overtures to Frank and Dean to stay in Chicago. I saw this at work and made my way to the bar where I found our driver. I asked how long it took to get to the airport.

"Thirty minutes, tops," he said.

"We're leaving at two," I said. "Can you be ready out front?" He nodded, yes.

As I turned away, one of our welcoming committee thugs was standing right next to me.

"Frank wants to stay," he said.

"That's great," I said. "Nice party."

He looked at me suspiciously and I waited for him to disappear. I worked my way back to Frank and whispered in his ear.

"Driver will be ready out front at two on the dot," I said. He nodded okay.

I rejoined our police chauffeur back at the bar.

"You attend these things on a regular basis?" I asked.

"No," he replied. "This is a first."

"Your superiors might get a kick out this," I said. "All these people work for Giancana?"

"No," he said. "In fact, Giancana isn't even the most important guy here."

He left the phrase dangling in the air. What? I looked around? Who in the room was more important than Frank Sinatra, Dean Martin, and Sam Giancana?

There are some things better left unknown and unsaid.

I looked at my watch and it was a minute to two o'clock. I tapped Frank and Dean on their shoulders and they simply followed my lead. In the noise of the party, it was as if no one saw us, which was impossible, but we got into the car and left without so much as a goodbye.

On our way to the airport, our police driver informed me that he knew a shortcut through the city dump.

"Fine," I said. "Just get us there on time."

We'd gone no more than a few miles when the car stopped dead. "What's wrong?" I asked.

"I don't know," the driver said.

"What the hell is going on?" Frank asked.

I looked at the driver and he pleaded his innocence. There was a local tavern across the street. I suggested to Frank and Dean that they make themselves comfortable while I looked for new transportation. There was nothing around, not a phone booth or store anywhere, so I went into the tavern myself. The bartender was madly fixing his new celebrity clientele drinks and laughing with the wide-eyed regulars.

"Can I call a cab here?" I asked.

"Sure, no problem," he said, but kept making drinks.

"We need it now," I said.

"Give me a minute, pal."

Dismayed, I walked outside to see if the driver had any luck calling the limo company for help. As expected, no such luck. But as I turned to go back to the bar, a Chicago police car nearly ran me down. Never in my wildest dreams could I have come up with a better solution. Through the graciousness of the Chicago Police Department and my new best friend, Sergeant Schmidt, Frank, Dean, and I made it to the airport on time, leaving the mob in our wake.

Our flight from Chicago took us to Cincinnati, where a limousine met us for the final leg of our journey to Madison. I don't remember if it was Frank or Dean, but, after a few airborne cocktails, someone came up with a great moneymaking scheme. Dean advised the driver that he wanted to stop off at the Beverly Hills Club, a Vegas-style casino in Covington, Kentucky, just over the river from Cincinnati. Dean and Frank wanted to make a run at the craps tables.

I had long since understood that everything worked by Frank's watch. So, gambling it was. They dropped ten thousand before either one could bust into a rendition of "Back Home in Indiana."

We finally arrived in Madison, a charming midwestern town, late that evening. Frank and Dean took up residence in a private home on the outskirts of town, and I checked into the local hotel, where the rest of the crew, including Shirley MacLaine and actor Arthur Kennedy, were ensconced.

As far as location filming, everything went along smoothly the first week. Then all hell broke loose.

I'd gotten word from my New York office that *Time* magazine had a reporter in Madison doing a story on the effect a Hollywood film crew has on a small midwestern town. I smelled trouble, at least for my client. It was a reporter's formula I knew all too well: how big money from Hollywood chews up and spits out small town bumpkins.

My first move was to advise Frank to stay out of this bombshell. He listened, said nothing, and went back to his residence for lunch. When I arrived at the house, I noticed two brand new Cadillac limousines parked in the driveway. When I say "new," I mean these cars were next year's models. I assumed they must have brought some local dignitaries around for lunch. I walked inside and there they were, Sam Giancana and the two members of his welcoming committee. The music was turned up and they were all drinking and eating pasta and laughing. I got Frank aside and told him about the Time story and suggested that if the reporter got wind of the arrival of his friends, that would make the story huge, and not in a good way.

"I had no idea they were coming down here," Frank said defensively. "They just showed up. They'll be out of here tonight and hopefully no one will notice."

"Notice?" I pleaded. "Did you see that fleet of tanks they showed up in?"

Yes, Frank was concerned, but he thought that meant very little. They were here already. A prompt exit would be equally suspicious.

"What can we do about it?" he asked, raising his shoulders.

The afternoon led into night, and the party continued with further additions to the cast. Jimmy Van Heusen and Sammy Cahn showed up and then baseball legend Leo Durocher. Cahn and Van Heusen were there to write songs for Sinatra's next movie, "Hole in the Head," and Leo said he had nothing better to do. The pasta festival continued for dinner with lots of Jack Daniels, Wild Turkey, and red wine.

Also joining in the festivities were Shirley MacLaine and two more of Giancana's pals. No one ever really heard their names other than the short one was Tony and the tall one was Johnny. In what little conversation I could get out of Tony, it appeared that he ran the state of Illinois and Johnny ran Indiana. And believe me, these characters were not in politics. In my brazen naïveté, after several glasses of wine, I got Johnny to show me how he carried large sums of money through customs when traveling.

"It's simple," he said, while removing his coat. "All you need is a good tailor."

With that, he turned his coat inside out, revealing six small zippered pockets hidden in various parts of the lining. He put the coat down, unzipped his pants, and showed me five more hidden pockets that were absolutely undetectable.

"I can go anywhere and never have less than fifty thou' on me," he boasted.

"Tony almost got caught in Mexico City. He has a bad ticker, and what with the altitude and all, he collapsed getting off the plane when he arrived. We rushed him to the hospital in an ambulance and all the time he appeared to be out cold on the stretcher but hunched in a fetal position clutching his crotch. Only I knew what he had his hands on," he laughed. "About twenty thou."

The evening proceeded rather smoothly, and after dinner we all adjourned to the game room downstairs, where Cahn and Van Heusen took up where they had left off earlier, at the piano. Giancana and Durocher took to the pool table, and the rest of us gathered around the bar. It was one of those parties right out of central casting and a good Hollywood movie: a couple of big stars, a couple of up-and-comers, a sports legend, the femme fatale, a couple of songsters to keep things light and a couple of mobsters to keep things dark. If I weren't sitting there, I wouldn't have believed the guest list.

Somehow the conversation got around to Frank and Dean's visit to the Beverly Hills Club and how they dumped all their cash in ten minutes. Tony went ballistic, venting all his well-chosen words on Johnny.

"How could you guys take advantage of our friends?"

Johnny pleaded back, "I knew nothing about it."

Then Giancana chimed in. "What are you two beefing about?"

When it was explained to Giancana, he too went ballistic and ordered that either Tony or Johnny or both get that money back to Frank and Dean as fast as possible, and no later than the next day.

Sam returned to his pool game with Durocher and Cahn, and Van Heusen resumed his songwriting. Pleasant conversation returned. And about that time director Vincente Minnelli dropped by to brief the stars on what he hoped to do the next day. And once again, all hell broke loose.

Giancana threw down his pool cue, picked up his drink, and threw it in Durocher's face. "Don't ever call me a dago you no-talent cocksucker!"

"Jesus Sam, no offense."

Before Durocher could utter another word, Giancana was screaming that he never ever wanted to hear that word, ever, ever, EVER! Frank and Dean were between the two of them, and as fast as it started, it was over.

Apologies and forgiveness were accepted, and Cahn and Van Heusen continued adding final touches to their newest song, conveniently titled, "Hole in the Head." I always wondered if Durocher realized how close he had come to serious injury.

Giancana and his friends did leave that night, and I took a deep breath.

The *Time* writer kept a low profile throughout his stay in Madison. As predicted, it was a hit job, and the writer was only divulged as a contributor when the story appeared a few weeks later. If he had done his homework, the story could have won a Pulitzer. There was the story on Giancana and Sinatra's Chicago side trip, losing money in the club, and not a word on Frank's growing unhappiness with Minnelli's direction of the film. But that was my job, suppression, which always made me uncomfortable. I preferred activity.

The shooting days dragged on, and Minnelli did nothing to speed things along. He'd wait hours before shooting a scene, blaming the shadows. On another occasion, he wasted two full days moving an entire set fifty feet for a better background. Finally, Frank told the studio chiefs at MGM that unless they removed Minnelli, he was removing himself. They got the message, and so did Minnelli. Things moved fast from then on.

The *Time* story covered not much more than what the locals thought of the Hollywood invaders. Unfortunately, the writer did somehow work his way inside the invaders' camp, where some unflattering words were uttered about the country folk. It bordered on wiretapping.

I'd convinced Frank weeks earlier that *Life* magazine would run a cover profile on him, and we'd have complete control of the text, captions, pictures, and cover shot. This was unprecedented, but I showed Frank the letter from Associate Editor Thomas Thompson stating, *"We are certainly not out to expose him or attack him in any way...Frank would, of course, have complete control over all the words published under his name...I will show the article to Mr. Sinatra before publication so that he can point out any factual errors or misquotations. We will show him all the pictures we are considering for the cover. We will expect him to select his own favorites..."*

Sinatra agreed. He didn't like the idea, but he agreed. By the time the *Time* story hit the newsstands, he had already sat for several hours of initial interviews with *Life*. As usually happens with bad news, someone got hold of an early copy of the Time article and showed it to Frank before I had a chance to ease him into it. I was reading the article when I got the call.

"James, it's Frank," he said. "Have you seen *Time*?"

"I'm reading it now," I told him

"When you're finished, do me a favor and call *Life* and tell them forget it."

"But Frank," I fought back feebly, "they're two separate magazines, different editors, different editorial."

He cut me off with a line I will never forget.

"They answer the same phone, don't they?"

With that he hung up. Six months of major haggling with *Life* was down the tubes with one thirty-second phone call.

But that was Frank, and he was done.

What was lost was one of the most insightful, honest, candid interviews I felt Frank ever gave.

The following are a few excerpts from my taped interview with Frank and writer Loudon Wainwright. These words from Frank Sinatra have never been printed before:

On the price of fame:

"There was a point in my life, a few years back, when things were a little rough for me, through nobody's fault but my own. I began wearing dark clothes, driving dark cars, and practically driving up back alleys because I didn't want to be seen. I didn't want to chance friction with anyone making a remark and abusing me because I wasn't ready for it. I was disturbed mentally about many things…Finally, I began to move around a little more and as I say, maybe the success I began to achieve, coming out of the so-called dark age that I went through was beginning to rub off on the onlooker, on the public or the fan so that I didn't have much trouble anymore. I am talking about the annoyances that happen…but that's part of the game… (I am not) public property. I don't think it should be that way. A performer wants to be loved by the public but not controlled like a puppet by the public. I doubt whether he wants that—I don't. I resent it very much."

On his relationship with the press:

"I've been known as the guy who fights with the whole press of the world. Strangely enough, I have more friends in the press than anyone realizes. I have close associations with, I would say, 99 and 9/10 percent of the press of the world. That's a pretty good statement to make for a guy who so-called goes around and takes punches at the newspaper guys. Men like Jim Bacon and Vernon Scott and Hopper and the rest of them…I've had associations with these people that have been twenty years old. That's a long time. I've never had beefs with them, it's ridiculous."

On his performances:

"I've been gifted some way. I rarely get nervous. Before a live performance, I'll get nervous like everyone else does, until you get past that first swing of the ball, until you get the feel of it. But when I am in my own surroundings such as when you are making a picture and you've got your whole family with you, the grips and the electricians, you're not playing to anyone who's kind of peeking through the curtain or who might bother your performance, because nobody's a critic on a soundstage…To clarify that, I don't like locations because I'm embarrassed on locations, where people can stand around and watch you work on the street. Consequently, the performance suffers because I feel silly. I'd rather be working in my own backyard. And then let them see the finished product."

On women:

"The basic theory is…nobody asks the other guy what happens in the bedroom. That's a rule of life that nobody dares defy. Anybody who does that is ridiculous. I have thought, and I believe, that no man or woman has the right—now I may be dead wrong, but I don't think so—since it is a direct invasion of privacy, of basic privacy."

On giving back:

"There are hundreds of people in our industry who have never raised a hand to contribute something that would give entertainment to somebody… This is unfortunate, but it is true…That is unfortunate, I feel, because I think that we have been gifted with a unique talent and it should never be used constantly for the benefit of earning power. It should be doled out in all directions. I truly get more fun out of performing when I'm not paid than when I do get paid. I don't know why that is, but I have more fun. Strangely enough, some of my performances when I've done this kind of thing have been fifty percent better than when I have worked for a salary. It's a kind of intangible thing that happens to you."

On performing live:

"I don't think there is such a thing as singing to anybody. I think it is a question of being direct and honest. People have said to me, "You give me a feeling of having sung to me." That is my aim and intent. To make you think that I'm singing to you. Actually, I am singing to you but not as an individual. I'm singing to an audience as a large individual. I think that is what is lacking in some of the younger kids who are working today. Of course, that comes with time and experience…I found myself working on stages in clubs or hotel rooms that were enormous, where one third of the audience to my right was in back of me and one third to my left was in back of me. I found myself pulling the microphone off the stand and doing the cardinal sin of turning my back to the middle of the audience. However, I had been working to that group in the audience for maybe five songs. An audience must be wanted. They must know that I know they're there. Otherwise, you lose two factions to the left and the right. That's why working in a place like the Coconut Grove is difficult, you've got a small center field."

On Elvis Presley:

"I don't think he's an entertainer but dollar-wise, exhibitor-wise and producer-wise, this man is considered a great entertainer...He's certainly not a great actor and he's not a great singer. As a matter of fact, I wish I could understand what he sings. I can't understand what he's saying. If Presley could prove to me as a listener that he's a great singer—I would like to hear him make an album of Rogers and Hart songs and convince me he understands those songs—I want him to run the gamut. Not the mumbling songs with the four-piece orchestra, I'm talking about working with a thirty-six piece orchestra."

On his association with the mob:

"I have been accused as you well know, and as the reader knows, of having consorted with gangsters, which is absolutely and ridiculously stupid. In my kind of life...I am sure hundreds of entertainers have come into contact with people who are considered to be undesirable people. That is not for me to judge—I am not the police department or the F.B.I. or any law enforcement agency. I'm an entertainer. If I work in a nightclub and I'm introduced to a man who might be one of these so-called undesirables or shady characters as they call them, it doesn't mean that I consort with them...While I have met these people who are called undesirables, I had an audience with the Pope, I knew President Roosevelt fairly well, I know Eleanor Roosevelt very well, I've met with Adlai Stevenson, with some of the people in the highest offices in the world. You can't say that I should only be allowed to meet that kind of person. There's no way of drawing a line with the kind of people an entertainer meets."

On discussing his own life:

"(It is) something I loathe. To discuss something in print logically, sensibly and theoretically is fine, but the person who writes a biography and begins to shed his laundry, I don't like it at all. I have no desire, never had and never will, to discuss my life as a child or my life with my family or my life today. It doesn't concern anybody but my family and me and my close friends. If we do have a problem, we try to keep it to ourselves. Sometimes we can't. That's why whenever I've been in print because of a marital problem, or whatever it might have been, I have clammed up so fast and refused to talk to anyone...I'd rather not air it to the world because it doesn't concern anyone else...There are a handful of idiotic people who thrive on reading about another guy's problems. It's a terrible indictment on our civilization today that there are still people who get their jollies by reading about another guy's problems. I don't believe the adage that people want to read or hear about it. That's a circulation manager's dream...I'm talking about scandal. If we discuss something that's constructive about a man in the public eye, I can understand…I feel bad when I read about a man's emotional problems. They bother me."

This is pure Sinatra, in his own words.

Chapter Twenty-Three

Renaissance Man Has a Cold

OF COURSE, MY business was getting ink, and getting the best ink I could muster for my clients. And so I had to live with Sinatra's media rages and somehow work through them. It wasn't easy. Each time I came up with a good story idea, I had to bite my tongue. Frank just wasn't interested. The more ideas I came up with, the more distant he became, even if he knew I was doing my best.

But I didn't stop.

One prime and early example of my trying and his suffering through the media came in 1965, when Sinatra's career was on fire. He was shooting a movie, *Assault on a Queen* with Virna Lisi, cutting a new Reprise album, creating an NBC television special (*Sinatra: A Man and His Music*), and then after all that each night he flew to Las Vegas to perform at the Sands Hotel. I wanted someone to capture the crazy, Herculean effort of it. The schedule would kill any mortal. For Sinatra, it was a walk in the park.

I found him at his five-room bungalow on the Warner Bros. lot and said, "Frank, I have a unique idea."

"You got a unique idea, James?" Sinatra said, with as much as sarcasm as he could muster. "I wanna hear it."

At this stage, Sinatra was more than press shy. He had grown to hate the thought of anything to do with the media. They were now the enemy. They nagged him with stupid questions and were only looking for the dirt and rumor, and Mafia connections. Like the kidnapping story, even when it turned out well, it never turned out well. My job now, more than ever, was to keep the press away—what he called the "garbage press."

Knowing all this, I still couldn't help myself. I mentioned a new kind of feature story, the concept of someone following him around like a shadow, never talking to him, just watching him, observing.

"It's a new style, with really good writing," I said. "It's a style piece to show what a hell of a worker you are. It's for the fans. Let's call it 'Sinatra, Renaissance Man.' It's unique, and I've got just the guy for it."

I pleaded with him to go along with me on this one. I told him about this new writer, Gay Talese, an Italian, and his award-wining stories in *The New York Times* and *Esquire*, mostly on Italian immigrants making a go of it in a new land. I knew the Italian angle would catch his attention, but I could tell he was angry just thinking about it.

"James, how the hell does this work?" he asked.

"A week, ten days max," I said. "This writer shadows you on the set, in the studio, hangs out at NBC, and I fly him to Vegas for the show. But here's the catch, Frank: he never talks to you. All he does is follow you and observe, sees how people react to you and vice-versa. It's never been done before. How could it? No one has a schedule like yours."

Sinatra was smoking pretty heavily then, and a cold was coming on. He took a long drag.

"I see what you're saying, James. If you think it's a good idea, let's give it a shot."

"It's a literary treatment, and you don't ever have to talk to him."

"Okay James, but I wouldn't get your hopes up."

Enter Gay Talese.

I had tracked down Talese, and pitched the idea to him over the phone.

Talese stammered at first. He couldn't believe what I was saying. It was a huge challenge, and he knew it. From the concerned tone of his voice and the questions he asked, I could also tell he was worried about Sinatra, doing him right, doing justice to the superstar, maybe he even feared letting down the Italians in New York and New Jersey. I could tell, even long distance, that he thought maybe this was too big for him.

"Before we do anything," I said, "check it out first with your editors at *Esquire*. They have to agree to the deal."

I'd been burned too many times before by jackass editors agreeing and then pulling the plug because of money or time or cold feet. It just made my clients angrier at the Fourth Estate, the so called moniker for professional journalism.

"Look," I said again, "we don't need this story. Frank doesn't even want it, but I think it's important for history, to bear witness to the hardest-working man in show business."

"Okay," Talese said. "It's a deal with me, but let me get back to you and make sure it's okay with the magazine."

"There are just two catches," I said. "First, you never talk to him, ever. All you can do is watch and observe him. Second, once you've finished your article, I want to go over it with you before you submit it to the magazine."

"We don't do that," Talese said.

"I don't mean I want to edit your copy in any way, but if there are inaccuracies, let's correct them before they go to print and become fact. We need to get this just right."

I wasn't pulling a fast one. I knew the game. I didn't want to wrest creative control, I simply wanted to get the facts right for this historic feature. It had to be accurate.

"Absolutely," Talese said. "As a matter of fact, since I won't be able to communicate with him, I'll need your help more than ever."

Talese called back the next day and said his editors give him the greenlight. Everything was a "go."

With the agreement and this kind of "fact check" deal in place (there was nothing unusual about it in the business), it was a "go."

Talese flew out the next weekend from New York to stay for a week. We got him a room at the Beverly Wilshire Hotel, across the street from my office. We started that Monday, and everything began swimmingly.

I introduced Talese to Sinatra at Paramount, where he was filming *Assault on a Queen*, and the two appeared to hit it off. We flew to Vegas and watched the show, played craps together, and flew back for some time in the recording studio at Western Recorders on Sunset. A Sinatra recording session was the hottest ticket in town, with room for ten people in the guest booth. Producer Sonny Burke and conductor Gordon Jenkins were making the album, *Moonlight Sinatra*.

Things were going so well that Talese extended his stay another five days, and even though Sinatra wasn't feeling his best (he had a cold), I couldn't believe this story was coming together without a hitch. It was ten days in and not one problem. It was going so well that I was starting to get nervous. Talese was in and out my office as if he worked there, and I felt maybe it was time to wrap this up before something bad happened.

Then one morning I got the call.

"Jim," Talese said. "I gotta come over and talk."

I could tell by the crack in his voice that he was in bad shape.

"Yeah, sure," I said. "Come on over right now."

When he was ushered into my office, he all but collapsed on the corner sofa. He looked as if he'd been up all night.

"You said you had a problem," I said.

"Yeah," he said. "I have a big problem. I can't do the story."

"What the hell are you talking about?" The staff outside my office heard this and so I toned it down. "This is the best goddamn story of your life. Jesus Christ, what're you talking about?"

"I'm sorry," he said, and he started to cry. He wept like a child. "I've never done anything like this before. It's impossible for me to do this without talking to him."

As he sobbed, tears streaming down his face, he looked up at me. "I can't do it, I'm so sorry."

"But that's the whole story angle," I said. "That's what you and your editors agreed to, now you want to do something else?"

He was broken. He stared down at the carpet. "I'm so sorry," he stammered. "New York thinks I've been out here long enough, and if I can't get some time with Sinatra either today or tomorrow, they want me to come home, story or no story."

How do I get into these shitty situations? My mind whirled. Frank didn't need this, and I didn't need this emotional little shit upsetting my client.

"All right," I said. "I'll do my best, but I can tell you he won't like it or like you for it. You're going back on your word, and my word. I really don't appreciate you and *Esquire* fucking up my relationship with him. I'll see what he says and get back to you. He may throw me out, and I wouldn't blame him."

Talese, still crying, blew his nose and mumbled more apologies. He limped out of my office, apologized again, and thanked me. He would wait for my call.

You don't want to be the guy delivering bad news to Frank Sinatra. Every morning, I'd check in with his staff to gauge the mood. Some staffers avoided him for days. This was not going to go well. It was likely that the up-and-coming star writer from *Esquire*, Gay Talese, would be on the next plane back to New York. I had to do this just right. It was part of my job, managing the twin beasts of Hollywood: the beast of the media and the beast of the celebrity. I was the guy in the middle, the lion tamer throwing scraps to the press and then getting my head chewed off by the client.

And maybe Talese was playing me, too?

When I arrived at Frank's office, I didn't even bother asking about the mood. It didn't matter. I had to be honest.

"The writer wants to talk to you," I said.

Sinatra looked at me with those searing blues. They saw right through me with a, "I told you so, asshole" glare.

"How much time does he want?" he asked.

"Half an hour."

He thought about it. "Okay," he said. "Bring him over to the studio this afternoon."

That was it. I nearly ran out of the office. I was flying. I'd pick up Talese at the hotel, bring him to the studio, he'd fire off his questions, and I'd take him to the airport and get him the hell out of town.

The plan worked.

Talese interviewed Frank for a half-hour, and the questions were pure vanilla.

"Where were you born?" was the first question.

What? Any asshole knows this stuff about Sinatra. He asked questions any bio or news archive could have answered. It was like he was scared to death to ask a real question. He talked to him like a bobby-socked teenager flummoxed by his idol.

I got Talese out of there fast, and afterward Sinatra said, "What the hell was that all about?"

I shrugged. "Who the fuck knows?"

It was at that moment I sensed that my "Renaissance Man" idea might backfire and was not going to turn out well. My brilliant idea was just another one of those "I told you so" press moments Sinatra scolded me for, and rightly so.

A few weeks passed, and I didn't hear from Talese. I called him and asked, "How's it going?"

"I'm still writing," he said.

Then, three weeks passed, and Sinatra asked me, "Whatever happened to that unique story idea of yours?"

I told him I was chasing Talese. "It's still in the works," I said.

But it was a month before I finally got hold of Talese again, and when I did, I asked him point blank, "Where's the story?"

"I don't really know how to tell you this," he said, "but I've turned the piece in to the magazine and they loved it."

"What?"

"Yeah, they loved it. My original was over a hundred pages, but they cut it down to fifty-five."

"Have you forgotten our deal? Have you forgotten that we were to go over it together to verify the facts?

"I know, I'm sorry," Talese said. "They told me it was against their policy to show any articles before they go to print."

"What do you mean, they told you? You and I had an agreement! You and I, not your editors. You gave me your word. You said you cleared this with your editors. What kind of creep are you?"

Talese listened to me rage on a bit longer before ending the call.

"I'm sorry," he said, and hung up.

The piece he wrote turned out to be the cover story, with the title, "Frank Sinatra Has a Cold." It was a prosaic, semi-fictionalized account of the man's coterie of hangers-on, comments from his haberdasher, and some gray-haired lady who supposedly carried a satchel of sixty hairpieces for him (not true). It was all about Frank's way or no way, and how an army of sycophants honed his ego.

I was an idiot to think I'd get something better, something about a man at the top of his game, something more than a long narrative that was adjacent to the truth. There are many ways to write a story. I didn't want a puff piece, but I also didn't want exploitation, false details, and generally sloppy reporting focusing on mob allegations, gofers, and side attractions surrounding my client, even if it was fun reading about it. And to make it worse, destroying Howard Strickling's number one rule: I was in the story too, as the "husky" PR guy.

The article was filled with errors, even the most basic one that his cold "plunged him into a state of anguish, deep depression, panic, even rage" was complete bullshit.

It was good writing, maybe even great, but complete and utter crap. I expected a reporter-writer, but what I got was some kind of ersatz fiction writer looking to pump up his copy.

It worked for Gay Talese.

Soon after the feature appeared, Gay Talese became known as one of the founders of a writing style called "New Journalism," a dicey brew of fiction and reportage.

The following are just a couple of examples of where his vision seems, shall I say, out of focus:

Talese writes: *"Sinatra had been working on a film that he now disliked, could not wait to finish."*

My Perspective: Sinatra was busy, very busy, and eager to finish all his projects so that he could take some time off. That didn't constitute dislike, or the perceived idea that Sinatra couldn't wait to get off a dog of a project.

Talese writes: *"(Sinatra was) worried about his starring role in an hour-*

long NBC show entitled Sinatra: The Man and His Music."

My Perspective: I can assure you if there were any cause for concern about Frank's performance, I, as his publicist, would never have had a journalist on the set.

Talese writes: Frank's having a cold can *"plunge him into a state of anguish, deep depression, panic, even rage."*

My Perspective: In all my years with Frank, if illness were ever a reason to not be able to deliver a perfect performance, the performance was canceled. Frank's cold could not and did not reach a level whereby his performance would or did suffer. Therefore, there was no possible way for Talese to have witnessed this range of emotions he stated. Frank was one of the calmest and coolly collected men I ever knew.

I can only assume that Talese ascertained these tidbits from hearsay... and that to me is not journalism, not even New Journalism. But the truth can be a bore.

All of that only happened in paragraph two. By the canons of journalism, he had now set a premise the rest of the article needed to back up. You can see where I may have had a few issues with his "voice" and "editorializing."

Clearly, for a man who staked his reputation on being impartial, Talese seemed to have gotten caught up in the celebrity of the whole thing and just couldn't handle it. The crowd at Elaine's, the Upper East Side watering hole for the city's intelligentsia, should have known this creep couldn't keep his word. My guess is that he never told his editors about our deal, and never had any intention of telling them. He bullshitted me from the beginning to the end.

I had to face the music with Sinatra.

I took a copy of the magazine over to his office as soon as it was on the street. I handed it to him. As soon as he glimpsed at the cover, an artistic rendering of him smoking a cigarette with multiple hands trying to light it, he looked up at me with those baby blues. I got the message. He didn't have to say anything. He threw the magazine in the wastebasket and turned away from me.

That was the end of my brilliant idea.

Working with Gay Talese was perhaps the worst experience of my career. It didn't matter how much I helped the writer. It didn't matter how much access to the client was granted. It didn't matter how much of my reputation I put on the line for him. Talese was going to fabricate what he wanted to make his story great, the truth be damned.

It worked for him. It made his career. Unfortunately for Frank, and somewhat for me, this work of fact-fiction, "Frank Sinatra Has a Cold," was heralded as one of the great literary feats *Esquire* ever published. But there are two people who know the real story behind the tale, and they are Gay Talese and Jim Mahoney.

Chapter Twenty-Four

Sinatra Strikes Back

AS MY BUSINESS began to grow, the number of mouths to feed in our family grew along with it. By the early 1960s, Pat and I had three kids, Jim Jr., Marilee, and Sean, and we had another son, Mike, on the way by 1962. By 1965, we had our fifth child, a girl, Monica. To say the least, the pressure was on to keep body, soul, and family fed, clothed, schooled, and under a decent roof.

There was a building boom going on all over Los Angeles, and in '62 we traded up to larger new house at 1730 Clearview, about a third of the way up Benedict Canyon. It was up against the mountain, where the kids could play safely, and the entire neighborhood was filled with Hollywood up-and-comers. A few doors down lived Ross Martin, of the TV show "The Wild, Wild West," and Joe Flynn of "McHale's Navy," and Burt Ward, who played Robin on the "Batman" television hit. A few years later, with the need for larger bedrooms for the kids, we moved around the corner to 9903 Anthony Place, a bigger house on a cul-de-sac. It was a two-story, fully renovated home, and all the rooms were now big enough for our family of seven.

By the mid-1960s, I was headed into my full stride in the business. Pat took the lead at home and I took the lead in bringing home the paycheck. The rules weren't written down, roles and responsibilities were just understood. Pat handled all the recitals, ballgames, Boy Scouts and Girl Scouts (with Pat and Debbie Reynolds as local den mothers), and I showed up when I could make it. Looking back it was as idyllic as "Leave It To Beaver," but I regret not being home more with Pat and the kids.

But the Hollywood PR life was never that easy to juggle, and I always felt the wolf was at the door. If I wasn't out there with Frank, or at the shop, or drumming up new clients, the whole thing could fall apart, and fast. With five growing kids to come home to, I felt that edge kept things afloat. Maybe my workaholic nature came from my father, his running up to look at jobs with my mother on Sundays, always being there for new clients or jobs. He was always on edge, too, always felt it was going to slip away. The anxiety of losing it all, like I saw happen with so many clients, stars, and friends, was the engine that drove me. It never stopped.

By this time, I had a pretty good relationship with the press, or what some call the Fourth Estate, but sometimes despite my best efforts they inflicted some unnecessary, even serious damage. For the most part, stretching the truth or printing outright lies were for a better story, a sharper headline, but there was always suffering to pay. It was usually at the expense of Frank Sinatra.

Sinatra was an easy target for fast and loose reporters playing with the facts. After more than a dozen years representing the man, it was my responsibility to attempt to quash them, but sometimes Sinatra himself jumped into the arena and took the bull by the horns.

In 1964, Sinatra was completely beside himself with anger at the Hearst newspapers, all of them, but especially *Herald-Express*. It was about the coverage of the trial of his son's kidnappers, inferring callously that the kidnapping was a publicity stunt. He was so angered by this that he wrote directly to William Randolph Hearst Jr. to declare:

"I have instructed everyone in my organization that with respect to all advertising under our control or under the control of any motion picture company that we contract with to distribute the pictures we produce, no advertising of our pictures is to be placed in any of the Hearst papers."

"I admit that in many instances, I could do nothing more than 'live with' unfair articles about my personal life. I resented the articles but enjoyed the personal comfort that I was strong enough, and good enough, from an emotional and professional standpoint, to continue to 'live with' these unfair and unfavorable articles—and to 'live well' both professionally and personally.

However, I found that 'personal strength' was not enough when my son was involved...After the trial was over, I was determined to do whatever I could do to correct this terrible injustice to my son and, more important, perhaps to do something which would cause 'the press' to hesitate before committing similar injustices to others..."

He could live with "unfriendly press," but at this point untruthful press was an evil that needed to be stamped out.

If there was a single shining moment for Frank in his retaliatory actions against the "unfriendly press," it came in 1973 when he took on James Reston, vice president of and a top editor at *The New York Times*. An article written by contributing reporter Wallace Turner angered Sinatra.

The crux of his frustration was the constant repeating of false rumors that had now seemingly become fact. If *The New York Times* was going to once again print rumor as fact, he might as well admit guilt for everything, that is, every crazy thing in the world. Why not?

To that end, Frank and I wrote this editorial response to the *Times'* story, and they printed it.

Here it is in its entirety.

New York Times contributor Wallace Turner went to the journalistic dung-heap August 15th and dug deep into a rotting lode of anti-Sinatra rumors. His resulting article should earn him a smelly little niche in the newspaper world's famed hall of garbage.

Typical of journalism's tiny hard core of character assassins, Turner's printed garbage represents that vicious brand of gossip mongering which hides behind irresponsible clichés: "knowledgeable sources say"; "unnamed friends report"; "there have been persistent rumors"; "persons in positions to know"; "a close friend reportedly said"; etc. etc. etc.

Turner's resurrection of rotten rumors is an old familiar song whose lyrics imply that I have "held high level political friendships—and lost some of them because of friendships with major figures in organized crime."

Instead of scrounging around the dung-heap of dishonest gossip and dirty rumors, Turner should have come to me. I would have given him sensational new evidence on my activities past and present.

He might have learned, for example, that on April 14, 1912, I was cruising on my yacht, the Christina, and towed an iceberg into the path of the Titanic.

He might have learned that on November 1, 1950, a buddy and I tried to shoot our way into Blair House in an attempt to assassinate Harry S. Truman, whom I dearly loved. My death sentence was commuted to life imprisonment by President Truman, one reason I dearly loved him.

Turner might have learned that on the night before Pearl Harbor, I tossed a big party and got the entire Naval, Air, and Ground forces completely stoned.

Who do you think was the real architect of the Bay of Pigs? Francis Albert Sinatra, and you'd better believe it.

Who do you think trained the police dogs for the 1968 Democratic convention in Chicago?

Who turned out the axe handles in his little basement workshop and air-

*mailed them to Lester Maddox? Who slipped into a National Guard uniform
and sang "I'll Do It My Way" while firing at anything that moved on the Kent
State campus?*

*Who do you think polluted Lake Erie? Well, I didn't personally pollute
it—I farmed out the Lake Erie contract to "certain mutual friends," "of Italian
lineage," "on a blacklist of persons barred from Nevada casinos" and "others
with interests in Berkshire Downs Racetrack", etc. etc. (Wallace Turner, see the
big scoops you missed by hanging around the dung-heap of rumor?)*

*How's this for a sensational tidbit? This is a right now kind of scoop! The
Watergate Seven did not break into the Watergate—I let them in with my
skeleton key!*

*Another recent notorious act of mine was the Russian wheat deal which,
"according to unnamed friends" who are "close to the source," has contributed
to inflation and boosted the price of bread. "At this moment in time" I'm trying
to corner the soybean market, thus bringing financial ruin to the cattle and
chicken producers. Mighty heady stuff for a kid from Hoboken, eh?*

*Be honest, Sinatra! Confess that the malicious gossip and the baseless rumors
are a pain in the heart.*

*Yes, it hurts; it really hurts. But how do you fight it? Malicious gossip is a
slimy, slippery thing. Take a swing at it and it squirts up in another location.
And even if you could fight it and win, some of the evil stench of it sticks in your
hair and clothing and the smell of it lingers on.*

*Maybe I can't fight it and win, but like the line in the great Rogers and Hart
tune, I'll try, by God, I'll try!*

*The only weapon I've got is the one Wallace Turner ignored—truth.
Fortunately, the Big Truth is easier to verify than the Big Lie.*

*My Big Truth is that I am not "a frequent associate of many known members
of the organized crime world" and have never been.*

*Like many other entertainers, I've performed in a lot of places and met a lot
of the great, near great and un-great.*

*In a Las Vegas nightclub, in a crowd of a thousand, there's certain to be
X-number of shady citizens. If one of them muscles in and tries to buy you a
drink, does that automatically make you, 1. An alcoholic? 2. A gangster?*

*But in the philosophy of Turner's garbage article, you sit down in a bus
next to a hood, then baby you're a hood too! That's based on the schlock-legal
principle known as 'guilt by association.'*

I once sang for Nikita Khrushchev. Does that make me a Communist?

*Sure, I've been introduced to a stray racketeer or two, or fifty for all I know.
But meeting a racketeer doesn't make you his kissing cousin, doesn't make you a*

"member of organized criminal groups." If it does, then every one of your Times *readers is a hood, because you meet plenty of hoods on the streets of New York.*

The Turner garbage contained nothing about the joy I get from knowing—not just meeting, knowing—many of the world's truly great men and women. Great because of their monumental achievements, their contributions to a world so desperately in need of the ingredients with which to make a better way of life.

I'm privileged to have friends who are presidents (and students) at our renowned universities. I'm proud to have friends who are pushing back the frontiers of medical research, who are closing in on the causes of birth defects, who are putting together the pieces of that grim puzzle, cancer.

I'm proud to have friends who create our masterworks of sculpture, of painting, of architecture, of literature, of music.

I know of no greater privilege than to have such a list of friends, which also includes a vice president and several officers and staff members of this newspaper.

There is not one "member of organized crime groups" on that list. And I strongly doubt that one Wallace Turner will ever make that list.

Finally, this—contrary to the August 15th story in the Times, *I am not a "G.O.P. insider." I don't want to be "inside" anything except the jacket of a hit record album; "inside" your TV tube with a crackling good special; "inside" the reels of a high-caliber movie.*

There's one other "inside" I want to be—inside the affection and respect of good Americans. The kind of Americans who think straight, talk straight, and cling to the beliefs which you Wallace Turners may consider corny illusions. The kind of people unafraid to speak up for what they know is right. Unafraid to speak out against what they know is wrong. People who've got the guts to stand up and be counted.

Being on that "inside" would, hopefully, keep me "outside" the reach of reporters whose typewriters are little more than manure spreaders.

I've had it up to here with the Wallace Turners, and with all the other Typewriter Turners of the journalistic underworld—who spawn and spread the rotten gossip and printed sewage so unworthy of the respected profession of newspaper reporting.

This commentary made the op-ed pages of *The New York Times*, and we both felt good about that, but things don't change that easily. The stories kept coming out, the rumors flew, the bad ink kept flowing, and there was nothing in the world a PR guy could do but just deal with it one byline at a time.

The truth, it would seem, is just not news.

Feeding the beast with Hollywood columnist Hedda Hopper and
song writer Sammy Cahn.

Peggy Lee and I at a London press conference. Is that all there is?

The King and I!

Debbie Reynolds and I at the LA
Coliseum. Always fun escorting
Miss Burbank around.

It doesn't get any funnier than
Mr. Warmth Don Rickles!

When I was rude enough to ask
Jayne Mansfield if "they" were real!

Tony Curtis working me for some print.

Making an entrance with Debbie
& Eddie Fisher, a relationship that
crumbled before my eyes.

photograph by Don Cravens

Eddie Fisher and me.
"He should have listened!"

On the set of "Pal Joey" with Kim Novack, another tough assignment.

Frank imparting his opinion on a young publicist.

Frank joins the paparazzi!

photograph by Lear jet Inc.
On the way to Vegas in Frank's Lear Jet

Exiting the Jet with The Chairman   Frank treated Pat like a Queen
of the Board

Frank and I in Rome with Al Liota, his
close friend and pilot and Brad Dextor
an actor who once saved Sinatra's life in
rough waters off Hawaii.

Sinatra scouring the tabloids on set of "Lady in Cement "
at The Fontainebleau in Miami.

Dining with Tina & Nancy Sinatra at the kid's table!

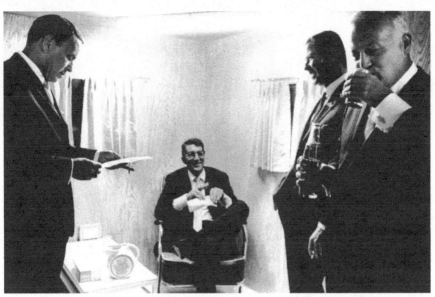

Back stage with Frank Sinatra, Dean Martin and James Bacon,
one of Sinatra's favorite columnists

Lee Marvin handed me his Oscar
for Cat Ballou and said,
"Here, it's yours!"

Me and a cast of thousands as Sinatra sets
his hands and feet in cement at Grauman's

Chapter Twenty-Five

Breakfast with The Colonel

THE WORDS CAME back to haunt me. It was what Henry Rogers said to me years before, during the Tony Martin debacle, about not being able to be picky when it came to clients.

Working for myself meant taking on projects and clients I may not have wanted. But being more and more like my father, I now had a different perspective on life and business. I had a roof to pay for and mouths to feed. A paycheck was the great equalizer between preference and reality. I understood the game. It was about managing a bundle of insecure personalities looking for fame. One minute you were a career shaper, the next a babysitter. But what the hell, it was their dime.

Early on, while working out of Sinatra's Beverly Hills office at the William Morris Agency, I started a morning ritual with an early breakfast around the corner at the Milton F. Kreis Coffee Shop in the nearby Beverly Wilshire Hotel, on the corner of Wilshire Boulevard and Rodeo Drive. I'd take a quiet back corner table and set out to read the Hollywood trade papers and any other daily papers, looking for my handiwork. The coffee shop was always a magnet for celebrities of all types, and you never knew who you might be able to get business from right there over a coffee and bagel. A frequent visitor to the coffee shop and to my back table was the legendary Colonel Tom Parker, Elvis Presley's manager and confidant.

I'd met the Colonel many times over the years. The first time was when interviewing Elvis backstage at the Pan Pacific Auditorium for *The Herald*. We met several times again over the years, mainly while I was working for Sinatra. The Colonel was easy to like, since there was something charismatic about the guy, something part snake-oil salesman and part politician, and you had to smile when he spoke.

The Colonel lived at the Beverly Wilshire while in Los Angeles, and the William Morris Agency represented Elvis. It was all very convenient and made for a comfortable existence. And the Colonel was all about comfort. He had his detractors, but there was no doubt about it, Colonel Parker was one of the great promoters of all time.

Everyone knew the stories about how he supposedly swindled and cajoled legions of unsuspecting "donors." If there was a buck to be made, no one had his hand out faster than the Colonel. But the one thing he can be credited for was his ability to promote, be it cough medicine or people. The Colonel was also a close friend of Howard Strickling, and like Strickling he took an almost fatherly interest in my business. I hadn't been in the business more than six months and was handling Lawford, Reynolds, Ladd, and the restaurants, among others, when one morning the Colonel sat down at my morning table and asked me how business was going.

"Fine," I said. "But it could always be better."

And from out of nowhere, he says, "How'd you like to handle Elvis?"

"Like breath to my body."

I couldn't believe my ears. It was as if I were in a dream. Here I was, sitting with one of the greatest promoters, con men, marketing mavens in the world, and he was asking me if I'd like to promote his top client.

"Are you serious?" I asked.

"Of course I'm serious," he replied. "I've been thinking that you could take over a lot of the pressure. He gets more requests than the President. I get bogged down with a lot of this stuff, and I think you could handle it."

"When do I start?"

"As soon as you give me $25,000."

The Colonel clearly had a sense of humor even when he wasn't joking. That's the way he operated… you paid him for the privilege of having Elvis as a calling card. In his mind, there was nothing unusual about this set up.

"I can't afford that kind of money," I said. Of course, I wouldn't have paid it if I could. "Okay," he said, "I'll make you a better deal on one of my other clients. How'd you like to handle Eddy Arnold?"

"Who the hell is Eddy Arnold?" I asked, not knowing the country market. When he explained, I wrote Arnold off as a shit kicker, a cowboy and not for me. Of course, Arnold was selling more records than Sinatra at the time, but what did I know about country singers?

Nevertheless, before breakfast was over, I had a deal. It wasn't to represent Elvis or Eddy Arnold. It was to handle the Colonel himself. My assignment was to do publicity for the top showman in the country.

All I had to do, within twenty-four hours, was to set up a luncheon to impress *Life* magazine at the MGM Commissary by inviting thirty people. All of this was to appear as a tribute to Colonel Tom Parker. And for this, he would pay me, a major coup in the world of the Colonel.

Having maintained a pretty good relationship over the years with Art Simms, who ran The Commissary at MGM, it wasn't too difficult to get a banquet-like table for the next day at noon. As an aside, Art Simms' success and legacy live on through his and his family's successful ownership and management of such Southern California eateries as Mimi's Café, The Kettle, Arthur J's, Simmzy's, Fishing with Dynamite (FWD), MB Post, and Tin Roof Bistro, to name a few. Getting a large group to attend the luncheon on a day's notice would be a chore. Getting *Life* magazine there would be an even bigger challenge.

Before leaving the hotel that morning, the Colonel noted that everyone I invited to the lunch had to bring a briefcase, if they had one.

"It's important for the effect," he said. He was a showman and a perfectionist.

"What's the luncheon all about?" I asked.

"Never mind, that's not important, but see if you can get *Life* there. I might have something for them."

I rushed back to my office and asked my secretary, Del Mertens, to go through my phone book and call out names from A to Z to me. If I said "yes" after a name, she was to check it off and call that person and ask them to lunch with me tomorrow, in honor of Col. Tom Parker, at the MGM Commissary at noon.

Basically, I stacked the luncheon with relatives and friends. Then I called my good friend Tommy Thompson at *Life* and told him that I wasn't representing Elvis but the next best thing—the Colonel—and it might not be a bad thing to attend this luncheon.

Not wanting to miss a possible earth-shattering Elvis announcement, Thompson agreed to not only attend the luncheon but he also wanted to bring a photographer. By three that afternoon, I had *Life* and thirty guests confirmed, none of whom had a clue as why they were going. And there wasn't much I could tell them. He wanted it to look like a tribute, yet I hadn't seen some of these people in years, and none of them, with the exception of Thompson, had a speaking relationship with Parker.

On the day of the event, the Colonel sat at the place of honor at the head of the table, flanked by Thompson and his photographer, Don Cravens, and we proceeded to have lunch while several hundred others in the restaurant wondered what this affair was all about.

When lunch was over, the Colonel got up, tapped his spoon on his glass for attention, and thanked everyone for joining him for lunch.

"However," he said, "there will be no announcements, nor speeches." Without another word he took off—the Colonel had left the building!

Every one of us at the long table was dumbstruck, though no one questioned the bizarre behavior. It was classic Colonel Tom Parker, and another one of his mysteries.

The Colonel and I continued to breakfast whenever he was in town, but I could never get him to explain what that luncheon was all about. Years later, long after Elvis had passed on, I had occasion to visit with the Colonel numerous times at the Hilton Hotel in Las Vegas. He was a paid consultant to the hotel until the time of his death. He also happened to be their biggest casino customer for a number of years, especially when Elvis was appearing there. He loved to play roulette and the $100 slots, but his favorite was the Wheel of Fortune, which any casino operator will tell you is the sucker bet of all time. On one of these Vegas encounters, the Colonel asked me if I remembered the luncheon.

"Sure, I remember it well," I said.

"Do you have any idea what it was all about?"

"Not a clue," I told him

"*Life* wanted to do a cover story on Elvis, and I thought the luncheon would move the project along.

"Did it?"

"It did somewhat," he told me. "But they never did the story."

"Why not?" I asked. "Elvis was as hot as one can get."

"Very simple," the Colonel said. "They wouldn't pay the $100,000 plus rights to the story and pictures outside the U.S."

And that's why the Colonel was called The Snowman. A lot of negative press has been written about Col. Parker for his P.T. Barnum approach to deal making and his alleged mismanagement of Elvis for allowing him to do all of those "B" movies. But you got to hand it to him, he swam amongst sharks his entire life and more often than not came out on top. He got Elvis to agree to pay him 50% gross on everything Elvis did, when all other managers were getting 15% max. Like Pierre Cossette, he's a Hollywood personality that they just don't make anymore.

Chapter Twenty-Six

I'll Take What I Want

STEVE MCQUEEN KNEW what he wanted from the very start: stardom. More than any other personality with whom I have ever been associated, McQueen's quest to be Hollywood's biggest star was unstoppable. No one was going to get in his way.

He mentally beat up everyone associated with him for this quest. I can't ever remember him being satisfied with anyone's effort on his behalf. His agents suffered unmercifully, even though they did an excellent job managing a career that was, from the very beginning, average at best.

McQueen didn't explode off Broadway like Brando or Newman, or any number of other megastars. His feature film debut was in the "The Blob."

I first became acquainted with Steve McQueen when I was representing Four Star Television. As previously mentioned, he was starring in one of their shows, "Wanted Dead or Alive." Four Star, originally founded by Dick Powell, David Niven, Joel McCrea, and Charles Boyer, was a very successful operation and produced such hits as "Zane Grey Theatre," "The Rifleman," and "The Big Valley." Onetime advertising guru Tom McDermott was running the company during this period, and one of his young stars, McQueen, was making life miserable for everyone. Nearly every meeting I had with McDermott had to be postponed because of "another problem with McQueen."

The problems were always something small, but annoying, like his dislike of a script, or the director wasn't any good, or they weren't paying enough for the supporting cast.

One day, McDermott said, "Jim, you'd be doing me a great favor if you'd go to work for McQueen and get him off my back."

As it happens, I did just that.

During this period, I was doing a pro bono piece of work for an agent by the name of Stan Kamen at the William Morris Agency. He told me if I'd do a pro bono Academy Award campaign for one of his new clients, who was crying poverty, he'd see to it that I'd be rewarded somewhere down the line. His new client was Peter Falk, and the movie was "Murder Inc.," what we all thought was a "B" picture. As it turned out, Falk went on to win an Oscar nomination for Best Supporting Actor for the role.

Kamen's payment to me was convincing McQueen he needed me as his PR man.

There's no doubt Steve McQueen had a certain style, look, attitude, and talent. We gave him the nickname, "The King of Cool." The TV show gave him a platform to play up this image, and with our well-placed "guest spots" on late night television and an occasional Bob Hope special, he was getting good exposure. He was a racecar enthusiast, and this kind of hip hobby helped, too.

Hedda Hopper took an early interest in his career and went out of her way to give him ink. He had charm, and when he turned it on, he was a killer.

Though he was a tough personality to manage, Steve and his wife, Nellie Adams, became good enough friends that he made my wife and I godparents to their daughter Terry.

McQueen had some bad habits that I believe carried over from his tough upbringing. They were all selfish, chickenshit antics, like refusing at the last minute to attend a press function because the limousine provided by the studio wasn't white, or that year's current model. But over time I came to understand the makeup of the man, indelibly scarred by a childhood I wouldn't wish on anyone.

McQueen's father deserted the family soon after he was born, and his mother, while hopping from marital bed to marital bed, left him with an uncle, Claude, in Slater, Missouri. Later, Steve couldn't even tell you how many times his mother married. But by the time he was twelve, she had settled in Los Angeles with the latest husband and sent for Steve.

You could have easily called Steve the original "Rebel Without a Cause," as he favored gang life to schoolbooks. And it wasn't long before young Steve was on a first-name basis with the local cops. After a few run-ins, his mother, who had taken to drinking heavily, had had enough and packed the wayward Steve up and sent him off to the California Junior Boys Republic in Chino—a penal colony of a boarding school. It was the first step toward, or the last step before, a visit to San Quentin prison.

After a few miserable years of incarceration, his mother, now widowed and living in New York, relented and sent for Steve to join her. Unfortunately, the reconciliation didn't last long, as she was quick to find a new husband and they both felt three was a crowd.

Steve, now sixteen, was in the Big Apple and on his own.

Without much of a trade other than steeling hubcaps, he ended up as a deck hand working on a tanker ship heading for Cuba. Even this was an underhanded venture, as he had to fake an identification to get working papers. In hearing this story much later, I could never really tell if a chapter or episode in his life was fact or fiction. He was shifty and would tell you whatever suited him best. He later told me his maritime service was short-lived and that he jumped ship in Puerto Rico and took a job in a whorehouse. Yes, a whorehouse. McQueen was the towel boy.

He returned to the States shortly thereafter and joined the Marines. Now, having served side by side with the Marines in Korea, I find it nearly impossible to believe that McQueen lasted any amount of time in the Corps. But serve he did between 1947 and 1950. He didn't speak much about it other than to say that he spent a considerable amount of time in the brig. And that I could believe.

But it was his time as a Marine that provided financial assistance through the G.I. Bill for McQueen to start studying acting. So, in 1952, he auditioned for the famed Lee Strasberg Actors Studio. Out of the two thousand who auditioned, only he and Martin Landau were accepted.

Because of his childhood and despite his Marine "discipline," when he got to Hollywood, he was the kid-in-a-candy-store, but still acting like a child in an adult world.

A typical example of this behavior was the terrible habit, when out on the road promoting his films at the studio's expense, at the studio's expense promoting his films, of loading up on the hotel bill. He'd hit the gift shop and sign for everything from electric shavers, portable radios, bottles of cologne and whatever else he liked. I called him on it once in Chicago when we were out promoting "The Cincinnati Kid." He told me nonchalantly that he deserved whatever he took.

"With all the shit they gave me making this film," he claimed, "I'll take what I want."

I waited for him to throw himself on the ground and hold his breath until he got what he wanted—another tantrum. I turned my back on these antics; the studio was paying for his and my expenses anyway. They could fight it out with him if they so choose. It wasn't my battle.

To make matters worse, on another occasion we were scheduled on a weeklong tour of six cities to promote another film and McQueen just arbitrarily decided to go home after the third day.

"You can't do this," I said, as he was packing.

"The hell I can't," he replied. "Just watch me."

Several years later, he got something of a comeuppance in a situation in which I took great satisfaction.

He was being chauffeured from a luxurious suite at the Waldorf Astoria to JFK in a brand new all-white limo en route home to Los Angeles when a horrendous snowstorm hit. He and his new white limo were stranded at a small hotel adjacent to the airport. For four long days and even longer nights, Steve was cooped up in a cell-like room when he could have stayed right where he was, in the lap of the Waldorf's luxury at the studio's expense. What made it best of all? There was no gift shop.

According to my old friend Tom McDermott, former advertising executive hired to run Four Star Productions, McQueen's troubles started the first day of production of the "Wanted Dead or Alive" series. McQueen's character was a Wild West bounty hunter, yet McQueen refused to have the character shoot anyone. This was a real head-scratcher for the producers, director, and writers.

It got worse.

When contract negotiations were underway during the production of the show, Steve faked a neck injury and halted production. But being the method actor that he was, he literally crashed a new Cadillac convertible into a wall in Hartford, Connecticut, to substantiate his neck injury. Both he and his wife Nellie, who was in the car with him, were safely buckled in and uninjured, but he sure faked it well. It cost Four Star a fortune in lost production.

When all was said and done, Tom McDermott and Four Star let McQueen out of his contract. The aggravation was just too much. In addition, ratings for "Wanted Dead or Alive" were not strong.

But the William Morris Agency nonetheless saw bigger and better things ahead for McQueen. They were the agency of record for both Four Star and McQueen, and they brokered Steve McQueen's future. But it seemed the harder McQueen's agent Stan Kamen and the Morris Agency worked for him, the more he and his manager, Hilly Elkins, complained. McQueen and Elkins were like piranhas that would never stop gnawing.

They were two of the most demanding people I knew and were by now notorious for their demands. Elkins, by the way, is the only man I've ever known to be physically banned from the William Morris Agency. He became such a pain in the ass, making such outrageous demands on behalf of McQueen, such as stating their three-year slate of multiple pictures lined up for the star was simply not enough, that they literally barred him from the building.

To their credit, however, with all their combined rude behavior, McQueen and Elkins got the job done. McQueen soon became the hottest actor in Hollywood—in spite of himself.

In the late '50s and early '60s, it wasn't an easy task to sell a TV star into feature films. They rarely crossed over. McQueen was probably the first to bridge that gap, even before Eastwood and Garner. I like to think I had as much to do with that move as anyone, and it happened quite by accident.

It was late 1959, and I was in a meeting with Sinatra and his producer, Howard Koch, at MGM. We were discussing his next film, "Never So Few," co-starring Gina Lollobrigida, Peter Lawford, and Sammy Davis Jr., which was set to go into production the following week. At the time, this was a critically important movie for Frank and his career.

We were discussing last-minute details, like what still photographers I wanted to use and other media promotion details when Sinatra took a phone call. He listened, hung up, and then went ballistic.

"He's out of the fucking picture, Howard!" Sinatra screamed.

Before we could ask "Who?" he said it again. "That's it! Smokey's out! End of discussion." Smokey was Sammy Davis, Jr.

When Frank calmed down, he explained that Sammy was being removed from the cast. Frank did another of his head shaking "No-Nos." Sammy was once again on Sinatra's shit list. This happened periodically, not only with Sammy, but also with other members of Sinatra's coterie.

Later on, I learned that Sammy had approached Frank about a loan that he could use to build a wing on his home in Beverly Hills for his and May Britt's expected baby. Sammy was always in need of money, and Frank had bailed him out on numerous occasions. Frank's heart got the best of him and he loaned Sammy the money again, only to find out later that it wasn't used for the baby's room, but a state-of-the-art screening room. Sammy wanted to entertain his guests.

"But Frank," Koch pleaded, "we start the picture on Monday and he works almost every day next week."

Frank was adamant. Sammy was history.

Sammy's part was not really that important to the film, but the character was in several scenes and quite flashy. The dialogue was flippant, and the part called for someone adept at driving a jeep in a carefree and reckless manner.

This was perfect for McQueen, I thought, and I made my pitch right there. Sinatra knew of the young upstart and approved. Within minutes, Koch was on the phone making the deal with Stan Kamen. From a PR standpoint, we made the most of that casting, touting McQueen as the first TV star to bridge the gap from the small screen to a major motion picture. We made the most of his "King of Cool" brand.

His next film, "The Magnificent Seven," a John Sturgis film, assured him of stardom. Sturgis saw some charisma in this ego-driven actor back when he did Sinatra's "Never So Few," and he never forgot. This was 1960, and by 1965 I was representing not only McQueen but also James Garner.

Martin Ransohoff, formerly the head of Filmways Productions, was also a client now. He had just signed a two-picture deal with MGM and was currently making the film "The Americanization of Emily." Garner was starring in the film, and Ransohoff was also producing McQueen's new movie, "The Cincinnati Kid," also at MGM.

One meeting I had with Steve McQueen was set for the cocktail hour at his home in Nichols Canyon in the Hollywood Hills above Hollywood Blvd. In the mid-60s, I was his PR guy, and we were meeting to discuss an upcoming trip to five eastern cities to promote the release of his latest movie, "The Cincinnati Kid." McQueen hadn't arrived yet, which didn't surprise me. The housekeeper apologized for his absence and suggested I make myself comfortable in the lovely living room with a fantastic view of west L.A.

I followed her advice and was rummaging through some newspapers and magazines on a coffee table when much to my surprise there was a 38 revolver. A strange place to store or keep a lethal weapon. I have an aversion to guns. I got my fill of them having served in Korea. Whatever, I instinctively picked the pistol up and checked to see if it as loaded. Satisfied that it was harmless I aimed it out the huge window and sighted in on a huge bird flying by, about thirty yards away. And I pulled the trigger. BOOM.....THERE WENT THE HUGE WINDOW....

The meeting was canceled. McQueen sent me a bill. I haven't touched a firearm of any kind since that stupid encounter. For months I was convinced that I'd read or hear about the authorities finding the remains of a decomposed body of a local or homeless hippie killed in Nichols Canyon. And of course, by his carefully groomed tough-guy reputation, McQueen would automatically be named a definite person-of-interest.

My clients were all working, life was good. But a few years later, on

McQueen's own pet project movie "LeMans," Sturgis saw the monster he created in McQueen. Sturgis was hired to direct on location, but by then McQueen's stardom and ego were in full bloom, with crazy demands, soaring budgets, no-shows, and daily changes to the script. Sturgis, a real pro, was fed up and walked off the film.

Remembering the Rogers & Cowan mantra "Activity Creates Activity" and not wanting to lose any momentum, I came up with what I thought was another brilliant idea.

"Marty," I said to Ransohoff, "why don't you make a deal with MGM for one of your upcoming commitments to remake 'Boom Town' with Garner and McQueen playing the Clark Gable and Spencer Tracy roles? MGM holds the rights, and they're perfect for the roles."

He liked the idea so much he was going to talk to the studio about it.

"Even if it doesn't work out," I said, "the publicity for 'Emily' and 'Cincinnati Kid' will be sensational."

"Go for it," he said.

I might add that Ransohoff was no wallflower when it came to the race for space—column space that is.

Since the fall of the studio system, many a producer or director understood the value of having your name in the papers, as if intrinsically following the R & C credo. More often than not, though, they would be perfectly happy seeing their names in the trade papers rather than jockeying for position in the entertainment columns. When Ransohoff gave his blessing, I ran with the story.

I gave the story to Louella Parsons and she loved it.

Of course, she wanted to verify it. Ransohoff was only too happy to wax on that this idea came to him as he wandered one day on the lonely back lot of MGM and came across the western street used in the original "Boom Town." He was more creative than I gave him credit. Nonetheless, it worked.

Louella gave the story a banner headline and five paragraphs. It was a major coup.

But then, at about eleven that night, I got a call from McQueen.

It was bad enough that he would call at that hour since Pat and the kids had just fallen asleep.

"Did you see Louella Parsons' column?" he screamed.

"Of course," I said, waiting for the big pat on my back.

"Where the hell did she get that shit?"

I couldn't believe what I was hearing.

"Are you serious?" I asked.

"Hell yes I'm serious!" he yelled back. "Where the hell did she get that shit?"

"From me," I yelled back at him. "I wrote the whole fucking story. And if you have trouble being associated with either Clark Gable or Spencer Tracy, you're even crazier than I suspected."

"If you wrote the story, then tell me what it said."

"Well," I explained, "she reported that Ransohoff was going to remake 'Boom Town,' one of MGM's greatest hits, which starred Clark Gable and Spencer Tracy, with Jim Garner and Steve McQueen in the starring roles."

"See?" he screamed. "You'll never learn, will you?"

"Learn what?"

"My name always comes first." With that, he hung up.

And so the lessons kept coming: in Hollywood, never underestimate the sensitivity of the precious ego.

It all caught up to McQueen, like it always does. He lost the co-starring role in "Butch Cassidy and the Sundance Kid" to Robert Redford. The reason: he wouldn't take second billing to Paul Newman.

You simply can't do enough for some people, especially if they're assholes!

Chapter Twenty-Seven

Is That All There Is?

PEGGY LEE LIVED a block away from Frank Sinatra in Beverly Hills. It was just a matter of time before we met.

Like Sinatra, she was a real pro. She surrounded herself with the finest musicians and arrangers. Also like Sinatra, she seemed to have a real fix on whom to work with in the recording studios, and who brought out her best.

Pat and I had seen Peggy's openings many times at clubs around town and in Las Vegas, but she was really known then as the toast of New York. At the time, she was dating John "Handsome Johnny" Roselli, one of the nation's more notorious mobsters. The rumors about the two of them were well known. It was Roselli, along with Sam Giancana, who was allegedly recruited by President Kennedy and CIA Director Allen Dulles to knock off Fidel Castro.

Peggy Lee and Johnny Roselli made a strange couple. It was a romance that would not last. Roselli ended up dismembered, placed in a fifty-gallon oil drum, and dumped in the waters off Miami.

Peggy was a major Big Band star and had many hit recordings, won an Academy Award nomination for a terrific performance in "Pete Kelly's Blues," and appeared on every top TV variety show several times by this point. In the mid-1960s, the Queen of New York nightlife was appearing regularly at Basin Street East, and you couldn't get in the place. The lines went around the block, even in freezing winter weather. When I finally signed her, she was making Las Vegas money in a place that seated less than a hundred people.

I've never known two performers who cared more about their performances, than Peggy Lee and Frank Sinatra. She'd get so concerned and worried before going on stage sometimes, she'd get physically ill. Still, with the stage as her bread and butter, she went on like a trooper. Her career was at a point where it would have been easy to shift into movies. She wanted to shift, too, but her agents at William Morris had other ideas. Despite the Oscar nomination, her agents were making far too much in commissions from club dates to ever advance her movie career. What was best for the client wasn't important. It was all about the money.

On one trip, Peggy and I were traveling to New York and we were 30,000 feet above Kansas when she turned to me and said, "I'm not going to London."

"What do you mean you're not going to London?" I asked. "You're booked for three weeks at the Club Pigalle, starting next week."

"I can't do it."

"Your musicians are already there and you're sold out, what the hell do you mean you're not going?"

The bottom line was that canceling at this late date would have cost her a fortune— money I knew she didn't have.

"I've been thinking it over," she said through tears. "I've never been there, and the newspapers are going to kill me."

Granted, the British press, along with the Aussies, are arguably the worst on celebrities. But there was no reason to believe they would be gunning for her. Yet she was adamant. She was canceling her gig.

After an hour and a half of persuasion, I finally convinced her that she had to make the trip. The reasons were numerous, too many to list, but not the least of which was her personal financial problems at that moment. Peggy Lee was also a world-class spender.

She agreed to make the trip but only on one condition—that I went along! That was out of the question, I told her. I knew this was not a matter of necessity but rather a matter of want. The bottom line was, it wasn't about the press or the place, she simply did not want to travel alone.

At this point, I was merely accompanying her to New York on the first leg of the journey because I had meetings there for a day and a half but was due back in L.A. for the weekend.

"Besides," I rationalized. "I've got two suits with me including the one I am wearing, one pair of shoes and no passport." The passport, I thought, was my best argument—the red tape alone would be prohibitive.

"Don't worry about your passport," she countered. "I'll get you one in New York tomorrow." No easy feat. Back then you needed at least three days and a birth certificate to get a replacement passport. Don't ask me how she did it, but I had a passport the next afternoon, and we sailed on the USS United States at dusk.

Peggy was a very persuasive lady. At 30,000 feet, after several cocktails, I got to thinking that going off to London wouldn't be so bad after all. I convinced myself that things were pretty well in hand at the office, so why not take a few weeks off? What the hell, I had never had a vacation, truly, and what red-blooded American boy wouldn't like to cross the Atlantic, first class, aboard the finest ship afloat, with the finest songstress in the business on my arm for dinner every night?

I convinced myself it was something I had to do. I called Pat when we landed, and said, "Pack your bags and meet me in London." Always a great sport about such things, Pat said, "Sure." She got on a plane the next day, dropping the kids off at their grandparents.

Knowing her penchant for the finer things in life, a few of Peggy's friends had sent four cases of Dom Perignon to be delivered to her stateroom for a crossing that was less than a week. It was going to be smooth sailing.

The ship's captain was all over Peggy during the trip. He wanted her at his table every night, which was a black-tie affair. It was one costume I had completely forgotten.

"Never mind," she said. "Meyer Davis has an orchestra on this ship, and he'll find one.

Good old Meyer found me a size 48, double breasted, baby blue tux with a broken fly zipper. I am a size 42 at my heaviest. We could only laugh and did, nonstop.

We had more fun at those nightly dinner dances worrying about my fly and whether or not people thought I was an exhibitionist or just another weird Hollywood type. Peggy introduced me as Dr. Mahoney, a psychiatrist acquaintance of hers from Beverly Hills, and I gave out more bad advice than I care to remember to more poor souls at the after-hour bars on the ship.

If Peggy ever had a fault, it was just that she did too many bad things in excess. Too much partying, booze, late nights, and smoking. It was the smoking that got my attention on the trip. She was the all-time chain smoker.

On the first day out, she told me that she had twenty cartons of cigarettes in her luggage. Twenty cartons presented a small problem, since British customs only allowed two cartons per person. When she found out that little tidbit, she was in a panic.

"Don't worry about it, Peggy." I assured her. "I'll be there with you, and when they ask what we have to declare, I'll handle the whole thing."

The next day, the first thing she wanted to talk about were the cigarettes, since her hairdresser had told her they were very strict about the customs rules.

"Peggy," I said, "these people are going to be so happy to see you, they won't know if you are bringing in the Lindbergh baby. Trust me, I'll handle the cigarettes."

This same conversation went on practically every time we were together—morning, noon, and night. The evening before we were to arrive in Southampton, I assured her once and for all that she had absolutely nothing to say to anyone once we got off the boat until we got on the train to London and met the dreaded press. I would do all the talking, and all she was to do was to stand there and smile.

We arrived with my carry-on bag and her twenty-six pieces of luggage. As the customs people stamped her bags for transfer and asked for autographs and pictures, one of the customs officers stomped up to me and asked, "Anything to declare?"

"No!"

Peggy overheard the interplay and asked, "What about the cigarettes?"

We missed the train and the press conference as they made her open all twenty-six bags, and the cigarettes were confiscated. At least it finally sunk in that when I say don't speak, DON'T SPEAK!

Peggy was a smash in London and everyone loved her, especially the press. She sold out every night and was the toast of the town. One titled Brit took more than a fan-like interest in Miss Peggy and she willingly responded. They made plans for a quick trip to the south of France as soon as she finished her engagement, to make sure this was the real thing. It appeared to be. And after a week of romance, they were going back to London to break the news.

The only problem was, "Sir Lancelot" was under the impression Peggy was rich, and Peggy was under the same impression of him. Neither one had enough money to pay the hotel bill. We wired her the money to get home.

As Peggy would ask, "Is that all there is?"

Chapter Twenty-Eight

A Rocky Yellow-Brick Road

AS THE BUSINESS began to grow, I soon realized I not only needed more office space, but some help with the new clients. I found nearby space across the street at 120 El Camino, directly across from the swimming pool at the Beverly Wilshire Hotel. About this same time, I also took new space in New York at 710 Madison Avenue. Business was good.

I was representing a fairly good stable of personalities as well as the Kennedy Foundation, which the Lawfords helped me sign as a client. The new stars I handled included Bob Newhart, Nick Adams, Hugh O'Brien, Tony Bennett, Robert Wagner, Julie London, Paul Anka, Roy Orbison, Robert Taylor, Vic Morrow, Jim Garner, Mort Sahl, James Coburn, and Andre Previn.

I was also being hired to promote various TV specials, series, and an occasional movie. It wasn't long before I had to hire two publicists and three secretaries to help do the work.

One of the first publicists I brought on board was Rick Ingersoll, an old friend whom I helped get the job replacing me at MGM when I went away to Korea. Another was David Foster, who'd just been let go from Rogers & Cowan and appeared to have a promising future. They worked well for a few years, but then proved to be my biggest nightmare and regret in those early days.

Neither one ever brought in or signed any new business the entire time they were with me, but they confronted me one day with an ultimatum that I either give them half the business or they were going to walk and take whatever business they wanted. Anyone in the public relations business knows this old story. And probably knows how it turns out.

Foster's father-in law, an incredibly wealthy insurance executive, had promised the lads that he would underwrite them for at least a year, with any new business they wanted to start. Among the few who defected was Steve McQueen, who had been promised a cheaper retainer. Good riddance.

Pat and I sat down and talked things over, and the decision was made to keep the whole business. I could always get more clients.

They left, and for a while things proved to be trying. I was left alone servicing my entire client list, and handling personalities is an all-consuming practice. It was critical to be there when they called, or they would find someone else who was ready for them.

Pat and I had another child on the way, and so things looked tough. I had to make some decisions, either scale back or hire for the future. Pat and I talked about it and we decided to look at the glass as half full. I started hiring.

Jay Bernstein, Guy McElwaine, Bob Dingilian, and Dave Gershenson joined the organization and brought with them a few very important clients, namely Judy Garland, Warren Beatty, and Bobby Darrin. I'd known McElwaine since he was a teenager. His father, Don, was one of Howard Strickling's top guns in the MGM publicity department, and he always took good care of me when I'd started at the studio.

At my shop, Guy had his hands full with Garland, who was always in one kind of jam or another, either with ill health, her soon to be ex-husband Sid Luft, agents, managers, studios, record deals, or suicide attempts. On one occasion, he burst into my office to tell me he'd just left the offices of Freddie Fields and David Begelman, Garland's managers. Judy had decided that she wanted to hold a press conference that very afternoon on the set of her new CBS television show, announcing to the world that she was not an unfit mother, as portrayed in the tabloids by hubby Sid Luft.

Luft, to his credit, was an impresario extraordinaire who was credited, along with Fields and Begelman, with resurrecting Judy's singing career by having her play The Palace in New York and her acting career by producing a remake of "A Star is Born," which she starred in. But for all their success in business, they were a mess in marriage.

Less than two weeks earlier, Jim Aubrey, then head of CBS, had engaged my services to not only promote Garland, which she was already paying us for, but for the show itself, which was getting battered by the critics. It was unheard of for a network in those days to hire an outside agency, but he confided that his people couldn't get close enough to talk with Garland, let alone get her to submit to their ideas to promote the show.

"You've got to be kidding!" I screamed at McElwaine. "She can't do a press conference telling the world that her husband is a deadbeat and a lousy father. It's bad enough that he's shooting off his mouth, but if she starts airing their dirty laundry, every legitimate newspaper, wire service, and TV newsroom will go berserk."

Guy acted as if he hadn't heard a word.

"That's what she wants," he said. "And she wants to do the press conference immediately after tonight's show."

"Is she crazy?"

"We'll invite the press to the show and when it is over, she'll come back onstage, make a statement, and then take questions."

"We're not doing a press conference tonight, tomorrow, or ever," I said, and then went to work figuring out how to stop this event dead in its tracks.

The problem with Judy Garland was that she didn't have an edit button on her own emotions. Who knows what she would say if she really got on a rant. By the time it hit the papers, it would not be about Luft but rather Judy's hysteria.

I immediately called Freddie Fields and told him this whole idea was insane and had to be stopped. He agreed but admitted that neither he nor Begelman could talk her out of it.

"You try to talk her out of it," Fields said.

"Okay," I told him. "Guy and I will meet you and David at the artist's entrance at CBS in fifteen minutes."

When Guy and I arrived at CBS, Fields and Begelman were there, accompanied by another of their associates, John Foreman—an old friend and co-worker of mine at Rogers & Cowan.

We all agreed it was crazy, but none of them would accompany me upstairs to talk it over with her. They wished me well. It was a pathetic display of spinelessness.

When I arrived on the stage level, the second floor, it was all eerily quiet. On tape days, there was always the usual hustle and bustle of a busy studio thoroughfare with set workers frenetically dashing back and forth, but that day it was totally vacant. Word was out, she was pissed, mad as hell at the world, and anyone with any sense would stay out of her way.

I proceeded down the yellow brick road that had been painted on the cement floor leading from the Garland stage door to her dressing room, a luxurious motor home decorated for a true star.

There was no answer to my first knock, or to my second. On the third try, she yelled angrily, "Who is it?"

"Mahoney."

"What do you want?"

"To talk."

"About what?" she yelled, and before I could reply, she flung open the door and motioned me in.

The place was a mess, but that wasn't surprising. She wasn't in very good shape either, obviously on something, either pills or booze, and certainly not ready for an hour-long performance on live television.

Seated rather uncomfortably in the corner, fidgeting with a script, was her producer and current director—her third at this point—Bill Colleran. He was not a happy camper. It was obvious I'd interrupted a meeting that wasn't going in his favor.

"Who's coming to the press conference?" she demanded.

"No one, we're not having one," I said. "Judy, this is not the way to handle this situation."

"What do you mean, we're not having it?" she screamed.

She then leaped across the trailer and took a swing at me, barely hitting my shoulder, but with enough force to knock me off balance and down on a sofa.

"Like I said, Judy," speaking as if it were a normal conversation, "we're not going to put you in such a compromising..."

Before I could finish, she was standing over me wild-eyed and screaming obscenities. My mind flashed back to those silly "Andy Hardy" movies and that sweet gal next door that Judy portrayed.

"You son of a bitch!" she yelled. "Don't you think I can act? Who do you think you are calling off my press conference?"

Before I could answer, she turned her wrath on Colleran, who was now cowering in the corner.

"You call the press conference," she screamed his way. "Get Vernon Scott and Jim Bacon. Get on the phone right now and call those people!"

She turned her back to me and, still screaming, ordered me to "Get the hell out of my sight." And as a sort of afterthought, she blurted, "You're fired too!"

At this point, she got my Irish dander up and I told her to do something physically impossible to herself. As a parting shot, I advised her she was three months behind in fees and expenses. With that, I was out the door and back down the yellow brick road.

There was still no one in sight on the second level at CBS. I advised the Garland braintrust awaiting me at the Artist's Entrance that I was pretty sure

I'd failed in my effort to call off the press conference. Colleran was not only her director and producer, but also her new press agent.

The taping finally got underway that evening at 10 p.m. and finished at 2:30 a.m.

What press had been called and showed up for the press conference tired early and were long gone by the time Judy was ready to talk. She was furious, but we ultimately achieved the desired result.

The next night was an opening at Dino's Lodge, and several celebrities had been invited, including Garland. I lived in fear that entire day of how she would belittle me in public if she did happen to appear. She did, and greeted me like a long-lost brother, and neither the press conference nor the dressing room blow-up was ever mentioned again.

Judy Garland was a breed apart, adrift in a sea of her own massive ego and unparalleled dysfunction.

Chapter Twenty-Nine

Me and The Karate Kid

ALTHOUGH ROBERT WAGNER and I knew each other from the old days at MGM, when I worked with Debbie Reynolds and she had a mad crush on him, I really got to know "R.J." when I was working at *The Herald* and when he was a contract player at 20th Century Fox.

For years, we casually spoke about the possibilities of working together, but it was golf that ultimately brought us together. And boy could he play the game.

I remember on one occasion, he'd been making pictures overseas and living in Rome for more than two years. He hadn't picked up a club the entire time, but when we went out to Bel-Air Country Club, he was three under par after six holes. Now, that's playing!

One morning, I picked up the paper on the way to the office and there on the front page was a picture of Wagner and an accompanying story. It described a harrowing account of how he fought off three toughs the previous evening outside a restaurant in the middle of Beverly Hills. According to the story, he and his wife, Natalie Wood, had just departed The Luau, a popular Polynesian restaurant on Rodeo Drive, when three thugs made some unflattering remarks about him and what they would like to do with Natalie.

It was a mistake. R.J. took on all three and they left bruised, battered, and arrested. I immediately got R.J. on the phone for the details, and in the course of the conversation suggested there might be an easier way to handle such a situation in the future, in view of the fact that his face was his fortune and it didn't make a lot of sense for him to end up some night with his fortune crushed against the pavement.

As a matter of fact, I told him a friend of mine on the Pasadena police force had just recently told me about this guy they imported from Hawaii who was an expert in karate. He was a world champion and had taught members of his organization the fine art. According to my friend, any member of this elite group could ward off two or three attackers with little effort. R.J. suggested that maybe we should meet this amazing master of self-defense. That very week, R.J. and I began a series of karate lessons with the legendary Ed Parker, whose clientele also included Elvis Presley. We practiced diligently in two-hour shifts every other day at Wagner's home on Canon Drive. Within no time, we were becoming quite adept at the art, or so we thought.

About three months into our blistering training schedule, I arrived mid-morning at the William Morris building. Sinatra's tough guy manager, the short, fat, and bald Hank Sanicola, asked me if I was starting to keep banker's hours.

"Hell no," I told him. "R.J. Wagner and I have been taking karate lessons."

"What the hell is karate?"

I explained that it was a form of self-defense, and the finest practitioner in the world was teaching us the skill. I went on to tell him that I was becoming very adept at some of the defensive moves, but wasn't into anything offensive as yet.

"What the hell you talkin' about?"

"Well," I persisted, "if some character in a bar or someplace looked as if he were going to take a swing at me, he wouldn't have a chance."

"What the hell are you talking about?" he repeated, getting off the couch. Sanicola was by no means the poster child for physical fitness. Out of shape as he was, I knew Sanicola could handle himself. He'd settled more than one confrontation.

"I'm just saying that if some nut wanted to make a move on me, he'd have a hard time. That's all."

"Show me," he said.

I began to feel a little feeble. "Well, if you were to make any move on me, like taking a swing or try to kick me, I'd be able to block the blow before you even knew what was happening."

"Okay. Block this."

With that, he made a move one way, feigned another, and before I could say "karate," his left fist was in my face. I was frozen like a statue.

Hank walked over to the couch and picked up his coat and was halfway out of the office when he turned and smiled.

"That karate isn't worth a shit, is it?"

That afternoon, I reported the incident to R.J.

We both laughed, but we never took another karate lesson. We continued to play golf together for many decades to come.

My life in golf and sports could be another book altogether. The game of golf was the one common denominator between the corporate world, Hollywood, and the growth of my business.

Chapter Thirty

Putting My Putter Where My Mouth Was

GOLF ENABLED ME to build a business that far exceeded my wildest dreams. I played around the world with some of the biggest names in entertainment, in business, and in golf. The game was more than a pastime, it was a business strategy.

From the very beginning, I never had a problem getting clients. I'd been very lucky.

And I'd been in the right place at the right time. But part of that strong combination of luck and timing was created by my love for the game of golf.

The first couple of months being in business for myself were a blast. I had the freedom to find clients, play golf, and build a business the way I wanted to. My work finished by eleven o'clock in the morning, and the rest of the day was available to seek out new business, play golf, or a combination of the two. Gable. Strickling. MGM. The *Herald*. Rogers & Cowan. All of it was invaluable training, and it gave me the foundation. Representing Frank Sinatra was like earning a doctorate degree in public relations and crisis management. But now I was on my own, and I loved it.

In the late 1950s, at Peter Lawford's insistence, I joined Riviera Country Club in the Pacific Palisades, and then in 1962 I joined Bel-Air Country Club, just down the road from Riviera. Even from the early days, when I snuck on the small practice holes at The California Club, I took to the game naturally. But now, with the push to get new clients, I found golf the perfect relationship builder. The long, breezy rounds on a beautiful golf course was a natural setting for telling stories, giving advice, and learning what was going on in the business.

I spent many afternoons and weekends sweating out five-dollar Nassaus—a smalltime betting game—with Lawford and other actors, producers, and directors who were either between pictures or just plain out of work. I won a lot of money in those bets, and people started complaining about it. They even gave me a nickname: "Crime." They called me that because, as the saying goes, "crime doesn't pay."

Ever since my father brought home that vintage set of irons and woods from that painting job in Cheviot Hills, golf and I became something of a partnership. I never bothered with a legitimate golf lesson. I taught myself by reading Ben Hogan's book, *Power Golf*, and watching professionals come through town.

Riviera, affectionately known as "Hogan's Alley" during the 1940s and '50s, was home for many years to the Los Angeles Open, and there I got the opportunity to play with many of the greats, including Hogan and Sam Snead. Then, I got to know the new generation of players, like Arnold Palmer, Jack Nicklaus, and Ken Venturi.

In January and February, they all came through town to play in the tournaments during the golf tour's California swing. Many of my clients were members and played there, and there was a natural desire to have them meet and play with golf's greats. My role became, as much as publicity generator, a golf matchmaker.

Since so much of my business was now conducted on the golf course, my game naturally improved. On the occasion of my first hole-in-one, a storied moment in any golfer's career, but mine happened to be at the famous 10th hole at Bel-Air CC. I was playing with Jimmy Stewart, a client. Our foursome was me, Stewart, Fred MacMurray, and football great Tom Harmon. My second hole-in-one was also at Bel-Air on the 5th hole, in the company of two other clients, George C. Scott and Jack Lemmon.

Being on my own changed everything. It was as if the universe opened its secrets to me. It was luck, timing, but something else, too. There was a mysterious positive force in the wind, and it was at my back pushing me forward into this new sphere of influence and connections. One connection built upon another, creating yet another until I was at a completely different level at my work and in my relationships with the greats of Hollywood. And golf was the common denominator.

One case in point. It was around the mid-60s and I was down in Palm Springs with Pat and the kids having some down time, if that was even possible when running your own business. Sinatra set me up to play at Tamarisk Country Club and said to just go over to the starter and tell him I was his guest. So I go over to the starter and am surprised to see that it's

Scorpy, an old caddy I've known for years that used to be at Lakeside CC in Toluca Lake, CA for years. Scorpy: "Ya got a game?" And I said: "No," whereby he says he's got a guy that I'll enjoy playing with. Around the corner comes Al Hart, the same Al Hart who furnished the $240,000 ransom for Frank Jr. years earlier. But since I never met the man and years had passed since the kidnapping, I had no idea who this short, bald, rotund man was.

On the first tee he asked me what I did. I said, "Publicity, in Hollywood." "Publicity," he said. "You know Columbia Pictures?" "Yeah, sure," I said. "That's mine!" he said.

Yeah, right, I said to myself, and teed off. Columbia was run by the legendary Studio Boss Harry Cohn. I figured this Al Hart guy was just some crackpot.

Somehow, horse racing came up and he said, "You know Del Mar Racetrack?"

"Yeah, sure," I said.

"That's mine!"

Now I'm thinking, "What an asshole.

Still later on he asked, "You like whiskey?"

"Yeah, sure," I said.

"You know Schenley's?"

"Yeah, of course!"

"That's mine!"

I stopped talking to him altogether after that, but then he asked, "You know banking?"

I didn't bother answering, preferring to wait for this nut's rejoinder. He must have gotten the idea, because he didn't ask me any more questions. At the end of the round, I wanted to get away from this buffoon, but he asked me to have a drink. I begged off, saying Pat and I had a dinner. That plan was dashed when Pat met us on the last green and casually said to Al, "Sure, we're not doing anything." Then, Sinatra happened to see us in the clubhouse and said, "Jim, I'm glad you met my good friend, Al. He owns City National Bank."

My ultimate "Ah Ha!" moment. It was all true. Al Hart was either the major stockholder or owner of all these companies. He had the goods after all, and the money.

Golf brought out many characters, and clients, and more than anything created the opportunity to build real relationships.

Baseball Hall of Fame icons Don Drysdale and Sandy Koufax loved the game, and they both hired me in 1966 to announce their salary dispute and threatened retirement from the Dodgers. They were asking for unheard-of salaries at the time. Drysdale wanted $105,000, and Koufax wanted $130,000. We made our pitch to management, and then went out and played golf every day until they came to their senses. It didn't take long.

World billiards champion Willie Mosconi was one of the best putters I'd ever seen. His touch on the greens was uncanny. Instead of a retainer, he wanted to pay me with billiards lessons. I opted for the fee instead.

When representing Perry Como television specials for General Telephone, Pat and I traveled to many of the garden spots of the world with the singing star, including Mexico, Bavaria, and Switzerland—and I played golf in all of them. I even had the pleasure of playing with royalty when Barron Hilton asked me to join him and the Prime Minister of the Polynesian Islands of Samoa for a round of golf on the island of Kauai.

But possibly the best of all were the many fun rounds of golf with another longtime client and pal, Andy Williams. He gave me singing lessons—on the course, no less. They didn't work. Somewhat in repayment years later, I introduced him to one of my Palm Springs golfing regulars Debbie Haas, an attractive redheaded beauty, who also knew how to play golf. They were married a few months later.

On another occasion I got a call from a man named Benny Binion. He said he owned a hotel and casino in Las Vegas, had heard of me and wanted to know if I was interested in helping him promote his hotel.

At this point, I was getting a lot of these kinds of referrals from people I didn't know. Word gets around when you handle the likes of Garland, Sinatra, McQueen, and Garner, but there was a big difference in promoting stars and promoting places, events, products, or companies. But these corporate referrals came from executives who thought that if you're good at publicizing top stars, you can publicize anything.

Mr. Binion wanted to know how much I would charge to do PR on his hotel and casino. Not exactly a golf story, yet, but stay with me.

I didn't know Binion, but I did remember there was a place in downtown Las Vegas that had a million dollars—He had ten thousand $100 bills in the window to make a Million Dollar display—framed and placed in a window so you couldn't miss it if you happened by the place.

The gimmick was to get unsuspecting visitors to come in for a free snapshot posing in front of the million dollars. The problem was, it took more than an hour to process the picture. By the time you got your photo, you lost whatever money you had on Binion's tables. What the hell did I have to lose? I told him I wanted $25,000 for one year, plus expenses.

"What are you talking about?" he shouted. "I can't afford that."

"Aren't you the guy with the million dollars framed in your picture window?"

"What the hell does that have to do with it?"

"Well, for one thing," I asked, "what do you think that million dollars in cash costs you just sitting there in the window for a year?"

"Not a goddamn thing," he said. "I own it."

We made the deal, and before too long we came up with another gimmick that put Binion's on the map. We created something called, "The World Series of Poker," a new, bigger version of his World Poker Championship. I really don't think I've met a more fascinating character than Benny Binion—all of five foot nine inches, rotund and balding.

Binion, despite his limited physical attributes, cut a dashing figure in his tailored western garb, his solid gold coin buttons, and custom-made cowboy boots. He was a true Vegas character. Giving him a run for his money in the character department were his number one son Jack, and the unforgettable players competing in the newly established "Binion's World Series of Poker."

The poker unforgettables were Doyle Brunson, Sailor Roberts, Jack Trout and the ever-popular Amarillo Slim. What fascinated me most about these players was that to a man, they loved three things: poker, ice cream, and golf. Before I got involved, Binion's poker championship was a closed affair, with fifty top players and friends kicking in $10,000 each. The winner took home $200,000. By the time I left the new "World Series of Poker," there were 10,000 entrants kicking in $10,000 each and the winner took home $8,000,000.

After a few years of promoting the Poker World Series, and knowing that all of these championship poker players were also golf nuts, we came up with another public relations idea that I thought would further promote and support both Binion and the Poker Championship. Thus begat the "Binion World Series of Poker Golf Championship," and all the poker players wanted to play in it. Jack Binion set the rules, the stakes, the pairings, the starting times, and whatever else there was to set. And the first rule was there were no rules.

You could tee up wherever and whenever you wanted, even in the sand traps. You could use any illegal ball, club, or piece of equipment known to man. And they did! One well known but illegal aid was to place a greasy substance on the face of a golf club, because when the ball is hit it will not only go straight but a long, long way. During that tournament, it was hard to find Vaseline in Las Vegas.

The wagering by these characters on the course made a joke of the stakes for the regular PGA tour events. If only the PGA Tour could sanction such a televised event, they would draw millions. Wagers were in the thousands of dollars per nine holes, and side bets included $5,000 golf cart races from tee to green on all par three holes. These guys could piss away money faster than anything I had ever seen, but it was all a hoot to them.

One of my favorite players was Jack "Tree Top" Strout, who was no better than a fifteen handicap on his best day. Strout stood at least six foot six and wore gloves on both hands. I never asked why. He had a bet of five thousand dollars a hole with a pal from Texas. But since Jack wasn't as good a player as his opponent, Jack could, at his own discretion, throw the ball instead of hitting it with a club, at least once each hole. They reached the eighteenth hole, and Jack needed a nine-foot putt to win $50,000.

Jack opted for the throw, and all six foot six of him stretched, reached out, and like a giant oak fell to the ground face down. He slam-dunked the ball in the hole for the win.

My game improved and my reputation among my clients increased to the point where I was getting invited to play in celebrity pro-amateur tournaments, like the Bing Crosby Invitational and the Bob Hope Pro-Am in Palm Springs.

One year, I won the Bob Hope Pro-Am with partners John Giumarra, a winemaker from Bakersfield, and Alex Spanos, owner of one the country's largest construction companies. After that, they both became clients.

Spanos is an interesting case in point on the power of golf.

Each year, Bob Hope hosted a private barbecue at his spectacular home in Palm Springs on the eve of his tournament. At one of these parties, Hope told me I had a lock on winning because it was clear to him that I had the best team in the field.

"Giumarra might be the best 18-handicap in the game...ever! And Spanos was good enough before he took the construction business seriously to play in the British Amateur. But more importantly," he went on, "Spanos might be the richest Greek in America and has the biggest plane at the airport. So, be nice to him because he lets me use that toy whenever I'm in need."

The next day on the first tee, I told Spanos that Hope had given me the rundown on him at last night's soiree.

"I'll tell you what we'll do Alex," I said. "We're going to win this tournament, and you're going to take me on the great big plane of yours to Scotland and Ireland for a golfing holiday to celebrate."

"Mahoney," he countered, "if we win this tournament, you've got a deal!"

We won the tournament.

But there was no trip to the old country. Instead he hired me to consult.

Spanos got his start feeding, housing, and caring for the immigrant farm workers in Stockton. California. He made a bundle. Next, he started investing in real estate. Then, he formed A.G. Spanos Construction Inc., which went on to become the most successful developer in the country.

Not long after my initial involvement with Spanos, he told me of his interest in buying a professional sports franchise, preferably football.

"I've got some connections," I said. "I can look into it for you."

These connections included my long-time friend and client Barron Hilton, who co-founded the American Football League with Lamar Hunt. Hilton owned thirty percent of the San Diego Chargers.

I had other connections, too. On my advisory committee were clients Howard Cosell, who knew as much as anyone about the workings of the NFL; Carroll Rosenbloom, owner of the Los Angeles Rams; and my best friend Don Klosterman, general manager of the Rams. My ace in the hole was Pete Rozelle, the NFL Commissioner and former head of PR for the L.A. Rams.

I started snooping around and asking some questions of my friends. It didn't take long to determine there were a few opportunities in other sports, too, such as the San Francisco Giants baseball team, but all were outrageously overpriced.

Spanos was able to spend upwards of $20 million if a team could be found. In a last-ditch effort, I asked… more like begged… Barron Hilton to talk with Spanos.

My relationship with Hilton began long before either of us even considered where destiny might take us. We were both kicked out of Loyola High School in 1945. Several years later, after he had successfully developed the Vita Pac Corporation, co-founded the American Football League "AFL," and created the Carte Blanche credit card, he answered his father's calling to help run the vast Hilton Hotel Corporation.

But when it came to Alex Spanos and his quest for a football team, Barron suggested we all talk it over at breakfast and over a round of golf at the Bel Air Country Club.

The next is a recount from Spanos' own memoir, *Share the Wealth*:

The end for me came during a USFL owners meeting in Chicago. I suggested that all of the owners put up a substantial amount of cash to ensure that the new league would have operating funds for three years. "No IOU's, no letters of credit," I added. Only one other owner offered to join me in putting up the cash.

Then someone stepped in to save me, in the place I had made so many critical contacts: on the golf course. I met Barron Hilton in 1981 through our mutual friend Jim Mahoney, a Los Angeles public relations executive who also represented Bob Hope and Johnny Carson. I'd also met Mahoney on a golf course, when we won the Bob Hope Classic in Palm Springs. Being in public relations, Jim spent part of his time introducing people. He invited me to play with him and Barron Hilton in Los Angeles.

I liked Barron immediately. After we hit our tee shots on the eighth hole at the Bel Air Country Club in Los Angeles, Barron and I rode together and talked about our mutually favorite subject, professional football. Barron's involvement with football dated back to 1959, when Texas oilman Lamar Hunt approached him with a plan to form a new professional football league, the American Football League (AFL). Hunt asked Hilton if he would be interested in taking the Los Angeles franchise. The idea appealed to Barron and he agreed to take what was then the Los Angeles Chargers.

When I met Barron, he still owned thirty percent of the Chargers. "Alex, I understand you are interested in going to the USFL. I don't think you belong there"…What he said next effectively ended my involvement in the USFL. "I own thirty percent of the San Diego Chargers, and I'd like to see you get involved with the NFL. I'd like to sell you ten percent, and with the ten percent you'll have the right of first refusal should Gene Klein ever want to sell the team. What do you think?"

What did I think? I would have rather owned ten percent of an NFL team than a hundred percent of the Los Angeles Express. I asked Barron what price he'd put on the ten percent.

"Four million dollars," said Barron.

"You've got a deal," I said, and we shook hands on it. From teeing off on the eighth hole to arriving on the green to putt, the deal took no more than eight minutes. I sent him a check for $4 million. No contract was needed. I trusted Barron implicitly.

More often than not, putting deals together or just putting people together was much more important than what went in or what was kept out of print. I felt as if I had done a good day's work.

A few days after the golf game, I asked Spanos how I figured into the deal, since it was my understanding if I helped him get into football, he'd "take care" of me. I was only looking for a rooting interest—maybe one percent. But Spanos went ballistic and said we had no such deal.

The next day, I dumped Spanos as a client.

Alex Spanos and I didn't speak for years, and it was more than uncomfortable running into him at La Quinta Country Club, where we both belonged.

But Barron Hilton stayed with me through thick and thin, we even laughed, begrudgingly, about Spanos and the deal, and we always found time to sneak out to Bel-Air at least twice a month to have lunch, talk business and relax. After taking his father's (Conrad Hilton) challenge in 1966 to run the family hotel empire, the company took off. I watched him override the Hilton Board and his father, and usher gaming into the mix of properties. He purchased the Flamingo and International hotels from Kirk Kerkorian in 1970, and things just started to take off for Hilton on a global level.

While representing Barron and the Hilton Hotel Corporation, we started some unique promotions, like the first-ever million-dollar jackpot slot machines and the Heavyweight Boxing Unification Series of prizefights, working with my client Don King. The unification series was a big deal, since it took the four or five heavyweight championship belts and combined them into one.

Barron and I traveled everywhere imaginable, including hotel groundbreakings and openings in Dublin, London, Brussels, Cancun, Australia, Hong Kong, and numerous trips to Hawaii. Never without our clubs. He took me for my first ride in a glider and I was his first passenger in a hot-air balloon at his expansive ranch, split partially in Northern California and partially in Nevada. The ranch was larger than the state of Rhode Island. We've also fished for trout on the East Walker River, for marlin off the coast of Cabo San Lucas, and for salmon in Alaska.

But the Spanos story always stuck in my craw, until something happened. Something I never expected.

Years later, at La Quinta Country Club during another Bob Hope Classic golf tournament, I was in the parking lot when I got a tap on the shoulder. I turned to find Alex Spanos staring squarely into my face.

"What is it with you?" he asked. "You never speak to me. You ignore me whenever we're together. Is something wrong?"

I couldn't believe what I was hearing.

"You're asking me what's wrong? Are you serious? After more than twenty years, you ask me what's wrong?"

"Yeah."

"You remember that Sunday at Bel Air on the eighth hole and the deal you struck with Barron?

"Yeah."

"I got nothing but shit and embarrassment from you. That's what's wrong Alex, in a nutshell."

He stood there stunned. It got his attention.

"You're absolutely right," he said. "I'm sorry, I'm truly sorry and I am going to make it up to you. "

I told him he knew where to find me if he was serious.

Two weeks later I received a note of apology, and a check for $100,000.

In the late 1960s and into the next decade, golf and Hollywood became a big business.

Everybody was on the course and playing at all the local clubs, from the Riviera to Bel Air to Lakeside. Stars would get a round in before or after their work on movies or television shows.

I probably spent more time on the golf course with Jack Lemmon than he's spent on a sound stage. We both played in Bing Crosby's tournament more than thirty times. Telly Savalas and I played, and won, a tournament in Barcelona, Spain, sponsored by Johnny Walker Scotch. Both Savalas and Johnny Walker were clients.

When Sinatra and I were in Rome for the filming of "Von Ryan's Express," we found time to play a few rounds of golf despite the ever-present paparazzi.

I also had the good fortune to play in, and win, my old MGM pal Howard Keel's celebrity tournament at the Mere Golf Club outside Birmingham, England. Glen Campbell and I had the pleasure on a misty Scottish morning to play the legendary North Berwick golf club with two-time Masters champion Ben Crenshaw. I birdied the 18th hole only to lose to Crenshaw's eagle.

Jim Garner and I spent every available morning or afternoon playing either Wentworth or Sunningdale golf courses, while in London for the filming of "The Americanization of Emily." The film's producer, Marty Ransohoff, was also a golf nut, as was James Coburn, one of the co-stars.

I soon switched over to a fulltime membership at Bel-Air Country Club. It was Gable, Strickling, and another client, Bob Sterling of the "Topper" television series, who, in 1962, sponsored me for membership at the club. There, the celebrities were thick and fun-loving, and the sky was limit for a PR guy in Hollywood.

After work in the morning, I'd head out to the course. I'd find Fred Astaire having lunch and we'd play nine holes. Astaire loved the game, and he was good. To say he had style was an understatement. He also liked to attend the L. A. Open Golf Tournament, and we went almost every year together. He was undoubtedly the shyest superstar I've ever known and would go to unbelievable lengths to hide his identity at these tournaments. He hoped for bad weather, so that he could bundle up in a raincoat, a hat and scarf, and dark glasses under a huge umbrella.

He got a big kick out of meeting the golfing elite. But I got a bigger charge from the reactions the golfers had meeting him. I'd say, "Please meet my good friend, Fred Astaire." By the time they realized who it was under the hat in the dark glasses with the collar turned up, they were speechless.

Soon, it wasn't just Fred Astaire, but many others I was spending serious time with and assisting with whatever issues or help they may need when it came to the press and Hollywood. Bel-Air opened up many doors to me. In fact, on one my first days there, I met Bob Newhart during a game of golf. Right away, I started representing him.

If not the most memorable, certainly the most poignant game of golf I ever played was with Clark Gable. It was right before he was to start filming "The Misfits." We laughed about the old MGM days and Strickling and those grand old times in Hollywood. I never got over how a kid like me could be in such rarified company.

It turned out that was the last game of golf Clark Gable ever played. Two weeks after filming "The Misfits," Gable died of a heart attack at the age of fifty-nine.

As I near the end of this chapter, expansive as it is in representing how far-reaching the game of golf was in my business, I would be remiss if I didn't mention another long-time friend and lover of the game of golf, the legendary *Los Angeles Times* sports writer Jim Murray. Winner of the Pulitzer Prize, inducted into the Baseball Hall of Fame, winner of the Associated Press' Sports Editors Award for best column writing, the Red Smith Award for lifelong achievement in sports writing, and many, many more. No sports columnist could put pen to print better than Murray. When others were covering stats, he was writing poetry. Ironically, it was Jim who first suggested that I write a book about my life in showbiz. Whenever we'd finish a round at Bel-Air CC we'd inevitably end up at "the smart table" in the grillroom, a table known to attract top entertainers and industry titans. The table is also famous for a small sign on it which reads: "If you don't have anything nice to say, pull up a chair." Jim and I would no sooner sit than multitudes would flock, just to be near him and hear him wax eloquent on any topic. One of my all-time favorite columns of his was one where he went on about losing his best friend. He goes through describing all of these great events and moments in his life that they shared together, and the reader doesn't find out until the end that he's referring to his left eye. It almost makes me tear up just talking about it. There will never be another writer like Jim Murray, and I was lucky enough to call him my friend.

One can tell a lot about a person by how they play the game of golf. As the sportswriter Grantland Rice once said, "Eighteen holes of match or medal play will teach you more about your foe than eighteen years of dealing with him across a desk." True to fact, I can usually size up a person, their character and/or temperament by the fourth hole. Golf is a game of honor. And if a person's prone to look for an edge on the course, they are more than likely going to do the same in business.

Chapter Thirty-One

No Thanks for the Memories

AS BIG A nut as I was for the game of golf, I was nothing compared to Bob Hope.

Granted, his name is legend in the world of entertainment, but the man was crazy about the game of golf. It was no act. He took a club with him wherever he went, and even had a short hole built in his Toluca Lake backyard. When home, he played at least nine holes at nearby Lakeside Country Club every day.

The thing about golf, though, is that it is so very competitive. And there are times that the competition can be an issue off the links as well as on. Never was this more evident than when having represented Sinatra and then subsequently Bob Hope in 1977, their rivalry played out for me not on the links but over the links.

Working for Hope was a real pleasure. He was not only a lot of fun but knew as much about publicity and promotion as any performer I've ever been around. And he knew how to use it. Given that he had a fulltime publicist, Ward Grant, Hope wanted me to concentrate on his television activities, since he liked what I was doing for Sinatra and his TV specials. This was a bit ironic, as Bob Hope and Frank Sinatra basically just didn't like each other. The Hope-Sinatra rivalry was built on a foundation of jealousy. Many times during my years of representing Sinatra, he wanted to know why Hope was "getting all the favorable publicity."

It bothered Sinatra that the press ignored Hope's obvious and numerous indiscretions, yet they would jump all over Sinatra for his slightest hiccup. By the same token, during my long association with Hope, he'd frequently ask why Sinatra was getting "such good press for doing nothing."

On one occasion when Hope complained about the lack of coverage, he asked me why my team couldn't be more creative.

"Like what do you want?" I asked.

"How about my picture on a postage stamp?" he asked.

"For that you have to die." I told him.

"Well," he stammered, "That's out of the question. Come up with something else."

Both of them had homes in the desert, Hope in Palm Springs and Sinatra in nearby Rancho Mirage. One day, Frank telephoned me with irritation in his voice. "How is it Bob Hope has a street named after him and I don't?"

The inference was clear, I had to lobby the town fathers to even the score, and it wasn't easy. Some city council members initially resisted, and I suspected Hope of stirring up the opposition. But to this day, traffic runs smoothly along both Bob Hope and Frank Sinatra Drives. They even intersect in Rancho Mirage. If both had it their way, they would have probably found a way to make sure that didn't happen.

Their hostilities went back to the time Hope and his then-manager, Jimmy Saphier, were putting together a television special for his sponsor, Chrysler. Hope, never one to spend a lot of money or any more than he had to on guest performers, agreed on a plan presented to him by Saphier and his agent at the time, Elliot Kozak. Rather than try and go after three or four stars with the $50,000 allotted budget, why not give Sinatra the entire $50,000 and put on a super, big time, two-man show?

Hope went for the idea, and Saphier contacted Sinatra's attorney, Mickey Rudin, who in turn presented the idea to Sinatra. Everyone agreed. The show was set. Not for long, however. Chrysler management wanted no part of Sinatra. He was not the image they wanted to project. They wanted to sell automobiles to "All American" families, not the Rat Pack.

"Broom Sinatra!" was Chrysler's order of the day.

Hope and his advisors found themselves between the proverbial rock and a hard place. Hope told Saphier to get out of the Sinatra booking and start recasting. Word of Chrysler's slam got back to Rudin and Sinatra before Saphier had a chance to call Rudin. Enraged and hurt by the snub, Sinatra told Rudin that as far as he was concerned, he had a deal and would settle for nothing less than the entire $50,000. He got it, and thus begat the spat. Sinatra later said that if the roles had been reversed, he would have told Chrysler "to go fuck themselves." And I believe he would have. But Hope wasn't Sinatra. Sinatra gave the money to charity.

Hope seized his chance to get back at Sinatra a few years later, but it was more the desert charities in Palm Springs that suffered the major loss than the singer.

Sinatra was always impressed with the success Bing Crosby had with his annual charity driven celebrity pro-am golf tournament at Pebble Beach, earlier known as the "Crosby Clambake." In the fall of 1965, Sinatra asked me to investigate the possibilities of his hosting a similar PGA event in Palm Springs. Hope had already lent his name to the Palm Springs Desert Classic. A year earlier, Sinatra had hosted a pro-am event at the Canyon Country Club. We called it the "Sinatra Swingfest."

It was hailed by celebrities and golf professionals and whetted Sinatra's appetite for a regular PGA tour event. The celebrity participation in this tournament was top notch. But then again, who's going to turn down Frank Sinatra?

Next, Frank wanted me to secure an annual PGA tour event under his name. I started setting up meetings with the PGA Tournament Committee. The committee was next scheduled to meet at Augusta National, during the famous Masters Tournament. I was invited to make a presentation at what might be considered the Sistine Chapel of Golf.

My meeting was set for a Thursday morning at 11:30. I arrived at 8:00 to catch some of the tournament, but when the meeting neared, I was told to wait under the large oak tree adjacent to the clubhouse. Someone would come for me.

It all seemed a little cloak and dagger, but I really got concerned around 11:45 when no one showed, and I sensed a foul up somehow. By noon, I was damned near beside myself. This was a one-time opportunity and it was quickly passing me by.

"Hey Mahoney," a voice finally yelled out. "Weren't you supposed to meet with us this morning?"

I turned, and coming toward me was my good friend and former Masters champion, Doug Ford.

"Yeah," I told him. "I was told to wait right here and someone would bring me up to the meeting."

I could tell right away that Doug was upset.

"Follow me."

We rushed into the clubhouse, down a few hallways, and into a small room where it was apparent a meeting was just breaking up. Still present were committee members Gardner Dickinson, Dan Sikes, Jack Nicklaus, and PGA officials such as Max Elbin and Leo Fraser, among several others.

Clearing his throat, Ford called out, "This is Jim Mahoney," loudly enough for everyone to hear. "Did someone forget he came all the way from Los Angeles to meet with us?"

I was definitely in a hostile atmosphere, and it threw me. They certainly knew I was coming to propose a new tournament, and it would mean more money for the PGA, the players, and, more importantly, charity. What the hell was the problem?

After the introductions came the interrogation. "What kind of tournament does Mr. Sinatra want?"

"That would be up to you people of course, but what he'd really like is something like Bing does at Pebble Beach," I answered.

Elbin asked: "How much of a purse is he willing to come up with?"

"I would assume that you people would tell us how much you want," I replied, "but we'd like to be at least equal to the biggest purse that you have."

"That's a million dollars," Elbin fired back sarcastically. "Does Mr. Sinatra have a million dollars?"

"On him!" I answered seriously but was able to break a bit of the tension—just a bit, though.

But that exchange gave me my first indication as to what the real problem was. "We already have a tournament in Palm Springs. Where would he like to have his tournament?"

"Palm Springs and only Palm Springs," I replied. "There is no reason a resort of that size can't handle two tournaments a year."

I wasn't making any headway. It looked like Doug Ford, and possibly Gardner Dickinson, a longtime friend of mine as well as of Frank's, were on my side, but the others never cracked a smile.

Then I was asked what kind of sponsors I thought Frank could bring to the table. I told them I was sure that Anheuser Busch would like to be part of the package, as would Singer Sewing Machines, and that there were probably many others waiting in the wings.

Still, I was waiting to be welcomed with open arms, but I was getting little more than the cold shoulder. The meeting adjourned as quickly as it began, and I was told they would consider the offer and put it to a vote with the players at their next meeting in New Orleans, a few months hence.

After that meeting, both Ford and Dickinson confirmed my fears. The powers that be within the PGA hierarchy felt an obligation to protect Hope and his territory, Palm Springs. They didn't think the area could or would support more than one tournament. But probably more important was the fact that Hope didn't want competition, and Sinatra would certainly bring that on big time.

Hope was well aware that Sinatra's tournament the previous year was voted the "Best Run Tournament of the Year" by the pros. In retrospect, any fear the PGA may have had that the area couldn't support more than one tournament was and is a joke and was proven in the years that followed.

In the ensuing weeks, between the Masters and the New Orleans tournament, I spoke with many of the tour players and they all thought the Sinatra stop in Palm Springs would make a great addition to the tour. I was assured that when the plan was put to a vote in New Orleans, we'd get our tournament.

I went to New Orleans to be on hand for the meeting and hopefully some good news. After the meeting, I was told the players voted for the tournament and their recommendation would go to the policy board, and I should hear officially within a few weeks. Both Gardner Dickinson and Doug Ford cautioned me not to get my hopes up. "The Hope camp is turning on the pressure, don't get too excited."

A few days later, I happened to run into Hope on the putting green at Lakeside Country Club. I asked him if he'd do me a favor and answer a simple question.

"Sure kid, what is it?"

"You probably know I've been trying to get a tournament in the Springs for Frank," I began.

"Right…"

"Tell me," I begged. "Are we ever going to get it?"

"No chance," he said.

I thanked him for being so candid.

I got word from the tour policy board the next day. They asked: "Would Mr. Sinatra consider a tournament in another city?"

The answer was "NO!"

It wasn't the end. CBS television golf producer/director Frank Chirkinian gave it one more try. He worked up a plan for CBS to create a new Frank Sinatra tournament and even wrote Frank a telegram saying the network was on board. It was a unique format, and Chirkinian sent me a different telegram outlining the new pro-celebrity tournament set up.

It read:

"An 8-week series beginning in mid-January running from 4-5 pm EST on Saturday afternoons. 8 top pros team with 8 celebrities in a team match play elimination tournament…the final would be 36 holes…winners get $50,000 each."

The legendary CBS announcers Jack Whitaker and Ken Venturi were to be the on-air commentators, and the event was scheduled to be played and recorded in December at Canyon Country Club in Palm Springs, the site of Sinatra's earlier success in the golf tournament business.

The only issue that remained, Chirkinian said, was getting the PGA to sign off on the deal. But again, Bob Hope's power at the PGA and in Palm Springs was insurmountable. The PGA, under Hope's weight, ultimately said "No" to the pro-am series.

Sinatra's reply was simple: "No Palm Springs, no tournament." Frank's beloved golf tournament was never to be.

As I mentioned earlier, Hope became a full-fledged client in 1977, and many times I had the good fortune to be with him on his travels around the world. We were in Tokyo some years back when a golf promoter was trying to put together a tournament similar to Hope's annual Palm Springs event, the Bob Hope Desert Classic. We'd just finished a successful press conference announcing the affair and were relaxing in the hotel's elegant Presidential suite high atop the Hotel Atami. It was nice to be back in Japan, but under more auspicious circumstances than the last time I was there as the odd Army sergeant in the Korean War. Word had just come over the news that a typhoon had flattened parts of Okinawa and was now bearing down on us. Rain pelted so hard that the streets were flooding fast.

"Let's go hit some balls," Hope said.

"HIT SOME BALLS?" I said, incredulously. "Did I hear you correctly? Have you looked outside?

"Yeah," he said calmly. "That doesn't mean anything. There's a place right here in the middle of Tokyo twice the size of Dodger Stadium that's covered, and you can hit balls to your heart's content, no matter what the weather. Get hold of that interpreter and ask the driver to be downstairs in ten minutes."

Within half an hour, we were in the middle of the wildest thing I'd ever seen, an indoor three-tiered driving range with more than a hundred separate hitting areas and every single one occupied. Adjacent to the driving range was a teaching area, and next to that, a huge putting green. To get to the driving range, you had to pass through the most elaborate shopping center for golf equipment I'd ever seen.

Hope and I took turns hitting balls for about half an hour. I got a bright idea. What a great picture this would make for newspapers and television back home. Again, golf was always the safe photo-op.

It didn't take long, especially in Tokyo, to find someone with a camera.

I was halfway through the first roll, getting these great shots of Hope hitting balls, with three hundred golf nuts doing the same thing behind and around him for as far as the eye could see, when out of nowhere this guy started screaming at me in Japanese.

"What's his problem?" I asked the interpreter.

"He's the owner and he doesn't allow pictures to be taken here."

I told the interpreter to tell the owner these pictures would make him famous. This was Bob Hope for Christ's sake. People clamored for his endorsement. What gives?

"No," said the interpreter. "That's just the point. If you take these pictures back to America, he's afraid someone will steal his great idea."

That evening, the weather worsened, so instead of remaining in Japan, we canceled a sightseeing trip to Mt. Fuji and headed back home to sun-drenched Hawaii, where we checked into the Hilton Hawaiian Village, also a client. Bob Hope and I played golf for three days.

Bob wasn't a Depression baby, per se, but a lot of his upbringing carried over to his adult life. One character trait that seemed to stand out more than others with Bob was that he was known for being very frugal. One case in point was when Alex Spanos told me that he gave Bob a plane of his use whenever he wanted it, and Bob gave it back. He didn't want to pay for the gas. Another time Bob tracked my son Sean down on the beaches of Cabo San Lucas. There were no cell phones at the time. When Sean finally came to the phone, concerned that there might be something wrong, Hope started telling him stories about when he and Bing used to go down there and the fun they had. Then he got to the point. He heard that I had signed up for the pay-per-view fight between Sugar Ray Leonard and Tommy Hearns and wanted to know if he thought it would be alright if he stopped by. Bob lived in Toluca Lake and I was in Beverly Hills, probably an hour away easily at that time of day, and the fight probably only cost $25 back then. And finally, Pat and I were coming home from La Quinta around the late 90s, and were not more than fifteen minutes on the 10 freeway heading towards L.A. when we decided to pull off to get In-N-Out burgers for the road. I got out of the car and as I approached the restaurant I saw Bob and his driver coming out. I said: "Bob, what the hell are you doing way out here at In-N-Out?"

And without hesitation, he reached into his pocket and pulled out a piece of paper. "Well, I've got these coupons!"

That being said, Bob and I had a lot of fun over the years. Whenever he'd call he used to open with a joke, and they were always killers. Dirty as hell, but hysterical. I used to love trading new jokes I heard, but they were never as good as his. Consistent with many of my high profile clients, he was another unique character whose likes we'll never see again. Thanks for the memories, Bob!

photgraph by John Engstead
We sent family Christmas photos every year
for nearly 50 years!

Sightseeing in England with James
Garner while filming
"The Americanization of Emily"

Hanging out with RJ and Rita Moreno.
Everyone wanted to hang out with RJ.

Andy's TV specials always made
Christmas memorable.

At sea with Peggy Lee on the
SS United States Luxury Ocean Liner

Lunch for Elvis' manager Colonel Tom
Parker at MGM. Another of his typical
PR stunts!

Perry Como & his Coachman with me on the set in London for one of his
many Christmas Specials.

The Duke demanded that Alex Spanos and I get
in the picture with he and Hope!

Do you think Arnold's trying to get our attention? My Par (short for partner)
Tony Jacklin and me at Pebble.
Credit: Peter Borsari

Garner was quite the Maverick on and off the golf course.

Teeing it up on The Old Course with George C., Lemmon and my son Michael.

RJ and I really got to know each other on the golf course, boy can he play the game!

Lemmon's lifetime goal, to make the cut at The Crosby.

Dean was a great golfer and even better friend.

Giving Hope a putting lesson or was it the other way around?

Newhart and I on a typically rainy day at Pebble

RJ hugging Pat, everybody loved Pat!

Partner Tony Jacklin and me at Pebble Beach. We were
told we won, only minutes later to be told otherwise.
Golf is a four letter word!

Alex Spanos, Jerry Pate, Barron Hilton and me at
Howard Cosell's All American's Golf Tournament.

photograph by Michael Jacobs

Nothing but laughs with Bob Newhart and Dick Martin.

Cheers to my good friend
Dick Martin!

Sir Nick Faldo, one of my favorite
"Crosby" partners.

Artist LeRoy Neiman, my favorite MGTD, and me.

Chapter Thirty-Two

Wasso's Star Wars

I FIRST MET Paul Wasserman, "Wasso" as friends called him, when he was working for United Press International. He worked for Henry Gris, the Hollywood foreign correspondent for the wire service. By the time I met him, he had ingratiated himself with journalists of all kinds and he knew everyone in town. He knew Hollywood inside and out, better than I did, and he had incredible relationships with members of the press who were literally unapproachable to most PR types.

Wasso had written an article about Bob Hope, and I always thought it was rather unflattering, but clearly the Hope camp thought otherwise. So, they hired him to work with their publicity team. Paul was bright, enthusiastic, generous to a fault, and affable. Everyone liked him, and it was as if he, like I, was tailor made for the public relations business.

One day in the early 60s, he came to me and asked, "You need an assistant?"

"Wasso," I said, "are you serious? Of course I need an assistant like you."

So, Paul Wasserman joined my company, and he took to the game like a natural.

There were personality quirks. He could be standoffish until you got to know him, and he had a strange sense of humor, equal parts acerbic and cerebral. For instance, whenever anyone would casually ask, "Hey Paul, how are you?, he'd reply, "Stop prying!"

Wasso's best asset to me, over and above his workaholic twenty-hour days, was that people in the music industry really liked him. Music publicity was his game. Even having worked with the likes of Sinatra, Vic Damone, Tony Bennett, Paul Anka, Roy Orbison, Andy Williams, and Peggy Lee, that still didn't provide me the kind of entrée to a certain part of the music business to which Wasserman was most adept.

He spoke the language of the Beach Boys, the Mamas and the Papas, and eventually Carly Simon, James Taylor, Paul Simon, Bob Dylan, George Harrison, the Rolling Stones, the Who, Linda Ronstadt, Neil Diamond, and U2, among many others.

When Wasserman came on board, we started representing them all. It wasn't long before this smart and well-connected associate was bringing in more business than I was. I saw the handwriting on the wall. I figured I had two choices again: lose the business when Wasso goes out on his own or make him a partner in the firm. I made him a partner, but with no financial ownership. Wasso stayed, and my reluctance proved prescient.

It was by now the early 1970s, a time when the music industry was changing and exploding at the same time. And so, Jim Mahoney & Associates became Mahoney/Wasserman Public Relations.

Wasserman simply earned his keep and earned his place on the letterhead. Selfishly for me, having his name there made it easier for the company to gain access to a whole new roster of clients. I personally had few dealings with Dylan, the Stones, and the rest of our new "A List" of clients that represented the new generation of music.

There was no question about it. Paul was simply the best PR man around when it came to this generation of musicians. Paul was also connected in other aspects of show business. He was personally responsible for landing several rather important film assignments, including "Easy Rider," "Five Easy Pieces," and "The Rocky Horror Picture Show," among many.

In this regard, I was somewhat taken by surprise one afternoon when my secretary buzzed to tell me Alan Ladd Jr. was calling.

I'd known "Laddie" for years, having spent many wonderful hours with him and his family at their home in Beverly Hills and their ranch in Hidden Valley. I watched his rise in the industry, from a gopher to agent to producer to head of production at 20th Century Fox. The man was a real Hollywood success story. But on this particular afternoon, Laddie had a problem.

"We've got this picture we really don't know how to position or sell," he explained. "We've got more than $20 million in it, but the good news is there's a slim chance Universal will take half of it. If I can't pull that off, and if you're willing, and if I could get the director to agree to putting you on the picture, we could do some business."

"That's a lot of 'ifs,'" I said, "but it sounds good to me. What's the movie and who's the director?"

Ladd hemmed and hawed, but he finally described it.

"It's a sort of sci-fi thing, it's called 'Star Wars' and other than a few of us, not many people around here are too high on its potential."

"Star Wars?" I asked.

"You'll have no stars to work with, and the producer and director will be of little help since they're up to their asses with the final edit. The picture opens in six weeks."

"Who's the director?" I asked.

"George Lucas, and he's no bargain to deal with."

As luck would have it, Universal begged off the partnership, Lucas okayed our hiring, and we were off and running on the new picture. Stumbling might be more like it.

Laddie set up a no-music, rough-cut screening of the film for my staff. He had the composer John Williams set up for the score later. After seeing the film, we all looked at one another and said nothing, but it was blatantly obvious that our work was cut out for us. A few of my in-house critics likened it to the old "Flash Gordon" serial flicks.

The so-called "stars" were young actors Carrie Fisher (none other than the daughter of Debbie Reynolds and Eddie Fisher, and my own kid's friend) and Mark Hamill. These were not exactly household names. Alec Guinness, at least a "name" actor, was unavailable for interviews, and another unknown, an actor named Harrison Ford, was off working on another film.

Making matters worse, Lucas didn't want any opinion makers or reviewers seeing any part of the film until he was finished. It's nearly impossible to sell a picture if you can't get the media to see it, especially banned screenings for the national media types. No matter how we looked at this project, it was going to be a tough sell. To make matters worse, Lucas wouldn't budge on his rules.

This is where Paul Wasserman earned his keep ten-fold.

Wasso had a writer friend at *Time* magazine who was a big George Lucas fan. If given the opportunity to see the film, she told him that she would write up a favorable review or not write at all. This was exactly what we needed to promote this turkey.

Fearing failure on the project more than firing, we invited *Time's* Martha Duffy to a secret viewing of the film. Laddie helped with this clandestine screening in one of Goldwyn's editing rooms. He was just as desperate for our success as we were, but somehow word got back to Lucas. He went ballistic. He wanted us off the picture and told Laddie to fire us, immediately. That was a Thursday. On Monday, *Time* came out with a cover story hailing "Star Wars" as "THE PICTURE OF THE YEAR."

Paul made it happen, and we were fired.

Less than a year later, Laddie left Fox in a battle with top management over bonuses for participants of this box office bonanza. Mahoney/Wasserman was not a part of this giveaway program and were never called upon to do another film for the studio.

The music business, from the earliest days of rock and roll and into the disco and club years, found recreational drugs simply part of the mix—as much a part of life as inspiration was to the music itself.

Despite being immersed in the world, surrounded by temptation, the one thing I could always credit Paul with was his resistance to that temptation. At this stage, he never partook of the drugs around him. In fact, he famously stumbled upon Janis Joplin shooting up during the Monterey Jazz Festival and assumed she was a diabetic.

Then, as was told to me by him, when working closely with one of our clients, the Rolling Stones, Wasserman was accused of being too straight and no fun.

"Try some of this," uttered one of the band members.

This time, he did. It was the beginning of the end for Wasso. It wasn't long before he was on the wrong side of a three-gram a day cocaine habit. Eventually, it took over. He even boasted while on tour with Bob Dylan of having snorted cocaine off the President's desk in the White House Oval Office during the Carter administration. And yet, strangely enough, it never cost us business.

He always did his job, but perhaps with a more intense, high-octane, frenetic fanaticism than was necessary. I should have seen the signs, but I never did. Wasso simply moved and maneuvered in a different world and at a different pace than I. Perhaps if I had known the signs, I could have changed things.

Fast forward a few chaotic years and it all caught up with him. It was over New Year's Eve, 1981. Pat and I were enjoying our usual sojourn to Las Vegas as annual guests of Barron Hilton. Paul, who had been working incredibly hard touring with the Stones, had opted to stay on in New Orleans for the wrap party following the tour's final concert performance.

I got a call on New Year's Day from Bill Wyman's girlfriend, Astrid Lundstrom. "It's Paul," she said.

"What's wrong?" I asked.

"He overdosed at the party or sometime after," she said. "He was on a binge, Jim. He's in a coma."

I went upstairs to what used to be the Elvis Suite at the Hilton, where they

held the New Year's party and now the subsequent New Year's Day brunch—
Bloody Marys and football on the television. I walked up to Barron and told
him what happened. Just then, one of his lieutenants came up to say they
were taking a group from New Orleans back home on the Hilton jet, a Bach
111, at noon.

"How many are there?" I asked.

"There are only six."

"When's the plane coming back?"

"As soon as we drop them off, we'll refuel, turn around and come back."

"Barron," I said, "do you mind if go along and hold the plane for a couple
of hours while I go down and see if Paul's all right?"

"Of course, stay as long as you have to."

I flew in the Hilton jet and arrived at the New Orleans hospital shortly
after midnight. Out in the hallway of the intensive care unit were three
people waiting: client Jack Nicholson, record producer Lou Adler, and
Wyman's gal Astrid. The doctors didn't think he was going to make it.

I sat there for a few hours, and the four of us talked about Wasso, what
a great guy he was, how he got in over his head, how we hoped he'd pull
through.

I left and flew home. There was nothing I could do. The best course of
action was to try to keep the business going, for my sake and for Wasso's.

Wasso, it turned out, was in a coma for three weeks. Once he awoke, he
immediately had a stroke. It took six months of rehabilitation in Los Angeles
to get him back to something close to normal. But when he did return to
work, he was never the same. He felt awful about what happened, but he also
had other ideas about his future.

"Jim," he said one morning. "I gotta do something on my own. I'm
quitting. I'm just not happy here."

I was shocked, but I understood. We parted as friends. I was truly sorry
to see him go. We had a really good thing going for a long time. He took
several of his clients with him and opened his own PR agency. But on his
own, his business, although successful for a time, began to unravel. He had
been so busy making the careers of others, he felt he had cheated himself.
He was always looking for the big deal. "Where's my $20 million deal?" he
often asked no one in particular.

Out of this need, Wasserman began selling a series of investments to his
friends and clients. He peddled shares in companies he formed, which were
funded, he said, by his lucrative clients, including Nicholson. Twenty, thirty,
forty thousand dollars was what he was asking for from his longtime friends

and associates.

Of course, there was no company and there were no investors like Nicholson. It was all made up. By the time reality crumbled around him, he was sentenced to six months in jail and five years' probation.

Wasso summed up his life best in a long interview with the *Los Angeles Times*.

"I've always liked living on the edge," he said in the article. "But I guess I realize I don't have the ability to kill myself, so now I'm facing the music."

I went to see him in jail, and I asked why he never offered any of his "bargain stocks" to me.

"You would have known it was bullshit from the get-go," he said.

Wasso died penniless in a convalescent home. Friends had to solicit funds for his entombment at Forest Lawn in Burbank. The Irish rock group U2, a big client, pitched in, and the Stones were approached, too. They replied, "No way, we paid him enough!"

Wasso's end was tragic, but he defied Strickling's cardinal rule: stay out of the story. Paul let his ego get the best of him. Like his clients, he craved being in the spotlight. He wanted to be respected and rewarded the same as his clients. Ultimately, this need sucked him into a downward spiral, he became the story, and it killed him.

Chapter Thirty-Three

Crisis Management

LOS ANGELES IS known for a few things, not the least of which are Hollywood and earthquakes. The earth is constantly moving all over southern California, from Palm Springs to San Diego and up the coast to Santa Barbara. In 1969, my family and I were confronted with a major crisis more personal in nature, when the earth started moving behind our house on Anthony Place in the hills above Beverly Hills, and the mountain behind us separated fifteen feet from its side. It was headed downhill, and the county authorities said the whole mountainside might bury our entire house and yard.

It was January, and I got a frantic call from Pat while I was playing golf in the Bing Crosby Invitational at Pebble Beach. I told her to get everyone out and over to our parents' places. We split the kids up and began looking for someplace new to live. We still owned the old house on Clearview, but it was rented out to another family. We were stuck, homeless, and searching for a new spot, maybe closer to Beverly Hills Catholic School where the kids were all attending, which is now called Good Shepherd after its affiliated church on Santa Monica Blvd. and Bedford Dr.

By a stroke a luck, we came across a couple looking to downsize from their home in the flats of Beverly Hills at 710 North Camden, and they thought our Clearview house was perfect. So, we swapped properties, sold the Anthony Place house (after the hill was stabilized), and put down some additional cash and moved into what would be the greatest house imaginable for the family and my work. From crisis came gain.

The house on North Camden was a full-fledged estate compared to our other homes, and was once the home of Jeanette McDonald and Nelson

Eddy, musical superstars of the 40s and 50s.

It had a beautiful large avocado tree and paddle tennis court in back, a large lawn in the front, and a French country feel. Later we removed the avocado tree, to my wife's chagrin because she loved avocados, and added a large pool. The bedrooms were bigger for the kids, and there was a cozy den and bar area for smoking cigars and having a cocktail. It was often the case that the kids would come home and find Sinatra and I having a drink and watching the fights in the den—or Hope, or George C. Scott, or Jack Lemmon, or Gene Kelly, or Sean Connery, or Howard Cosell—or any number of celebrities sitting in my little haven.

On the professional front and now moving into the mid-1970s, the Mahoney PR machine was in full-gear. From the early beginnings on my own in Frank's William Morris office on El Camino, to getting my own space nearby at 120 El Camino, to eventually being the proud owner of my own building on Little Santa Monica Boulevard, immediately adjacent to the soon-to-be Peninsula Hotel, across from the Friar's Club. Things were nonstop growth.

The constant irony of the new office building was imagining the ghost of old L.B., Louis B. Mayer, my old boss, who had his final office in the same building and space as mine after he was pushed out at MGM. There was something spooky about that, but I got over it. I was too busy to think about anything but my eight to ten employees and maybe fifty clients to keep happy. Every phone call was a piece of new business, someone pissed off, or someone firing us. I got to where I hated hearing the phone ring, and that dread has never left. But more and more it seemed to be ringing for a crisis.

Crisis management is nothing new in Hollywood. In fact, Hollywood may have invented it. MGM Police Chief Whitey Hendrey was one of the early practitioners. Most of his job was burying the bones, and all the studios were good at that. They had the machinery in place, and more importantly contract players had little choice but to toe the company line. The end result: those hurt were compensated and the rest disappeared.

When the studio system collapsed, the business of cleaning up the mess was left to us, the PR pros. Call them press agents, publicists, communication counselors or just plain flacks, if you got in trouble and didn't have one of us around, it was as good as flying solo. Crisis management was the most difficult part of our profession, where we earned our stripes … and pay. And over the course of my career (and I've had my share of success in tough situations), I've been helped by four rules:

Rule One: Money talks.

Rule Two: Pay big and pay fast.

Rule Three: Keep it out of the press.

Rule Four: Rules One and Two usually make Rule Three much easier.

I had just sat down in my den to watch the evening news when the Hilton Hotel in Las Vegas flashed on the screen. It was going up in flames—a real "Towering Inferno." This is one of those nightmares that has to play out. You simply can't predict the ending, and you don't want to spin misinformation. Just months earlier, a similar fire hit the MGM Grand on the strip and killed eighty-four people.

I immediately called Barron Hilton and was told he'd just left for his plane en route to Vegas. I left the house immediately and luckily caught up with him at Santa Monica Airport just as he was boarding. I got on the plane with him, and when we arrived the fire was still raging.

It was intense, reportedly traveling from the 8th story where it began to the 28th in just fifteen minutes. There were 4,000 people in that hotel, including the casino, and 2,700 rooms.

My responsibility was to concentrate on what the fire was doing to the client. These were not the pictures and images a hotel man wants circulating on newscasts and newspapers for weeks to come.

Once in Las Vegas, with the firefighters still working to put the fire out, I couldn't help recalling the media disaster the MGM Grand suffered. As a result of that fire, hotel guests up and down The Strip were requesting rooms below the fourth floor. Even Barron Hilton himself insisted on staying in the lower floors after the MGM tragedy, when he previously always stayed in the finest Hilton penthouse suites.

The disaster at the MGM escalated because the hotel had no plan. Management was totally caught off guard by the speed and magnitude of the smoke and flames. MGM hotel executives were being interviewed on television while their guests were literally jumping from windows of the high-rise structure down to the streets below.

Adding insult to injury, they had no answers for the inquiring journalists. They all just stood by helplessly. MGM was decimated with the ensuing coverage and, in fact, was subsequently sold to Bally's, which renamed and rebranded the hotel to eliminate the taint.

It looked as if Hilton might suffer the same fate. Flames were licking the exterior of the building from the rooms. But worse still, eight people had died—an elderly man and his wife in a tenth-floor bathroom and one woman on the twenty-first floor. One man died after being found by firefighters in the rubble, and still another one jumped and landed on the pool deck. In addition to the other three who lost their lives, another 198 were taken to the hospital with various injuries.

I told Barron, customarily cool and collected, that we had to find the cause immediately and get that story out. "We have to control this with the press," I said.

He looked at me and said nothing, but then he nodded. "Let's find out and then let's get it out," I said.

It's important that you control the press and don't let the narrative control you. Fortunately for Hilton, it was quickly determined by Las Vegas Fire Department inspectors that this blaze was the work of an arsonist. The hotel fire prevention system was up to code, and the Hilton was as safe a hotel as there was in the country at the time.

To help lend credibility, I found the Las Vegas Fire Chief, Roy Parrish, and got him to give me a quote detailing what happened. Within an hour, every major wire service, network and news organization in the world got the story, with the details of the arsonist. I also suggested to Hilton that he offer a $100,000 reward for anyone with information leading to the arrest of said arsonist.

That evening, I asked the governor of Nevada, Robert List, if he would preside over a press conference the next morning along with the fire chief and the president of the hotel. I suggested to the governor that with the importance of tourism in his great state, it might go a long way with recovery if he were to make a special point of mentioning Hilton's diligence and care for all concerned parties during this emergency. He was eloquent.

Lives were lost, people were injured, and that is never easy to take. It was a dark time for Hilton, but the communications helped. My job was to make sure the Hilton organization also didn't die that night.

Not all disasters and tragedies can be controlled.

Alan Ladd was one of my first clients and one of the most loyal, but he had serious problems, not the least of which was vodka. His two big films, "This Gun for Hire" and "Shane," made him a box office superstar. But when a career fades, everything fades. He was no longer interested in anything except a steady supply of vodka with a splash of water. Guests believed he was sipping a tall glass of water, when some of us knew otherwise.

On one occasion, I was with a visiting journalist from *Better Homes & Gardens* magazine and was showing off Ladd's unusual wardrobe. His slacks were meticulously hung in a specially designed closet, which rolled out from the wall with a press of the button. Everything was either beige or white.

Unfortunately, I pressed the wrong button and a bunch of empty bottles of vodka tumbled to the floor. Fortunately for me that episode didn't make the magazine.

One evening I got a call from Sue Ladd, Alan's wife, saying that Alan was up at their ranch alone, and had just shot himself.

The Ladd ranch was in Hidden Valley, a small celebrity enclave about an hour's drive north of Los Angeles.

"Can you get up there right away?" she pleaded from their other home in Bel-Air.

"How bad is he hurt?" I asked.

"I don't know," she answered rather matter-of-factly, given the circumstances. "He just called to tell me he shot himself, said goodbye, and hung up."

If he were able to make the call, I assumed he was alive. "Who else have you called?

"No one, just the ranch foreman, and he said he couldn't get in the house but saw Alan through the bedroom window."

She was oddly cool. And it was always intriguing to me how, in a moment that should have triggered hysteria or irrational thought, some people stay cool, calm, and collected. That being said, it also struck me as odd that the first person Sue Ladd decided to call other than the ranch foreman was their publicist.

But Sue Ladd was an exception; she had been a publicist herself and knew that if the shot wasn't fatal this story inevitably would have to be spun. She was Ladd's second wife and a successful actress before entering the agency business, and eventually managed Ladd's career. She hadn't even called the police. Smart move, from a PR perspective.

"The foreman says Alan appears to be just sitting up in bed... I'm calling the doctor... please hurry," Sue calmly asked.

When I arrived at the ranch an hour later, Sue and a doctor she'd called were in the kitchen. They advised me that Alan had in fact shot himself, and it was one of the most bizarre self-inflicted gunshot wounds of all time. He was shit-faced drunk and couldn't even shoot straight. The result was a messy flesh wound that looked far worse than it was.

When I went in to see him he was resting, but the doctor said he had to get him to the hospital immediately. "Just in case," he said.

"Can we avoid the hospital?" I asked. "With a gunshot wound, every newspaper and national television news show will be going with it within hours. Anyone reading between the lines would see or at least suspect this was an intentional effort." It was well known that Ladd was a gun nut and had an unbelievable collection of firearms.

"I'll say it was accidental," the doctor said. "He's going to be okay."

Ladd survived, and we were able to make the best of it. We got lucky. Alan suffered from acute depression and took his waning career hard. But no matter what the circumstances of this bizarre moment, the case was officially written up to this day as an "accidental shooting."

Crises have a way of coming at you in clusters. Word gets around town fast when you become known as a media fixer. And for better or worse, my name always came up when something went wrong in Hollywood. Thus, "Get Mahoney!"

Now being adept at the crisis of celebrity gunshots, another shooting came my way. I got a call one day from a reporter for one of the wire services checking on a story about Cher shooting at Sonny Bono in their living room in Sherman Oaks. My initial reaction was to deny the story. Whenever confronted with potential negative press, denial was always my natural first reaction.

"I just got off the phone with Sonny," I said. "As a matter of fact, they were going over the script for this week's TV show and discussing what songs they'd be singing."

Sonny & Cher were spotted as potential TV series talents when they appeared on big shows like "American Bandstand" and Merv Griffin's talk show, which was one of our clients. Soon, they had their own comedy and variety show, and that show became a client, too. "The Sonny & Cher Comedy Hour" started as a five-week 1971 summer replacement series, and it quickly became a huge hit. As the show got bigger and bigger, Sonny & Cher's fame increased exponentially. By 1973, gossip began to engulf the duo. There was talk of off-camera fighting, canceled concerts, and even physical violence.

"I want to speak to Sonny right now," the reporter demanded.

"That's no problem," I said, "I'll have them both call you."

I rushed out of my office looking for Bill Barron, our firm's television show specialist who also handled Sonny & Cher and the Beach Boys, and found him pounding the keys on his aging Royal typewriter.

"We've got a problem," I told him.

"*WE'VE got a problem*?" he answered sarcastically.

I told him of my conversation with the reporter and would he, could he, get a definitive answer from either one of them? Within minutes, Bill was in my office with the story.

"Yeah," Barron said. "There was a shooting, but no one was hurt."

"Christ, that's good."

"Seems Cher found Sonny doing something 'rude' on the living room couch with one of her assistants."

I got on the phone with Sonny who, if not morally questionable at this moment, was at least a smart enough businessman to know how devastating this news could be. There were things to protect: a TV series, recording deals, and concert dates all on the line.

"Are you two insane?" I shouted. "You do know what could be lost here."

"So, what do we do?" Sonny asked.

I spelled out my plan for them, which was to get on the phone with the reporter and convince her everything was fine.

Luckily, Sonny and Cher understood the ramifications. They both agreed to call him and explain that the story was a figment of some sicko's imagination. It was an Emmy Award-winning performance.

On several occasions, the crisis management issues I was asked to handle revolved around one piece of violence or another. And Sinatra had more scrapes than most when it came to being on the periphery of violence.

On one occasion, the setting was the famed Polo Lounge in the Beverly Hills Hotel. This was one place where you wanted to avoid a public scuffle.

The Polo Lounge was a mecca for everything from business dealings to romantic trysts. The maitre'd proved to be part seat coordinator, part diplomat, and part magician whose innate knowledge of who's who in town made sure that business rivals and former lovers were never seated within close proximity. The Polo Lounge boasted a phone jack at every table. Given the prowess of the Lounge to cater to every need of the entertainment personality, it is no wonder it was a place where a rumor started, or ended.

So, on one particular night, Frank, Dean Martin, and Frank's good friend Jilly Rizzo, as well as two young ladies who just happened to be African American, were seated at a round table. Frank had asked if I wanted to join them and I begged off, always wanting to keep a certain distance from clients socially. Celebrities are definitely a breed apart, and too much time around them often creates a negative aura, similar to the old adage "familiarity breeds contempt." Also in the room was a rather prominent businessman, Frederick R. Weisman, who was well known for his art collection and philanthropy. He was celebrating his son's wedding engagement and it was near closing. There were just a few tables occupied.

Weisman started to mouth off about how loud Frank's party was and then uttered something near fatal, the "n-word." It was aimed at the two women at Sinatra's table. There was an exchange of words, and then things got heated. One shout led inevitably to another and then a punch was thrown, at Sinatra.

Rizzo, with a legendary short fuse, was ferociously protective of Sinatra, and so he picked up a large glass ashtray and smashed it over Weisman's head, knocking him out cold. As for Rizzo, the ashtray shattered into shards and cut his hand severely enough to require stitches.

It's at times like this when you need to pull in favors. From the bartenders, to the waiters, maitre'd, and nearby customers, they were all kind enough or smart enough to keep the details to themselves. What was reported was, Weisman struck Sinatra, friends intervened, and Weisman accidentally slipped and fell, smashing a cocktail table and inevitably causing a self-inflicted wound. The reality was, Weisman suffered a fractured skull and lay comatose near death for days.

Weisman never fully recovered. One mouthy moment changed his life, but not the lives of anyone else present. That story made the papers, but the true details never did. And so, another crisis averted, another career keeps moving forward, and the public remains no wiser.

Sometimes, a client is smart enough to come in out of the rain.

You never know how a crisis will present itself. It could be a midnight call from a reporter, or while you're playing golf on the fourth hole at Bel-Air Country Club.

One afternoon, I was at Bel-Air, far from the clubhouse, when I noticed a club assistant barreling down the middle of the fairway in a golf cart. I knew he wasn't bringing drinks, and this wasn't going to be good. It was going to be a message from Pat about one of the kids, or again a client in hot water. Either way, the stomach juices started churning.

This time, and much to my surprise, the message was from a dear old friend and ICM agent, Ben Benjamin. The golf cart messenger said Benjamin had to talk to me immediately.

As luck would have it, there was a phone behind the fourth green. So, as my foursome went on to play the fifth hole, I made a call.

"Would you consider working for Burt Lancaster?" he asked.

"Of course," I said. "When do I start?"

"As soon as you can get over to his office, he's there right now, I'll tell him you'll be there within the hour."

Burt, like most major stars, kept an office from which to work between pictures. Despite lavish homes in Los Angeles and getaway second homes in places like Palm Springs, many big names preferred to work out of a dreary space in some utilitarian office block. Perhaps it was their need to feel like a regular workingman, or just to get out of the house.

When I walked in, he was just finishing up his lunch from Burger King. Even for me, this was an odd image to process, one of the America's greatest film stars and physical specimens sitting in a nondescript office eating fast food. Despite that inauspicious lunch, I was taken by how well preserved he was at seventy years old. He was the he-man of the movies, a former circus performer, and star of "Trapeze," who clearly kept his number one asset, himself, in the best of shape. When he got up to greet me, he moved with precision, like a cat.

"I'm told you can keep things out of the papers," he said, as his way of introducing himself.

I took what he said as a compliment and told him that I'd had some luck in that area.

"This will more than test your luck," he said. "I'm being sued for more than a million dollars for punching someone out."

"What's his name?" I asked.

"That's part of the problem," he grimaced, "it's not a he, it's a she."

"Jesus, Burt, when did this happen?"

He said the incident occurred about a month earlier on location in Cuernavaca, Mexico, during the filming of "Little Treasure."

He and his co-star, Margot Kidder, were rehearsing a scene that called for somewhat of a verbal confrontation between the two of them, but nothing else. She had a different reading on the scene and came on pretty strong, eventually slapping him on the side of the face.

"I reminded her that the scene didn't call for any rough stuff," he said, sitting back behind this desk. "I asked the director, Alan Sharp, to work it out with her before we shot. She didn't get the message, or she chose to ignore it. When we went for a take, she whacked me again. Instinctively, I whacked her back."

"Jesus, Burt."

"Then all hell broke loose," he explained. "She came at me like a whirling dervish, clawing and slapping, so in that frenzied moment when no one stepped in, I instinctively turned and just knocked her on her ass."

I sat back and listened and took it all in. Nothing surprised me anymore. We both knew this could be a catastrophic for what remained of his career, and his legacy.

"What happened afterward?" I asked.

"We shot the scene the way it was supposed to be shot and finished the film," he said. "Things didn't improve between us, but we finished the movie and that was that. Now, I'm being sued for a million dollars."

I thought for a moment.

"Well, Burt, this isn't good for you, nor her, nor for the business. This is the kind of thing the tabloids would kill for and run with for weeks. Maybe I can talk to her attorney and see if they can be reasoned with. Do you have the name of her attorney by any chance?"

"Yes, it's right here," he said. "It's a Century City firm called Bushkin, Kopelson, Gaims, Gaines & Wolf."

"We might be in luck," I told him. "Bushkin is a good friend of mine. We both represent Johnny Carson. I'll get hold of him this afternoon and see if we can work things out."

When I finally tracked down Bushkin later that afternoon, he confirmed his firm represented Kidder and, though it wasn't his case, he assured me they were going ahead with the filing. I told him that from a public relations standpoint, if there was any way to handle this situation other than litigation, we'd all be a lot better off.

"This is the kind of thing that will be on the front page of every paper and a lead story on every newscast in the country," I added. "And God knows what the tabloids will do with it both here and overseas. Your client already has a reputation for being hard to deal with, and this will just scare off future producers all the more. Burt is an icon in the eyes of the world, and we don't need this type of press at this stage in his life. Isn't there some way we can work this out with maybe a charitable contribution to the Motion Picture Home and an apology of some kind?"

"I don't know," Bushkin replied. "I tend to agree with you, but they tell me around here that she is hellbent for reprisal and won't be swayed."

I told him that whatever he could do would be appreciated and to please get back to me. Especially get back to me if they were going ahead with the filing so I could brace for the onslaught.

The next day, Bushkin called.

"Mahoney," he said. "You're in luck. We convinced her that a lawsuit doesn't really work for anyone. You're right, it's bad press, but she does want an apology from Burt and a $25,000 donation to a worthy charity."

"Fantastic," I said. "You're the only guy I know who could have helped with this one. I really appreciate your help. I owe you one, a big one."

I couldn't wait to meet with Lancaster. There isn't anything a press agent likes more than to give a client good news. I was really full of myself. I'd not only saved Lancaster upwards of a million dollars, plus legal fees, but also his unblemished reputation in the community and from the harassment for the rest of his life by groups who don't take lightly to men who beat up women. I sat down with Lancaster and started to tell him the good news. I got no further than the word "apology" when he exploded.

"APOLOGY! Are you serious?" he screamed

He was now out of the chair and coming toward me.

"Apology? I am not apologizing to anyone. What do I have to apologize for? Holy shit, Mahoney, I'm seventy years old and I'm not apologizing to anyone for anything. I don't care what they sue me for. Let them sue. Fuck 'em."

He was standing over me now and fuming. If he punched her for lousing up a scene, God knows what he was about to do to me for screwing up the deal. I had nothing left to do but roll the dice.

"Jesus Christ, Burt, calm down. You asked me to get you out of this mess and try to straighten things out. I have. I've just saved you a ton of money and a lot of aggravation. Let me work on a note and if you like it, fine. If not, so be it, let the suit begin."

The fire was out.

"How much money do they want?" he asked.

"Bushkin suggested something like twenty-five thousand," I said.

"All right. Let me see what you have to say in the note. Just remember, I'm not apologizing for anything. You understand?"

I told him he was doing the right thing and I'd be back with a note for his approval the following day. When I got back to the office, I phoned Bushkin and told him I was sure everything could be worked out within twenty-four hours.

I worked on that note that afternoon and, surprisingly, the next morning Lancaster approved the wording with very few changes. He assured me that the note and a check would be in Bushkin's hands within hours. He was in a much better mood, and I can only assume he was happy to have this episode behind him.

His mood changed when I told him my fee.

"Let's just hope this is the last I hear of this; I've got a gut feeling it isn't over," he said, as we shook hands and parted.

A few weeks passed and I had forgotten about the whole episode when I got another urgent call from Ben Benjamin.

"Burt wants to see you," he said.

"What about?"

"He'll tell you. He needs to see you in an hour at this office."

I rushed back to his office. He was seated behind his desk, and this time he didn't look particularly well, more pale and drawn. He motioned for me to take a seat across from him.

"Look at this," he said, flipping what appeared to be some correspondence across the desk to me. "Read that… and you thought it was all behind me."

The letter was from Margot Kidder's husband. He was incensed, infuriated, insulted, and much more.

I read the handwritten note scrawled with the words, "Duel to the death." It went on to say the weapon would be of Lancaster's choice, and the duel would be at a mutually agreed-upon setting.

I looked up at Lancaster. He was staring a hole right through me. I continued to read. I thought maybe a moment of levity might break the ice.

"What the hell, Burt," I said. "You've never lost a duel. Take him on. I'll be your second."

He went ballistic. He was on his feet again, and the color in his face was turning redder and redder.

"Are you serious?" he screamed. "This guy is for real. He wants to kill me. I'm on a plane to Paris tonight at ten o'clock. Coincidently, that's where he lives. He's there right now, and I'm on a plane tonight." He was starting to repeat himself, the way a boxer will psyche himself up before a fight.

"Burt," I told him calmly. "Don't worry about a thing. I'll handle this guy. There will be no confrontation or embarrassment of any kind. Just don't get yourself all upset over nothing."

"Nothing!" he screamed again. "A fucking death threat and you're telling me to stay calm?"

"I told you I'd take care of it. Burt, it'll be handled. Just get on the plane and forget about it. Paris undercover police will be notified, and you will be met at the airport. Just put this whole thing behind you. I'll call you later this afternoon."

I don't know why I told him that, as I don't know what Paris undercover police would do or even if there was such a thing as Paris undercover police. I did call Bushkin and told him of Burt's dilemma, and he told me he would take care of the irate husband. "Not to worry," he assured me.

I called Burt later that afternoon and told him everything had been taken care of and he would have no problem in Paris.

"What did you do?" he asked

I simply assured him again not to worry and that the whole matter had been handled.

Sometime later, I ran into Lancaster at the Crosby Golf Tournament in

Pebble Beach, and he walked right up, looked me in the eye, and said, "No one met me at the fucking airport!"

Chapter Thirty-Four

My Wild Ride With *Kid Shalleen*

HAVING EARNED MY stripes in dealing with big stars and big egos from my days at MGM, I thought I was well prepared to handle the ornery, hard-drinking ladies' man Lee Marvin. But I wasn't.

Lee won the Best Actor Oscar for the 1965 film, "Cat Ballou." Insiders in the Academy's upper echelon told me they were astounded that he drew more votes than Lawrence Olivier and Richard Burton. And it was a comedy! This was a first, but I also heard he blitzed the field that very same year in the Best Supporting Actor category, too, for his role in "Ship of Fools." But something happened at the Academy. Martin Balsam won the award for his supporting role in "A Thousand Clowns."

We'll never know how the actual count led to another name being read out that night, but it happened. Both Lee and I heard the same story. He won both! But who knows what's true and what's not true in Hollywood. Typical of Lee Marvin, he couldn't have cared less. All he did was shrug his shoulders and say, "Fuck 'em." That was Lee.

I first met Lee at MGM when I was shepherding press to the set of "Bad Day at Black Rock," starring Spencer Tracy. What I liked about him from the first was his no bullshit attitude. He was a man's man and told it like it was. The fact that he was an actor on the way to becoming a star was simply a means to a paycheck.

Later on, when I was working with Harrison Carroll, I visited with Lee many times on various films, including "Pete Kelly's Blues" and "Raintree County." I didn't go to work for him, however, until 1962, when he was filming "The Man Who Shot Liberty Valance" with another of my clients, Jimmy Stewart.

The most amazing thing about Marvin's career is that he managed to make the transition from a character actor who specialized in subhuman villains to a leading man of style and talent. His rich and varied career was proof that in Hollywood in those days, it was often better to be interesting than good-looking.

Marvin was never a sex symbol, nor did he care to be, but women loved him. His high forehead, big teeth, and battered nose made him, even in heroic roles, look like a man you didn't want to mess with. His baritone voice gave him authority, but it wouldn't be mistaken for sensual. But this only added to a feeling that in the persona of Lee Marvin, the movies had discovered a new kind of villain, and hero.

Marvin's formal training came at the American Theater Wing in New York, after he had drifted into acting almost by accident. His father was in advertising, his mother a fashion editor, and there was no precedent for an acting career in a long-established, well-to-do family.

Lee was an early maverick. Like me, he was expelled from a string of schools, mostly expensive private schools, and he dropped out of high school before graduating to join the Marines at seventeen. He was seriously wounded in action in the Pacific Theater, having had a good chunk of his ass shot off, and spent more than a year in the hospital before being discharged. Suffice it to say, he paid his dues for his country.

Marvin first attracted public attention with a series of memorable bad-guy roles. In films such as "The Wild Ones" and "The Big Heat," Marvin helped define the post-World War II villain. Totally amoral, physically unattractive, and uneducated, this bad guy represented the sociopath end of the spectrum, an area in which prewar Hollywood had barely dealt. When Lee threw a pot of boiling coffee in Gloria Grahame's face in "The Big Heat" or threatened the one-armed man played by Spencer Tracy in "Bad Day at Black Rock," audiences knew they were being presented with a new form of screen villain, one with no restraints.

But Marvin also had a mellow, likeable side, which helped him win the Oscar. In "Cat Ballou," "Paint Your Wagon," "Monte Walsh," and "Donovan's Reef," he displayed a pleasing comic persona made up of equal parts drunkenness, affability, and straight acting. In "Monte Walsh," he even had a romance, on and off screen, with Jeanne Moreau.

To fans and acquaintances, Marvin was always a tough, two-fisted, irreverent, loud, no-nonsense kind of a guy who at times could be gentle, loving, sensitive, and even a lonely human being. And what you saw on the big screen was what you got in life.

It took a lot of time and patience to truly understand Lee Marvin, and he liked it that way. Co-workers never really knew how to take his frequent irreverent and, more often than not, rude exclamations and remarks. He loved to shake up the status quo and couldn't have cared less who was there to be shocked or insulted. Directors and stars alike, including John Ford, John Wayne, Jimmy Stewart, and even Richard Burton, gave him a wide berth. He arrived on the set of "The Klansman" one morning, and within earshot of the entire crew, advised his co-star Richard Burton that Elizabeth Taylor "gave lousy head."

On the same set, he told Associated Press correspondent Bob Thomas he was going to kill him for something he wrote about Elizabeth Taylor. Those remarks would get one's attention, and Lee liked that. Sean Connery was restrained from tearing into Lee one night at a dinner party after Lee advised an elderly lady that he'd bet she had "the prettiest little clit in town."

I'll never forget the time Lee was being interviewed by a lady from the *Christian Science Monitor* who asked, "in what place of importance Lee had put his golden Oscar."

Without missing a beat, Lee told her he'd "rubbed it with Vaseline and sat on it."

Crudeness was nothing more than cheap shock value comedy to Lee. And I was not immune.

An invitation to Alcatraz is hard to turn down, especially, when it's not a one-way trip. Marvin was filming "Point Blank" in the summer of 1969 on location there and asked me to join him for a couple of days. It was his first film with director John Boorman and co-starred Angie Dickinson, Carroll O'Connor, and Keenan Wynn. Wynn was one of Lee's Malibu drinking buddies.

Lee was on a roll, having won the Oscar for "Cat Ballou," having garnered great reviews for "Ship of Fools," and his two latest films "The Professionals" and "The Dirty Dozen" were cleaning up at the box office. Newsweek wanted to do a cover story on Lee and asked if I could get a photographer to shoot Lee behind bars.

The studio set Lee up in the same suite at The St. Francis that I had shared with Clark Gable almost fifteen years earlier. Lee had a late call the first day of shooting, which enabled us to have a leisurely breakfast before heading out to The Rock.

As I was carefully watching my step from the dock onto the barge, one of the deckhands grabbed my arm and in a hushed tone only loud enough for me to hear whispered, "Be careful, asshole."

I looked up to see one of my old high school pals, Dick Enoch, whom I hadn't seen for more than twenty years—and with good reason. Dick had spent a good deal of that time in the slammer. I'd never really found out for what offense, a hijacking of some kind, but whatever the case, Dick had been serving some serious time.

I don't know why, but at that moment all I could assume was that he was still serving his jail time on this barge, taking people back and forth to Alcatraz. I was wrong. He had done his time and was trying to go the straight and narrow. Lee came over and, after the introductions, we spent the trip talking over the good old days at Hami High.

Lee enjoyed this camaraderie and insisted we all get together for dinner that night. After just two nights in the Bay Area, Lee had already settled on a favorite restaurant and suggested we meet at Scoma's, out at the Fisherman's Wharf section of town.

The next day at Alcatraz, I wanted to see Al Capone's cell, to which Lee gladly brought me. As I stepped inside, I heard a sound I didn't want to hear—the lock of the cell door. Lee thought it would be funny to lock me up. It wasn't that funny, especially as the hours ticked away. He left me in the cell for half the day, and I was madder than hell. He just laughed it off. His sense of humor was more than most people could take, and up until then, I had been able to take most of what he could dish out. But this was a costly move. It cost not only him, but also weeks of work by me, the cover of *Newsweek*. Since I was literally "in jail" and nowhere to be found, John Boorman wouldn't allow the photographer on the set.

That night, we went to The Cliff House on the coast just south of the Golden Gate Bridge, and like most evenings with Lee he started out fine, but after a few cocktails things changed. It was at this point in my life that I really became aware of the effect alcohol had on people, especially Lee Marvin.

We met Dick for cocktails and dinner as planned, and I could tell Dick was nervous. He had never been around someone like Marvin and wasn't sure how he should act. I also sensed that he didn't want to embarrass me in any way. He couldn't have, he was an old friend. But it wasn't long before I regretted the introduction.

Lee got enough liquor in him to start asking questions about Dick's prison time.

When the interrogation got to the "butt fucking" stage, I wanted to crawl under the table.

Fortunately, Dick, still being on probation, told me it might be best for him to call it a night and get out of there before he got himself into trouble. I apologized for Lee's indiscretions and told him it was the booze talking and that Lee was really a good guy. I never saw Enoch again.

Lee and I closed the restaurant with too many cognacs, and I called for the check and asked for our car. Lee told me he'd given the driver the night off.

"Don't worry," he said, "we'll get a ride."

We waited forever for a nonexistent cab. Finally, Lee stood in the middle of the road and stopped traffic. The first car that stopped was a Volkswagen bug. When the driver recognized the celebrity hitchhiker, he couldn't believe his luck. He and his bride of less than twenty-four hours were about to give an Oscar winner a ride they'd never forget.

After introductions, I thanked the couple for their good Samaritan efforts and how important it was that we get back to the St. Francis.

"No problem," said the young groom. "We're just driving on through to Napa." He went on to tell us that they had just been married hours earlier in Carmel and were looking forward to their honeymoon.

"Have you fucked her yet?" was Lee's opening shot.

From there, it got worse. I couldn't believe what I was hearing. What's more astonishing was that the honeymooners were breaking up with laughter. They were in hysterics. The more descriptive Lee got with his suggestions of what they should do, or what he would do to the blushing bride if the bridegroom had any reservations, the more they broke up. They dropped us off at the hotel and were still laughing as they drove off to the wine country.

Lee wanted to go to the bar. I convinced him we could have a nightcap in the suite— hoping that he might forget the offer by the time we got up the stairs or so I could at least keep him under control once inside. I went to my end of the suite and started paring down my clothes. I was down to my shorts when I heard Lee calling from the living room.

"There's no fucking ice! Where's the fucking ice?"

Fortunately, I had a full ice bucket in my room and came to the rescue.

By now, Lee too was out of his clothes and down to his undershorts and, hopefully, in for the night. It was wishful thinking.

Lee had a way of getting to a certain stage of inebriation that totally changed his personality. In a matter of seconds, he could go from somewhat coherent, considering the amount of alcohol he consumed, to an almost zombie state. By the time I'd fixed a nightcap, the transformation had happened. These days, you would call his state Post Traumatic Stress Disorder, a clear and present byproduct from his service to his country.

He was seated on the couch and mumbling in what sometimes seemed like another language. I'd witnessed these seizures before and truly believe those transgressions were the scars left on his psyche from more than a dozen landings in the South Pacific as a Marine sharpshooter.

He wasn't one to discuss war stories, but he did tell me on one occasion about the time he was pinned down by Japanese machine guns for several hours with half his ass shot off and his best buddy lying dead on top of him. He still had the wallet he carried that day, which was cut in half by the same piece of shrapnel that stopped him. I firmly believe that Lee felt some kind of weird guilt that he wasn't able to remain with his unit for a dozen more landings. Instead, he spent more than a year in the hospital recovering. I came to understand his drunken transgressions.

Lee put his drink down on the coffee table, and from underneath a pile of newspapers he pulled out a knife that looked like a small machete. "Heeeeyahhhha!" he screamed. "Heeeeyahhhha! I'll kill that son of a bitch."

With that, he was on his feet and waving the knife at his imaginary foe. Most of what he was saying was unintelligible grunts and groans in a foreign tongue, not unlike those heard in a samurai movie. He then systematically took on the table lamps in a style of the old Errol Flynn movies, when the great swordsman would clip candles while fencing the enemy. First one, then two, then three went flying, and then he took on a standing lamp before leveling the only quarry left, the coat rack. Before I could attempt restraining him, he was out the door once again, screaming that he was "going to kill the son of a bitch!"

Lee went from door to door, pounding on each one of them, screaming his threat to kill. He slashed and decapitated all of the hallway lamps along the walls as he proceeded down the hall, ranting and raving. Doors were opening and closing further down the hallway, and it looked like a Laurel & Hardy comedy. Unsuspecting souls would peer out, see this crazy lunatic stumbling down the hall yelling obscenities in nothing but boxer shorts, and immediately slam their doors shut.

When Lee got to the end of the hallway and pounded on the last door, he hit pay dirt. It was then that I realized who he was after. Earlier in the day, Lee had mentioned that his stand-in, Boyd Cabeen, was nowhere to be found, and Lee had to do all the standing in for his stand-in.

The purpose of a stand-in was to allow actors to prepare for a scene while the director and the crew set up the shot. Lee had been standing under the hot lights where Cabeen should have been. Two or three days of doing his stand-in's job had gotten on Lee's nerves big time.

I recognized the female voice from behind the last door. It was one of the wardrobe assistants from the film who just so happened to be shacking up with Cabeen. She pleaded from behind the locked door that Boyd had been hospitalized that afternoon and wasn't there. She was telling the truth. Ironically, I found out the next day, he had been hospitalized for an overdose....of vodka.

As quickly as Lee had gone berserk back in the suite, he calmed down and leaned against the wall, seemingly exhausted. I asked him for the knife, and he gave it to me, and we quietly retired for the evening. Besides the normal apologies to staff and guests, again nothing made the papers. Lee was free to rant another day.

Lee and I traveled a lot together, and when we did, it was tough to run a business. So, I created an interesting arrangement during our frequent trips to New York. Since Lee was the original party animal, with a knack for attracting trouble, I always ordered a chauffeured limousine for Lee. It was at the ready whenever and wherever he went. What Lee didn't know was that the chauffeur was an off-duty policeman. That kept everyone safe, and it made my life a lot easier.

One of the things Lee dearly loved about visits to New York was spending time with his old friends and drinking buddies, columnist Jimmy Breslin and the dwarf actor Michael Dunn, who appeared with Lee in "Ship of Fools." More often than not, they'd spend their afternoons and evenings at one of the East Side watering holes, with Dunn hoisted to a seat on the bar and Breslin and Lee on either side of him.

One night, I was awakened at an early hour by a gruff voice over the phone. The voice introduced himself as Officer Malone of Central Park Division. He wanted to know where he could find Lee Marvin. He was wanted for questioning and possible booking.

Still half asleep, I advised the officer that Lee had gone to an early Mass and I'd have him call as soon as possible. When in doubt, always defer to a religious alibi or something equally as devout. Fearing the worst, I asked what the problem was with Lee.

"Seems there's a lady who's been admitted to New York Hospital," he explained, "and her mother says Marvin put her there. Her mother is raising hell with us and wants him arrested."

"For what?" I gasped, now fully awake.

"I'll have to get permission to tell you more, but I can tell you one thing, the girl is L.O.B. at New York Hospital and your friend had better come up with some pretty good answers."

"Officer Malone," I pleaded, "we're here to open an important new movie on Friday night, and the last thing in the world I need right now is some bad press."

I promised Lee would call as soon as he returned from church.

"I'm sure it's some kind of misunderstanding," I added. "Please, let's not let anyone notify the papers."

He said he'd do his best, but I'd better get back to him within the hour.

I jumped out of bed and went searching for Lee at the other end of the suite. There in the living room, strewn everywhere from one end to the other, was female clothing. Everything right down to the pantyhose and brassiere. But there was no body to go with them. I then eased my way back to Lee's room and there he was, out like a light, spread eagled on the bed, naked as a jaybird. But he was alone.

I looked under the bed, behind chairs, in the closet, and still there was no one. I then retraced my steps and checked every nook and cranny in that suite. All the time I was looking, I was thinking what the hell is L.O.B? I even looked in my room, under the bed and in the closet, thinking that sick son of a bitch may have hid her in my room as a practical joke. No one was there. Whoever it was, she left the suite with none of her clothes.

Then the phone rang. It was the manager of the Regency, a normally staid individual, who was now filled with anger. Never, in all his years as an innkeeper, has he been so embarrassed and dishonored.

"I am the laughingstock of Park Avenue!" he wailed.

Still, I had no idea what he was ranting about "Wait a minute…," I said.

"I want you and your client out of here by ten o'clock," he continued, cutting me off.

"Would you please explain what's going on?"

"Naked women!" he screamed. "That's what's going on, and in the lobby of my hotel. Naked women passing out on my doorstep! That's what's going on, and I want no part of it. You and your friend need to get out!"

By referring to Lee as my "friend," it was clear he had no idea who he was dealing with, and it was going to take more than star cachet to get us out of this one.

"We'll leave, but not without some explanation," I said. "I've been staying at this place since it opened and brought a ton of damn good business!" I screamed back. "I'll be down in the lobby in fifteen minutes, and we will talk this out face to face."

I hung up and the phone rang again.

"Officer Malone on the line, Mr. Mahoney." His tone was totally pleasant this time around. "It seems everything is going to be okay."

"And how's that?"

"Well, it seems the young lady is okay and has convinced her mother to forget the whole mess. The girl is terribly embarrassed about what happened and hopes Mr. Marvin isn't upset."

Now I was really confused. "Just please tell me what happened."

"Well Mr. Mahoney, the young lady passed out on the sidewalk in front of your hotel at four o'clock this morning and lay there for an hour or so until we could send over paramedics. The only thing she had on was Mr. Marvin's sport coat, with his wallet and identification. Her mother naturally thought Mr. Marvin had done some dastardly deed to her daughter and wanted him strung up. I'm thinking it was the other way around," he chuckled.

"I appreciate your help, officer," I said, taking a breath. "And would it be okay to have someone drop off the coat and wallet? I'd really appreciate it. I'd also appreciate it if you'd call the manager of this hotel and tell him you have Mr. Marvin's coat and wallet you recovered from someone who you think took if from him at this hotel. And by the way, let me know how many tickets you would like for the premiere of "Paint Your Wagon" for you and the boys."

Before I hung up, I had to ask, "One more thing. What the hell is L.O.B.? I am familiar with D.O.A. and D.U.I. but what the hell is L.O.B.?"

"It's code for Liquor On Breath. The girl was shitfaced when we picked her up."

An hour later, the apologetic hotel manager returned Lee's wallet and coat along with a bottle of Dom Perignon.

Lee was fast asleep.

The film "Paint Your Wagon" was an expensive musical made in the fall of 1969 on location in Bend, Oregon. It was adapted by Paddy Chayefsky from the 1951 musical written by Lerner and Loewe and directed by Josh Logan. Logan was a big musical talent, but a little weak for Lee. Lee needed a stern hand, and Logan's softer approach just wasn't working for him. But it was nonetheless the happiest cast and crew with whom he'd ever worked.

"Everyone's fucking everyone, but nothing's getting done," Lee said. "Logan just sits on the set and stares into the forest." He went on to say that there were rumblings that Logan was going to be replaced. "I know I'm gonna get blamed for it, too," he said.

Sure enough, Marty Rackin, the head of Paramount Pictures, called me and asked if I'd come over to see him at the studio. I'd been no more than ushered into his elaborate office suite when he laid into me about Lee, his habitual drinking, and how he was costing the studio thousands of dollars a day.

"What Lee really needs is a good old-fashioned shit-kicking," Rackin said.

"Do yourself a favor," I told him calmly, "don't try it."

"I'll tell the press what a drunken asshole Marvin is," he said.

I'd heard this plenty times before. They never followed through with the threat, since they knew the negative publicity might destroy the movie.

It was a very short meeting. I talked to Lee about the rumors concerning the problems on the set, and he told me they were all blown out of proportion. He also suggested that I come up and see for myself.

"Michelle and I have this great big house all to ourselves," he told me. "You can stay with us." Then he added sardonically, "That is, if you can take it."

Lee's turbulent and highly chronicled romance with Michelle Triola began quite innocently on the set of "Ship of Fools." Michelle was a dark, attractive, petite, well-built chanteuse who happened to be a friend of the film's writer, Abby Mann.

For some reason, Mann considered Michelle a good-luck charm and found her a small part in the film. She might have been good luck for Mann, but proved to be snake eyes for Betty Marvin, Lee's wife of fourteen years and mother to his children. Michelle and Lee were soon an item.

By now, the rumors about the film's troubles were in print. Columnist Joyce Haber of the *Los Angeles Times* reported everything that I had heard word-for-word. Upon my arrival in Bend, I went directly to the location, and even before tracking down Lee, I ran into an old Hamilton High School buddy, Bill Randall, who was the sound mixer on the film.

"You're not going to believe this group," he laughed. "It's Peyton Place meets Tobacco Road. Everybody's doing everybody. It's wild, man."

Rackin tried to replace Logan with Richard Brooks, but the irascible Brooks told him to take a hike. What Lee finally did was have a long heart to heart with Logan, and everything got back on track. Logan later admitted being totally intimidated by Lee.

I spent the day on the set, and as far as I could see, there were no problems. After work, on the way back to town, Lee told me that Logan was going to stay on the film. Logan, according to Lee, had a few mental seizures early on, mostly from indecision, which bothered Lee, but there would be no change. These same problems concerned the other cast members, Clint Eastwood and Jean Seberg.

On the day I arrived, Michelle hadn't had such a good day. She had been stopped by a motorcycle cop who couldn't quite figure out from the identification she was carrying whether she was Michelle Triola or Mrs. Lee Marvin. This was a problem that was rapidly becoming chronic. Lee didn't want to marry Michelle, but he would introduce her on occasion as Mrs. Marvin. He felt it was easier than trying to explain their traveling, live-in relationship with every new acquaintance. He was sort of old fashioned and puritanical in this regard. Also, she was using his credit cards.

The incident with the cop was just enough to set them off arguing for the evening. One night was all I could take, and I decided to cut short my visit to Bend. Naturally, more problems arose once I left Bend, including a strike by more than 200 local actors for a $5 increase in pay each day. Little did they realize they should have asked for three or four times that amount.

The film finally got made for about twice the money Paramount had budgeted, and after all the work and aggravation, got so-so reviews. As far as Lee was concerned, the picture did two good things for him. First, it put him in the million dollar-per-picture bracket; and secondly, he now had a new career: recording star.

His feeble rendition of "Wand'rin' Star" was the number one record in Britain and was climbing the charts in the U.S. He was besieged with offers to perform the song on television. He wasn't really singing at all. He spoke it lyrically. But it was a chart-topper, and so it goes in Hollywood.

On Sunday evenings, "The Ed Sullivan Show" was as important a television show as one could ask for to promote a record or a movie at the time. Paramount was all over Lee's agent, Meyer Mishkin, to book him on the show. I wasn't so sure it was a good idea. I knew the song was put together with smoke and mirrors in the recording studio. Lee was no recording star. But before I could get a word in edgewise, he was booked on Sullivan's show.

"Jesus Christ," I told Meyer, "this is suicide, Lee's never sung in front of an audience, let alone Ed Sullivan's audience. It took them three hours to get the number done under perfect conditions in the recording studio."

"Not to worry," he tried to reassure me. "It's all been worked out with Paramount and the Sullivan people. Lee is going to lip sync the record with the West Point Glee Club in the background."

"Does Lee know this?"

"He likes the idea," said Meyer. "In fact, what he likes about it is going to New York and getting away from Michelle for a few days. Pack your bags, we leave Friday morning."

We arrived in New York, checked into (where else?) the Regency Hotel, and had a pleasant dinner at the restaurant 21. Saturday was supposed to be a free day, and the three of us went our separate ways, agreeing to meet up later in the afternoon and go to dinner. I visited my New York office in the morning and didn't get back until after lunch. My message light was blinking and, although I know they blink at a set pace, mine registered "frantic."

Meyer left several urgent messages saying the Sullivan people were double crossing us. They had called Lee directly at the hotel and asked him if he'd like to come over to the studio and see a run through with the West Point Glee Club. Once he arrived, Sullivan and his producer, Bob Precht, convinced him that they could save a lot of time and bother if they shot the number Saturday afternoon. It was a typical cheap Sullivan trick. By doing this, he could save the money it would take to house the Glee Club overnight in the city. Meyer was somewhere in Jersey and couldn't get back in time, and he urged me to get over to the theater and hopefully delay the taping twenty-four hours.

No such luck.

By the time I got there, Lee was already putting on his tuxedo in a closet-sized dressing room two floors above the studio. I heard him yelling long before I got off the elevator.

"Get this fag son of a bitch away from me!"

Lee was rudely referring to the wardrobe man who was vainly attempting to get Lee's tie on properly. It was apparent Lee was already into the sauce and was in no condition to tape anything, let alone "Wand'rin' Star" with the men of West Point. I suggested to the dresser he find one of those clip-on ties and to leave us alone for a few minutes. I tried to convince Lee to do the taping tomorrow, but he would have no part of it.

"Let's get this damn thing over with!" he slurred. "What the hell, let's get it done and get out of here."

I could see this conversation was going nowhere, and I told Lee I would be right back. I set off to find either Ed Sullivan or Precht. By the time I caught up with Sullivan, it was too late. Lee was downstairs and on the set, ready to tape.

The number called for Lee to begin lip syncing the song to a playback upstage and to slowly saunter or walk through two rows of cadets, who stood shoulder to shoulder, to a point center stage where he would finish the song to thunderous applause. Sullivan was then to join him for a brief chat.

The music began, and I could see in the television monitor Lee was in place. For a brief moment, I honestly thought this might work. His first move downstage was smooth, but he wasn't singing the song. He appeared to be having brief chats with each of the cadets as if he were inspecting the troops. The music played on, and Lee kept talking. It was as if it wasn't really happening. The crew kept on shooting, and the taping went along.

All of a sudden, Lee was in front of one cadet and appeared to be berating the hell out of him. The music stopped, and you could hear a pin drop except for Lee's ranting and raving.

When I moved closer, I realized he was upset with the ribbons one of the cadets was wearing on his tunic, most likely given for academic or other military achievements.

"What the fuck are you doing with a Silver Star, soldier? Where the fuck do you get off wearing a Silver Star, you asshole? You know how to get a Silver Star, motherfucker? You die! Do you understand? YOU DIE!"

Of course, you don't have to die to get one, and there was a very real possibility that the cadet had already seen combat before entering his West Point training. So on all kinds of levels, Lee was wrong.

He turned and spotted me. "Mahoney, let's get the fuck out of here."

With that, Lee was on his way, with me in close pursuit. He walked right by Sullivan, who sat transfixed on his stool. I started to offer some kind of an explanation or apology, but Sullivan just uttered three little words I'll never forget: "The demon drink."

Lee wasn't finished.

As he got downstage, he turned and leered out at the makeshift Saturday audience and couldn't resist. "Fuck you too!" he shouted at them.

Fortunately for all involved, this incident was never tipped to the press. Sometimes, you get lucky.

Outside the stage doorway were the usual photograph hunters and paparazzi. Lee brushed by all of them in search of the limousine Sullivan had provided. One of the neglected fans yelled out something about Lee's fancy patent leather pumps and whistled a few sort-of "come hither" notes. Lee spun around at the whistler.

"You fucker, you wear them!" And with that, he took off his shoes and threw them at the startled fan.

As we settled into the limo, the driver (who was Black) turned and asked, "Where to, gentlemen?" word.

"Why don't you take us to where you fuckers drink?" Lee shouted, using the "N word."

This was Sullivan's driver, and there was little he could do about his belligerent passenger. But by the look on his face, I didn't want to meet up with this guy in another place or time.

Before another word was spoken, I suggested we just make a turn at the next corner. I was sure we'd find a bar soon enough. We hadn't come to a stop before Lee was out of the car and through a restaurant door. As I entered, close on his shoeless heels, someone was already telling Lee that the place was closed. But Lee ignored this admonition and was on his way to the bar. I explained to the gentleman, who just happened to be the owner, that we might have a minor problem, but to please bear with me and I'd have Lee out of there in no time.

"I don't give a shit who he is!" the owner fumed. "This place is not open yet, and it's against the law to serve drinks before five. You want me to lose my license, pal?"

By now, I could hear Lee arguing with the bartender. He not only turned Lee down for a drink but also had the unmitigated gall to ask him for an autograph. Lee was halfway over the bar when the owner and I arrived on the scene.

"Give the guy whatever he wants," the owner screamed. "But one drink, that's all. You guys have got to get out of here. I could be shut down."

Lee's reply was simple and direct: "Fuck you."

I finally convinced him we'd be better off back at the hotel with all we wanted to drink and no one to contend with. Lee had the bartender in stitches, bent over laughing. Every time he'd ask for an autograph, Lee would insult the hell out of him and finally threatened to kill him. The bartender thought he was kidding, but I knew better.

As we were leaving the restaurant and getting back into Sullivan's limo, Lee spotted a group of elderly women gathered together on the sidewalk. It appeared they were saying their goodbyes following an afternoon at the theater. Lee walked over and eased his way among them. All of a sudden, they recognized him and started acting like schoolgirls. For a moment, it was a really pleasant sight.

"I've got a great idea," Lee told them.

"What's that?" they asked in unison.

"Let's fuck," he said. And they scattered like a bevy of quail.

Lee's next movie was "Hell in the Pacific." It was filmed on the South Pacific isle of Palau, and this time Michelle accompanied Lee.

Sometimes, she was good for Lee on "out-of-towners," those films shot on location.

With a little booze, he could be tough to handle, and sometimes she handled him better than any of us. However, their continual bickering not only drove Lee crazy, but everyone else, too. His agent Mishkin cut short his visit to Palau because of it. It was all based on marriage. Michelle wanted it.

Lee didn't. I've always found it somewhat ironic that Michelle, inadvertently, had more to do with the final separation with Lee than anyone or anything else, including the daily booze.

The inadvertent part came when Michelle entered into an agreement with producers Hal Landis and Bobby Roberts. They told her she'd earn a "producer's fee" if she got Lee to do their movie, called "Monte Walsh." Neither Landis nor Roberts had a film credit to their names, nor much Hollywood experience. But they were smart enough to know that if Lee Marvin was tied to their script, they had a good shot at getting a studio to buy in.

Michelle knew Lee was encouraging his good friend and ace cinematographer Bud Fraker to direct. She mentioned this to Landis and Roberts and told them to cut a deal with Fraker. The arrangement would snare Lee. It worked, and "Monte Walsh," was on the drawing board.

Legend has it that Michelle suggested the sexy French star Jeanne Moreau for the part of Lee's love interest in the film. It was inadvertently Michelle's undoing. Lee took to Moreau like breath to his body, and the feelings were mutual. She had such an incredible effect on Marvin that he literally quit drinking, for a short period of time.

When the film finished, Moreau asked Lee to accompany her back to France. Moreau mesmerized Lee, but he was realistic. He knew her lifestyle and his would never mesh, so when she flew back to Paris they promised to keep the flame alive.

Moreau called Malibu often, and Lee took the calls without even trying to hide his desires. This only fueled Michelle's fears of losing Lee. The two fell into deep bickering, and Lee resumed his heavy drinking. Separation and "divorce," even though they were never married, was only a matter of time.

There was no getting around the fact that New York and Lee made for a strange brew. New York, New York! It's a wonderful town, and we were lucky to get out with our lives, and our asses. We were opening the film *"Hell in the Pacific,"* in which Lee co-starred with the legendary Japanese actor, Toshiro Mifune. Mifune was basking in the afterglow of his starring role in *"The Seven Samurai."* He was the Japanese equivalent to Lee Marvin.

Lee had just finished *"Paint Your Wagon"* when he immediately turned around and shot *"Hell In the Pacific,"* and was literally drained from the long and arduous experience of back-to-back-to-back films, as well as his on-and-off screen affair with Jeanne Moreau.

We were once again back in New York for the opening, and Lee brought along Michelle, who knew about the Moreau situation. Nothing got by

Michelle, and though she had long put up with Lee's antics, this time things were starting to unravel. He was trying to distance himself from her while she was trying to stick close. Lee and Jeanne were not hiding their mutual feelings, but Michelle was doing her utmost to derail the affair.

On the afternoon of the *"Hell in the Pacific"* premiere, Michelle, Lee, and I had just returned from lunch, when she informed Lee that she had nothing to wear that night. "You've got the fucking plastic," he said. "Why don't you get yourself something?"

She did, and then some.

In addition to the right costume for the evening, she returned to the hotel with two new fur coats. With those charges, Lee went into a rage and he started drinking early, at four o'clock, and I sensed we were going to have a serious problem as evening approached.

Arrangements were made for the customary limousines to pick us up at the hotel, along with Lee's co-star, Mifune. We were to be delivered to the theater with enough time for the flashbulbs, interviews, and hoopla accompanying a premiere. We were ushered into our seats just seconds prior to the dimming of the house lights. Since we'd all seen the picture a number of times, it was preordained we'd leave shortly after the film started rolling and be off to a nice quiet dinner at 21.

Upon arriving, our host, Jerry Burns, seated us at one of the most visible tables across from the bar and inquired if we'd like cocktails. What a question! "Martinis," blared Lee. "Everyone will have a large gin martini."

Mind you, we all knew that Lee had a head start. The last thing he needed was another martini. Even Mifune could sense impending disaster.

I'll never forget the look on Mifune's face. It was not unlike those wonderful facial expressions from his many great film roles. This one was of sheer terror. He'd seen Lee in action and had a pretty good idea of what was to come. Mifune didn't speak English, but he certainly understood certain phrases and was trying to explain all this to his gorgeous date, who had accompanied him from Japan and understood less English than he.

The waiter returned with a tray full of large martinis, and as he was about to deliver the first to Michelle when Lee reached over to assist. The entire tray poured into Michelle's lap.

"You motherfucker!" she screamed. It stopped the entire restaurant.

One of the bartenders absolutely froze in place while pouring a drink and didn't seem to move for a full minute.

"You cocksucker! Look what you've done to my dress!"

Mifune looked as only Mifune could look in a jam. He understood these words. I was seated next to Michelle and took some of the hit and grabbed for a napkin to clean up the mess. At the same time, I tried to calm her down. Lee was his usual passive self and actually appeared to look as if nothing had happened.

"Take it easy," I pleaded with her. "It was an accident, and we'll have it fixed in a minute." All eyes were on us.

"Fuck you!" she directed her wrath at me. "You always side with him. Let me out of here. I'm leaving. I've had it!"

Lee finally had had enough, too, and said, "Let her go."

Michelle almost pushed me off my seat as she got to her feet. I told her I would accompany her back to the hotel.

"Don't bother, I don't need any help getting anywhere."

Mifune looked as if Godzilla had arrived. I wanted to tell him Godzilla had been here all along. As Michelle turned to leave, Lee suddenly came to life again and roared, "Wait a minute!" In that great booming voice, which had the attention of every ear in the restaurant, he bellowed, "There's just one thing…one thing."

From across the room she screamed, "What?"

When he was sure he had the attention of all, even the cooking staff, he yelled, "Just don't fart!"

It was inevitable. And so it came, the divorce. The problem was, Lee and Michelle were never married.

The legal battle of "Marvin vs. Marvin" was as big as it got in Hollywood, and it had the distinction of creating the new legal phrase: "palimony."

This wasn't the first time Lee Marvin was in court because of a woman. By the time Lee was filming *"Ship of Fools"* and seducing Michelle, he had displayed booze-fueled, abusive, off the wall behavior with any number of women wherever he happened to land, day or night. It was too much for his first wife, Betty, to handle, and that marriage ended with Lee giving Betty everything. But she didn't want everything. She settled for $6,000 a month in alimony and $1,000 a month in support for the children. A pittance.

As background for the legal drama that was unfolding next, one has to remember that Lee and Michelle were at first the picture of domestic bliss. They settled into a small house on the Pacific Coast Highway in Malibu, within earshot of the Sheriff's Station, which was convenient.

Things went well for the first few years. Michelle even had some kind of control over Lee's wild behavior. It wasn't until that ill-fated trip to San Francisco for the location filming of *"Point Blank"* that Lee started complaining. He didn't trust her anymore. Lee, as crazy as it sounds, was a one-woman guy, as long as he felt that one woman was with him and him alone. But seeds of doubt always crept in and around the edges. Lee was troubled. A smell of treason was all it took for him to get deep into the sauce. Theirs was a classic "love/hate" relationship, and for weeks at a time everything would be lovey-dovey, and then all hell would break loose.

On one occasion, Lee got so bombed he literally drove to Camp Pendleton, at least a two-hour drive down the coast and tried to reenlist in the Marine Corps in an effort to get away from her. Not too long after that, he called and asked that I pick him up at the Malibu house as soon as possible. When I got there, he was waiting on the highway.

"I've got to get away from her!" he shouted.

"Where do you want to go?" I asked.

"Anywhere," he replied. "Anywhere she can't find me."

"What about Hawaii," I suggested.

"She's got my money and credit cards."

I told him that was no problem. "How's about me taking you to the airport and buying you a ticket on the next flight?"

I gave him what cash I had, and he hid out in Kona for about a week before cooling off and coming back for more.

Another time, he called and told me he was stuck at the house and couldn't leave. "What do you mean you can't leave?" I asked.

"She's threatening to kill me and she's just crazy enough to do it. Right now, she's sitting in a car across the street and half zonked. She said if I try to leave here, she'd either run me over or ram whatever car I get into."

"Sit right there and don't move," I instructed him. "I'll get back to you in a few minutes. Just stay patient."

I called my friend, Under Sheriff James Downey, and explained the problem.

"What would you like me to do?" he asked.

"Have your guys in Malibu pick her up and book her. She's sitting right out there on the highway in broad daylight half bombed."

"Then what?" he asked.

"Just keep her overnight. That should give Lee enough time to disappear."

I felt like Howard Strickling must have felt back in the old days at MGM. I understood now what it was like to have friends in high places.

Michelle was taken to Malibu Sheriff's station and was held in the slammer under Citation Number B169351, Violation 647(F) PC disorderly conduct—drunk until the next morning when her old friend Ruth Berle, wife of Milton, bailed her out. By then, Lee was hiding again, this time in

Mexico.

Still another time, following another reconciliation, Lee called and said I'd better come down to Malibu right away. He was worried something was seriously wrong with Michelle. "She won't wake up."

Fearing the worst, I asked, "What do you mean, she won't wake up?"

"Just get down here and hurry."

There was an urgency in his voice that I had never heard before. I sensed this might call for more than PR expertise. I asked my neighbor, attorney Ed Hookstratten, if he'd like to take a nice ride with me to the beach. After all, what else would he have to do on a pleasant Sunday morning?

Granted, the first thing I should have done was to call an ambulance or the fire department. That was the right thing to do. But calling either of them to Lee Marvin's Malibu pad would have brought headlines we didn't need.

On the way, I explained the problem to Hookstratten. He was not pleased. When we arrived at Lee's place, I made a quick introduction and Lee ushered us through the entrance hall and living room and right into the bedroom. Michelle, wearing nothing but a flimsy negligee, was motionless on the bed. She looked bad, near white and cold. I checked her pulse and it was weak but, luckily, something was still there.

"What the hell happened?" I asked.

"I don't know," he answered. "She's been like this since yesterday."

"Yesterday!" I screamed. "Jesus Lee, do you have any idea or clue as to what is
wrong with her?"

"She said she was going to kill herself with sleeping pills, but she's always saying things like that. I just thought she passed out from the booze. When she didn't wake up, I thought I'd better get some help. That's why I called."

Hookstratten and I agreed that we'd best get her to an emergency room, and fast. We chose the Hollywood Presbyterian Hospital. It was hardly the closest, but Hookstratten knew someone there who wouldn't ask questions.

Thankfully, Michelle Triola was not a household name, and she was admitted to the emergency room with no questions asked. She was put into intensive care, where she stayed for the next two days. Hookstratten and I slipped away unnoticed. Michelle recovered in less than a week and went right back to Lee's Malibu pad as if nothing at all was wrong. It was just another day in Hollywoodland.

The Marvin-Triola palimony trial was planned well in advance of its actual filing. It was fully orchestrated by Michelle, who saw the end coming.

She had a plan and she needed a divorce attorney who understood her plan, a creative co-conspiring lawyer who would help her make new law. The one she found to fill this role was Marvin Mitchelson.

My first inclination of the separation came one afternoon when Lee called to warn me that Michelle was going to ask for my advice on a few things.

"Like what?" I asked.

"Well," he stammered, "she's been getting a lot of shit from store managers and salespeople when she uses my credit cards, and she wants to get cards with her name."

"I thought she had cards?" I said.

"She does, but she wants them to read Michelle Marvin and not Michelle Triola."

"That's bullshit! Lee, she's been using your credit cards with no problems for so long any store owner on Rodeo Drive would probably question any changes now."

"I don't know," he said. "That's why I thought you ought to talk to her. I'm just tired of bickering and whatever you decide, I will go along with."

That evening, I got a call from Michelle. "Jimmy darling, Lee tells me you had a chance to talk about a name change."

"The name change?" I asked coyly. "What do you mean name change? Lee merely said you wanted some Michelle Marvin credit cards."

"Well that too," she proceeded. "But I really think if I had a legal name change, it would make it a lot easier for me wherever we go, be it shopping or traveling or whatever."

"You've got to be kidding, Michelle," I said. "To get a name change, you have to go to court and explain to a judge why you want it. And if the judge doesn't like your reasons for the name change, he'll deny you the request and you'll be the morning joke in every newspaper."

"That's not true," she interrupted. "My attorney tells me you can have it done with no problems, no press, no stress."

When she mentioned the word attorney, I felt a chill go up and down my spine. "Attorney?"

"Oh, you know him," she said, nonchalantly. "He's an old school chum of yours, Marvin Mitchelson."

Mitchelson was a shameless self-promoter of a lawyer who had no one's interests at heart except his own. Maybe it's a sixth sense, but at that moment I knew Lee was going to have the fight of his life with the Triola-Mitchelson combination. Mitchelson was a well-known divorce attorney whose practices were extremely suspect. Our relationship dated back to high school, but quite frankly, I can't remember from which of the five I attended that we were acquainted.

"Jesus Christ, Michelle, if Lee wanted to change your name, he'd marry you. Why are you pressing him like this? No wonder he's drinking." Now I was grasping for reasons that might just get her attention. "What about your parents?" I asked. "Do you realize what an embarrassment this kind of caper would cause them? I've never heard of such a thing. My advice is to forget this idea and forget that you ever met Marvin Mitchelson."

She wasn't giving up that easily.

"What about when we go to Japan?" she asked.

There were plans afoot for Lee to go to Tokyo for the opening of "Hell in the Pacific," and she obviously assumed she'd be accompanying him. "We'll be meeting the King and Queen and they're old fashioned. If I'm not introduced as Mrs. Marvin, they'll think I'm a fucking whore."

That won't be all they'll think, I thought, if she calls the Emperor and Empress of Japan the "King and Queen."

Name changes were hardly in my job description, but Lee was one of those clients who, when pushed to the wall on any number of issues, uttered the only words he knew: "Get Mahoney."

Not long after that, Lee took off. He flew to New York for one last sweet parting with Moreau. More than a week passed before he surfaced. His father was ill, he said, and he'd gone to Woodstock, New York, to visit him. In the meantime, Lee asked his agent to tell Michelle that he wanted her out of the house. She wouldn't budge. But then Lee's attorney, Dave Kagan, got involved, and she said she'd vacate the house if she got $1,000 a month.

It was nothing. Lee would pay her $5,000 a month just to leave him alone. So, he agreed, and we all assumed the nightmare was over.

I heard from Lee a week later. He was still in Woodstock. He was jubilant. "Guess what?" he asked.

Before I could hazard a guess, he said, "I'M GETTING MARRIED!"

"You've got to be shittin' me?" was my initial reaction.

Could it be that he had second thoughts about Michelle, or had he gone off the deep end and succumbed to the beauty and charms of Moreau? While these thoughts were banging around in my head, he told me to set up a wedding some place as soon as I could.

"You're going to love Pam," he said. "And we want you and Pat to stand up for us."

"Pam?" I asked incredulously. "Who the hell is Pam?"

"You've never met her," he went on excitedly. "We've known each other for

Jim Mahoney

years, long before I married Betty. We went together a long time ago, after the war, and we drifted apart after I started acting and moved to California, but that's all behind us and we're now back together. See what you can do about getting us married and I'll call you as soon as I get in tomorrow."

I hung up the phone and was in a state of shock. I sat there and stared at the phone and wondered how it was again that I got into this line of work? Jesus Christ, I thought, maybe I'm not cut out for this shit after all.

That same afternoon, I got a call from Michelle.

"Have you heard from Lee?"

I told her I had, but nothing more.

"Has he told you?" she asked.

"Told me what?"

"Don't play games with me Mahoney!" she shouted. "You know damn well what I mean. How could he do this to me? Have you talked to him about this? This is humiliating. What can I tell people? I'll be a laughingstock."

She started sobbing and then, when I could finally get a word in edgewise, I assured her that I was as surprised as she was about this new woman.

Michelle finally regained her composure and said, "I want the Malibu house. It's the least he could do for the years of devotion and now this."

At the time, it seemed a reasonable trade off. She was threatening court action through Mitchelson, and her getting the house might end it fast. I told Lee this too, saying he'd have her out of his life for good. It was "pay the two dollars and have it done with" concept. Lee wanted no part of that deal.

"No way does she get the house!" he declared.

I shook my head. "Okay," I said. "But this is going to cost you a lot more now."

And so, the "palimony" trial was set into motion.

My next call was to Barron Hilton, who had only months before bought the International Hotel in Las Vegas from Kirk Kerkorian and renamed it the Las Vegas Hilton. I confided with Barron about the marriage plans and asked who in his organization I could speak with about pulling off the Lee-Pam wedding without the media going crazy. Without a pause, he suggested Greg Dillon, who at the time was not only Barron's closest advisor, but also in charge of all acquisitions for the Hilton organization.

I took a chance and called Frank Sinatra, too, in hopes that he would be his usual generous self and agree to fly the bride and groom to Las Vegas in his Lear jet. Frank had always admired and enjoyed Lee, though they only worked together once and briefly in the film "Not as a Stranger." He made the plane available wherever and whenever. He told me to give the bride and groom a big hug for him.

When Lee called, I told him a limousine would be waiting in his driveway the next morning at 11. I told him to put on his best costume, bring his fiancée, and meet me at the Santa Monica Airport. If all went well, I assured him, he'd be back in Malibu by the cocktail hour a happily married man.

Pat and I met Lee and Pamela Feeley as scheduled, and we were airborne, sipping Dom Perignon, thanks to the ever-thoughtful Mr. Sinatra.

Greg Dillon and the staff at the Las Vegas Hilton did a remarkable job with the wedding, especially on such short notice. They not only had a limousine meet us and whisk us downtown to the courthouse for the license, but they also hired a minister and set up a makeshift chapel loaded with flowers in the Elvis Presley Suite on the 30th floor of the hotel, with its 360-degree view of The Strip, the desert mountains, and the world beyond. Pat and I were the only witnesses, and after the minister pronounced Lee and Pam husband and wife, the minister offered the couple a few words of advice.

"Before you go to sleep at night," he said, "be sure you resolve any differences." Lee, never one to pass up a one-liner," leaned over and whispered in my ear, "Bullshit!"

We took photos, cut the cake, drank champagne, and we were back in Sinatra's plane winging westward in less than two hours. As promised, the newlyweds were well ensconced in their Malibu pad by the cocktail hour.

By the time Marvin vs. Marvin hit the downtown L.A. courtroom, the newest phrase in the legal lexicon was being heralded in Hollywood and around the world: "palimony."

It was a clever legal fiction created by Michelle's attorney to argue a contractual bond for an unmarried ex-spouse to plead, and it put Marvin Mitchelson where he most liked to be: center stage.

It never ceased to amaze me how fast love could disappear in Hollywood. Lee was now happily married to Pam, and Michelle had taken up with actor Dick Van Dyke, a Malibu neighbor who, allegedly, she had been quietly having a longtime affair with on the side.

The crux of the Mitchelson case was an "oral agreement" that Michelle would give up her career as a singer to become Lee's companion. In return, Lee would support her for the rest of her life. In essence, it was a contractual relationship.

Mitchelson was relentless. He subpoenaed everyone close to Lee, which made for a media frenzy as the names dropped. Every day, the paparazzi camped out in front of the courthouse, and each day I was there for the circus. It figured to be a precedent-setting case with plenty of money-starved exes all over Hollywood rooting for Michelle.

We all knew Mitchelson would do anything to win, and Michelle knew how much Lee hated all of this, which only fueled her fire. One afternoon, as court was adjourning, Mitchelson approached me. He said, "Jim, I'm calling you as a witness."

"Marvin, you don't want to put me on the stand," I said.

"Mahoney, I'm putting you on the stand."

Sure enough, I was subpoenaed, and a few days later I was called to the witness box. The courthouse was packed with media, and the crowd was so loud the guard shouted for everyone to "be quiet."

Mitchelson started in on me. He began slowly, with the usual questions about the length of the relationship I had with both Lee and Michelle. And then he led me toward the name change issue.

I knew this line of questioning wasn't going to be good for his client. But his line of attack continued. I explained that she initially told me that it had become increasingly difficult and embarrassing to be using his credit cards when shopping, that she'd have to explain why she had Lee Marvin's credit cards and that the whole matter could be resolved if the cards had the name Mrs. Lee Marvin, or Michelle Marvin. And then the shopkeepers wouldn't keep questioning her.

"And what did you find wrong with that?" he asked me with all the lawyerly bravado he could muster.

"I told her quite simply that if he wanted to marry her, he'd have married her."

It stopped him, for a moment. "Why did you say that?"

"She assured me that as her attorney, you had told her it would be a very easy process to change her name to Mrs. Marvin."

That came as a surprise to him. It slowed him down. I went on to state everything I had told her over time. None of this was sounding good to the judge. And then I dropped the bombshell.

"When she reminded me," I said, "that they were going to the Far East for the opening of the movie *"Hell in the Pacific,"* she told me that they were going to be meeting the King and Queen of Japan."

That drew a snicker around the courtroom.

"She was very concerned," I said, "that the King and Queen would think she was a two-bit hooker."

With that, Michelle screamed, cried, and collapsed.

The judge pounded his gavel and shut down the trial for the rest of the day, and that ended my testimony. At the end of the eleven-week trial,

Michelle was awarded just under a million dollars, half the money he had earned during their six years together.

Later, the award was reduced to $104,000, two years' worth of salary based on her highest weekly earnings as a singer, for "rehabilitation purposes... to reeducate herself and to learn new, employable skills." At the same time, the judge warned that the odds of her returning to a singing career were "doubtful." That award was eventually overturned on appeal. In the end, Michelle Triola ended up with NOTHING!

Lee died much too early. He was just sixty-three. He was buried at Arlington National Cemetery, between the graves of the great Heavyweight Champion Joe Louis and a nineteen-year-old Vietnam vet.

John Boorman gave the eulogy. In closing, he said, "There'll never be another like him."

A few months after we said our goodbyes to Lee, after he was lowered into his grave, I received a package in the mail. There was an accompanying note from Pam Marvin. It said the item enclosed was something for me. She explained it was something Lee had carried with him ever since he was a Marine in boot camp. It was the machete-sized knife he wielded that one crazy night we spent in San Francisco.

"Lee would want you to have it," she wrote.

Lee Marvin was a true original, and as crazy as he was, I miss him every day.

Chapter Thirty-Five

The Good, the Bad, and the Ugly

YOU DON'T STAY in business without some long-term clients. The transitory clients usually need help with a single project, an event, an issue, or a tragedy. In some cases, it's just the chemistry. A "click" is either there from the start, or it isn't.

I've worked with clients who fit all descriptions. One perfect example of a long-term client was Bob Newhart, who I represented for many years and remains a good friend. In fact, Bob and his wife Ginnie are Godparents to our daughter Monica. With Bob, there was never a problem. Maybe it was his Chicago upbringing, or his humble beginnings as an accountant, but either way Newhart understood my work and the value it brought to him. Bob and I had a running joke, where he'd say in his best Newhart stutter, "Jim, I ..I...I understand that you handle Frank and everything, and... and that's all good....and I know how Frank doesn't want to be in the press. That's all fine... but... but with me, I...I WANT TO... TO BE IN THE PAPERS!"

On one occasion Pat and I joined Bob and Ginnie at a nightclub that used to be on Sunset near Doheny Dr. where a hypnotist by the name of Pat Collins had a nightclub where she performed as "Pat Collins, The Hip Hypnotist." Most people don't know this, but Bob had a big fear of flying, which is not a phobia to have when your work takes you around the world. So Bob thought if he could get a post-hypnotic suggestion from this hypnotist then it might help cure his fear of flying. So to make a long story short, we all go and the highlight of the show is when she asks everyone to stand, and she proceeds to put some of the audience under in some hypnotic trance. About ten people went under, and they were asked to please step on stage while the rest were told to please sit. Ms. Collins then proceeded to ask questions to the people on stage and they related stories that were not only funny, but ones that they probably wouldn't reveal if not in a trance. So she got to Ginnie Newhart, who is very sweet but on the shy side, and asks her if she knows any of Bob's comedy routines. "Oh yeah, all of 'em!" she says, as the crowd laughs. Which one is your favorite?

"Oh, probably 'The Driving Instructor,'" she says.

Ms. Collins, "Oh, so would you like to do that now for us?"

"Absolutely!" says Ginnie. Ginnie proceeded to do Bob's routine to a tee, every pause, every facial expression, every hand gesture, it was as if Bob were up there doing it. Needless to say, the crowd was in hysterics, and Bob was blown away. I don't think this night out helped Bob much with his fear of flying, but he did discover a very capable, trustworthy new stand-in.

Another time Bob and Ginnie took their kids up for a "working vacation" while Bob performed nightly at Harrah's in South Lake Tahoe. Pat and I had rented a big RV camper for several summers in a row, and when Bob heard about the fun we had he thought it might be a good idea for the Newharts as well. It also alleviated the air travel issue. So Bob and family pack up their new RV and set out for Tahoe. Everything is going perfectly, kids weren't fighting, they're making good time, and they finally reach Tahoe's South Shore and Harrah's. But as Bob pulled in he miscalculated the height of the hotel's entrance ceiling and sheered off a third of the RV's roof. The bad news was the RV was trashed, the good news is he used that story in his act for the next ten years.

And then there are others, like the great Anthony Quinn.

Quinn hired me just before leaving for Europe, where he was filming two pictures back to back. He wanted representation at home while he was gone, and so he wanted his name in the gossip columns and trade papers on a regular basis. Like a lot of big names, he feared he'd be forgotten.

With him out of town, I admit, he was out of mind. I did a lousy job, no question about it. I took his monthly fee and did very little while he was gone. I still regret it. I was so oblivious to Quinn that I didn't even realize he had wrapped up his work and was back in town. Then, one morning the phone rang. It was Quinn.

"Jim," he said. "Let's have lunch."

"Anthony," I said. "You're back in town?"

"Been back for a while, Jim. Meet me at Frascati's at 11:30, okay?"

"Sure," I said. I knew something was up, but you never knew what in this business. Maybe he had a new project. Maybe he wanted a report on what I was doing for him. I scrambled to pull something together, but there was precious little to show him.

Frascati's was on Wilshire Boulevard, across from the Beverly Wilshire Hotel, and Quinn, a big, querulous man, was as charming as ever all through lunch. He never brought up the subject to be discussed. I let him talk and talk. All the while, I was digging deep into my bullshit repertoire for something to say in my defense, if the subject arose. But there was nothing to say, and I knew it, and so did he. It was agonizing. When the plates were removed, Quinn finally got to the point.

"We're going to call it quits, Jim," he said. "It's not working out the way I had hoped."

"I understand." And by way of an apology, "It's my fault, I fucked up."

"Hey," he laughed. "I don't mind getting fucked, that's to be expected, but how about a kiss once in a while?"

I'm happy to say there weren't many of those conversations where I knew I was at fault. But more often than not, it was the other way around. Usually, my staff and I were spending way too much time and energy on a client and not getting paid a fair return. Or it was all about taking on a new client, untested, with no name, who wanted a front page feature on day one. That was more typical.

One of my all-time favorite clients was Jimmy Stewart, a gentleman in a manner that only old Hollywood could create. Having cut my teeth working with iconic stars, I appreciated and admired Stewart greatly. Once again, and not unlike my experience with Anthony Quinn, I fell short in delivering. I was spending too much time on film locations and personal appearances with Sinatra and Marvin and George C. Scott, and maybe playing too much golf. The others felt ignored, and I suppose they were right. By the same token, I never fooled myself. A lot of these clients were coming to me only because I handled Sinatra.

Whatever the case, I'll never forget one afternoon with Jimmy Stewart when I set up interviews for him with the *Christian Science Monitor* and the Armed Forces Radio Service.

We met for tea in the late afternoon, and the writer, a woman, came equipped with a prewar reel-to-reel type tape recorder. It was so large it came in a suitcase. She had a terrible time getting the tape connected from one spool to the other, as well as closing its plastic cover securely.

We were about two minutes into the interview when Stewart noticed the tape wasn't operating and assumed it was because the top was not closed. Interrupting the interviewer seated across from him, he mentioned innocently, "You're thing is open."

I don't have to remind the reader that Jimmy Stewart had a way of stammering and stuttering certain phrases, which could and did add a certain comic drama to what he was saying. To this day, I don't know if he was testing her mettle or sense of humor.

"Oh," she exclaimed. "I'm so sorry."

She then proceeded to press her knees together and continued with the interview as if nothing had happened. I had to excuse myself, but Stewart, always the gentleman, never even cracked a smile.

The 1970s and 1980s were a strange time in Hollywood. It was a time of passing ships, the Golden Agers and the Rock and Rollers. In one afternoon, we'd pitch *Life* magazine for stories about Frank Sinatra or Jimmy Stewart, and the next we were meeting with *Rolling Stone* to sell stories about the new Irish rock group U2.

Things were moving so fast we often had to make rapid decisions on strange requests that came to us due to the unique nature of our clientele. This often meant that we made a decision without the counsel of the client's manager, lawyer, or accountant. We had no business making these decisions, but we did and sometimes it paid off, and sometimes it didn't.

I received one such inquiry regarding the Rolling Stones. It was a million-dollar decision. I asked my partner at the time, Paul Wasserman, to check it out. Negotiating financial arrangements for celebrities is hardly ever, nor should be, the responsibility of the publicist, but we were often the only ones answering the phones.

The Stones were set to appear at the Los Angeles Coliseum on an upcoming Thursday, Friday, and Monday, and this particular call came from a man who wanted to book the band on that open Saturday. He told me that if there were any questions we might have as to his legitimacy, we were to call his lawyer or his banker for verification of his ability to pay.

This promoter, who we found out was in fact for real, had made arrangements to take over the Rose Bowl in Pasadena and wanted to pay the Stones $1 million free and clear, no expenses, for one performance on Saturday afternoon. And he wanted a quick answer. Once again, let me remind the reader these were 1980s dollars.

Since the Stones' financial advisors were ensconced in Switzerland, Paul thought he'd just put the offer in directly to Mick Jagger over the phone. Paul was in my office the next day when Jagger called. They talked over a variety of subjects and the conversation appeared to be about over when Paul asked Jagger if he'd given any thought to the Rose Bowl offer.

"Okay," was all I heard, and then Paul hung up.

"What did he say about the $1 million offer?" I asked.

"He said, 'The boys don't want to work on Saturday.'" For the rest of the day, I couldn't get that line out of my mind. *The boys don't want to work on Saturday.*

That afternoon, I had a meeting with Johnny Carson at NBC and told him about this incredible million-dollar offer that had been turned down with such nonchalance. Carson's response, without so much as batting an eye, was, "I can understand that."

He went on to explain that since the group would have to split the million dollars five ways, and since their wives or girlfriends would probably want to go shopping on Rodeo Drive on Saturday... I tuned out Carson for the rest of the explanation.

These people really are different.

And truly, one of the most "different" people I ever worked with was the British comic actor Peter Sellers. The problem with Peter was that he was nearly impossible to get to know. He always seemed to be playing a role from one of his films.

For instance, when he was shooting "The Party" in the fall of 1968, he staged an actual party at his rented Beverly Hills home. He strolled among his celebrity guests, hands behind his back, cordial but quite dignified and aloof. At times, he paused to offer a marijuana cigarette from a tray, acting as the very soul of courtesy. After a few moments, I realized he was playing the character from the movie, Hrundi Bakshi, an out-of-work Indian actor who stumbles into a Hollywood party, not unlike the one Sellers was hosting.

One afternoon, I arrived at his house for a meeting. His wife, actress Britt Ekland, escorted me to the den where he was waiting. I opened the door and found myself in total darkness. The shutters were closed, the drapes were drawn, and the lights were off.

"Sorry about the darkness," I heard Sellers say from somewhere within the blackness. "I can concentrate better when it's dark. You'll get used to it in a moment." For the record, I never got used to it, even after my eyes had dilated enough to make out the figure of Sellers.

Eklund interrupted our meeting at one point to ask an absolutely innocuous question about an Indian dialect. Sellers went ballistic. It was like a scene from one of his "Pink Panther" movies. Here we were in this darkened room, barely able to see each other, and he is screaming at his wife because she is "just so fucking stupid."

I couldn't understand why this beautiful woman was living with this nut. In fact, they separated a few months later and divorced the next year. His grip on reality seemed increasingly tenuous to me. At another point, but still during the shooting of "The Party," he decided that he had to have a new Pontiac in a certain color, with a special interior, tires and sound system. And he had to have it NOW! We found the car after a frantic daylong search, with the help of John DeLorean, then a General Motors executive and also a client.

The Pontiac was delivered to the set of "The Party," and Sellers spent the rest of the day—still in make-up and costume—driving and photographing his new toy. Less than two weeks later, he tired of the Pontiac, and we went through the same exercise with a Chevrolet Corvette, which was airlifted in from Detroit.

The line between genius and madness was getting thinner by the day, and by the client.

Through all the chaos of this time, I somehow managed to see my family. My eldest son, Jim Jr., was graduating from grammar school in 1969. I promised him that I'd take him to his first U.S. Open Golf Tournament, being played at the Champions Club outside of Houston. We'd been invited to stay with an old friend, Don Klosterman, who at the time was the general manager of the Houston Oilers, and a record-setting quarterback for Loyola University in Los Angeles. He played a little professional ball in San Diego and Canada, but his career was tragically cut short by a skiing accident that left him partially paralyzed from the waist down. In spite of this tragedy, through will power, guts, prayer, and determination he taught himself to walk again and became a damn good golfer, and the best golf partner one could ever hope for.

Three years later in 1972 Don came to L.A. as general manager of the L.A. Rams under owner Carroll Rosenbloom, and we became inseparable. I considered Don part of our family, and he ours. We played golf regularly at Bel-Air CC, we spoke daily about everything from soup to nuts, and we closed down more watering holes than I care to remember. He was a mainstay at our weekend barbeques where he often brought not only current and former football greats, but guests like Ethel Kennedy, Joey Heatherton and Carol Lynley, to name a few. When Don passed away in June 2000 from a heart attack a part of me died with him, and I'm not alone. I've never met anyone who was more loved and respected—he truly had no peers.

Don met us at the airport in Houston and told Jimmy that he had a real treat set up for him the very next day, a trip to NASA's Space Center.

As we were leaving the airport, Don asked me who my favorite sportscaster was.

"I don't know," I replied.

He was insistent. "You must have one you really like."

"Maybe my old friend, Tom Harmon," I told him.

"How about Howard Cosell?"

"He's an asshole!"

Most of America thought Cosell was both the most beloved and hated man in television. Why should I be any different? Don was smiling by now.

"Well, Mahoney," he said, "that asshole is your roommate for the week. He's staying with us, and he's sharing your room. I'm putting Jim Jr. in with my son Curt."

Cosell was in Houston to announce the ABC telecast of the Houston Open golf tournament. This visit to Houston marked the beginning of my long and often turbulent association with the man, who was smart, funny, acerbic, obnoxious, egotistical, but unquestionably the premier sportscaster of his time.

Cosell displayed all these characteristics from the moment we met. His well-honed bravado wasn't a sudden development. It didn't start with the advent of "Monday Night Football." He literally won me over within minutes, and I can't even tell you why. Perhaps it was a mix of genuineness, brilliance, and an off-the-cuff quick wit. From our first conversation, I knew Howard and I would be lifelong friends.

Much has been written about Howard, and not a lot of it praise. Early on, Howard took on most of the nation's sportswriters and ripped them whenever he had the chance. Cosell started in radio and had a running feud with the "bought and paid for" print media guys. He knew he had an advantage over them. He knew he could be on the air in minutes after the game with locker room interviews, player analysis, and postgame critiques a full eight to ten hours before the print press got their stories in the morning papers. It was a ceaseless battle between the radio guys and the print guys.

This game got serious, too. The print reporters would use loud and foul language to booby trap Howard's tapes, making them unusable over the airwaves. He never forgot this treatment, and when he got into a position to really answer back, he did, with both barrels.

Following the debut of "Monday Night Football," Howard became one the nation's favorite speakers on the guest lecture circuit. He was besieged with offers, be it for breakfast, lunch, or dinner. And, more often than not, his target was the members of the Fourth Estate.

He believed fully that any criticism he received was "fanned" by jealous and dull-witted print naysayers. But knowing him, I think he got a kick out of this battle, and even from reading the barbs and critical reviews of his work. He enjoyed seeing his name and likeness in print, for better or worse. With a kind of child-like naivete, he believed the reader was smart enough to see through the criticism and realize the writer was an ignorant fool.

Unfortunately, most readers believed what they read. The image they created of Howard Cosell, the bombastic blowhard, was what the world remembered Cosell to be for the rest of his life. Eventually, he would come to embrace himself as that caricature, but it took time. Meanwhile, he had a bad case of the Hollywood disease, insecurity. Howard lived in a world of fear. He believed he was "on the precipice of professional peril" every day of his life.

The visit to Houston was a memorable one for me, but unforgettable for my son. Howard took him by the hand to the locker room at the Champions Golf Course and introduced him to all of golf's superstars, including Ben Hogan. The same afternoon, Jimmy was given a personal walk-through of the space center and was shown how to land a spacecraft on the moon by none other than the only man to ever hit a golf ball on the moon, Admiral Alan Shepard.

That evening, we took in a baseball game at the Astrodome, as the guest of legendary Judge Roy Hofheinz, who just so happened to have built the place. We spent the first three innings in the judge's box above the Astros dugout, and the rest of the game having dinner in the judge's apartment high above the playing field with Arnold Palmer, Jack Nicklaus, and Jackie Burke. Roberto Clemente hit a home run as the Pittsburgh Pirates edged the Astros by a run.

Howard and I became fast friends after that trip. We stayed in close touch and spent a lot of time together when I visited New York, which was bi-monthly in those days. We even spent some time together in London and in the south of France. I enjoyed accompanying Howard when he covered the fight scene, and I just might be one of the very few who watched from ringside as Muhammad Ali got beaten more than once.

Shortly before the first "Monday Night Football" game, Howard called and asked if I would work for him.

"Just what did you have in mind?" I asked.

"I don't know," he replied honestly, "but I've got things going on, what with football, my radio show, and whatever else they want me to do. Our first game is next week between the Jets and Cleveland and then we go to Baltimore. Why don't you meet me in Baltimore and we can talk?"

There is very little PR you can do with a character like Cosell except to paint him in the best possible light through philanthropy or cast him as a man who simply "gets" the joke that his personality was bigger than life. Otherwise, you're in denial of the obvious.

I took on Howard as a client, and as luck would have it our old friend Klosterman had just made a deal with Carroll Rosenbloom. Don was now managing the Baltimore Colts. Once again, we were slated to move in as his favorite houseguests. Don also invited former University of Texas and Detroit Lion's football great Bobby Layne as an added houseguest, and the place was rockin'.

Howard's reviews for the first "MNF" performance were horrendous. When Don and I met him on the following Saturday evening at the airport, he had the look of a man facing the gallows. We did our best to cheer him up. We told him not to let the "bought and paid for" get under his skin. By the next Monday, Howard was back to his old feisty self.

After the game, we returned to Klosterman's, and the party was on. Bobby Layne had imported a singing cowboy from somewhere in Texas, and Howard grumbled about how he hadn't a clue as to the results of the night's telecast. The director, Chet Forte, had assured him everything had gone smoothly. Roone Arledge, the legendary head of ABC Sports and the hands-on producer, promised Howard that he'd drop by the house later for a drink, but first he wanted to get some immediate feedback from affiliates around the country.

Then unexpectedly, Bob Cochran, head of broadcasting for the NFL, entered the house, apologizing for the intrusion, and asked if he could have a word with Howard alone. Cochran and Cosell went into Don's den.

Cochran was a Harvard man and an ex-Marine who looked like a linebacker. He had a reputation for not backing off, and from what we could hear Howard had his hands full. According to Howard, Cochran read him the riot act. I don't know from what authority, but he told Howard, in no uncertain terms, that he was jeopardizing the entire package and sponsors wanted out. Cosell told us later that Cochran had the audacity to say he was just "too Jewish" for football. Cochran left without saying a word to the rest of us. An understandably shaken Howard called me to join him in the den.

"That's it," he said, "I'm through. You've got your first assignment, Jim. When Roone gets over here, tell him I'm through, finished, it's a wrap."

Howard then went to bed.

Arledge arrived a few hours later with different news. The country, he said, loved the show, and all was well. Howard heard this and came back downstairs to hear it again. Roone assured him it may be choppy seas temporarily, but there was smooth sailing ahead. Howard, in his robe, lit up a big cigar and smiled.

"I think I'll have that drink after all," he said.

Howard must have quit that show ten times over the course of its run. There was always someone at ABC who would stroke Howard and bring him back from the edge. Leonard Goldenson, the founder of the network, was like a father figure to him, and Elton Rule, the ABC president, was like a brother. Howard and Roone had a love-hate relationship that, to the best of my understanding, no one ever figured out.

But Howard's real problems began with the success of "Monday Night Football." Suddenly, Cosell realized what success made available to him, and it gave him options he longed for. He felt he'd become a star in the wrong business. He wanted to be a network anchor and told Roone about these ambitions. Roone promised him a position in the spotlight at the network's news division. The offer dangled for years in front of Howard's nose.

The problem was "the mouth that roared" was so vilified by the nation's sportswriters after five years at "Monday Night Football" that it was impossible for Arledge to give him any straight news assignment. This was despite the fact Arledge had also been given the added responsibility of running ABC News. He had the power to do for Howard whatever he pleased.

Howard never understood that his success was built on his opinions mixed with fact. He was a superb commentator and a most colorful one at that, but a strict journalist he was not. Howard also had eyes for political office. He enjoyed his visits to Washington to appear before various Congressional committees. He told me at one point that he was considering running for Daniel Patrick Moynihan's seat in the Senate. Howard Cosell's ambitions never ceased.

These grand positions and places were just a few of the things that vexed and tormented the man. With all his success, a loving wife and caring family, and more money than he ever dreamed of, he never felt he made it, or made a difference. He was always left wondering what could have been. For all the supposed detractors and the thousands of words of criticism hurled at Howard, I was on hand only once when he was literally stopped in his tracks and left speechless.

We were at the Waldorf Astoria for a dinner honoring All American Collegiate golfers, and many celebrities and golfing greats were on hand. At a reception following the dinner, my wife and I were seated with friend and client George C. Scott when Howard approached the table.

Now, Howard knew I represented Scott and had told me many times how much he admired him and looked forward to meeting him. Before I could get to the introductions, George was all over Howard. I knew George was opinionated and had his likes and his dislikes, but never in my wildest dreams did I think George C. Scott would pick this forum to level Howard.

"You're a supercilious, pompous asshole," Scott began. And it went downhill from there.

He told Howard point-blank what he thought of his work on "Monday Night Football," and none of it was good. Howard never said a word. He turned on his heels and was gone. Rarely have I been speechless, but Scott's outburst left me there. It didn't matter. When Scott was drinking you could never talk rationally to him, nor would he remember.

I didn't hear from Howard for several days. He wouldn't return my calls. Finally, I got a call from his wife Emmy who said Howard wanted to talk to me. Finally, Howard got on the phone.

"How could you allow that to happen?" he asked.

"How the hell did I know what he was going to say? I had no idea he felt that way. I do know he is a nut for the Detroit Lions. Maybe you said the wrong thing about them."

"I've never been so humiliated," he continued. "No one... no one... has belittled me like that in public. What is wrong with that man?"

I'm sure it didn't help matters, but I told him Scott was drunk and he went off the deep end when he drank, and he wouldn't remember what he said anyway. And, I said, "Maybe he read some of the 'bought and paid for' press reports."

Howard suffered greatly from this kind of regular public abuse. He believed deep down that he wasn't valued, or at a minimum greatly undervalued, and he continued to harbor his grudge against Roone Arledge for not keeping his word about the news anchor slot. Arledge, as Cosell proclaimed, promised him that he would eventually be named co-anchor of the nightly news and the host of the new ABC "20/20" newsmagazine program.

Neither happened, and Cosell felt cheated, forever.

When one thinks of a movie star, a real living iconic Hollywood movie star legend, for me only a few come to mind, and I was lucky enough to actually work for them. There are, of course, Clark Gable and Fred Astaire, but I can't help but think of John Wayne, too. It doesn't get any bigger or iconic than Duke Wayne.

I first got to know Wayne when I was working for Harrison Carroll at the

Herald Express. I'd meet him on the film sets when I was with Lee Marvin or other clients. I got to spend real time with him during the filming of "Donovan's Reef" and "The Man Who Shot Liberty Valance." Marvin was in both of these films and was one of Duke's favorites. They were a lot alike, not an ounce of bullshit between them.

One night in Sacramento in 1970, when Ronald Reagan was running for re-election as California's governor, a group of Hollywood stars was put together by Frank Sinatra, a staunch Reagan supporter, for a political fundraiser.

On this particular night, Sinatra invited Wayne, Dean Martin, Joey Bishop, Gregory Peck, Kaye Stevens, Sammy Davis Jr., and me to fly up on his jet, leaving Burbank Airport at 5 p.m. Arrangements were made for us to be picked up in Sacramento, taken to the auditorium, do the show, return to the jet, and be back in time for a late dinner at Chasen's.

Everything ran smoothly until the end, when we found two hundred antiwar protesters assembled outside and blocking the auditorium stage door. We couldn't get out to leave. I suggested we have the limousines move around to the side door. And I further suggested that when Sinatra, who closed the show, started singing his final number "My Way," the group depart through the side entrance and get in the limos for a fast exit. I'd wait behind for Frank, and we'd meet up with them at the plane.

Sinatra nodded his approval. It was then that I heard a loud, "Ma-hone-ee!" John Wayne had that distinctive voice, what we called Wayne-eze.

"Ahm not gowin' out no side door!" he shouted. "Ahm goin' out that back door and you're goin' with me."

Sinatra shrugged his shoulders and smiled. "Don't worry about me, I'll ride out to the airport with the governor. He's coming back to L.A. with us."

"Alright," I told Wayne half-heartedly, "if you want to go out the back door, I'm with you."

About half an hour later, Sinatra began his closer, and the group headed out the side door to the limos. All except Wayne. He looked across the room at me and smiled. "You ready, Ma-hone-ee?"

"No," I confessed, "but let's do it."

I opened the stage door and the mob was screaming, yelling, honking horns, beating on drums and waving anti-Vietnam War posters. It was no place for any sane person.

The moment Wayne stepped out the door, all six-foot-four of him, they realized who it was, and the bedlam came to an immediate stop. It suddenly became church quiet.

The entire crowd was mesmerized as John Wayne slowly moved through the masses. The crowd parted as if he were Moses at the Red Sea.

We got to the car and he opened the door.

"After you, Ma-hone-ee."

As I stepped in, he turned to the crowd and just stood there for several seconds smiling and finally waved goodbye. They started to applaud, and suddenly there was cheering. In less than a minute, he transformed an angry mob into a group of enamored fans. As he got into the limo, he looked at me with a huge grin.

"That, Ma-hone-ee, is how you make an exit."

Always an event with Sammy Davis,
Howard Cosell & Flip Wilson

Fred Astaire, best dressed man in Hollywood,
and a true gentleman.

The world's best Willie Mosconi showing me some trick shots.

Another Saint Patrick's Day celebration with the neighbors!
Cheers to Gene Kelly and Jim Jr.

Jack Lemmon's favorite response when asked if he'd like a drink: "Who said, NO!"

Howard Cosell was once voted, "the most liked and disliked sportscaster of his era." A true genius of sports.

Evel Knievel paying off a golf bet.

The Rhinestone Cowboy Glen Campbell and me on our way to Pebble Beach.

Sinatra's pal and confidante Jilly Rizzo, and
yours truly. We had some great times.

Wine tasting with Frank

Tiny Bubbles were never far when
Don Ho was near!

Barron Hilton, The Yankee Clipper and
me at the Las Vegas Hilton

Promoting "Hell In The Pacific" with Lee Marvin and Toshiro Mifune,
a great actor and perfect gentleman.

White House visit with Hollywood types.
Credit: Alan Berliner

Frank wanted his portrait painted, so I called Norman Rockwell.

photograph by Scott Redd by Pacific Skipper 1979

George C. Scott thought it would be fun to take a boat to Pebble,
thank God we decided to drive instead!

Johnny Carson, the gold standard of talk show hosts

There goes Johnny! My wife Pat and I out on the town with
Johnny Carson and his wife Alexis

Hanging out with my favorite Stone,
Keith Richards!

Uptown girl Christie Brinkley
favors Cuban cigars!

5 o'clock at Barron Hilton's ranch with Baron, LA Rams GM Don
Klosterman and Mr. Cobra himself, Carroll Shelby.

Chapter Thirty-Six

And So, The End Is Near

IT WAS MY first visit to Scotland, and I was there as the guest of a new client, Teachers Scotch. They were happy with the work we'd been doing on their behalf and extended an open invitation to see how they produced their blended scotch. It was July, 1974, and being a golf nut, I timed the trip to coincide with the 101st British Open in Blackpool, England.

We spent several days in Glasgow and in the Highlands with my friends from Teachers. My son Jim, in his late teens then, and I hightailed it down the coast to the historic Royal Lytham and St. Anne's Golf Club, the site of many Open events. Jim was now very interested in golf, and I knew this would be an experience we both would never forget. The Open is to golf fanatics what Wimbledon is to tennis fans.

As we rushed across the jammed parking lot, anxious to set foot on the hallowed turf, a familiar voice cried out, "Mahoney, is that you?"

I turned and there standing in the doorway of one of the many television trucks ready to beam the tournament to the world was a longtime friend, former PGA champion and TV analyst, David Marr.

"What the hell are you doing here?" he asked with a certain surprise, which indicated I clearly should not be there. "Your client's in jail in Australia, shouldn't you be there?"

There was a familiar smirk on his face, so I thought he was kidding. Deep down, I knew that his intonation said he wasn't.

"Don't bullshit me," I said. "This is the first time I've taken time off in I can't remember when, and I don't need another problem."

His tone turned serious. "I'm not kidding, I just heard it on the radio coming over here. Seems Frank arrived either in Sydney or Melbourne and caused some kind of flap with the press. It's escalated into an all-out war and the Prime Minister isn't going to give him fuel for his plane until he apologizes to the nation."

My heart sank. So much for my visit to Lytham and St. Anne's.

I left Jimmy on the course and hurried back to the hotel in hopes of reaching Frank somewhere Down Under. I must say, these types of crises with Sinatra didn't surprise me anymore. Hell, during my tenure with Frank I dealt with everything from his teeth being knocked out in Vegas by a bouncer, his being kicked out of Mexico and banned from ever coming back, to consoling Mia Farrow when she was informed by Frank's attorney that their marriage was over. This had become a way of life. He was never boring. But the threat of some sort of forced captivity in Australia and the Prime Minister's involvement all seemed a bit much, even for Frank.

The only person who seemed to be happy with what was happening was President Nixon, who, hip deep in his Watergate scandal, had finally been knocked off the headlines, if not the front pages, with what was fast becoming an international incident involving my client.

It was July 11, and the real news of the day was about Henry Kissinger, then Secretary of State, being forced to testify in the trial of Daniel Ellsberg, who was part of the Watergate scandal. A sitting Secretary of State had to testify in a criminal case! That was big news, but the headline splashed across *The Los Angeles Times* read, "VIRTUAL PRISONER IN HOTEL: SINATRA WON'T SAY I'M SORRY."

Clearly, this was going to take some undoing.

Before I left for Scotland, I had discussed the PR side of the tour in detail with Frank. I offered to accompany him on his tour of Japan and Australia, but he didn't think it was necessary, since the tour was sold out. It was an eight-city, thirteen-concert tour, culminating in Sydney. We had sent out the necessary press materials and the pre-publicity details before his arrival. Headlines spoke of the astronomical $20 ticket price, a sort of badge of honor for those who purchased them, and even quoted Sinatra directly from my release: "I knew I had to play Australia when I returned to the world of one-night stands…to me Australia is the new frontier, the new world."

Australia loved Frank Sinatra, and he said there "was no need" for me to be on this trip. In fact, he didn't want to do any press. He was romancing the next Mrs. Sinatra, Barbara Marx, at this time, and since she was accompanying him on the trip, he didn't have time for anyone else.

As for my little family trip to Scotland, he was just as excited as we were that we were taking the time off. As a matter of fact, he had a super dinner party for about thirty of us at Chasen's the night before we took off for Scotland, and he to Japan.

Frank had plenty of company on his tour. In addition to Barbara, he brought along his attorney Mickey Rudin, his close pal Jilly Rizzo, his make-up man Layne Britton, and a new British valet.

Back at the hotel in Scotland, I finally heard a radio report of what had happened. When Frank arrived in Melbourne, a few members the hotel staff were actually undercover reporters from local papers. They were masquerading as bellhops and waiters. He had been chased and harassed all day, with his security detail eventually getting rough with the pushy and overzealous paparazzi.

By evening, while talking to a sold-out audience, Frank blew his top and called the members of press, "Bums and parasites who have never done an honest day's work." He called the local press "dollar-and-a-half hookers."

Generally, you don't want to piss off an industry that buys ink by the gallon. The papers blew it all out of proportion, with one woman reporter writing, "At a dollar-and-a-half, I'd give change back." And overnight this "Frank-ism" became a national insult.

Soon, the Stagehands Union refused to work with him, which threatened to cancel the tour. The Waiters Union refused to serve him food or room service, and the Transport Union refused to refuel his plane to leave. The unions demanded an apology and pressured the government to step in and make him an example. The treatment was surreal.

For three hours, I tried to reach Frank. I fully expected to hear that the Phone Operators Union wasn't putting calls through. Finally, after trying every number I'd been given in advance of the tour, I took my last shot. I told the overseas operator that I was having a terrible time reaching a client of mine who was having a serious problem in Australia, and if I gave her his name, I was sure if she contacted an operator in Melbourne, that operator would know exactly where the client was staying.

"Highly unusual," said the well-mannered operator. "Give me the name and we will give it a go."

In less than two minutes, I was connected to Sinatra's suite.

Frank's newly acquired valet was on the phone and was interrogating the operator as to who might be calling from Blackpool. He refused the call, admonishing the operator for connecting "...one of those creepy Fleet Street gossipmongers to Mr. Sinatra's suite. Mr. Mahoney is in Beverly Hills and knows very well how to reach Mr. Sinatra." The line went dead.

My final recourse was to try the family, and I finally did reach his daughter

Tina in Los Angeles and told her of my dilemma. She told me she would talk to her father. She called back shortly and told me she hadn't spoken to Frank, but had spoken to Mickey Rudin, who told her that everything was under control and "you needn't worry."

This went on for a few days, with politicians and pundits weighing in hourly. I was trying to enjoy the family vacation, but the whole affair sickened me. I was constantly on the phone, checking the news, calling Los Angeles and Australia for updates.

Finally, a meeting was convened between Frank, Rudin, and the Australian Council of Trade Unions President, Bob Hawke, to iron out an apology of sorts. It was not a complete mea culpa but enough of one to get Sinatra's plane refueled and his group on to their next venue. Privately, Frank vowed he'd never go back.

We returned from Scotland, and by this time Frank had taken off for Biarritz, France with some pals. I always called him to check in, no matter where he was in the world.

It was getting harder and harder to reach him. I started to get the message when Rudin was also avoiding my calls. It started to dawn on me then that the Australia debacle was going to come back to haunt me. I should have gotten on the next flight out of London.

I didn't understand the magnitude of what happened there. Then, the details on what had occurred in Australia were relayed to me by Frank's make-up man, Layne "Shotgun" Britton, and I started to put two and two together.

Shotgun confirmed that most of what was reported in the world's press was accurate, except that the Aussie press corps brought it on themselves. He explained that some reporters had literally dressed like waiters and maids to infiltrate the very hotel suites in which Sinatra's party was staying.

"They'd do anything to get an exclusive picture or quote from Frank," he said. "Anything about Frank was gold."

He went on to explain that Frank's quote about "bums and buck-and-a-half hookers" was exactly what he said. Shotgun told me the problem wasn't so much with Frank as it was with Rudin, who Shotgun always referred to as the "Frontier Rabbi." Shotgun, a legend in his own right, had nicknames for everyone in the Sinatra organization, and he worked with everyone in town, from Jane Russell to Bob Hope to John Wayne.

According to Shotgun, I started getting the blame for the entire Australia incident, even before the story made the news. He overheard Rudin sarcastically asking Sinatra, "Where's Mahoney when you need him?"

It really came as no surprise, since Rudin had been on my case for a long time. He continually berated the quality of work we'd been doing on Frank's behalf, while on the other hand we were praised for these same efforts.

Rudin was a natural complainer. Everything was a problem. Frank loved him for his wisecracking, critical thinking. He complained about practically everything and every major story done on Frank, most of which was my handiwork. That included cover stories in several major publications worldwide including *Life, Look, Time* and *Newsweek*. They were never good enough, and Rudin knew full well that Sinatra seldom cooperated on any of these major stories. A lot of it was done with smoke and mirrors, feeding the press what they needed to get the ink we needed.

The simple truth was that to promote Frank, but without using Frank, I'd have to get the people all around Frank to talk—co-stars, directors, producers, musicians, even his children. Frank's reluctance to work with the press got so bad during one period of time, when we were trying to promote one his TV specials for Budweiser, that I literally trapped him into doing an interview.

We were at NBC in Burbank to do "The Tonight Show." I told my old friend Vernon Scott, of United Press, to position himself by the entrance to Stage 4 at 3 p.m. on the day of the taping and have no more than three questions to ask Frank, and at least one of them had to be about the show. I knew there was no way Frank would brush off Vernon, since he was a trustworthy friend. But when you're forced to play these games to orchestrate what passes for an interview, it was never easy.

Nonetheless, for Rudin, it wasn't good enough. Rudin felt I had too many clients, and therefore not enough time for Sinatra. Rudin's sarcasm and side comments started to work on Frank. Rudin knew what he was doing sowing these seeds of discontent, and once he saw some life coming from them, he planted more.

Sinatra, like everyone else, paid me a monthly retainer for my services— whether he needed me 24/7, or just occasionally. I always made sure my clients were serviced, and I had the staff to do it. But it was hard explaining this to Rudin or Sinatra because the mood had shifted, and when that happens the best solution is to stay out of the way and wait for the mood to shift again.

Unfortunately for me, Rudin was the one person, and practically the only person within the entourage, to whom Sinatra would listen. As the old cliché goes, Rudin knew where the bodies were buried, and I might add, the money. To make matters worse, the one job I supposedly wasn't doing was getting positive press in Las Vegas. This hit me hard.

With Frank Sinatra, the past has a way of coming back to haunt you, and Rudin was no help in leaving dark ghosts behind.

There was that time in Miami when Frank declared that *The New York Post* columnist Earl Wilson was never to use Frank's name in print, and then banished him from the ringside seat at his opening at the Fontainebleau in Miami. Well, that moment was about to come back to sting me.

A show business publicity man, Lee Solters, handled the press for Caesar's Palace, and Frank had long since made this casino his new home away from home when in Las Vegas. At each opening, Solters would call the cadre of press for coverage—one of which was Earl Wilson. Wilson, who always blamed me for his falling out with Frank, never missed an opportunity to let Solters know that he wouldn't cover Frank's events at Caesar's Palace because he couldn't, thanks to me.

So as not ruin his own reputation with his hotel client, Solters in return complained to the Caesar's brass that Jim Mahoney was the reason he couldn't get the casino's name into Earl Wilson's column. And they in turn complained to Rudin.

In was all insane and Frank knew better, but he listened to the chatter. Rudin even complained that I should stop "giving Frank away." Frank really listened to this line of argument. He hated people taking advantage of him. Now, I was one of those people.

By "giving away" Sinatra, Rudin felt I had coaxed Frank into doing too much for nothing in return, monetarily that is. Hell, it was my job to cultivate and nurture charitable events that promoted Frank in a positive light, just as much as it was his manager and agent's jobs to find and procure him paying gigs. Rudin never caught on that charity and benefit work created a good image and over the long run was worth its weight in gold.

It should come as no surprise to anyone that when I went to work with Frank, his image had been tarnished, and in some quarters he was considered persona non grata. For one reason or another, even to this day, there are some people out there who never appreciated his vast generosity and talent.

When Sinatra worked, he wanted to get paid. On many occasions, Sinatra would not only agree to appear at a benefit, but he'd also bring an accompanying act or two as well as an orchestra. And he paid for everything. He did this routinely for his pal, Princess Grace of Monaco and her Red Cross Ball, and also for the Queen of England and her favorite children's charities.

I took particular abuse for setting up an appearance to raise scholarship and endowment funds for the Communications and Drama departments at Santa Clara University. Actually, I believe Sinatra would have done the gig with or without my involvement. His old pal, Father Walter Schmidt S.J., was in charge of the affair and headed up the university's Board of Fellows, of which I was a member.

But the biggest lambasting I took was for, once again, getting Sinatra to do something for nothing—something that ultimately turned out to be tremendously successful, at least as far as I was concerned. But this was certainly another nail in the coffin of Rudin's distrust of me.

Going back into my memory banks, in the spring of 1965 we were hired by Budweiser to promote a new Sinatra TV special. Taking a different approach to promote this show, I contacted an old friend of mine, Don Hewitt, who was producing news for CBS. I noticed CBS had done personality type interviews on Sunday nights—in a precursor to what became "60 Minutes." Don was not immediately floored by the idea of an entire hour on Frank Sinatra, but the longer we talked the more interested he became.

"Sinatra's a true Renaissance man," I told him. "He's doing movies, television specials, recording albums, and appearing in Vegas and in concerts throughout the world for charity. It would be a super show if you just follow him around with a camera for a few days, maybe a week." If this pitch sounds familiar it should; it was a revamped version of the same concept I pitched to Gay Talese later that same year, with a few more wrinkles in it.

"Would he give us full access?" Hewitt asked.

"I think I can get him to do that. But there are a few things I need from you."

"Like what?"

"First of all, I don't want any personal questions about his love life or about alleged connections to the Mafia. And I want the show to air the Sunday night before his next TV special."

Hewitt said he'd get back to me, but it sounded like something he'd like to do. I went to Sinatra and I explained this Sunday night vehicle could be one of the all-time great promotional tools.

"CBS will be giving you an entire hour of promotion for your show," I said. "We couldn't buy that much time."

Whatever the case, he seemed pleased, and said if Hewitt wanted to go ahead with the project, he'd like to meet him. What follows is an excerpt from Hewitt's book, "Minute by Minute," that details the meeting.

My acquaintance with Frank Sinatra—it was never a friendship—began in early 1965 when Sinatra's press agent, Jim Mahoney, took me to Sinatra's office.

Jim and I had agreed earlier that old blue eyes came as close as anyone to being show biz's Renaissance man.

Jim knew the sale had been made, but I didn't, so I was selling like crazy. Sinatra, who had already made up his mind to do the documentary, figured he'd needle me a little to find out what kind of guy I was. Mahoney can't recall precisely who said what to whom, but he says that my recollection that it went more or less like this isn't far off.

"Frank, this is Don Hewitt," Mahoney said. "Hello Don, what's on your mind?" Sinatra said. "I want to do a documentary about you." "Why?"

"Because like Jonas Salk and Hubert Humphrey and Joe DiMaggio, you are a part of the times in which we live." God, how I was selling.

"You're part of the fabric of the fifties and sixties. People I grew up with remember WHO they were with and WHERE they were by WHICH Frank Sinatra song was popular at the time." Andy Rooney gave me that line.

Sinatra warmed up a little. I thought I was doing great. Then he asked, "What's in it for me?"

I wasn't prepared for that one and it called for some fancy footwork.

"Let's face it," I said, "you haven't enough money to buy a CBS news documentary on yourself. CBS doesn't have enough money to pay you what you're worth. Let's call it a wash."

What I didn't know was that "What's in it for me?" didn't mean money. "How do I know I can trust you?" came next.

"Frank," I said, "I'm going to ask you to sit in a seat opposite Walter Cronkite. That's the same seat Dwight D. Eisenhower, Jack Kennedy, and Lyndon Johnson sat in. If you don't think you're big enough to sit in that seat, I wouldn't do it, if I were you."

He grinned and said, "I'm recording tomorrow night. Want to start then?"

We did. It was the night he recorded "It Was a Very Good Year" for his "September of My Years" album.

I'd heard that he was difficult, but that night he couldn't have been more cooperative. Frank Sinatra was playing… "Frank Sinatra"…the man on the album cover.

I wish the rest had been as easy. It turned out to be a bitch.

Before we started filming other sequences, Sinatra's attorney, Mickey Rudin, flew to New York to set up some ground rules: what we could ask and what we couldn't— specifically no questions about the Cal-Neva

Lodge, the (Nevada) casino Sinatra had interest in. Rudin had lunch in the CBS cafeteria with Fred Friendly and me. Either Sinatra would do it no-holds-barred or we weren't interested. Rudin said that unless we agreed to stay clear of those areas, Sinatra wasn't interested. So, it stunned me when Mahoney called a few days later and gave me a list of things Sinatra would be doing that we could film. My guess is that Rudin had gone back and told Sinatra that we had agreed to his ground rules because several days into the shooting, during a lull in the interview with Cronkite, Sinatra called me into the next room and told me I had broken all the rules.

"What rules?" I asked him. "Mickey's rules," he said.

"We never agreed to those," I told him, but he didn't seem to believe it, and from that moment on, he marked me as a bad guy. We never spoke again."

The fact that Rudin had gone to New York to negotiate a deal or renegotiate what had already been agreed upon was a complete surprise to me, too. As a matter of fact, Hewitt didn't inform me about the Rudin-Friendly-Hewitt luncheon until much later. Why should he? Nothing new had been agreed upon when I called him with a proposed shooting schedule. He assumed we were all on the same wavelength and everything was a go. Sinatra never said a word to me about Rudin's arrangements, and I haven't a clue as to what transpired between the two of them on the subject. I can only assume Rudin convinced Sinatra he actually did make a deal with CBS and they had reneged.

To Don Hewitt's credit, he sent us a transcript of the show, as it was to play out with the sound bites of the Sinatra/Cronkite conversation. Rudin went ballistic, in letter form, claiming the show "deviates substantially from the subject matter of Frank Sinatra as an entertainer and goes into matter which has no relationship whatsoever to Frank Sinatra as an entertainer."

What bothered Rudin most was the following passage that he wanted CBS to excise from the final broadcast.

Walter Cronkite:

Do you think that moral standards have declined in this country in the last twenty years?

Frank Sinatra:

Yes, I do.

Cronkite:

Well let me ask you this very directly. Do you think that by any chance those who have been in a leadership position, idolized as you have been for instance, have you had any part to play, do you think, in that by any chance?

Sinatra:

Well, I haven't directly or purposely. I don't believe so. What I do with my life is my own doing. I live it the best way I can. I've been criticized for many, many occasions because of…of acquaintances and what have you, but I don't do those things to have anybody follow me in doing the same thing.

Cronkite:

Frank; let's speak of those acquaintances just for a minute. Rightfully or wrongfully, there have been a lot of stories associating you with a gangster, hoodlum element in the nation. Can you tell us how you feel about those stories and to what degree they're true or untrue?

Sinatra:

Well, there's no degree of truth to begin with, and secondly, it has been uttered and printed so many times and we just can't continue to try to fight something that has no basis because you just tire of it after a while. It's just as…I meet all walks of life…people in all walks of life in my business I think as you do. That doesn't necessarily mean that there's any relationship.

Cronkite:

But that impression has been fostered, hasn't it, by your involvement at one time in the Cal-Neva Lodge…a Nevada gambling casino?

Sinatra:

The fact that I used to be involved was a legitimate business reason. We built a hotel in Las Vegas, and finally there was so much work to be done on my own natural vocation—pictures, singing, recording— that I just dropped all the fringes of business. As a matter of fact, not only Las Vegas, but all of them.

It all seems harmless compared with today's invasion of privacy tactics used in interviews, but back then there was a sense of implication simply by posing a question. If Cronkite wanted an answer, the question must have had some basis in fact. De facto, Sinatra was a gangster trying to justify his associations.

To compound this mess, I got a call from Rudin days before the show was set to air advising me Sinatra was suing the network for millions.

"Why?" I asked.

"Invasion of privacy."

In his gut, Sinatra knew Hewitt had done a good show. Sinatra was in effect doing my job for me. Needless to say, the story made the front page of every major newspaper and was featured on every television and radio newscast. The network ignored the lawsuit and aired the show as scheduled.

Ironically, and no surprise to me, Hewitt's documentary on Frank Sinatra was an incredible tribute and garnered better ratings than the Sinatra Budweiser special. After it aired, the legal proceedings were dropped.

And so, fast forward a decade, the letter came. It was short and to the point. I was no longer Frank Sinatra's PR man. I was fired. Mickey Rudin wrote it, signed it, and sent it. I was history. Even after all the years being at Sinatra's side, as close as one might think they are to the man, when you're history with Frank Sinatra, you're history. And to add insult to injury, I was asked to send over all my files on Sinatra to his new press agent, Lee Solters.

I wasn't alone. I was just one in a long line of disenfranchised associates, co-workers, or friends, who woke up one day to find the door closed. I could only assume that the Australian incident was my downfall, but a few insiders said it was due to too many clients, too. It was no secret where they got that idea.

At that point in time, Sinatra's entourage took on a new and rather strange persona. When I ran into them on the street or at one of the studios, it was like I was radioactive, that they shouldn't be seen talking to me.

It's rather fascinating how Sinatra had the ability to be so friendly and charming and gracious one minute, or in my case years, and the next minute be shut off. It was like a light switch. Some people, like Peter Lawford, never recovered from Sinatra's rejection. Others, like Lauren Bacall and the late actor Brad Dexter, bristled at the mention of Sinatra's name. Dexter was not only his closest pal and co-produced movies with him, but also braved pounding surf and riptide to save the singer's life in Hawaii.

And legend has it, onetime girlfriend, Bacall was "broomed" for having the audacity to confide to a friendly journalist, Hedda Hopper, that she and the singer were mulling marriage.

Sinatra's most notable kiss-off was Mia Farrow.

As fate and that Big Clock running things would have it, I was with Mia the day time ran out for her. She was filming "Rosemary's Baby" at Paramount, and she asked me to lunch. She was visibly shaken and well into a bottle of wine when I met her in the studio commissary. Drinking in the middle of the day, for Mia, was somewhat surprising, but in the middle of a production as important as this one, it was astonishing.

"What are we celebrating?" I asked innocently. "My divorce," she cried, barely audible. "Mind if I have a glass of that?"

She explained that Mickey Rudin had just visited the set to advise her that Frank wanted a divorce. Hard to believe, but that's how things happened with Sinatra.

It was hard to talk about it directly with her, but the world knew what

happened. It was a classic case of an older man trying to find his lost youth
and a younger, much younger, woman trying to find her father. Her father,
director John Farrow, had died two years earlier. Mia was twenty years old
when they married, and only a few grades ahead of Frank's daughter, Tina,
at Marymount High a few years earlier.

Mia was a beautiful, flawless, wood-sprite of a young woman, full of life
and with a wide-open future. She danced when she entered a room and was
always the center of attention, a glowing presence that made any man smile.
She called Frank "Charlie Brown," because he was such a softy with her.

Frank was hitting his 50th birthday and was still pained by the kidnapping
of Frank Jr., Kennedy's assassination, Ava's fading love, and an impetuous
failed engagement to long-legged dancer Juliet Prowse. He was looking
for stability, a woman he could settle into, and a time when he could stop
searching. He wanted someone he didn't have to compete with, that he could
shape to his desires and wishes and needs. Mia was the farthest creature
imaginable for this ideal.

Frank never talked about his loves to anyone, but sometimes he broke
this code, after many drinks, after many long hours talking deep into the
morning. He did say to me, and to others, that all he wanted from Mia were
"two good years." He had to get through whatever he was working out, and
he knew this was a mistake, but he needed just two years of peace. It was a
modest proposal, I thought. All you could say to him was, "She's beautiful,
Frank. I don't blame you."

Frank had Mia agree to leave her work on the hit television series, "Peyton
Place," and worked her into his script for his next film, "The Detective."
Frank knew the perils of being separated for long periods of time. Time
apart was a big factor in the destruction of his relationship with Ava. It was
all set. Mia agreed to the role and production schedules were drawn up. But
then she got the offer for "Rosemary's Baby."

The Roman Polanski film would be her first starring role, and she couldn't
pass it up. Frank agreed but didn't like it. He juggled schedules and waited
for her, but deep down he was embarrassed. It was unprofessional to hold
up his crew.

Of course, there was more to it than that. There was the differing politics
of the Vietnam War, her late-night clubbing, and her travels to India to
meditate with the Maharishi and the Beatles. Frank wanted her to drop all
the crap, the Polanski movie, and all the late nights. He wanted her by his
side. She was stalling, trying to work out some kind of compromise. There
was her career and reputation, too, she said. Frank's ultimatum was left

hanging until that afternoon at Paramount when Rudin told her it was over.

We had another bottle of wine. Needless to say, she didn't return to work that afternoon, and neither did I.

What might have been my downfall with Sinatra—having too many clients—proved to be my salvation. If I had listened to Rudin's advice and limited my company's growth and left it to the capriciousness of Rudin and Sinatra, I'd be out of business.

Thankfully, even with Sinatra's name off the roster, my business prospered. The loss of Sinatra actually freed me up to do existing business and gave me time to explore new areas of growth. Two weeks after Rudin terminated my services, I got a call from Bob Hope asking if I would be interested in doing work for him. A week later, I also went to work for Neil Diamond. Not such a bad turn of events after all.

Sinatra had a favorite expression: "What goes around comes around." And boy did it. Shortly after he married Barbara Marx, he fired Mickey Rudin.

I worked with Sinatra so damned long that it was easy to take his talent for granted. The truth is, I can only paraphrase the words I heard from others: "With his songs, he took the listener where he or she wanted to go: Chicago, New York, or old London town. He took you way beyond the lyrics."

There will never be another like Sinatra—not a client, a man, a friend, or a talent.

Chapter Thirty-Seven

Booze, Drugs, Needles & Guns

INSECURITY IS HOLLYWOOD'S hidden disease, and it's rabid. It strikes hardest at the stars one assumes are most immune. And the disease comes in many guises.

Lee Marvin was a prime example. He never thought his work was worth a damn. While shooting one of his last films, *"The Big Red One,"* for director Sam Fuller in Ireland, he told the *London Daily Mirror's* Ted Macauley that his "entire body of work sucks."

"You know what hurts," he told the reporter. "I mean what really hurts deep down is I'm no good. In seventy-five films, I've been a failure. I mean, how many of my films can anybody remember? They've all been lousy, and so have I."

Bob Hope often told the story of a time he visited Fred MacMurray at his lavish Santa Monica home. Hope noticed a small structure on the back part of the MacMurray's estate. He asked the actor what it was for.

"That's where I plan to move when things go bad," MacMurray said. "We'll be able to rent out the main house." He was absolutely serious! Fred MacMurray was well-known as one of the richest men in Hollywood.

There are some 160,000 dues-paying members of the Screen Actors Guild, and it is safe to say that at any given time less than five percent are making a living at their occupation. Of those who do, even those that strike it rich, few are happy and even fewer have found satisfaction with their work.

There are exceptions, but the list is very short, in my experience. The happy ones I knew of were Fred Astaire, James Cagney, and Jimmy Stewart— but no actresses fit the bill. Don't get me wrong, there are periods of manic euphoria, but it's later, between jobs or when things are drying up in general, when life becomes unbearable. Fame is one strong drug in and of itself, but when fame dims something has to fill the void. The usual remedy comes in the comfort of booze, drugs, pills, and sometimes a gun.

Booze, pills, and drugs, have taken their toll on many who lived in the glare of Hollywood. This includes the best and most iconic actors and actresses in the business, including Marilyn Monroe, Judy Garland, Alan Ladd, William Holden, Natalie Wood, Ava Gardner, Lee Marvin, Steve McQueen, Errol Flynn, Spencer Tracy, and Richard Burton, to name just a few of the greats.

When I was a fledgling publicist at MGM, I often came across a nattily dressed, smallish, rotund, middle-aged balding man who was known as "the company doctor." Later, I discovered that every studio had one. If an actor or actress wasn't feeling their best, or wasn't "well enough" to go in front of the camera, the doctor had the answer in his little black bag. Later, people like Eddie Fisher's "Dr. Feelgood" took over that practice.

But Hollywood's drug of choice, the one that did more damage than anything else, was simple alcohol. Hard drinking was the way of the world in old Hollywood, and still is. Some people, the smart ones, found treatment or just plain stopped, but the ones who needed help most never saw the problem coming. Booze was the giant killer. I saw it plenty, and besides Marvin (who deserved top billing in this category), the one who stands out the most was George C. Scott.

The first time I met Scott was on the set of "Patton." I wasn't working for him or the movie. My client was Franklin Schaffner, the director of the movie. Both Scott and Schaffner went on to win Academy Awards for the film, but despite having the Oscar on his mantle, Scott had a low opinion of Hollywood, the acting profession, and certainly of those of us in the promotion game—namely me.

But in 1974, his manager, Jane Deacy, summoned me to a meeting in Puerto Vallarta, Mexico. Scott was in Mexico putting his own money up to produce, direct, star in, and distribute the movie, "The Savage is Loose."

Knowing a little of Scott's disdain for the process, the politics, and the practicalities that go into moviemaking, I was stunned by his investment. Perhaps this was his way of cutting down on the banalities of the business. But, nevertheless, everyone in the business knows the old saw: "Never spend your own money."

Thanks to John Huston, Puerto Vallarta had taken on a chic mystique. It was where he shot "Night of the Iguana," starring Ava Gardner and Richard Burton. A visiting Elizabeth Taylor fell in love with the Mexican Riviera and it quickly became a playground for her and Burton, putting it on the jet-set radar. Scott had chosen the location for much more pragmatic reasons—an unspoiled coastline and cheap production costs.

When I finally arrived, we met out on the patio of a cliffside hacienda that Scott and his wife, actress Trish Van Devere, had leased. It was late in the afternoon, and cocktails and hors d'oeuvres were being served. The ocean view was spectacular, but a little unnerving. A rickety railing was all that separated us from the waves crashing on the rocks a hundred feet below.

I began the conversation, post pleasantries, by explaining what Scott should do to help promote the film, like taking time out to be photographed and interviewed. I pitched hard, for at least an hour. Marketing this movie meant marketing George C. Scott, I explained. And this would take up a considerable amount of Scott's time with the media, on and off the set. Of course, this would be easier said than done for a man who I would soon discover didn't see his own worth in the acting pantheon.

As I spoke, he looked increasingly annoyed, bored, and uninterested. He wanted to spend his energy on getting into production, not making nice with some magazine writer.

"Forget this publicity and marketing shit," he bellowed. "I've got no time for it, I've got a fucking picture to make."

"Mr. Scott," I countered, "why don't you do what you do best, direct and act, and I'll do the fucking marketing?"

He rose to his feet and glared at me for a long moment, gulped down what was left of his drink, and bolted from the deck. After an agonizing silence, Trish observed, "You'll never know just how close you just came to taking a swim, and if you haven't noticed... there is no pool."

What I mercifully didn't know but would come to understand intimately, was just how volatile a person Scott could be, and that Trish wasn't joking. Just as I was about to make my apologies and leave, Scott returned as if nothing had happened.

"All right," he said, "let's get started, I'll put up with some of this bullshit, but not a helluva lot."

That was the start of a friendship that lasted more than twenty-five years. George and Trish would ultimately move a block away from us; they were over all the time, and they liked to refer to me as "Gooch" because I tended to wear Gucci loafers at the time.

Scott was a big, difficult man, and when it came to drinking, he had national ranking. His drink of choice was a double-vodka with a beer chaser, and he never wanted to see an empty glass. We spent many an afternoon golfing at the Bel-Air Country Club, and afterward George liked a game of bridge or a little gin rummy. Unfortunately, these forays, with the help of the demon drink and a glass that was never empty, led to some very uncomfortable situations.

On one particular occasion, he ran late for dinner, a common theme, and this infuriated Trish, who also had a volatile streak when provoked.

On this night, Trish's dinner had come and gone when she finally called the club. She was told he was still playing cards.

Presumably under the influence herself, she took it upon herself to drive to the club and then gunned her brand new Mercedes through the club's front glass doors and into the lobby.

I wasn't there for the actual scene, but as usual it didn't take long for it to land in my lap. The next day, I got an early call from one of the parking attendants who told me what had happened and that, thank God, no one got hurt. The first thing I wondered was how George got home. Strange, I know, but it's my job to wonder where the client ends up. One of the attendants had driven him home.

"Is the mess cleaned up?" I asked.

"As best we can," he replied.

Needless to say, the front of the place had to be boarded up and was eventually repaired.

I told the attendant that if anyone asked to tell them that I accidentally backed into the doors. I paid for all the damages, and no one at the club ever knew the difference except the parking attendant, who Scott took care of.

I asked Scott one day when it was that he started drinking. In retrospect, this was a very intrusive question. The underlying accusation was, "When did you start drinking to excess?"

"The Marines."

"What did you do in the Marines?"

"Have you ever been to Arlington National Cemetery and seen the guards at the Tomb of the Unknown Soldier?" he asked.

"Yes," I said.

"That was me. When I wasn't posting guard, I was part of the burial detail, an average of at least two burials a day. That's what I did for a few years. It was very depressing, and that's when I hit the bottle."

It was how he started drinking, but it wasn't the complete story. Much of the rest, the ugly excess, was naturally fueled by insecurity. He thought very little of what he did as an actor, believing it to be little more than child's play. He thought of acting as a fraud. It wasn't real work. He never thought what he did had any special merit and believed that any kid in a playground could do what he did. He barely acknowledged it was a profession. And yet, he was brilliant at it. All that insecurity and self-doubt welled into a crescendo of bad behavior and recklessness.

Later in our relationship, this recklessness became dangerous.

The year was 1988. It was just prior to the first AT&T National Pro-Am Golf Tournament at Pebble Beach. The tournament was formerly known as the Bing Crosby National Pro-Am, or simply "Bing's Clambake," or "The Crosby Clambake," or finally "The Crosby." AT&T hired my firm to help ease into the name change with the press and the public. They knew fully well that the Crosby name was still magic, and they wanted me to help smooth what could turn out to be a rocky transition.

A few Crosby loyalists grumbled about this, and some never got over it. A lot of old timers, including myself, still referred to the event as "The Crosby."

Though not on a retainer, I had already been helpful to the tournament with my access to the best golfers in the entertainment industry. Bing had asked me years earlier if I'd help the tournament committee to wrangle these celebrities. The payoff was great. I got to play in the event for more than thirty years straight, and in this particular year the tournament had invited none other than George C. Scott.

Scott was a notoriously mercurial golfer. I remember a time at Glen Eagles in Scotland where, after a bad round, he demanded, "Get me a car."

I asked, "What about your clubs?"

"Burn 'em," he said.

A few weeks prior to the Crosby tournament, George stopped by our house in Beverly Hills for a cocktail—not an uncommon occurrence. But on this specific afternoon, he'd come up with what he thought was a great idea for the upcoming trip to Pebble Beach.

"Let's go by boat!" he said. "I've chartered a huge yacht, and let's have the Mahoneys and the Scotts take a leisurely cruise up the coast to Pebble Beach. We can anchor off the beach club and live a life of splendor aboard the yacht."

I had spent enough time with George to know a boat was awfully close quarters for that length of time.

"I've got too many meetings prior to the tournament," I said.

Scott understood, but he chartered the yacht anyway and headed up the coast. The Monday before the start of the tournament, Scott had the boat docked in Morro Bay for the night. The next day, the captain of the yacht strongly suggested that the weather was not favorable to head to Monterey. Typical of George, he ignored the advice with a gruff, "Bullshit, we're on our way to Monterey, let's go!"

Reluctantly, the Captain took the boat out into the sea.

It was then, just past the calm of the harbor, when a massive wave crashed over the vessel, ripping apart the upper deck's super structure. Everyone on board scrambled for safety, but Trish fared the worst with a broken leg. But, as George demanded, they got to Monterey. When it came to George C. Scott, reckless turned into danger with a speed I had never seen before, even with Lee Marvin.

This became blatantly apparent to me a few years later, again on the way to Pebble Beach. This time we were flying. George had hired a limo for the airport run, and he told me he'd pick me up. How dangerous could a limo ride to the airport be, I thought? So, I accepted. As we headed through Beverly Hills, he turned to me and asked, "Do you know where I can buy a gun?"

I didn't ask why. I am not sure I wanted to know why. I knew an upscale sporting goods store, Kerr's in Beverly Hills.

"We could stop at Kerr's," I suggested. Certainly, he didn't need a gun in Pebble Beach, but there we were, stopping at a gun store. Without a word, he picked out a revolver, a .38, and after paying for it, the salesman handed George the legal forms and told him the gun would be ready in two weeks.

"What do you mean two weeks?" he asked indignantly.

"Well, it's a law," the salesman stammered. "You just can't come in a store and buy a gun. Those are the facts. It's the law. I'm sorry."

"Well, I want a pistol now," George bellowed.

Thankfully, the salesman held firm and didn't let George have a .38 revolver that morning. Scott was headed to New York after Pebble Beach, and so I told him I would pick up the gun for him when it was ready. The salesman agreed with the plan.

I kept that weapon away from George for a year through various ruses, such as telling him the gun was at my place in Palm Springs—even if it wasn't—and I had left it there thinking he would be coming down. It was a game of cat-and-mouse, and as it progressed, I made up more and more excuses to keep the firearm away from him. And on more than one occasion he would show up at my house, drunk, looking for the gun.

Unfortunately, George lived only staggering distance from me in the flats of Beverly Hills, which made these drunken intrusions a fairly easy and regular occurrence.

It was my fault he lived so close.

One day, the telephone rang.

"I need a house in L.A.," he said. "Can you find me one?"

"Sure, what kind of house do you want?"

"I don't know, get me something like you've got."

Pat and I looked around the neighborhood and sure enough found a place two blocks away. When I told him about it, he sent me a check and bought the house sight unseen.

So, needless to say, his visits were now frequent. My kids often opened the door to an inebriated George C. Scott showing up at the door unannounced. On one of these visits, my daughter Marilee didn't recognize a bearded George returning a coat he had borrowed. She thought he was Larry the deliveryman from the dry cleaners. She took the jacket out of his hand, thanked him, and shut the door in his face.

Of course, I knew why he wanted that gun, and he knew I knew. He wanted to kill himself. He was quite simply that unhappy—with no apparent reason to be so. It was a sad day when I finally had to turn it over to him. And I prayed long afterwards that it never be used.

He was very unhappy for the last few years of his life. He and Trish had separated, and he was living in a one-bedroom condo in the San Fernando Valley—a far cry from the huge estate in Connecticut or the lovely home in Malibu he'd acquired after the constant annoyance of tour buses drove him from Beverly Hills.

I visited him quite often. Mostly, we'd watch whatever sporting event was on television. He started writing a book, which I took to be a positive sign, on the Mexican revolution. In addition to being a history nut, he was a very good writer, having graduated from the University of Missouri's prestigious School of Journalism.

But his health was shaky. He wasn't eating properly and he loved the sandwiches I'd bring him from Nate and Al's delicatessen in Beverly Hills. He stopped drinking under doctor's orders, which I told him was a mistake. I felt that such a dramatic shift in his habits might shock his system. Of course I wanted him to stop drinking, but I wanted him to taper off slowly. He was suffering from a life-threatening abdominal aneurysm and refused the necessary surgery. He claimed the doctors told him they could operate, but that it was a very delicate surgery.

"Fuck it," he replied.

I urged him to have the operation, but all he'd say is, "Sooner or later, I'm gonna die. And I'd like it to be sooner."

In the end, it wasn't the gun that got him. On September 22, 1999, at the age of seventy-one, he was taken by a ruptured abdominal aortic aneurysm.

Chapter Thirty-Eight

You Don't Know Jack's Wife

SOMETIMES, PR CAN be a family affair.

One day in 1983, my son Jim Jr. was over for dinner, celebrating his having recently passed the California Bar exam. He lived down in Manhattan Beach, which was thirty miles from us, so instead of him trying to make it home after a few cocktails, I suggested he snuggle up on the couch and make that trek in the morning.

Around midnight, I got a call from my good friend and client Jack Lemmon, who was in a full-blown panic.

"That damn Felicia, I'm just going to kill her!" he promised.

"Jack, what the hell's going on?" I asked, not really wanting to hear the answer.

Jack proceeded to tell me that his wife, Felicia, had been arrested in the city of Alhambra, about eight miles east of Downtown L.A., and been taken to the Alhambra Police Department. He added that if she wasn't bailed out in an hour, they would be taking her over to the Cybil Brand Institute, an old rundown women's jail in nearby Monterey Park.

I told Jack I'd come pick him up, and we'd go down together.

"By the way, I might bring my son Jimmy," I told him. "He recently passed the Bar exam, and we might need an attorney."

So, I made my way over to Jimmy, who was out cold on the living room couch, and nudged him.

"Hey counselor, I think I might have your first case," I said.

We both dressed and went directly to Jack's house, only ten minutes away. On the way to the Alhambra PD, in between multitudes of "Damn that Felicia!" and "She's really in trouble for this one!" Jack explained what happened.

It was opening night for Jack's play "A Sense of Humor" starring Estelle Parsons, Polly Holliday, and himself at the Ahmanson Theatre in downtown LA. The play went flawlessly, everyone sang its praises later backstage, and there was much celebration. The pre-play plan was for Jack's guests Walter Matthau and his wife Carol, director Richard Quine and his wife Diana, and Jack and Felicia to go out for a late-night dinner after the play in Beverly Hills. But when they all exited the parking structure, they couldn't find the freeway ramp heading west.

So, at a red light, Jack jumped out of his Rolls Royce and ran up to Walter's car to ask for directions. Felicia, feeling no pain from the after-party and in no mood for waiting around while the men figured it out, jumped over to the driver's seat, put the car in gear, and took off. Flying past a stunned Jack, Felicia hopped on the first freeway entrance she saw, Interstate 10 heading east.

Realizing that she was going in the wrong direction, Felicia got off the freeway a few miles down the road. At the bottom of the ramp was an Alhambra police car with a female officer issuing a traffic citation to another driver. Felicia pulled up and, and in a less than sober manner, asked the officer if she knew how to get back to Beverly Hills. The cop told her to pull over. An exasperated Felicia, in no mood to comply, uttered a few choice words to the officer as only Felicia could.

The cop immediately called for backup, and before you know it Felicia was being booked and carted off to jail. There being no cell phones at the time, Jack had no recourse but to have the Matthaus take him home and wait for Felicia.

The whole ride down to the station, Jack was saying how that was it, he had to put his foot down in this situation and it would never happen again. When we got to the police station, I suggested to Jack that he stay in the car just in case somebody had called the press.

Jimmy and I went into the station and told them that we were there for Felicia Lemmon. By that time it was close to 3 a.m., but I assure you every officer in the Alhambra PD on duty that night was present and observing. This was probably the most celebrated booking the Alhambra cops had ever been involved in. I told Jimmy to stay back while an officer took me back to Felicia. She was a mess, makeup smeared all over her face, her clothes disheveled and filthy, one high heel broken. I helped her to her feet and assisted her as she walked out toward the main police station area, where Jack had now joined Jimmy.

Just as Felicia was going through the swivel doors that separate the front of the station from the jail area in the back, she bent over and screamed, "I hope I don't lose the baby!" Felicia was in her 50s at the time, and the expressions on the officers' faces when they heard that were priceless—all shock and disbelief.

As we left the station and were heading back to the car, Jack turned toward Felicia and said with a measure of pride, "Damn it Felicia I was prepared to lay into you for what you did tonight! "But I gotta tell ya, that was one hell of a line!

And with that he put his arm around her as we all walked back to the car and drove home.

As a follow up Felicia received her booking report, and asked if I could have my son review it with them and explain their options. We met at the old Hernando's Hideaway at the Beverly Wilshire Hotel in Beverly Hills.

Jimmy started reading the report:

Officer: "What is your full name?"

Felicia: "F- You, bitch!"

Officer: "What is your current address?"

Felicia: "None of your F-ing business!"

Jimmy started to laugh, as the dialogue on the report got progressively worse. Felicia was arrested for driving under the influence, resisting arrest, assaulting a police officer, and driving without a valid driver's license. Jimmy retained a DUI specialist, and together they got her off on all charges.

In all honesty, this scenario could have happened to any of us. But for some reason when celebrities are involved, it just takes it to another level. They are clearly a breed apart.

Chapter Thirty-Nine

Take the Money and Run

SOMETIMES, NO MATTER how clever or attentive you are as a publicist, there is nothing you can do to please the client. In those times, you take the money and run. Such was many an experience in the world of television.

Whether deserved or not, over the years I achieved a reputation for being able to handle difficult actors and undesirable situations. A big part of this was the "clean up" of Sinatra's public persona during the late fifties and into the sixties. Quite honestly, most of the perception transformation would have happened with or without my help. The media, certainly the majority of writers, championed him following the success of "From Here to Eternity," his private life seemed to be sailing smoothly, and he was singing better than ever. However, just by virtue of representing such high profilers as Sinatra, Garland, Astaire, McQueen, Hope, Marvin, Lemmon, Johnny Carson, and George C. Scott, it helped perpetuate whatever talents my staff and I might have had in keeping good news flowing, and the bad news safely under wraps.

Because of this, we'd get calls from harassed studio heads, agents, or producers, asking for media guidance on troublesome projects, be it an actor, a movie, or a TV show. And when it came to television, the landscape was filled with such devilish situations. I often think back on that memo I sent to Howard Strickling in March of 1953, urging MGM to get into television. His response was, "Think of television as the enemy." Maybe he was right.

And so one morning, I got a call from Lee Rich, who, along with another old friend, Merv Adelsen, was running Lorimar Studios. Their television success was legendary and included the shows "Dallas," "Knot's Landing," and "The Waltons." Rich asked if I'd come out to the studio and chat with him and Merv about doing some work for them. Naturally, I told him I would be delighted.

"You might not be," Rich warned.

By now, my office staff had grown significantly, and the client list had increased proportionately. I'd moved our offices into the building I'd bought across the street from the Friars Club in Beverly Hills on Little Santa Monica Boulevard. Ironically, it was this very same building that housed the office once occupied by Louis B. Mayer when he left MGM. It was still an odd feeling knowing how things had come full circle in the blink of an eye.

We were handling several television series, both on network and in syndication, and big ratings TV specials for Ford and Chevrolet. We worked hard for these clients, merging their specific branding messages with our own brand of publicity, and it was not always an easy marriage.

I met Rich and Adelson in their new Lorimar offices in Culver City. It turned out they were situated in a new, impressive building on the corner of Washington Boulevard and Overland Avenue, a corner that was part of the old MGM lot. It was strange being back at my old stomping grounds, high atop this new massive structure looking out over the old studio complex. So much of the infrastructure remained the same while so many other changes had taken place. It was like going back to your childhood home after some other family had moved in and redecorated.

Rich and Adelsen had little time for small talk. They got right to the point. "We're having some problems with the cast of 'Dallas,' they refuse to do any publicity, and just thought you might be able to help," Rich said.

"What kind of problems, exactly?" I asked.

"Can't get them to sit for interviews or photos," he explained. "Can't get them to do anything! "We think that a new and different approach might make a difference, something or someone like you."

What a piece of cake, I thought to myself. "Dallas" was the hottest show in television. I took the job with relish and couldn't wait for the start of the new season, with production scheduled in two weeks in Dallas at the famous Southfork Ranch location.

The next weekend, Pat and I were invited to a birthday party for my neighbor and friend Gene Kelly at restaurateur Jean Leon's Malibu home. The very first person Leon introduced me to was none other than J.R. Ewing himself, Larry Hagman.

It wasn't much of a conversation. Among many Hagman quirks, he didn't speak on Sundays. He rested his voice. So, at Leon's party he was mute. Also, and unbeknownst to me, he carried a portable fan with him at all times. This was to clear the air in case some fool dared to smoke in his presence.

As I approached Hagman later on with my usual cigar in hand, he whipped out his fan and blew it directly back in my direction, again without saying a word. This was going to be an interesting assignment. He was a legend in Malibu, too, with his Fourth of July antics. Each summer he drove his neighbors crazy by hiring the Pepperdine University Marching Band and leading them up and down the beach playing marching songs.

Despite Hagman's non-speaking, I told him that I looked forward to the "Dallas" assignment in Texas. Little did I know what I would be getting myself into.

Our publicity machine got lucky and *People* magazine assigned a photographer to cover the first few days of production at Southfork. It was a good beginning. My old MGM friend, Howard Keel, was playing patriarch Jock Ewing, and he introduced me around to some of the stars and set workers.

I advised the production office that the photographer from *People* was coming the next morning and I didn't want any last-minute surprises, so we told everyone in advance to be ready. I'd learned early on that you don't surprise anyone on a set with a photographer, especially actors or actresses.

The story angle we agreed to with *People* was the introduction of a new player in the cast, the young Christopher Atkins of the film, "Blue Lagoon."

Atkins, all grown up, was to play the new heartthrob, and his first scene called for some simple dialogue with the ever-affable J.R. Ewing. It was nothing complicated, just a simple scene between the two on the porch at Southfork. For publicity, it was a perfect first scene. Again, I couldn't have asked for a more amenable introduction to my new assignment.

Atkins was the picture of cooperation. He said the photographers could shoot anything they wanted. When Hagman arrived, I re-introduced myself and followed with, "As you know, *People* has a photographer here today, and I was hoping he could get a shot of you and Chris Atkins, sort of welcoming him to the cast."

I didn't mention the "new and old" angle to the photo, knowing all too well how an actor would react to anything suggesting age.

"What?" he asked rather incredulously.

I repeated myself and went through the whole set up again.

After a long pause, Hagman answered, "No, no, no, no, no, no, no, no, no, no, no, no...No!" His delivery was like a Gregorian chant. And he continued. "No, no, no, no, no, no, no, no."

At this point he was getting louder, loud enough to get everyone's attention on the set. I was getting embarrassed and suddenly realized why Rich and Adelsen called. He broke out of the chant when he realized he had all the attention he needed.

"Do you know what they will do with those pictures?" he asked. Before I could answer, he repeated himself.

"I know what I would like them to do with them," I shot back.

"No, no, no, no, no, no, no." Off he went again.

At this point, I wished I had never taken that call from Rich and Adelsen. This was *People*, for Christ's sake, the most celebrity-friendly magazine there is. What would he do if I had a serious request?

"I'll tell you what they'll do with those pictures," he went on.

By now, I was wondering what he thought they would do with them. Would they sell them? Did he think all pictures of him belong in the National Gallery or the Smithsonian?

His voice was now fevered. He answered his own question. "They'll put those fucking pictures on the cover of their chickenshit magazine," he said. "That's what they'd like to do, but they're not going to because they are not going to get any."

With that, Hagman bolted from the set and took off for his dressing room. *People* cancelled the story.

Larry Hagman was the highest paid man on television. Money changes a person. It seems there is a direct relationship between how much money you make and how selfish and uncooperative you become. The less money, the easier, but with more money the brain starts to revolt against the exact machinery that brought the bushel baskets of cash in the first place.

For the most part, the entire cast, with the exception of Howard Keel, was either out of work or completely unknown before the series. Other producers were not fawning over any of them when they landed the series. Yet, they got so carried away after the show started to climb in the ratings that they actually demanded a day's pay, each, in order to assemble as the entire cast to shoot a publicity photo.

Imagine it: some of these people had gone from earning nothing to more than $100,000 a week. Instead of being gracious and beholden to the system that made them rich, they held the company up for ransom for a day's pay, and for a photo designed to make them even more famous and even richer.

On the corporate side, things were not a bed of roses, either.

Ford Motor Company, for example, was no walk in the park. There was Ford's Easter Sunday special, "The Robe," that we were handling. It was the 1953 Easter movie classic with Richard Burton, Jean Simmons, and Victor

Mature. Publicity for the promotion should have been a slam-dunk with such notable talent.

The previous year, we had great success promoting the classic "Mutiny on the Bounty" for Ford. The ratings were at the same level as the Super Bowl. We got lucky. We discovered a true descendant of the mutiny, Fletcher Christian III. He was living in Tahiti, and so we brought him stateside and toured him around the country. We had him on every talk show and in every newspaper and magazine imaginable.

But with *"The Robe,"* it wasn't quite so simple. The original cast of Burton, Simmons, and Mature were unavailable, dead or uninterested. That was not unusual. So much of public relations is coming up with a creative "Big Idea," and so my idea for this promotion involved art.

I'd just returned from Stockbridge, Mass., where I'd arranged to have Norman Rockwell paint a portrait of Frank Sinatra. Frank had gone through a period where he wanted his portrait painted by famous artists. In dealing with Rockwell, I found him to be pleasant, easy to work with and, above all else, a gentleman in an almost grandfatherly way.

"What if," I suggested to Ford's marketing executive, "I could get Norman Rockwell to paint his version of 'The Crucifixion' for a *TV Guide* cover for Easter week?"

Ford had deep enough pockets to pay for such a thing. I called Merrill Pannitt, the managing editor of *TV Guide*, and proposed the idea. He thought it was fantastic but doubted that I could get this great but aging artist to agree to do another magazine cover, let alone for *TV Guide*. He also cautioned me that his wasn't the final word, since a committee decided cover choices, but as far as he was concerned, it looked like a slam-dunk. He suggested I feel out Rockwell.

I discovered while working with Rockwell that he had a hearing problem and always had his wife on an extension while using the phone in case he missed any part of the conversation or misunderstood any of it. This was a blessing.

"Absolutely no way," was Rockwell's immediate reaction when I called. "I don't do covers anymore, and I certainly wouldn't do one for a TV magazine."

I started to explain that this wasn't just any TV magazine, but a magazine with one of the biggest circulations in the business. He asked me if I could hold on a minute. He may have thought he put me on hold, but I could hear his conversation with his wife, who was obviously in another part of their house. I'm sure the neighbors heard as well. She thought it was a good time for him to do a religious cover, and she liked *TV Guide*. That was all the convincing he needed.

He told me that he'd have the "Crucifixion" done for me in three weeks and asked where I'd like it shipped. First of all, I told him we should agree on a fee and far be it for me to have any idea what he charged for this type of work. He told me that he would waive the fee, but to see if I could get the Ford Motor Company to send a donation to his favorite charity.

I couldn't wait to tell Ford. I called Merrill Pannitt and told him the great news. We both were thrilled, and Merrill told me that he was meeting with the committee the next day and would have an answer for me after lunch.

The next afternoon, Pannitt called as promised.

"I'm sorry, Jim," he said, "but the committee passed on your Rockwell idea."

When I relayed Ford's response to Rockwell, he said: "Good, I didn't really want to do it anyway. My wife's religious, she likes *TV Guide*, but I could care less."

It's easy to become jaded in this business, but you can't let it get to you. The good thing is that all these ideas can be recycled to different clients and re-packaged as fresh.

One of the strangest calls came from my good friend Gary Nardino, who headed up Paramount Television. Nardino had six highly rated shows on various networks at the time, including: "Family Ties," "Cheers," and "Happy Days." He needed a favor. Penny Marshall, who played Laverne in another of his comedy hits, "Laverne and Shirley," refused to talk to Shirley—that is, her co-star Cindy Williams wouldn't speak to Marshall. Mind you, they were each being paid $50,000 a week to star in the show.

"Can you find a solution?" Nardino asked.

Where do you start with something like this? Like a dysfunctional Hollywood family, they were arguing over who got better laugh lines?

"I'm not a shrink," I said. "I don't know if I can help with this, but I'll try."

That same afternoon, I found myself in Nardino's office sitting next to Penny Marshall, but Cindy Williams never arrived. Marshall showed up as a courtesy to Nardino, who was doing his best to keep the show going.

I sat and listened and realized pretty fast that PR wasn't going to solve anything here. This was an issue of ego, on both sides. After the meeting, I said, "Gary, this is beyond me. I think the show is in trouble and you're just going to have to accept it."

He thanked me and, as it turned out, no one could help. The show eventually went into the tank and died. But Nardino called again, this time to handle another of his shows, "Cheers."

We ran with "Cheers" for over six years, and that was when I recycled my old art idea, but this time I turned to noted artist and good pal LeRoy Neiman.

LeRoy and I originally worked together on the Sinatra film, "The Detective," much of which was shot on location in New York. I'd convinced Leroy to do a number of sketches of Sinatra and the cast in various scenes to illustrate an article for *Playboy* magazine. In addition to his colorful paintings of famous athletes, athletic events, beautiful people and gorgeous locations, LeRoy was well known for painting famous watering holes like Toots Shors, 21, and the Polo Lounge.

What better or more famous bar was there in the country than "Cheers"? I felt it was a perfect subject for Leroy to capture.

I presented the idea to LeRoy and he was interested, but there was one problem. Who was going to pay for it? One of the things I learned early on with Leroy was that he was not only a gifted artist, but a great businessman. Right up there with Andy Warhol and Peter Max, Neiman's business acumen made him one of this country's most successful artists.

I agreed that the question of who would pay for it was a good question. I'd get back to him with an answer. LeRoy cautioned me that "Cheers" might be a very good subject for him, but he wouldn't fully commit to the painting until he saw the actual bar set for himself. He also told me, grudgingly, that for me, he'd only charge $25,000 for the original painting.

Once again, I checked with *TV Guide* for their possible interest in using it for a cover. They said okay, provided they could see it once completed.

Assuming Paramount would jump at the chance for an original LeRoy Neiman painting of the "Cheers" bar, I called the head of TV publicity, John Wentworth. He not only didn't have the money in his budget for such a "harebrained scheme," he didn't like Neiman's work.

My next call was to the show's producer and director, Jim Burrows, who loved the idea. "Don't worry about the money," he told me. "It's a marvelous idea, and the lithos and prints will make for great gifts."

I called LeRoy with the good news, and he said he'd be on the coast in a few weeks and we'd go over to Paramount and check out the set firsthand. LeRoy didn't do the actual photographing of the angles. That was the job of his assistant, and she shot no more than two or three photos when the camera's flash caught the attention of someone at the other end of the bar.

"Whomever is shooting pictures in here can stop right now," said the female voice. "Get the fuck out of here and take the camera with you."

One of the show's production aides emerged from behind the set and apologized for the scheduling mix-up, asking if we could do this photography "thing" later.

"Who the hell was that?" I asked.

"Shelley Long," he replied. "She's having a bad day."

He said their rehearsal schedule was changed and he was sorry we weren't advised. He didn't have any idea as to when the stage would be free for us to shoot the photographs LeRoy needed. LeRoy never went back to the stage of "Cheers," and as a matter of fact, neither did I.

So, I tucked the art idea away for another time and place. Public relations is like that. It takes creativity, determination, and the right client to make it work effectively. But without a willing client, you've got nothing but a bunch of dreams. Dreams are cheap, and they don't get you ink.

Chapter Forty

There's Talk Show Hosts, and then
There's...... Johnny

AT ONE POINT, I thought of titling this book "A Breed Apart." What brought this title to mind was Johnny Carson. Carson epitomized the vast gulf between how the stars of Hollywood lived and how mere mortals like I lived. I never forgot which side of that equation I lived on. I was not a breed apart. I was still fighting the beasts, hanging on for dear life, winning clients faster than I was losing them, and putting a good spin on it all.

Over the years, I handled my share of talk shows and hosts, starting with Joey Bishop and his daytime TV show in the 60s. Talk was still somewhat in its infancy at the time, so there was very little precedent for how things worked. It was not a lot of fun early on, and Bishop was a sarcastic and abusive piece of work. He was nothing like the jovial comedian he portrayed. On more than one occasion, his sidekick, Regis Philbin, was reduced to tears, and it bothered me. But egos in the world of talk television live on a different plane, even from the giant egos of film and music. We struggled along with Joey, did some good publicity work, but ultimately the show was cancelled.

Several years later I got a call from Mike Douglas to work on his show. Since they were on television daily, the usual profiles in magazines didn't cut it in terms of publicity. You had to come up with gimmicks or events that shed new light on what people consider already very familiar.

For example, with Douglas I suggested a golf tournament, but a different kind of tourney.

Douglas' show was based out of Philadelphia, and on his estate he had a one-hole course. It just happened that a major tournament, the U.S. Open

Championship, was being held at nearby Merion Golf Club.

The idea was this: open up Douglas' estate to the greatest golfers in the world for a "closest to the hole" contest. Pros like Arnold Palmer, Tony Jacklin, Tom Weiskopf—ten in all—came over for the event, and later a party with the press.

It was a raging success, taking Douglas off the entertainment pages and onto the sports pages. And Mike loved it, primarily because he won his own tournament, beating out Palmer by inches.

That relationship lasted a few years and left me with fond memories. One benefit of the show was that Mike and I were exactly the same size. I could wear his suits without any alteration. As with all the talk shows, clothing companies and top designers vie for the privilege of having a mention or a credit on the show. In Mike's case, he was a clothing nut and didn't wear the same suit more than two or three times before taking it home and putting it in the closet.

Douglas lived in a palatial estate in Philadelphia until 1978, when his show moved to Hollywood. Every closet in the house was filled with new suits, and every time I stayed with him at this magnificent home, I made off with two or three new suits. Instead of asking him for a periodic raise, I'd just visit Philly, and he happily went along with this trade. Eventually, he sold the house to pop and soul singer Teddy Pendergrass.

By now my business was doing well, by any yardstick. I sold my office building on Little Santa Monica, made a good profit, and moved my staff of twelve to Robertson Boulevard, next door to the Ivy, the place-to-be-seen restaurant in Beverly Hills. It was the early 1980's, and I still had my New York office, an outpost in Hawaii (for the Hilton Hawaiian Village business), and a staffer in Las Vegas. The younger kids were growing up fast, and television and corporate work were dominating the business.

It was at this time that I was hired by Merv Griffin. Griffin, as it turned out, was one of the sharpest, most creative personalities in the business. But he was as tight with a buck as anyone in town.

I started with his personal publicity and was later asked to handle the television show—at no additional fee! I didn't mind so much, as they really did go hand in hand. But not too many months later, I was asked to kick in and help another show Merv created get off the ground, and run the promotional blitz campaign behind it.

When I asked for a bigger fee for this new show, which was to be called "Dance Fever," to help defray the additional costs, I was told there was no more money in the budget. So we were now handling Griffin personally,

"The Merv Griffin Show," and "Dance Fever," all for the same single fee.

Around this same time, ABC management told Merv they needed the Hollywood Palace Theatre, where he was taping his daily talk show. After thoroughly scouting the town for new studio space, Merv discovered he had nowhere to go. The town was totally void of studios or theaters equipped to handle his needs.

Another client, Trans America Video, headquartered just three blocks from the Palace on Vine Street, was looking to unload a parcel of property that just happened to house an old theater.

I told Merv about this Vine Street opportunity, and within a day he not only leased the building with an option to buy, but moved the entire show there permanently. Ultimately, Merv Griffin bought the entire block, which included the landmark Music City building on the corner of Sunset and Vine. Still, I received no bonus and no raise for this real estate work. I advised Merv's tightfisted manager Murray Schwartz that it was time for some serious financial review.

"We can't consider any raises at this time," he said. So, I took a walk from Merv. Sometime you just have to know when enough is enough.

It was probably all for the best, since I got a call about this time from an old golfing buddy from the Bel-Air Country Club, John McMahon, who was putting together a production company under the Johnny Carson banner. He wondered if I'd be interested in representing the new venture and getting involved with Carson. Who wouldn't? It's the way it worked in Hollywood. One door closed and a window opened. You jumped through that and landed in a garden, until the sprinklers turned on and you got soaked.

Over the years, I'd met Carson many times backstage at "The Tonight Show." I was there with clients like Hope, Sinatra, Newhart, Marvin, and many others. But I didn't really know Johnny. I'd spent no time with him socially, but I learned he spent little time with anybody socially. The only really extended time I shared in his company was in St. Louis in the mid-1960s, when Sinatra put on an all-star show to raise money for a Catholic charity called the Dismas House.

Father Dismas had befriended Sinatra years earlier and asked him to raise money for his charity, which was doing a remarkable job in rehabilitating criminals before they rejoined society. Sinatra got Dean Martin, Sammy Davis Jr., and Joey Bishop to join him in the show and asked Carson to emcee.

One of the things I noticed early on with Carson, unlike say Martin or Davis or even Bishop, was that he was never "on" until he was really on.

In person, Dean Martin was one of the most natural comics ever; he just had a mind that thinks funny. Others with this God-given talent were Don Rickles, Jonathan Winters, Bob Newhart, and Bob Hope. But Carson, until he was onstage, or had a few drinks under his belt, wasn't much fun to be around. In fact, he wasn't good company, period.

With all his success and big late-night ratings for NBC, Carson could ask bosses for the moon, and get it. Everyone did their best to please him. Every time his contract came up for renewal, his attorney, Henry Bushkin—who in many a comic bit would be referred to as "Bombastic Bushkin"—would go into the negotiations and write his own ticket. Toward the end of his long run, Carson had very little to ask for in the way of more money, so he opted for fewer workweeks and fewer workdays. He got whatever he wanted.

What Buskin also opted for were production commitments from the network. That amounted to Carson putting together a production team to produce his own movies, television shows, and specials under his own banner at NBC's expense. This was the dawn of Carson Productions.

To run this new entity, Carson hired his old friend and my golfing buddy, John J. McMahon. "J.J." as his friends called him, hailed from Chicago and never let anyone forget it. He started as a TV ad salesman before joining ABC where he rose through the ranks to eventually run the Los Angeles affiliate. He was such a success that NBC later hired him to run their West Coast operation in Burbank. This was when he and Carson became good friends.

Carson Production Group, Ltd. was formed in the early 1980s and was headquartered in a small office not far from NBC on Riverside Drive, in Burbank. My function was to create a positive profile for Carson, the new company, his company's executives, and whatever specials, shows, or films they were producing.

There was one problem: image. Specifically, Carson's image.

The Hollywood business and trade press was resentful of Carson. They wrote about his heavy-handed treatment of NBC, how he threatened to quit if it did not give in to his and Buskin's demands. The media, and a lot of insiders, couldn't wait for Carson to fall flat on his face with this new venture. They didn't have to wait long.

The company's early television pilots were dreadful and panned instantly. McMahon took the blame, but there was plenty of blame to spread around.

About this same time, George C. Scott was complaining to anyone who would listen about the quality and scarcity of good roles coming his way. I saw an opportunity and asked him if he'd ever consider going back to television. After the failure of his first series "East Side, West Side" some twenty-three years before, Scott swore he would never do another series.

"Sure," he replied gruffly, "but only under my conditions."

Needless to say, his conditions were extensive.

"What're those?" I asked.

"Everything," Scott said. "I want approval of everything from where I work, with whom I work, script approval, everything."

"Okay," I said. "Let me see what I can find."

So, with a tacit agreement, a few days later I visited Carson in his dressing room. I told him that "if the project was right" and "with a lot of unusual contractual obligations and perks" he could get George C. Scott to star in a series for Carson Productions. Such matters as "unusual contractual obligations" were nothing new to Carson. He and Buskin wrote the book on those details.

"Come up with the right role for him to play, be it a cop, doctor, lawyer or whatever," I said, "and if the scripts are quality, you will have probably the best actor in the business working for you."

Carson was ecstatic and told me he would get on it right away.

Within no time, a deal was hammered out for Scott to do a half-hour weekly comedy series, under the Carson banner, portraying the President of the United States. The aptly named series, "Mr. President," would add to the cast the extremely talented Madeline Kahn and the affable Conrad Bain and, as such, was considered a sure winner for the new Fox Network lineup.

How could we lose? We had an Oscar winner in the title role, a comic genius co-star, a television icon's production company backing the production, and a network bending over backwards to fulfill an obligation. For my efforts, I received, the publicity assignment, a production credit on the show, and an additional $5,000 per episode. Such a deal!

It was a disaster from day one.

The ornery Scott said the scripts were weak and he took an early dislike to the producer, director, and head writer. Unfortunately, all three were the same person, Ed Weinberger. Again, instead of trying to work together to fix a problem, Scott retaliated by refusing to even talk to the man. Carson promised to make the necessary changes to ensure a smooth-running production.

But Carson did nothing.

Needless to say, you can't have a star hating the scripts and refusing to speak with the director. The writing, and possibly the best writing credited to the show, was the writing on the wall. The project folded in very few episodes, and no one walked away friends.

But, of course, in Hollywood no good deed goes unrewarded without a good kick in the ass.

I'll never forget when Scott turned to me and said, "Carson dumped us, and you should have done something about it."

He blamed me because I put the deal together and he thought I could control Carson. That was really a shock to me. In George's mind, I had failed him. He thought I had the kind of clout with Carson that would allow me to step in and correct the problems. Little did he know, or refused to understand, that no one had that kind of clout with Carson.

To dissect the reasons for failure of these early productions would fill a book in itself. To be fair, some of them were quite good. In fact, Carson's initial movie effort, "The Big Chill," not only won Oscar nominations, including one for Best Picture, but tremendous reviews, many awards, and lots of money.

Part of the package Bushkin sold to NBC, in addition to the series and movie deals, were a series of one-hour specials, some of which were to star Carson. It seems Carson was obligated, whether he wanted to fulfill the commitment or not. With Carson's clout at the network, he could have packaged ninety minutes of Buddhist chanting and all ninety minutes would have made it to air. But instead, Carson opted to return to his roots, Norfolk, Nebraska, for what was billed as a the "heartwarming 'Johnny Goes Home' television special" in 1982, replete with old-time friends, teachers, and local moments. And as it turned out, Carson's first foray into this world of specials was also to be his last.

We hadn't been in Norfolk twenty-four hours when it looked as if I'd said the right thing to the wrong person at the wrong time.

After the initial day of filming, Carson invited Bushkin, J.J., his agent Bill Haber, and me to join him for an Italian dinner at an old school chum's restaurant. It was all very folksy and uneventful. After dinner, we returned to the glorified motel where the entire production company was being housed, and Carson suggested that we have a nightcap before retiring. The moment we walked into the bar I knew it was a mistake. Over the years of hanging out with celebrity types, if you're lucky, you acquire a sixth sense of when and where not to be. This was definitely one of those times.

The bar was part of the motel we were staying in, and it didn't take long for my internal radar to kick into high gear. I looked around and saw most of the customers were locals, and they were taking exception to the "Hollywood types" invading their territory.

I felt the tension and looked around at Carson and J.J. to see if they picked up on the vibe. To make matters worse, the barmaids and waitresses were all over Carson, trying to take his drink order, while ignoring the regulars.

Carson was on a roll and didn't catch on to what was going on behind him. One couldn't help but hear a few off-handed remarks from the bar and adjacent tables about the "big star," and "show biz" and "Johnny who?" I knew McMahon and Bushkin heard the noise and we looked at each other, like "Maybe we better get out of here."

Part of my job, as I learned over the decades with Frank Sinatra, Lee Marvin and George C. Scott, was to shield the client from potential trouble. And even in a tiny town like this, a small mishap can mean big news.

We hadn't been in the place ten minutes when Johnny ordered another round. "No John," I said, "we're going to bed."

Silence.

"We'll have another round," he said, louder this time.

"No John, we're going to bed," I said as I stood up. "We have a big day of filming tomorrow."

Carson just glared at me, got up, and asked me to come with him. It was more an order than request. I followed him out of the bar, up the stairs to the second floor of the motel and, for what seemed like an eternity down a long walkway to his room at the far end of the property. He fumbled with the keys for a minute, opened the door and beckoned me in.

"Don't ever, ever speak to me like that again!" he bellowed. "Do you understand?" I just nodded. "And furthermore, you can't come to the football game tomorrow!"

It was all I could do to keep a straight face. But thank God I didn't so much as crack a smile. The game he was referring to was somewhat of a celebration of Johnny's return to the community with a packed stadium at his old high school. I turned, left the room, went to mine, and considered packing. I'd blown another client. As amusing as it was to ban me from the football game, in reality it was a blessing. We'd be shooting outdoors most of the afternoon and evening, and the temperatures were in the twenties. That, simply put, is not my kind of weather.

The next morning came all too soon with a knock at the door. It was Jeff Sotzing, Carson's nephew and associate producer for the special. He wasn't smiling and had obviously heard about the incident the night before.

"Johnny wants to see you as soon as possible," he whispered. I told him I'd be right over as soon as I showered. "By the way," Jeff added, sort of as an afterthought, "there was a hell of a fight after you left the bar."

Carson's door was ajar when I got there, and seeing me, he beckoned me in before I had a chance to knock.

"About last night," he began, "I really appreciate what you did and I want to apologize. I was totally out of line. I'm really sorry. Okay?"

"Okay" I said, "But under one condition."

"What's that?"

"I don't have to go to the football game."

No smile from Carson. He didn't appreciate my humor.

Once ingratiated into "Team Carson," I was asked to get involved with "The Tonight Show." This was somewhat of a touchy situation, as Carson had never had a personal publicist. The show had always been handled by the NBC Press Department. It was a delicate situation for a while, but they grew to live with it. Historically, they could never get Johnny to do any press, so any help was appreciated.

Once a year, Carson would agree to a few, a very few, interviews with selected members of the press and visit the network photo gallery for new photographs to help promote his anniversary show. This was his only exposure. He had grown to distrust the press, and with good reason. Like Sinatra and so many other superstars who've rightly or wrongly been raked over the media coals, Carson would rather have a root canal than do an interview. Like Sinatra again, he thought there wasn't anything left to say.

It took time to get to know Carson. He didn't warm to people quickly, or ever. It was made easier for me with the help of McMahon and Bushkin. To crack the Carson family inner circle was nearly impossible. Carson was often somber, gloomy, and very private. He spent most of his free time at home without much entertainment. His real passion was tennis, and he tried to play at least once a day. More often than not, his tennis partner was one of the local professionals and, frequently, top players in the world.

Johnny Carson was a regular fixture at Wimbledon and the U.S. Open Tennis tournaments. When he was doing "The Tonight Show," it was easier for producers to get Andre Agassi or Boris Becker on the show than Clint Eastwood or Tom Cruise. And the next day, you can bet that player would be on Carson's court before breakfast.

When he sold his one-time Malibu estate to Jimmy Connors, he made sure he wrote into the escrow agreement that he'd get ten hour-long lessons as part of the deal.

When you thought you knew Carson, you were always surprised by what you didn't know. He was stingy with his time. He awoke early in the morning and read every paper available. By ten or eleven, he'd worked out, played tennis, had breakfast, and called into the office with ideas he might have come up with for that night's monologue.

Carson usually arrived at his combination office/dressing room beneath his studio, Stage 1, around one p.m. Then, he immediately met with the writers to discuss that evening's monologue, and with the producers to go over the evening's guests. Carson had little to do with the booking of guests on the show. If Johnny had a problem with you, you didn't do the show. No ifs, ands, or buts, you never did the show. It didn't matter how big a star you were.

For instance, Carson would agree to Bob Hope's guesting on the show, but always reluctantly. No matter how strong a deal Bushkin would make with the network, they stood their ground when it came to Carson promoting other NBC shows.

But Hope's TV specials were always a big deal. The problem was, Carson felt Hope was a terrible guest, that he never listened. But what Carson didn't realize was that Hope was going deaf. He couldn't hear half of what was said to him.

What made it worse was that Hope couldn't care less what Carson had to say, because he was only doing the show to promote his upcoming special.

It got to be hilarious if you really knew what was going on, but confusing as hell if you didn't. Carson might ask Hope, for instance, how his golf game was, and Hope would tell him, "Dolores sings on the show Monday night with the Mormon Tabernacle Choir." Carson, inevitably and famously, was then caught looking off camera to his producers for help.

Once Carson arrived in Burbank and entered his dressing room, he rarely emerged before five to take a thirty-step jaunt to makeup, which took little more than ten minutes to complete. Other than to say hello, no one was to talk to Carson unless he initiated the conversation.

Adjacent to the make-up room were the guest dressing rooms, and Carson made it a practice to avoid talking to any guest prior to the show. He felt it would diminish any spontaneity they might have once on camera. Fair enough, but it did nothing except to add to his reputation as a loner. He rarely broke his rule except, of course, if the guest happened to be an important "dignitary" like Bill Clinton or Colin Powell. He felt there would be no spontaneity there, anyway.

After make-up, Carson returned to his bunker and went over final editing of the evening's monologue, placing each comic gem in the proper order. About this time, the show's producer, Freddie DeCordova, arrived and went over the rundown for the show, and Bobby Quinn, the show's director, would arrive with last-minute best wishes and good luck.

Then, with minutes before the show started, Carson finished getting dressed in the outfit selected earlier in the afternoon, when there were four or five outfits suggested by the costumer. By this time, Doc Severinsen had already started playing for the audience, and at five-fifteen— you could set your watch by it—Ed McMahon would ritualistically stop by to wish Carson good luck. At five twenty-five, Carson, followed closely by DeCordova and Quinn, departed the bunker for the backstage area. Once again, if you weren't spoken to, you didn't dare approach Carson.

And then it was, "Heeeeeeeeeeeeeere's Johnny!"

Immediately following the show, Carson bid adieu to the audience and his guests, made a beeline for his dressing room, followed in quick order by DeCordova, Quinn, and associate producer Peter Lassally.

Once behind closed doors, they would review the show. Never, ever did a show get anything but a good or sensational review in those closed-door meetings. I became privy to many of these sessions, when Carson would ask me to join him after the show to discuss one problem or another. These ranged from getting divorced, getting married, or a crisis such as Joan Rivers brought with her defection as guest host.

The closest I ever heard to something remotely resembling a critical review of the show was when it was occasionally agreed that one of the guests didn't come across well for one reason or another.

Before these reviews began, Carson excused himself to get out of his coat and tie and into something more comfortable. When Carson was out of earshot, I took great pleasure in suggesting to his trio of production heavyweights that they level with him at least once and tell him the show was a piece of shit. I wish I had a picture of the expressions and nervous reactions this comment always elicited. No one dared to ruffle Johnny's feathers. I'm not sure if it would have mattered. Johnny wasn't really close to any of them. No one was in jeopardy of ruining a friendship.

The mini-reviews were wrapped up in five minutes. Unless Carson had something to go over with me, or his secretary, he was out the door with his security guards escorting him to his car. Carson drove directly home ninety-nine percent of the time. With any luck, he was home by 7:30 p.m. This was the life he led for more than twenty years while the show was in Los Angeles.

On a rare occasion, always initiated by J.J. McMahon or Bushkin, we'd go out after the show for dinner. It didn't take me long to realize that Carson, the man who made millions laugh every night, was a lonely and lost soul.

After a couple of cocktails, and I do mean a couple, he was ready to rumble. His marriage to Joanne was in the early stages of disaster about this time, and he was not too subtle when an attractive lady showed interest.

It didn't make much difference, however, given he'd be zonked by eleven and we'd be trying to figure out the best way to get him home. Many times, it was by limo since all of us had had too much to drink. I must say, for the two or three hours on any one of these given evenings out on the town, after a few drinks, Carson was as amusing and fun to be with as anyone I've ever known. But as I was to learn, every time Johnny was on the town drinking, it was a near-brush with disaster.

On February 27, 1982, Johnny and his wife Joanna were driving home from a night out when he was stopped along La Cienega Blvd. The police claimed they pulled over the late-night star because of a broken taillight, but my guess is they were looking for a reason to talk to Johnny. After a few words with Carson, the officer suspected Johnny had been drinking more than his quota and cited him.

I got a call near midnight from Bushkin advising me of the incident and asked that I meet with him and Carson the next morning at 9 at Carson's Bel-Air home. When I arrived, Joanna greeted me at the door.

"What happened?" I asked.

"He was shit-faced," she replied.

I thanked her for her candor and headed into the house.

There, sitting in the living room, was Bushkin and another man who was introduced to me as Robert Shapiro, a defense attorney who later surfaced as part of the O.J. Simpson legal team.

After considerable discussion, it was decided that Carson should fight the drunk driving rap, and Shapiro, who Bushkin explained to us rarely lost DUI cases, would lead the charge. When the two counselors finished their sales pitch and took off, I told Carson I thought he should seriously reconsider this decision.

"Get it behind you," I advised. "Go on the air tonight, apologize for doing a stupid thing, like thousands of others have done before you, and get on with your life."

Carson was adamant. No way was he going to apologize. He had convinced himself by this time that he was completely sober when he was pulled over. Sometimes people just want to dig their own grave and jump in.

Shapiro dragged the court proceedings on for four months, getting his name in the papers alongside Carson's with regularity. What could have been put to bed in hours had developed into a public relations nightmare.

Even the Mothers Against Drunk Driving (MADD) group got on Carson's butt, stating that they were monitoring his case to make sure he was not getting preferential treatment. Nevertheless, Shapiro pressed on for the trial and the fight for exoneration.

By October, it had reached a crisis, and Carson agreed to enter a no-contest plea—something I had urged from the beginning.

"The no-contest plea is entered against my advice, but with my consent," Shapiro told the court.

As a result, Carson was placed on three years' probation, fined $603 dollars, ordered to complete an alcohol treatment course, and had restrictions placed on his driver's license for ninety days.

"He could have done this from the very beginning, what took him so long?" Barbara Bloomberg, president of the Los Angeles chapter of MADD, asked the press.

In the end, Johnny got on the air and apologized.

Eventually, I sensed a coming disaster in another division of the Carson Empire.

One night, Carson, J.J., and I were invited over to Bushkin's Century City condominium complex to see a movie. What initially got my attention came when I arrived at the garage entrance to the Bushkin unit. There in the garage was a fleet of new luxury cars, including a new Ferrari and a Rolls Royce Corniche Convertible. I knew Bushkin was doing well, but I had no idea *how* well.

I've been to condos and I've been to condos, but this was right out of Architectural Digest, from the furniture to the art on the walls. Carson was equally taken aback. After a brief tour of the place, we settled into the lush couches in Henry's state of the art projection room.

"Holy shit," Carson shrieked. "I'm living on food stamps at the beach and Clarence Darrow here is living like King Farouk!"

He was kidding that night, but it was the beginning of the end, not only for Bushkin, but for all of us. The visible extravagance was an eye-opener for Carson, you could see it in his eyes and his demeanor, as he realized that it was he who was paying for all this luxury. Carson wasn't Bushkin's only client, but he certainly was his most important. So immediately after that night, Johnny started sniffing the books.

Though Bushkin handled most of Carson's business affairs through his law firm, Bushkin, Kopelson, Gaims, Gaines & Wolf, there was always someone from out of the woodwork hitting Carson up with business schemes of one sort or another. As insulated as Carson was, he was still vulnerable. And how did they get to him? Where else, but on the tennis court.

One of these new pals, Michael Klein, a stockbroker and son of former Charger football owner Eugene Klein, suggested Carson package his empire and take it public. Carson was reluctant to even discuss the plan initially, but after hearing some of the possible numbers and dollars, his tennis companion got his attention.

Carson foolishly gave his okay for Klein to look into the matter, and that was really the beginning of the end. The going public thing meant Carson had to open his books, deals, and investments and subject them to close scrutiny. Not surprisingly, Klein looked for and eventually found several deals and investments that Bushkin and his associates got Carson involved with that weren't too healthy. Early in 1982, the Bushkin cabal got Carson involved in a Westside banking operation. They also got him involved in a real estate development deal in Houston, Texas, and a radio station in Albuquerque, New Mexico. These were big-time investments, in the millions of dollars, and all were losing money or going bankrupt. Bushkin also had detractors from within. Johnny's current wife at the time, Alex, was not a fan of Henry's, and his ex-wife Joanna was alleged to have said some disparaging things about Henry to whomever would listen.

The coming months proved to be some of the most interesting of my career as a Hollywood Press Agent.

Let's face it, not every investment is a winner; not even the "Oracle of Omaha" Warren Buffett himself bats a thousand. But let's give Henry his due here. In his twenty some odd years of handling Carson he gained Johnny ownership over the entire Carson "Tonight Show" library, Johnny went from working five nights a week to three, NBC footed the entire bill for his film and television production company, and upon his death on January 23, 2005 his estate was estimated to be in excess of $450 million dollars, almost exclusively from Henry's negotiations.

But by now the financial and emotional strains on the Carson-Bushkin-McMahon relationship had hit its peak, and when Bushkin fired McMahon seemingly out of the blue, Carson had had enough. Besides Bushkin, McMahon was the only solid player Carson had on his team. The firing came on the heels of McMahon's wife allegedly suggesting to Carson's wife Alex that Carson Productions would be doing a lot better if "Bushkin didn't have carte blanche control of the company." It was also alleged that Bushkin charged the company for the fancy projection room in his condo, among other things.

Around this same time, in his autobiography entitled *Johnny Carson*,

Henry also tells of a potential offer that came in from Coca-Cola for the possible purchase of Carson Productions, with the suggestion that he and Ed Weinberger would run it. Knowing that Johnny really didn't enjoy the production business Henry thought it might be a possible fit for both sides, so he presented the opportunity to Michael Klein with the caveat that he not tell Johnny until it became real. Klein agreed to not tell Carson, but according to Bushkin Klein immediately turned around and told Johnny, who blew up. Carson suspected a coup, with Henry and Ed Weinberger trying to "steal" his company.

Hearing and seeing enough, Carson fired Bushkin and hired Beverly Hills attorney, Ed Hookstratten, my former neighbor who helped me bail Lee Marvin's pal, Michelle Triola, out of her drug overdose.

Hookstratten immediately assured McMahon that he'd get things straightened out between he and Carson, and if nothing else have him properly paid off on his contract. He never did. The irony of it was Hookstratten negotiated McMahon's initial Carson Productions contract with Bushkin.

Hookstratten and I went back many years. In fact, as neighbors, he even babysat our children when he was still attending law school. I helped him sign his very first celebrity client, Peggy Lee. But despite all that history, one of the first moves he made as Carson's attorney was to fire me.

The extent of his dismissal letter to me went as follows:

Re: Carson Tonight, Inc. / Johnny Carson

Dear Jim,

With reference to the above and entitled matter as to our recent telephone conversation, please be advised that effective January 31, 1989, The Tonight Show, as well as Johnny Carson, will cease to require public relations services for a certain indeterminate period of time.

Very truly yours,

E. Gregory Hookstratten

I knew it wasn't his fault. He had his marching orders, but that didn't stop me from not speaking to him for a long time. No matter what anyone says in this cutthroat business, it's never easy swallowing being fired, especially by surprise and with a few days' notice. There's an old saying in public relations: "The day you win an account is the first day you start losing it."

We're used to the wins and to the losses, but the pain of losing always makes more of an impact than the joy of winning. PR people go to work every day trying to do a good job for their clients. After winning the business, toiling to help the client in whatever way possible, developing a rapport, and building up a history of good work, the cold suddenness of being fired can take your breath away. Loyalty counts for nothing. Still, you want to protect your clients, or at least make sure they are not unprotected.

Clients don't know what we do behind the scenes. And if they are in a position where they don't want publicity, the work seems even less valuable, less tangible. Keeping the press away takes time and money, but few clients really understand what their press agents do all day.

The daily barrage of calls and returned calls is ceaseless. The media doesn't go away. We can't ignore them. We need them for the next client. Every action someone like Johnny Carson or Frank Sinatra takes is potential international news. Then, when the shit hits the fan, you're expected to handle it without cooperation, or additional pay. It's a thankless task, but that's what we bargained for once we threw our hats into the three-ring circus. The beasts were never satisfied.

I started to take stock of things after Carson. I sat down with one of my old associates, Richard Leary, and we went through our work for Carson over the years. Rarely do PR people look back at the weekly reports and itemize all the work completed, all the calls taken, all the ideas generated day by day. It's worth taking a brief look at some of the work that we performed in the background for our clients, in this case Carson, without them ever really seeing it, understanding the effort behind it, or placing a value on it.

When Joan Rivers, for example, sandbagged Carson, I made it my personal mission to make her look like an ungrateful bitch while positioning Carson to the media as justifiably hurt. When Carson was getting his latest divorce, the *National Enquirer* had eight full-time reporters assigned to the story. Our staff fended off those reporters nearly every day with counter stories. Of course, not helping the situation were leaks from inside NBC to the tabloids. The tabs had paid sources within NBC to shovel dirt their way, and this only infuriated Carson more, blaming us for not stopping these leaks.

Mind you, this was all basic PR craftwork, the kind that every public relations agency handles every day. We are paid well, but we're not living the lavish lifestyle our clients imagine when they see the negative morning stories, and they burn over it. We were paid monthly retainers by our clients for performing on their behalf. Those retainers ranged from $800 for young personalities moving up the ranks of stardom to $5,000 for big shows and names like Hope, Sinatra, and Carson.

But it didn't seem to matter. Our monthly fee was always too much. It was too much because they often didn't see what we did, or they never read our daily reports, and that was our fault. The only thing that matters in PR is the story that either was in news that morning, or the one that wasn't.

As I went through my Carson file, it made me proud of the work I did on Johnny's behalf. I rarely looked back. I'm a forward-looking guy. But this was encouraging. It made me realize that no matter what our clients thought after we were fired, we did our best, and we helped them in ways that they cannot even imagine.

For example, in order to make the competitor show, "Nightline," look good, ABC planted a story in *The Wall Street Journal* that "The Tonight Show" was slipping in the ratings. This kind of negative news, which was false, can spread like wildfire, but we immediately put out the real ratings facts. In addition, Ted Koppel, the "Nightline" host, had his PR team quite intentionally put out all the dirt they could about Carson's shaky business dealings, in an effort to foment distrust among viewers and, more importantly, with Bushkin.

The details in our reports made for some good reading, and if nothing else was good primer for up-and-coming Hollywood PR agents. Looking back, you realize that PR is often an everyday, full-on battle, with strikes and counter strikes.

My old boss was even in on the Carson battle, too.

Warren Cowen used his creative PR magic to attack Carson by setting up romantic dates between their client Julio Iglesias and Joanna Carson to hype the Spanish singer's American debut. It was great press for the singer, but it drove Carson mad.

Of course, Mothers Against Drunk Driving had a field day with Carson's DUI arrest, and the Robert Shapiro debacle that ensued for the next six months. We managed the daily slings and arrows from this unnecessary event, but sometimes you can't help a client who won't listen to you.

There was one time when a phony producer in New York got the wire agency PR Newswire to run an announcement that said Carson was cast opposite Lauren Hutton in the movie, "The Eileen Ford Story."

Of course, it was completely false, but the trade magazines didn't bother to fact-check the story before giving it front-page treatment. We spent days trying to put this lie to rest. Some press couldn't believe that a story could get into print when it was 100 percent fake. The nut wouldn't stop, either, even after being enjoined by a court to halt the false casting stories. Then, he put out an announcement that he had fired Carson off his phony Eileen Ford picture, and that story ran in the trades, too.

The oddity of PR in Hollywood is that when there is this incendiary brew of bad press and big egos, blame can only flow in one direction—the PR person. No matter what kind of job one did in muting and beating back the attacks, or halting the exploitation of a client's image, the steam generated by the client's anger vents hot at the only thing it knows—the PR agency he or she is paying five thousand a month to prevent this sort of news.

With Johnny Carson, who hated interviews, the media perceived his reticence as pure arrogance. And by not playing the game, he paid. It doesn't matter how many fans you have, or what the facts are, the Hollywood media relishes cutting a big shot down to size.

But the press can be fair, too, like when we handled damage control during automotive innovator John DeLorean's trial for selling cocaine to prop up his failing auto company. We got the call from the Associated Press at 9:30 a.m. on a Friday. The editor at AP said, "The chief prosecution witness in the DeLorean case just declared under cross-examination that DeLorean boasted that the coke was from Johnny Carson. We can hold the wire for five minutes, no more, for Johnny's response."

Now, this was major global news, and we needed to respond. DeLorean's lawyers brought this false information out to show how full of crap the prosecution witness was, but if the media spread this out without a response, the lasting impression would be that it was true.

What followed was the fastest, all-out mobilization for PR damage control we ever took on. We immediately got Carson to give an authorized response in time for the wire and we spent the rest of the day making calls to the media saying it was absolutely clear he was an innocent bystander, and that dragging his name into the DeLorean trial was an outrage.

NBC's Press Department helped, too. Later that same day, they aired tapes of Carson's on-show statement sent to all NBC TV stations. But it was left to us to handle the immediate rapid-fire responses required to set the record straight through the day and week. Anything else would have been disastrous for Carson and the network.

It wasn't all about Johnny, either. We had *People* do profiles on producers Fred DeCordova and Shirley Wood, and we arranged a *Los Angeles Times* Calendar cover story on talent coordinator Jim McCawley.

It all sounds like great PR, until the insecurity kicks in and the ego raises its ugly head. Carson liked these "staff stories" at first, but then he grumbled about them taking too high a profile. The show, after all, was about him, so the fun of letting the staff share in the spotlight faded.

You would think that you'd get used to being fired. You don't. It's always a big-time rejection—the bigger the star, the bigger the rejection. But you learn to live with it.

Hopefully, a new, bigger, better client will come along, a star who will appreciate the sometimes difficult effort it takes to keep their image intact.

Some weeks after being fired, I got a call from Carson. I kid you not. Among other things, he told me he was going out of town, and as soon as he returned, he'd call and we'd have lunch.

Not too many weeks later, we were hired by Paramount TV to promote "The Arsenio Hall Show." It paid $8,000 a month, and we helped position it as a hip alternative to the usual nighttime talk and entertainment shows. It worked, but I never heard from Johnny again.

Chapter Forty-One

Statue Envy

THIS WOULDN'T BE much of a book on Hollywood publicity if I didn't mention the granddaddy of PR events, the Oscars.

The golden statue is given out each year to the best in film by the nearly ten thousand members of the Academy of Motion Pictures Arts and Sciences, but the Oscars are little more than a self-aggrandizing pat on the back.

For the uninitiated, the Oscar nominees are voted on by peers. In other words, actors vote for actors, directors for directors, and so on. Once the nominees are selected, all voting members can vote for the winners in all categories. While the Oscar itself is an independently voted upon prize and above the taint of being bought, the race for the Oscar is anything but.

To even approximate the money spent each year to secure an Oscar is impossible. Given that the studios barely admit to spending dollar one to secure a nomination, their campaigns amount to millions of dollars in ad revenue for the trade papers *The Hollywood Reporter*, *Daily Variety* and *The Los Angeles Times*' "The Envelope" section, along with *Deadline Hollywood* online.

Planting stories for potential Oscar-winning films or performances gets started even before the cameras roll. The earlier one can plant the idea that one will see an Oscar-worthy performance or element of filmmaking, the better. After all, the biggest fans of the film industry are the actual members of the industry itself, and most especially the Academy members. No one takes a bigger interest in the Oscars than those voting for them.

If the work is indeed Oscar-worthy, then the press agent is halfway home. If the work is "good" and, by hook or by crook, you can get Academy members in that particular category to see it, you've got a leg up on the field.

There is the "sympathy vote," too. The sympathy vote worked for Elizabeth Taylor for "Butterfield 8" after losing for "Cat on a Hot Tin Roof" in 1958, when her indiscretions with Eddie Fisher likely cost her a much-deserved win.

There's also the "it's about time" vote.

John Wayne took home an Oscar for "True Grit" when everyone agreed it wasn't really that role he deserved it for, but his body of work, and since he was getting on in years Hollywood needed to honor him pronto. The same could be said for Henry Fonda, who was literally at death's door when he won for "On Golden Pond" in 1982. How do you compete against an aging or dying Hollywood icon?

An Academy campaign is not unlike Chinese water torture. Its success depends on the continual drip, drip, drip of press coverage. But these abundant mentions of a potential nominee need to have taste and tact. This is key. Eventually, or at least the hope is eventually, the voting members will have heard the name associated with the category enough times to simply believe a win is a foregone conclusion. Once a campaign becomes obvious, all can be lost.

For many years, I had a perfect record in Oscar campaigns. It might sound crazy, but every time I set out to win an award for a client, he or she won. Granted, I was pretty selective about with whom I would work, but I batted a thousand for a long time.

More often than not, the clients I took on were real dark horses and incredible challenges. Bear in mind, I started all these campaigns either before the picture went into production or during production. I had time to set the groundwork, and that paid off.

Two of the most interesting campaigns were Shirley Jones for "Elmer Gantry" and George Chakiris for "West Side Story." Another was Franklin Schaffner for his direction of "Patton." But the most fun was working with Lee Marvin and his incredible win for "Cat Ballou."

Jones had never done a dramatic role; no one had ever heard of Chakiris before or since. The odds against Schaffner were overwhelming. But Marvin was the biggest thrill of all. He beat out Richard Burton and Peter O'Toole for their roles in "Becket," Peter Sellers for "Dr. Strangelove," and Anthony Quinn for "Zorba the Greek."

I started on the Marvin campaign an hour after he read the script. I remember it as if it were yesterday. He was doing a television show at MGM, and I was scheduled to meet him for lunch. When I walked into his portable dressing room on Stage 30, he was more excited than I think I'd ever seen him.

"Here, take this script and read it right now," he said. "It's fantastic. If we can pull this off, it's one of the greatest parts ever written."

But no one bats 1000% over an entire career. I had some legendary strikeouts, too.

Take the case of Peter Falk. In 1959, he was a virtual unknown. He was an Off-Broadway actor, scruffy by Hollywood standards, blind in one eye and making $30 a week. Life changed for Falk when Twentieth Century Fox started filming a little movie called, "Murder, Inc."

Falk was cast as Abe "Kid Twist" Reles, the crime syndicate's number one hit man. It was a sensational bad guy role. Falk's character was as evil as Richard Widmark's portrayal of Tommy Udo, the giggling psychopathic killer in "Kiss of Death."

The reviews were fantastic, and suddenly Falk found himself a hot commodity. He came to my attention via William Morris agent Stan Kamen, who told me his boss, Abe Lastfogel, thought Falk had the potential for an Oscar. If I took care of Falk, that is, did a mercy campaign for little or no money, they promised me payback, a good account down the line. Falk was told by Lastfogel, and then Kamen, that it was important to work with me to handle an Oscar push. We agreed and went to work for zip.

The point of an Oscar campaign is to suggest to Academy members... simply suggest through the media... that a role is Oscar-worthy. You begin by placing buzz about the movie and the stars with the gossip columnists. You pitch stories about who is talking about your star, their potential next roles, and who wanted to work with this person. The trick is to make sure that when their name appears in print, there are words and phrases like "award-worthy" or "Oscar hopeful" written alongside your client's name. Unfortunately, these legendary gossip columnists of old Hollywood no longer exist.

Winning an Oscar is an actor's greatest achievement, but getting the nomination is the tough part, and that's where publicity can be the deciding factor. There are hundreds of movies, and thousands of potential nominees every year. To hone that down to five per category, and have your client be one of those five, is no easy task.

The night of the Oscars in 1960, I attended the awards with Falk and walked him through the press maze along the red carpet. The fish-out-of-water actor was stunned by the attention. It was a long shot, but here we were, nominated and in the mix. That alone was an accomplishment, a win. The category, Best Supporting Actor, was traditionally one of the first awards to be given out. Breath held!

"And the winner is....?"

The first word I heard was "Peter." I couldn't believe my ears. It worked! But then I heard the second word: "Ustinov."

As soon as the word "Ustinov" was read, Peter Falk turned to me and said, "You're fired!" And he was serious.

That was one long award show to sit through. Despite the non-win for Falk, William Morris paid off on their promise to take care of me when they brought me Steve McQueen later on down the line.

In the case of Fred Astaire, it was more of a case of an aborted effort rather than a full-scale campaign gone awry.

As previously mentioned, I'd first met Astaire at MGM in 1950, when I was working for Howard Strickling. In addition to my assignment to work with unknown Debbie Reynolds in the small but attention-grabbing portrayal of Helen Kane in "Three Little Words," I was also to get publicity for the other stars in the movie, namely Fred Astaire, Vera Ellen, and Red Skelton.

I became better acquainted with Astaire while working on his subsequent movies, and when a decade later I'd gone into business for myself, the ever-dapper Astaire hired me to promote his own projects.

Most of these projects were his television specials, for which he won a mantel full of Emmys. Astaire was unquestionably my favorite, a true all-around artist. He could do anything. Few people remember that he introduced, either on Broadway or via film, more hit songs than anyone of his day. A few of the classics were "Night and Day," "They Can't Take That Away From Me," "Cheek to Cheek," and "The Way You Look Tonight." Irving Berlin always wanted Fred to introduce his songs because he sang them exactly the way Berlin intended them to be sung.

Astaire's acting was always overlooked because of his legendary dancing skills. I always thought one of his greatest straight-acting performances was with Ava Gardner in the film, "On the Beach." But few remember this performance.

Fred Astaire was extremely fastidious and perfectly groomed at all times. He headed up all the "Best Dressed" lists and incredibly, except for the clothes the studios tailored for his films, he bought clothes straight off the rack.

I asked him one day what his secrets were to being the "best dressed."

"Taste has a lot to do with it," he told me, "and of course putting the right colors together. But to really look well-tailored, you must stay in pretty good shape and buy your suits and jackets one half-size smaller than you normally would."

One afternoon, I got a call from Fred. He wondered if I could stop by for a drink and shoot a little pool. He was quite adept with a cue stick and got more of my fee back than I would like to remember. His latest film, "Finian's Rainbow," had just opened across the country, and reviewers were given it and him good ink.

After cocktails and a few games of eight ball, he got around to what he really wanted to discuss.

"What about this Academy Award business?" he asked.

"What about it?" I asked.

At times, Fred had what one might liken to a Jimmy Stewart stammer, and this was one of those times. Proud and soft-spoken as he was, Fred didn't quite know how to approach the subject, even with his press agent.

He knew I represented Lee Marvin with his Oscar campaign a few years earlier, as well as some others, and he wanted some serious insight into how the process worked.

"Well, er, ah," he stammered, "we got pretty good notices with "Finian's" and, well, I, uh, well, I was just thinking, what would you think about it?"

I told him I thought it was a pretty good idea.

"What would you do?" he asked more lucidly.

I told him there was a lot that had to be done in advance, including getting the studio's support for an ad campaign in the two most important Hollywood trade papers done tastefully, and not to appear as if he had anything to do with them. But more importantly, the voting members of the Academy had to be reminded that this was an Oscar-worthy performance, and we'd do that in the coming weeks by various means.

I let Fred know that it might be necessary for him to kick in a few thousand dollars for additional ads, depending how far the studio would go. And he might have to do some additional interviews, once again to attract the voting members. I reminded him that this wasn't a national political campaign and that we only had to reach those several hundred acting members of the Academy.

"Actors nominate actors," I said. "We have to reach them, where they live and read."

I also informed him that there would be an extra fee included for me in an Academy campaign because of the extra effort. He said he wanted to think about it overnight.

He called the next morning and said he should just forget about the Oscar campaign.

"If it happens, it happens," he said. "If it doesn't, so be it."

It's always interesting how fast humility and modesty fade when frugality is just underneath. It was unfortunate that we never did the campaign. I think he had a shot at winning. I wasn't too long after that that Fred passed away, and the thought of him not having a fair shot at this Oscar saddened me. Maybe I should have done it for nothing.

A few months after Fred's death, his wife Robyn presented me with a gift. It was one of Fred's Emmy Award statuettes, for his 1959 television special, "An Evening with Fred Astaire."

"I know he'd want you to have something that was dear to him," she said.

There were many other Oscar efforts that I lost, and won, but my aborted Oscar campaign on John Wayne's behalf came about in 1967.

I was called by his agents, Harry Friedman and Jack Gordein, and asked if I could bring Academy attention to his performance in the film "El Dorado," but without him knowing.

I was taken aback by this kind of clandestine campaign. We needed the star to cooperate, to give interviews, and play up the film.

They said that Wayne had a Victorian attitude about the Oscars and believed that if the Academy members voted him one that would be just fine, but he wasn't going out to try and solicit or promote himself for one. Friedman and Gordein were aware of the Academy campaigns I'd conducted and thought it was time Wayne held one of the golden statues.

I told them it was possible, but it would be difficult.

The only time I represented a performer without contact was when a manager, Ray Katz, asked me to represent his client, the comedian Jack Carter. I told Katz I really wasn't interested in the business because Carter was certifiably mad and too much aggravation. He could be described as an angry comedian, not only on stage but off stage as well. He was known to work best when he was really hot under the collar.

At the Friars' Roasts, they used to put him on last because he would get so steamed at the other comedians for supposedly stealing his material. And the longer he steamed, the funnier he was. You saw the anger build on his face as he sat at the dais. When he really got mad, he was brilliant. I agreed to handle Carter if, and only if, I didn't have to talk to him. That relationship didn't last, and I was worried the same might turn true with John Wayne. I didn't want that to happen.

Agents Freidman and Gordein gave me the go ahead to work secretly. They'd pay me, but Wayne was not to know of the deal at all costs. About two weeks into the effort, I got a panicked call from Gordein.

"Stop everything," he said. "I'm worried about this. If he finds out, he'll not only fire you, he'll fire me too."

He was probably right.

Wayne won his Oscar later, for "True Grit," and there wasn't a man in the world who was happier or more deserving. And he did it on his terms.

But maybe the greatest statuette coup of all was the way I worked with Rapid-American Corporation millionaire Meshulam Riklis and his sexy, young, entertainer wife Pia Zadora.

It was the early 1980s when the nearly sixty-year old Riklis, the power behind his twenty-six-year old spouse, came to me with the idea of winning a Golden Globe for her. The little blonde bombshell had starred in the Riklis-backed film "Butterfly," and he wanted the world to know how good she was in it. The Hollywood Foreign Press Association, which runs the Golden Globes competition, had a category it called "New Star of The Year in a Motion Picture." Riklis wanted Pia to grab it.

The only problems I saw were that the film wasn't seen by anyone, it was dreadful, it had not yet been released in the United States, and the other competitors included the actors in the movie "Ragtime," Elizabeth McGovern and Howard Rollins. Kathleen Turner, another newcomer, was up for the hit movie "Body Heat," too. To make matters worse, the critics who did see "Butterfly" labeled her performance as "spectacularly inept." It was not a good start.

Pia Zadora had talent. She was vivacious and she could sing and dance. In Las Vegas, she drew crowds to the Riviera Hotel. Of course, it helped that her husband owned the place. Still, she put on a good show.

I knew Vegas inside and out, and I knew how to work the foreign press. They were suckers for free trips and free food. I knew this lure might swing a few votes, but Riklis wanted more.

The only chance Pia had, despite being a true Broadway child star and another Hoboken-born entertainer like Sinatra, was a full-on blitz of free food, entertainment, and whatever else I could dream up.

"It's going to take a sustained effort," I said.

"Whatever it takes, do it," Riklis said.

"We're talking jets, rooms, booze, food, the shows," I said. "And not just once, but several times. Plus, we'll need a full-on publicity and ad blitz."

"It doesn't matter," Riklis said. "Do everything you can."

I explained it still might not work, but at least we'll give it our best shot. With the green light, in early November of 1981 we flew out a dozen Hollywood Foreign Press members to Las Vegas for a few nights' stay at the Riviera. There was lunch, dinner, deluxe rooms, private screenings of "Butterfly," the Pia stage show, and whatever else they wanted.

Next, we did the same at the Riklis mansion in Beverly Hills. Then, we placed articles in *Playboy* and *New York Magazine*, and anywhere else we could find a reporter willing to listen. It was a full-on, two-month onslaught, with Pia doing a lot of the publicity work herself, on television and radio talk shows. We used every tool we had to reach the eighty Golden Globe voting members.

In January of 1982, the awards show was held and the "New Star of the Year" award was announced to the world: Pia Zadora for "Butterfly."

It was a shock to Hollywood, but Riklis and Pia beamed. The win, however, wasn't good for either. Sometimes in this business, a win is a loss. We were accused of buying the award, and the media backlash was severe. Our tradecraft was standard in the industry, but we just did it on a more massive scale.

In 1982, Zadora also won the Golden Raspberry Award for "Worst Actress" and "Worst Star" of the year. She was so despondent over all the negative press that she wanted to give the Golden Globe back. In fact, the rumor of us buying a Golden Globe for our client persisted to the point where after 1983, the Hollywood Foreign Press stopped handing out the "New Star" award altogether.

We did our job, but perhaps in this case, we did it too well.

Chapter Forty-Two

Full Circle: MGM's Final Bow

SINCE THOSE FIRST early days in the late 1930s when I crawled under the fence at the Selznick Studio to watch the making of "Gone with The Wind" and then later lucking my way into MGM's publicity department with the help of my father, Clark Gable, and Howard Strickling, I have always had a fond place in my heart for MGM. It was my neighborhood playground, my place of work, and where it all started.

So, it was both sad and ironic when I was there for its end, too. The MGM I knew was gone forever. Its iconic status as one of the great Hollywood studios had come to a close. The curtain had fallen.

MGM has lived on in various incarnations, but L.B. is surely rolling over in his grave. The studio lot is owned by Sony, the giant Japanese electronics conglomerate, and the rest of it, the brand, the archives, all of what was salvageable, was most recently purchased by Jeff Bezos and Amazon for $8.5 billion.

The irony is one of my clients, Kirk Kerkorian, was the last individual owner of the studio, when it was still a true studio. So much has been written about the L.B. days and now of the corporate raiding and pillaging, stripping away the assets for quick fortunes, but no one has told the story of the studio's last days as a real studio. The man pilloried for its demise was my client.

My job, as I saw it, was to clear Kerkorian's name as a corporate raider and restore it as that of a shrewd and smart businessman. Maybe I was the only one left in Hollywood who could appreciate the irony. I was pitching MGM's last story. It was no easy task.

Kirk had a tough skin, tougher than anyone I had ever come across. He started his education at the infamous Jacob Riis High School in downtown Los Angeles—a school for malcontents and incorrigibles, one step shy of the penitentiary. The exact school they threatened to ship me off to if I didn't clean up my act at Hamilton High. Kirk learned fast and early how to handle himself. Part of that was learning how not to take the bait, a handy skill during most media interviews. The writer comes in with an agenda, a bias that slants the interview from the start, and Kirk could spot it instantly.

I worked with Charles Fleming, a writer for *Vanity Fair*, about doing an in-depth article on Kerkorian's success. I turned to *Vanity Fair* for two reasons: one, the article would have substance and not just a few column inches; and two, the magazine is considered a bible for industry insider knowledge.

A good feature in *Vanity Fair* was tantamount to Moses coming down the mountain with chiseled marble. As we began, Fleming assured me that the facts about Kerkorian and his dealings with MGM would come out in the article. I felt comfortable with Fleming. I made certain Kerkorian's camp would be available for interviews. I even convinced Kirk it was better to cooperate with the writer because, as titillating a story as MGM was at the time, *Vanity Fair* would probably do the story with or without our cooperation.

Kerkorian gave his blessing to the story but declined to be interviewed. With others cooperating, I thought we'd at least get the core of a new MGM message out to the industry.

Over the years, the myth had been that Kirk systematically dismantled the revered den of Leo the Lion. Kirk had, instead, bought the studio in near-bankruptcy and tried his very best to make it work. He brought in the best talent in Hollywood as heads of production, and they failed him miserably. He poured millions into films his creative executives suggested. They produced one colossal bomb after another. Kirk, as captain of the sinking ship, took the blame and financial hit.

Kerkorian never read a script nor gave a greenlight. He occupied a tiny office at the studio and never so much as asked for a screening pass. He left it all to those he put in charge.

But he was busy, too. He purchased United Artists from Transamerica Corp. and merged them. He figured that one would buoy the other during a rough patch. He even asked the company's board of directors to let him put more money into the operation by buying back outstanding shares, meaning if the studio lost, he would lose the most. But the board rebuffed his offer.

Eventually, in order to fund the hemorrhaging company, Kerkorian sold the lucrative film library to Ted Turner. But that wasn't enough. The studio also needed to strike box office gold.

The first executive who Kirk hired to take the helm was Jim Aubrey, the onetime golden boy president of CBS and lionized in Jackie Susann's bestseller *The Love Machine*. Then, in rapid succession, came Lee Rich, then a brief stint by Jerry Weintraub, and finally Alan Ladd Jr. All were given free reign.

There were a few successes on Kirk's watch like "Rain Man," "A Fish Called Wanda," and "Moonstruck." Being the brilliant businessman that he was, and not looking to take any more of a beating than he had, Kerkorian finally made the financial move to put the studio up for sale.

He made a deal with Ted Turner for $1.5 billion, but shortly after making it, Turner confessed that he didn't have the money and wanted out. Kirk agreed to buy back the studio and logo, but Turner had quickly sold the lot to Lorimar, ironically a company co-founded by Lee Rich, my old friend who hired me on the "Dallas" fiasco.

Kirk took the heat for selling the studio acreage, which was seldom used for filming and was a tremendous tax burden. He wasn't alone in selling off prized assets. Years earlier, 20th Century Fox did the same thing when they sold their back lot after colossal cost overruns on the Richard Burton/ Elizabeth Taylor fiasco "Cleopatra," the land now a real estate bonanza called Century City. Before that Columbia Pictures sold their studio and their legendary ranch in Calabasas. Hal Roach and Selznick's "40 Acres" in Culver City were now industrial parks. Yet the business media treated Kirk like he was bulldozing the White House.

Kerkorian also took a lot of heat for selling the studio wardrobe and a storehouse full of old props—12,000 props and 120,000 costumes in all—for $1.5 million. It was costing more to maintain the warehouses than it was worth. In 1970, David Weisz, the auctioneer who bought the stash, started selling it off. And yes, there were some treasures: a chariot from "Ben Hur," Fred Astaire's hat from "Easter Parade," the blue and white gingham dress Judy Garland wore in "The Wizard of Oz," and probably most desirable and sentimental, the ruby slippers from the same movie. Collectors scooped up everything, and even Debbie Reynolds got into the bidding by sinking $100,000 into this Hollywood history.

In the year of that auction, MGM lost more than $8 million in bad movie write offs and gained more than $9 million in asset sales. With all the stinkers his executives were producing, Kerkorian had to protect his shareholders. So, he took the steps he had to, as unfortunate and difficult as they may have been for the lovers of old Hollywood. But he knew as well as anyone that old

Hollywood was never coming back.

One of my great regrets was not investing whatever savings I had at the time with Kerkorian and buying MGM stock when he bought the studio. As luck would have it, I enjoyed a financial windfall with the sale of my small office building in Beverly Hills, the very day Kirk bought MGM. Instead of putting my sudden fortune into MGM stock, my broker convinced me to buy San Francisco school bonds, which went south within no time. If I had put the money in MGM stock and continued to invest it with Kerkorian in his various companies, my investment would have quadrupled within three years.

And so, my goal with bringing in writer Charles Fleming of *Vanity Fair* was to capture all this, bring out the facts, and cut through the misconceptions of Kirk Kerkorian as corporate destroyer. But my effort backfired.

Fleming did little more than rehash the misconceptions and previous erroneous reporting that followed Kirk everywhere. It was hard to take. The cover story headline was, "The Predator."

From the title onward, it went downhill. The entire article took the premise that Kerkorian was a money hungry corporate raider, a billionaire who couldn't get his fill. And he stayed a client and friend until the very end.

Chapter Forty-Three

And The Circus Never Stops

PERHAPS THE BEST metaphor I have of being a publicist in Hollywood is that of the lion tamer. I had a chair and whip, but they often weren't enough to fight off the media beasts on one side and the beast of Hollywood egos on the other. I held the beasts at bay as best I could, but like all of us in the Hollywood ink business, we have our wounds.

James Garner fired me because my representative in Paris sent the wrong colored pair of shoes to his wife, Lois. That was it! All the work over all the years on films, movies, playing golf together, it didn't matter. I was told later that Lois thought that their neighbor, Steve McQueen, was getting more attention and better press from my services than her husband.

For a press agent, from the moment you sign a client, you are everything and nothing in particular, and you can never forget they are a breed apart. Why do we put up with it? For me, it was always because I looked at the bigger picture, at all the great opportunities. I pushed aside the ego-driven chickenshit and focused on the prize ahead. Unfortunately, the chickenshit was often what was more important to the client.

On the opposite end of the spectrum, I fired a few clients, too.

I stopped working with Peggy Lee and Hugh O'Brien in little more than an hour one night in New York. I was in a bad mood and I just snapped. I was fed up with the personal crap they demanded, and enough was enough. I regretted it, but what was done was done.

And there were surprises galore, too, like when MGM handed me its first ever out-of-house publicity assignment, the marketing for the movie "Dirty Dingus McGee." They never hired outside, but I suppose my years of service and loyalty paid off. After that, MGM turned over their entire TV publicity operation to my company. It's these acts of reward that keep you looking to the future, to the big picture.

Similarly, after saving Sonny Bono's ass with the gun incident and the press hot on his heels, as the newly crowned mayor of Palm Springs, his city council rewarded me with a $100,000 retainer to promote tourism. With that, we came up with the still highly-successful Palm Springs Film Festival, among other promotions.

I sometimes look at public relations the way weathermen look at meteorology—it's not an exact science, but we can predict certain things based on patterns and history. But publicity, unlike the weather, can be manipulated, just not fully predicted. And as you are dealing with creative types and egos the majority of time, you can be pleasantly surprised by a warm breeze and then just as quickly be deadened by an unexpected frost.

After Sinatra, or rather his hit man Mickey Rudin, fired me, he and I went on to have a very good long-term friendship, long after our working relationship ceased. It rekindled in Palm Springs.

In the early 2000s, Pat and I bought a place in La Quinta, a beautiful place on the golf course, and we started to shift things more and more toward the desert. It was part of our long-term plan. After the kids were grown and out of the house, we would sell it all, get out of the circus, and move. We both loved the desert.

One evening at a Palm Springs restaurant, Pat and I ran into Barbara Sinatra. She asked me to join the board of directors for her charitable foundation, the Barbara Sinatra Children's Center at Eisenhower Medical Center. I served for many years and am grateful to have been part of the good works Barbara did for abused children.

And even in his later years when Frank was ill and not always lucid, he still referred to me whenever we crossed paths as his "favorite Irishman." I also went on to work with the Sinatra children and served on the board of the Sinatra Foundation. So, when Frank finally passed, it was his daughter Tina Sinatra who offered me the opportunity for a final chance to a say a private goodbye.

One afternoon, the phone rang. It was just after the news of Frank's death had been announced. Tina was on the line.

"Jimmy, would you like to say goodbye to daddy?" she asked.

This was a private invitation, and the arrangements had been made with a funeral parlor in Inglewood for the family and special friends to pay their respects. I planned on attending the public funeral, but I said that I would join her and the family. As close as I had been to Frank over the years, this would be our last time together.

I was picked up, and I assumed we were heading for a kind of intimate wake. In the car were Bob Finkelstein, Tina's close friend and the family consigliere, and the family accountant, Sonny Golden. It was just the four of us, and an interesting group of intimates for sure. All they did for the entire trip to the funeral home was bitch about Barbara. I had no idea they loathed her so much.

As was Hollywood history, Barbara had married Frank after divorcing her aging husband, Zeppo Marx of the famed Marx brothers. From day one, the kids and the first "Mrs. S." had been very protective of Frank. This latest marriage didn't sit any more comfortably than had the marriages to Ava Gardner and Mia Farrow.

Primarily, it was about the money.

There was an agreement that Barbara would always be taken care of, but no one knew what that meant. Frank had a diversity of business interests, everything from movie ownership to record labels and rights to a Budweiser distribution company. How was this all to be divvied up? It was a lawyer's field day.

When we got to the funeral home, there were security people everywhere. Even in death, Frank Sinatra required a security detail—if for no other reason than to protect against people sneaking in cameras to sell the "final shot" to the tabloids.

It was strange seeing Frank in the casket. We had had so many fantastic times over the years, and now here he was in a dark suit and tie, cold, stiff, dignified. The fixed visage of death was hard to take. I would have preferred to remember the vibrant, entertaining, charismatic Frank, the "Renaissance Man," the man who held the world on a string.

Then, as I had come to expect from my years in the business, the unexpected came visiting, even in death.

Tina decided that she didn't like her father's positioning in the casket and asked that he be propped up. So, sure enough, the staff of the funeral home cranked the casket in such a way as to raise Frank to a near sitting position. There was just something fundamentally odd about the scene, but once he was positioned, I knelt and paid my respects. But as I did, I noticed a nice rosary wrapped in his hands, but on his finger his ever-present signet ring was missing.

"Where's his ring?" I asked.

"According to Barbara, he didn't have any jewelry," Tina said somewhat sarcastically.

I knew from years of traveling and just simply hanging out with the man that he owned enough jewelry to open a store.

"Are you serious?" I asked.

"We can talk about it later," she said.

There is always a point when these moments, no matter how touching or final, become awkward. It wasn't long before we had all paid our respects and were starting to stare at one another looking for direction.

"Do you want to kiss Poppa goodbye?" Tina asked.

No, I thought. But she stood and stared at me as if it wasn't a request, but a mandate. After an awkward pause, I leaned over and kissed the dead Frank Sinatra. If he could, I think he would have slugged me.

After some forty-odd years pounding the pavement in Hollywood, I was getting tired, and the world was changing. The Big Clock was talking to me. The hands sweep us all away sooner or later, making way for the new. It was big business now, and everything was about the "brand" or shareholder value or message points. There were still too many late-night calls from troubled clients or inquisitive reporters or unhappy staff. It got to where I hated the ring of the phone, any phone. Still do.

The clients I liked, and liked working with, represented a bygone era. Nightclubs, openings, and events had all taken on a new form and were being invaded by two-bit celebrities, not stars.

Hollywood publicity and public relations was now more of a crisis and branding game. It was no longer about putting names in columns. It was no longer about getting ink with features and cover stories. It was no longer about "Activity Creating Activity." Hell, there weren't any iconic columnists left to pitch stories to, save for a handful in New York. We don't even use the word "press," it's the "media," in all its many and growing digital forms, platforms, tweets, blogs, and viral YouTube videos.

What kept me and my team going, was the creativity, the ideas. We were inventing new ways of getting the media excited, new ways of generating awareness for our clients. We created possibilities. We created stories.

The crime of public relations in the era of new media is that the creative engine no longer seems to be running it. It's become a relic. We used to have to come up with clever stories to earn our column inches. Now, it's about walking down a red carpet in the right or wrong dress accompanied by the right (or wrong) date. No one seems to care about who the people are, just what they're wearing. And in turn, the celebrities are a walking conundrum. They have a rabid disdain for the notion of publicity while clamoring for fame.

By as early as 1991, I was starting to tire of the battles. I loved winning the business and coming up with great story ideas, and I never lacked for getting new clients. But the business was changing, and the image of the business was changing along with it. You had to be a big global player in order to be able to do it all. I thought I was doing fine, but my staff urged me to go "upscale."

I was told that the Ivy location where we did business was no longer good enough. And so, I bit the bullet and moved the office to the most expensive place in town, on Maple Drive in Beverly Hills. I never thought it was necessary, but the business needed sizzle, I was told, and so I went along. We had close to twenty expensive professionals in the office, and now we had a custom-fitted HQ that said, "We've arrived."

The 1990s was the age of the merger, too. Big worldwide marketing companies craved a foothold in Hollywood. They wanted to sell their corporate business with celebrities to maximize exposure across many fronts. And they were paying top dollar to do it. Burson-Marsteller, a division of advertising giant Young & Rubicam, had their eye on me and mine, and I was interested.

At the time, Burson-Marsteller was the largest public relations agency in the world. Not that I relished becoming a cog in someone else's bigger machinery, but I saw the writing on the wall. Gone were the days of old Hollywood where the publicity world was primarily a man's world. Now the business was being run by an army of smart aggressive women like Pat Kingsley, Nancy Seltzer, Nancy Ryder, Leslie Dart, and Annette Wolf, to name just a few. And of course, it was only right that more women were being given opportunities in this profession, but it was also a reminder to me that times have changed, and maybe it's time for me to go.

The approach had changed, as well. Now, it was not so much press agents as it was "suppress" agents. And, it was that alluring but elusive magic of cross-pollinating celebrity with corporate America. I am all for that. In fact, I believe I helped pioneer the packaging concept with companies like Ford and General Motors. Granted, I did my fair share of gatekeeping with Sinatra and others, but it was always a game of pro-action, getting the ink, the positive ink. I had no desire to sit on movie and television sets to prop up young egos.

You no longer called the press to plant stories. Now, the media called you, and you held them at bay, with not a lion tamer's chair and whip, but with the hold button. The business had become all about the word, "No!"

I knew the numbers coming in and the numbers going out. The flat-fee business of old was not keeping pace with the rising costs of staff and offices. Here I was still busting my ass in my sixties, chasing new clients and current clients for overdue payments, and trying to appease a staff that wanted more and more, and I had nothing more to show for it. So, I sold to Burson-Marsteller. It was business, nothing personal. It saved my ass.

After ten more years of consulting, in 2002 I decided to get out of the game altogether. My major clients were all either retired or dead. Bob Hope was dead. George C. Scott was dead. Jack Lemmon was dead. Lee Marvin was long dead.

Yet, despite the aging-out of my Rolodex, the company was doing well. My army of young publicists was more than capable of getting the job done, but I was personally burned-out. I had gotten out from under the weight of expensive offices and staff, and the ship was level and moving forward. I had no interest in dealing with Hollywood's new batch of egocentric hatchlings. It was time to quietly bow out, and the timing could not have been better. Finally, I put down the whip and the chair.

I've forgotten more clients than I remember. We did a lot of good work, but there was nothing distinctive about it, and name-dropping is not an art I care about. I just focused on the work at hand. If it was a big name or little name, it didn't matter. It was about the story and creating something from nothing. If they were interested in doing something great, I was there for them. If not, and they just wanted their egos stroked, I'd hold their hand, tell them they were the greatest, and take their $4,000 a month.

There are dozens and dozens of names, and projects, I have not mentioned in this book. If you like names, here are just a few of the others we handled: Don King, John DeLorean, Theodore Bikel, the Smothers Brothers, Jack Jones, Carroll O'Connor, Tammy Grimes, Julie London, Robert Culp, Connie Francis, Robert Taylor, Eleanor Parker, Fabian, Frankie Avalon, The Beach Boys, Linda Ronstadt, Bob Dylan, George Segal, Mort Sahl, Liza Minnelli, Vic Morrow, Mr. Blackwell, Jim Aubrey, Hugh O'Brian, John Ireland, Joni James, , Ellen DeGeneres, James Taylor, Neil Diamond, Peter Max, George Allen, Wayne Rogers, Fred Silverman, the Los Angeles Rams, Joey Heatherton, Francis Faye, the 1974 World's Fair in Spokane, the 1984 New Orleans World's Fair, the Kapalua Resort, Meat Loaf, Lee Van Cleef, the Bee Gees, Freddie Prinze, Chuck Connors, the Righteous Brothers, Bobby Darin, Mel Tillis, Robert Goulet, Mickey Rooney, Paul Anka, Robert Evans, Blake Edwards, Samuel Bronston, Ray Anthony, Gene Barry, Norman Jewison, Shirley Knight, Ben Gazzara, Glenn Ford, Carol Lynley, Glen Campbell, and Sammy Davis Jr.

We also handled movies, television series, and TV specials, including "Von Ryan's Express," "Easy Rider," "Five Easy Pieces," "The Fall of the Roman Empire," "55 Days at Peking," "Prizzi's Honor," "The Smothers Brothers Comedy Hour," "Annie Hall," "Star Wars," "The Goodbye Girl," "Starsky and Hutch," "Looking for Mr. Goodbar," "The Grammy Awards," "The People's Choice Awards," "thirtysomething," "Family Ties," "Dynasty," "Rowan & Martin's Laugh-In," "Shogun," "Love American Style," "Mannix," "The Winds of War," "Space," "War and Peace," "The Beverly Hillbillies," "Petticoat Junction," "The Addams Family," "CHiPs," "Fame," "Late Show With David Letterman," the City of Reno, "Law & Order," "Wings," "Frasier," The Kerlan/Jobe Clinic, The Arlington Million, The Kennedy Foundation, and plenty of others. Come to think of it, maybe there's another book in me!

When I set out to write down these stories, I never intended for them to be interpreted as a textbook or primer on public relations. But looking back, I can see how some of the lessons I learned are still relevant today, even if the delivery method is different. One thing that has not changed: the egos of Hollywood.

There is no question that I skirted the truth and altered facts occasionally in dealing with the press, but it was always in an effort to protect the client. If there's going to be a backlash from the media, it's always better for the publicist to take the hit, to sacrifice self, in order to keep the stink off the client.

One of my pet peeves is the non-response to a media inquiry, the non-comment you see that so often goes like this: "His spokesperson was unavailable for comment."

That line drives me up the wall. What does a publicist do if not answer a question from the press? To me, a non-response is tantamount to admitting guilt. By the same token, if there's truth to an accusation, it's best to face it head-on immediately and get it behind you.

The practice of public relations has grown by leaps and bounds since its inception at the turn of the twentieth century. It was weaponized by its early creative practitioners, like the legendary public relations founders Edward L. Bernays and Ivy Lee, to name a few.

Bernays' great line about PR was, "Perception is as significant as reality."

In his book "PR! A Social History of Spin" by Stuart Ewen, the author writes at length about Bernays, who invented the term "counsel or public relations" eliciting, according to Ewen, *"a deliberate association with the legal profession" and urging practitioners to become "the creator of circumstance."*

Bernays believed that you could control the masses' behavior without their knowledge. He called this maneuver "the engineering of consent." He was so right, and today we see it everywhere in our smartphone newsfeeds and in our specialized cable news channels. You don't have to look any further than Murdoch's conservative spin on the Fox News Channel or the more liberal spin on MSNBC.

The same principles are at play right now. They apply whether you are trying to sell a politician, an actor, an automobile, a movie, or a television show. If you can convince the public you've got the best product, something they need, can't do without, or is a "must see," the public relations practitioner is ready to do the job. But it's not advertising. If you want to control the message and measure it scientifically, PR is not what you want. You want advertising.

Public relations is "non-paid" awareness building. We use editorial space to get the message across. When done well, it's seamless and powerful, since it uses the third-party independent authority of the publication and its reporter's credibility.

The catch is that you can't always control it and you can't easily measure it. The good news is, if you know how to artfully work the media, it's far less expensive than paid media, like advertising, and it can actually drive greater sales or awareness. And when it's weaponized and delivered through social media platforms, it can change the outcome of elections. You only need to look at the recent social media election campaigns to see its direct effect. A full-page ad has much less power than a full-page story about the same subject, or customized social media "news" posts targeted to select audiences.

If you hold back a popular star client from the media long enough, everyone wants their story when they finally have something to sell. In this case, you can cherry-pick your options, take the best cover, or blast the story out to everyone. And most stars will sell their souls for a major magazine cover.

At the height of my time as a press lion tamer, *People* and the popular British magazines *OK* and *Hello* actually paid top dollar for "exclusive" wedding pictures, baby pictures, or honeymoon snaps. And the television show "Entertainment Tonight" even offered free flights on chartered jets for the grieved mourners at Anna Nicole Smith's funeral. Is this paid or non-paid media? Is it a form of checkbook journalism? Yes, PR has its paid components, and as such the business often dwells in the gray area between editorial and advertising.

It's easier to get your client's message out today, if it's good. It's a well-worn path to parade your unwilling or uninterested client for a one-day junket from "Good Morning America" to "Rachael Ray" to "ET" to "Stephen Colbert" in just one day, in one city, and hit all major dayparts of the television viewing audience. Is any of it creative? Will the star have anything different to say from any single five-minute appearance to the next? Probably not, but the publicist's obligation will be satisfied.

Today, we aren't making stars like Elizabeth Taylor or Frank Sinatra or Debbie Reynolds or Lee Marvin, but we're creating a far less talented genre of the star known as "celebrity." They can't sing, or dance, or act. They are famous for being famous, for being celebrity style-makers. The Kardashians and YouTube stars are the modern queens of this business. So be it.

But what becomes of the legacy of Hollywood? Will we really be talking about it in thirty years the way we still talk about Elizabeth Taylor? Will we even remember Anna Nicole Smith the way we remember Marilyn Monroe? I hate to see it, but Hollywood as a state of mind or institution is going the way of the studio system. MGM used to brag of having "More Stars Than There Are In The Heavens." We know how that ended.

If publicity does what it's supposed to do, to create activity that begets more activity, then there is a chance for the new stars. There is always talent waiting to be discovered and shaped. There is not, however, always talent and creativity in the minds of the current young publicists. As I said, today it's more the art of "suppress" and the catchy tweet.

Eventually, someone will discover the world of creative publicity again and re-brand it as new. I already see the concept of "brand journalism" and "native advertising" sneaking into major media outlets, including *The New York Times*. We used to call it advertorials or, in television, infomercials.

These are corporate stories written by staff writers, paid for by the advertising corporations, and printed in separate "editorial sections." They aren't fooling anyone. The stories are straight PR pieces, and some of them are written damned well. The corporations love them, even if they pay through the nose. They use them for internal and external marketing campaigns using the moniker, "As seen in the New York Times." It's a form of corporate advertising in an editorial guise.

We all understand that the media has to make a buck, too. The digital world is clobbering the old schoolboys. And so, a little "paid for PR" can keep the real writing and reporting alive.

I preferred to work in the world of shaping the real reporting, to finding and telling stories. To me, that's where the action is, that's where the real creativity lives. It's mano-a-mano with the writer and the editors. You work the relationship, you pitch great story ideas, you drink and laugh together, and you get the ink. And when it works, when you get Hollywood ink, there's no better feeling in the world.

Then, you do it again.

About the Author

From Gable to McQueen; from the Rolling Stones to U2; Jim Mahoney's job as a Hollywood press agent was to polish stars and make sure they continued to shine brightly. He earned a reputation as one of the best "suppress" agents in the business. He lives in La Quinta, CA and will be 95 in February.

With a felt tip pen and Pat's lipstick LeRoy Neiman worked his magic
on the menu at Tavern on the Green!
Perks of the job!